AF521846

Between GOD and TSAR

Between GOD and TSAR

Religious Symbolism and the Royal Women of Muscovite Russia

Isolde Thyrêt

NORTHERN ILLINOIS UNIVERSITY PRESS DeKalb

Published by the Northern Illinois University Press, DeKalb, Illinois 60115

Manufactured in the United States using acid-free paper

Design by Julia Fauci

Library of Congress Cataloging-in-Publication Data

Thyrêt, Isolde.

Between God and tsar: religious symbolism and the royal women of Muscovite Russia / Isolde Thyrêt.

p. cm.

Includes bibliographical references and index.

ISBN 0-87580-274-5 (alk. paper)

1. Empresses—Russia—Religion. 2. Empresses—Russia—Public opinion. 3. Religion and politics—Russia. 4. Russia—History—To 1533. 5. Russia—History—1533–1613 6. Russia—History—1613–1689. I. Title.

DK 100.T48 2001

947—dc21 00-05842

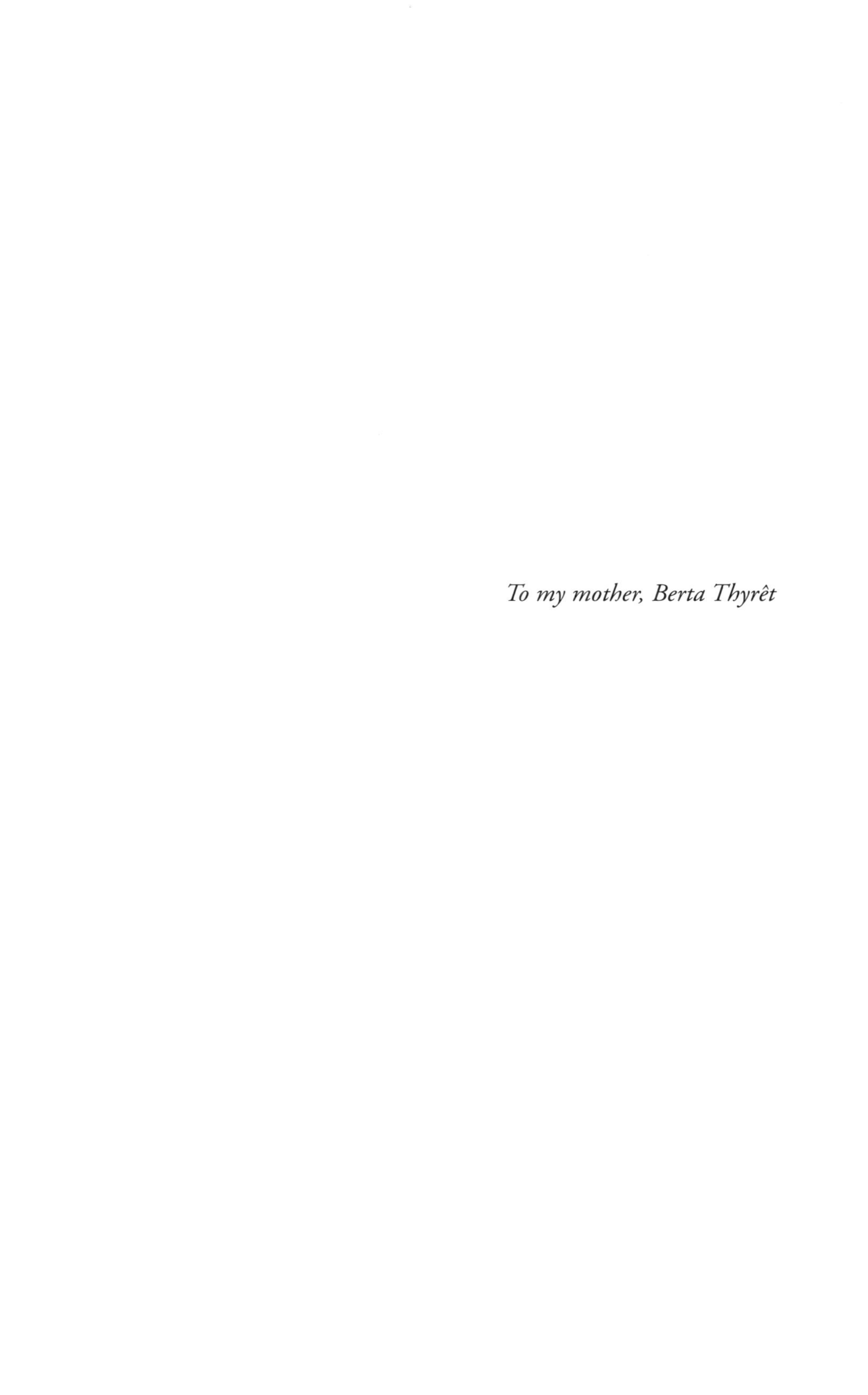

To my mother, Berta Thyrêt

Contents

List of Illustrations

Acknowledgments

THE CONCEPTUALIZATION AND WRITING of this book took many years during which I was fortunate enough to enjoy the continued support and intellectual stimulation of many colleagues and friends. I owe special gratitude to Caroline Bynum for kindling my interest in the issue of medieval women's spirituality and for encouraging me to strike out on my own in the relatively unexplored area of the religious life of the Muscovite royal women. My advisers during my doctoral studies at the University of Washington must be commended for their decision to allow me to approach the subject in an interdisciplinary fashion. Michael Williams's critical questions about the nature of Eastern Orthodox spirituality have been invaluable in my exploration of the piety of medieval Russian royal women. The art sections in this book would not have been possible without Anna Kartsonis's tireless efforts to sharpen my appreciation of Byzantine art and to caution me about the pitfalls in studying the depiction of women in medieval Russian icons. I hope the art historical method I apply in my study meets her expectations.

Most of all I am indebted to my dissertation adviser, Daniel Waugh, who not only provided me with an essential grounding in the field of medieval Russian history but had the wisdom and patience to let me pursue my own ideas. Throughout this project he has pushed me to reach for fresh answers without disregarding the complexities of the medieval Russian subject matter and source base. His standards of scholarship will always be a model to me.

In addition to my dissertation advisers I am deeply indebted to many colleagues both in the United States and abroad who have encouraged me in my research and provided many valuable suggestions over the years. The anonymous readers of the manuscript and Mary Lincoln, the editor, have done an extraordinary job in engaging its arguments in detail and providing insightful suggestions for improvement. Their reviews have been not only substantive but also inspiring. Nancy Kollmann, Eve Levin, Valerie Kivelson, and Daniel Rowland have provided me with useful suggestions over the years and have been instrumental in helping me decide the final format of the book. The enthusiasm they expressed for my work and their continued encouragement have been invaluable.

I also would like to express my deep appreciation to Engelina Sergeevna Smirnova without whose help it would have been difficult to complete the art historical work for this project. Her lectures on Muscovite art at Moscow State University in spring 1990 shaped my understanding of the subject decisively. Not only was Engelina Sergeevna instrumental in arranging access to the materials of the Tret'iakov Gallery at a time when these materials were inaccessible to the public but she tirelessly worked to supply me with scholarly literature and the visual materials necessary for this project. I am deeply grateful to her for the hospitality and generosity she displayed on several occasions during my stay in Moscow.

The source base for medieval Russian royal women and Muscovite religious culture is so scattered that the contributions of colleagues who provided me with materials or suggestions on individual subjects have been invaluable. Liudmila Vladimirovna Chizhova must be commended for her patience in trying to arrange my visit to the Golden Palace of the Tsaritsy in the Kremlin in 1989–1990. Ernst Kitzinger helped me develop my views for the discussion of the depiction of Mariia Il'inichna in icons. Hugh Olmsted graciously provided me with letters of Maksim Grek to Muscovite women. Paul Bushkovitch engaged me in stimulating discussions about Muscovite religious life and the use of medieval Russian miracle tales as a source for the spiritual life of royal women. Gelian Mikhailovich Prokhorov extended to me the hospitality of his home and worked closely with me on several manuscripts during my stay in Leningrad in 1990. Vladimir Mikhailovich Kirillin shared with me his interest in the cult of Sergius of Radonezh and made my work at the manuscript division of the Lenin Library a pleasant one. Karl Christian Felmy from the University of Erlangen was a wonderful fellow-researcher in the archives of Moscow and Leningrad and enhanced my understanding of Russian Orthodox culture. Mariia Semenovna Fomina shared her knowledge of medieval Orthodox didactic literature. Marshall Poe made valuable travel literature available to me. Christine Havice shared with me her knowledge of Byzantine illustrated chronicles. Martha Vinson provided a copy of her unpublished translation of Saint Theodora's *vita*. Aleksei Mikhailovich Lidov and Andrei Leonidovich Batalov made useful suggestions regarding my discussion of the theme of miraculous birth.

Among innumerable people who showed interest in my project I wish to express my particular appreciation to Natal'ia L'vovna Puskkareva, Shirley

Glade, Ann Kleimola, David Miller, the members of the Kent State Medieval Colloquium, the Women in Slavic Studies Discussion Group, and the Early Russian History Workshop at the University of Illinois Summer Research Laboratory, as well as my graduate students Kirsten DeVries, Denise Rinn, and Craig Bonnie. Tat'iana Viktorovna Shemakhanskaia at the Moscow Archival Institute (MGIAI) removed many obstacles associated with my stay in Moscow in 1990. Mariia Andreevna Alekseeva kindly gave permission to reproduce several illustrations. Elizabeth Zelensky graciously allowed me to cite her dissertation. Claudia Jensen, Shirley Wajda, and Christine Worobec each read portions of the manuscript and not only made valuable suggestions for changes but tirelessly strove to improve the prose of a non-native English speaker. Kirsten DeVries helped reformat the notes and the bibliography. To all these people and many others who have given me advice and encouragement, I wish to express my deepest gratitude. Finally, I wish to thank the staff of the *Russian Review* for permitting me to republish an article ("'Blessed Is the Tsaritsa's Womb': The Myth of Miraculous Birth and Royal Motherhood in Muscovite Russia," *The Russian Review* 53, no. 4 [1994]: 479–96) on the myth of the tsaritsy's miraculous womb as a part of Chapter 1.

Generous support from various institutions has enabled me to do research abroad and at home and to complete the manuscript in a timely manner. Research for this project was supported in part by a grant from the International Research and Exchanges Board (IREX), with funds provided by the National Endowment for the Humanities, the U.S. Information Agency, and the U.S. Department of State, which administered the Soviet and East European Training Act of 1983 (Title VIII). A dissertation fellowship from the Social Science Research Council and a Foreign Language and Area Studies Fellowship (FLAS) allowed me to write drafts of several chapters of this book. As a research scholar at the Kennan Institute for Advanced Russian Studies in Washington, D.C., I was able to perform the research necessary for Chapters 4 and 5. The institute also provided an intellectually stimulating environment that shaped my views on medieval Russian royal women decisively. A postdoctoral fellowship awarded by the Joint Committee on the Soviet Union and Its Successor States of the American Council of Learned Societies and the Social Science Research Council gave me the much needed time to finish the manuscript. I am also grateful to Kent State University for cosponsoring a one-semester leave of absence to allow me to achieve this goal.

Over the last decade I have been fortunate enough to utilize the resources of a number of archives, museums, and libraries in Russia and the United States. I would like to thank the *sotrudniki* of the archives of the Russian State Archive of Ancient Acts (RGADA), the Russian State Library (RGB), and the State Historical Museum (GIM) in Moscow and the Russian National Library (RNB) and the Library of the Academy of Sciences (BAN) in St. Petersburg for creating a comfortable working environment and for providing me with an abundance of materials. Natasha Borisovna Rogova at the manuscript division of RNB went out of her way to make my two short stays in St. Petersburg in 1990 productive ones. I would like to express my appreciation to the entire staff of the Sector of Old Russian Art at the Tret'iakov Gallery for granting me free access to all visual materials I requested and for introducing me to their restoration workshop. Natal'ia Aleksandrovna V'iueva from the Kremlin Museums in Moscow was kind enough to lead me on a personal tour of the Great Kremlin Palace in 1990, which included a visit to the Golden Palace of the Tsaritsy.

In Seattle I benefited from the help of the interlibrary loan staff at the Suzallo/Allen Library, notably Ruth Kirk and Anna McCausland, who tirelessly obtained materials from the Lenin Library for me. Work at the Art Library of Princeton University, the Library of Congress, and the libraries of Ohio State University (notably the Hilandar Collection), the University of Illinois, and the University of Michigan has rendered materials vital to my project. I am particularly grateful for repeatedly gaining access to the Byzantine Library of Dumbarton Oaks. On several occasions the staff of the Slavic Reference Room at the University of Illinois have retrieved rare materials for me.

This project took nearly a decade to complete, during which my thoughts on the religious role of Muscovite royal women gradually evolved as I discovered more evidence. I am aware that this book touches on many controversial issues and advances a number of hypotheses. I assume full responsibility for any errors I may have committed.

I am humbly aware that hard work, discipline, and a scholarly approach alone did not lead to the completion of this project. Over the long years I researched and wrote this manuscript, I enjoyed the support of loyal friends who put up with me in difficult times and cheered me on. Esther Muños has been a firm believer in the value of my research and one of my most loyal supporters throughout my years as a graduate student and during my professional career. Bernie Kreidler extended her hospitality to me on numerous occasions when I did research in Seattle. Bridgett Mullins literally held my body and soul together during the final two years of this project. Kim Gruenwald was there as a friend whenever I needed one. Glee and Dorothy Wilson opened their home when I wanted just to talk and hang out with their dog, Elton. Finally, I would like to thank my mother, who has also been a true friend, for her infinite patience and her unshakable faith in my success. It is to her that I dedicate this book.

Note on Transliteration and Names

THE READER MAY BENEFIT from a discussion of the terminology and linguistic conventions employed in this work. I refer to the Russian rulers and their wives in the appanage period as grand princes and grand princesses, while I use the terms *tsar* and *tsaritsa* flexibly. Although, strictly speaking, the latter two terms reflect the title of the Russian ruler and his wife from the mid–sixteenth century on, I often employ them in the sense of "ruler" and "ruler's wife." I tried to avoid referring to the tsaritsy as queens since the Muscovite tsaritsy did not enjoy the same legally defined and ritually expressed position as their western counterparts. Since the English language, however, does not possess a word that reflects the connotation of the medieval Russian adjective *tsarskii, -aia, -oe* (the word *tsarist* carries a much narrower meaning), I have used the adjective *royal* throughout the book. In order to convey the quality of the status of a medieval Russian ruler and his family, I have opted for the use of *royal* for two reasons. First, its meaning is flexible enough to apply to both grand princesses and tsaritsy. Second, although technically the status of a tsaritsa was higher than that of a grand princess, I have avoided translating *tsarskii, -aia, -oe* as "imperial" to distinguish the Muscovite period from the era of Imperial Russia.

Translation problems also arise occasionally with regard to the symbolism relating to Muscovite royal women. The medieval Russian language, as the medieval Greek and Latin, was rich in body and gender imagery, which could be used to inform religious concepts. Womb and fertility imagery applied to the tsars' wives can present challenges to the modern researcher who strives to provide not only an adequate translation but the correct historical meaning of a term. In my translations I have tried to provide a balance between both considerations.

The reader should be aware that biblical citations are taken from the King James Bible. With regard to transliteration practices, I follow the Library of Congress system. In general, Russian names are presented in their original form. In the spirit of this book, the female endings of the last names of Russian women are retained. In order to distinguish Orthodox foreigners from native Russians, I have anglicized the name of the former. This does not apply to foreign Orthodox clerics who lived most of their lives in Russia. Whenever convention favors an anglicized name, I have followed it. Thus I refer to Sofiia Alekseevna's successor as Peter the Great rather than Petr Pervyi. In the case of Sofiia Alekseevna I have retained the Russian spelling of the tsarevna's name to set it off from the theological concept of Sophia the Wisdom of God.

Between GOD and TSAR

Introduction

The tsaritsa gazed at the chapter headings—
letters out of red gilding.
She lit the crimson lanterns
and humbly prayed to the Mother of God.

Over the book of Deep Wisdom,
the tsaritsa's dark blue nights passed by.
And from the dove tower,
white birds came flying to the tsarevna.

The tsarevna scattered the seeds
and the white feathers splashed.
The doves cooed submissively
in the *terem*—under the filigree door.

—Aleksandr Blok (*Polnoe sobranie stikhotvorenii,* 1946)

IN THE EARLY FIFTEENTH CENTURY the Greek Photius (Fotii), who had been appointed Metropolitan of Kiev and All Russia in Constantinople, assumed his spiritual office in Moscow. According to received opinion, the customary presents for the Russian church the hierarch brought with him from Byzantium included the so-called great *sakkos* of Metropolitan Fotii, a richly embroidered liturgical vestment that features both traditional religious iconographic themes and contemporary ruler portraits (see Figure 1).[1] The front of the *sakkos* features scenes from the life of Christ such as the Annunciation, Christ's Entrance into Jerusalem, the Last Supper, the Crucifixion, and the Resurrection along with selected scenes and figures from the Old Testament. The placement of the images—the relegation of the Old Testament images to the sleeves and sides of the garment; the central location of the themes of the Crucifixion and the Resurrection—expresses the pivotal role of Christ in Christian salvation history. The connection between the periods of the Old and New Testaments and the post-Scriptural human race is marked by the presence of the Old Testament kings Solomon and David and the saintly Byzantine ruler Constantine the Great and his mother, Helena, in the central composition. Immediately below Constantine and Helena (at the bottom edge of the *sakkos*), one sees the standing figures of the Byzantine emperor John VIII Paleologus and his Russian wife, Anna, on the left and Anna's parents, the Muscovite grand prince Vasilii I and his Lithuanian spouse, Sofiia Vitovtovna, on the right. The two ruler couples are linked by the busts of three Lithuanian saints who died as martyrs on April 27, 1347.[2]

1. The great *sakkos* of Metropolitan Fotii (Kremlin Museums, inventory no. TK-4). The *sakkos* was brought to Russia from Byzantium in the early fifteenth century. It features the Byzantine emperor John VIII Paleologus; his Russian wife, Anna; and her parents, the Muscovite Grand Prince Vasilii I and Grand Princess Sofiia Vitovtovna.

The portrayal of the Russian grand-princely family is striking for a number of reasons. The *sakkos* represents the first depiction of a Muscovite grand prince and his family.[3] The appearance of Vasilii and Sofiia in the complex arrangement of religious themes suggests that the Russian ruler and his wife were considered part of the Byzantine Commonwealth, which, because of its adherence to the true faith, was assured of the promise of salvation.[4]

The inclusion of women in the array of ruler portraits on the lower edge of the *sakkos* is particularly noteworthy. The iconographic details and inscriptions surrounding the portraits in the great *sakkos* attest to the important role of the Russian royal women in the political and religious framework of the Byzantine Commonwealth. The betrothal and eventual marriage of "John Paleolog, faithful emperor in Christ God" to Vasilii I's daughter elevated the grand princess to the status of the "most pious augusta Paleologina" (both inscriptions are located on the *sakkos*). Her imperial position is marked in the liturgical vestment by a halo, a scepter, and purple shoes, features found also in the depiction of John VIII. The creation of a dynastic alliance with the Byzantine emperor undoubtedly brought the Russian ruler prestige, but Anna's marriage did not convey any imperial privileges to Vasilii and Sofiia. The inscriptions refer to the two simply as "Grand Prince Vasilii Dmitrievich" and "Grand Princess Sofiia." Neither of Anna's parents wears a halo or purple shoes, and their dress is distinct from that of the Byzantine ruler couple. Vasilii holds a simple cross in his right hand while Sofiia raises her hands in prayer. The Greek artists were careful to insist on the superiority of the Byzantine emperor over the Russian prince regardless of the marriage ties between them—one notes the unique crown of John VIII. Still, their rendition of Vasilii I and Sofiia Vitovtovna suggests that the two had the potential to imitate their Byzantine overlords through their adherence to the Orthodox faith. Vasilii I's display of a cross and Sofiia's praying pose both speak of their religious disposition. Moreover, the Russian ruler and his wife could demonstrate their commitment to the Orthodox faith by showing respect for the Lithuanian martyrs who had been put to death by Sofiia Vitovtovna's pagan forebears. Vasilii I and his spouse were expected to work for a united metropolitanate of Russia and Lithuania under the aegis of the church of Constantinople, a notion that Sofiia's father, Vitovt, challenged.[5] If Vasilii and Sofiia upheld Byzantine Orthodox interests in their realm, they could both follow in the footsteps of the saintly model rulers Constantine and Helena. Although in the Byzantine mind foreign royal women could not transmit the imperial dignity to their natal families, these women were considered able to assure the success of the realms of their parents and husbands through their personal commitment to the Orthodox faith.

The great *sakkos* of Metropolitan Fotii raises several important questions regarding the status of royal women in Muscovite Russia. The absence of ruler portraits of Muscovite grand princes and their families before this time invites a closer scrutiny of the relationship of husband and wife in the Russian ruling family. What role did the Muscovite royal women play in politics, society, and culture? In view of the sobering message of Fotii's *sakkos* that Russian imperial brides could not confer imperial status to their fathers or brothers, to what extent did Muscovites accept foreign, Byzantine definitions of the role of the rulers' wives and apply them to their own royal women? What role did religious symbolism play in Russian efforts to interpret the position of the wife of their ruler? To what degree did representatives of the established Orthodox church guide these efforts? Finally, what part did Muscovite royal women play in the construction of their own image? This book seeks to provide answers to these questions by examining the development of the role and image of the Muscovite ruler's wife from the time of the consolidation of the Muscovite grand principality in the late fifteenth century to the end of the Muscovite period in the late seventeenth century.

While the bulk of the research presented here deals with the image of the wives of the Russian tsars and its basis in the political, social, and cultural life of Muscovy from the mid–sixteenth century to the time of Peter the Great, a true appreciation of the creativity Muscovites displayed in the development of the concept of the tsaritsa is only possible if we consider the tsaritsa's part in the process of the creation of the institutional and ideological foundation of the autocracy, which stretched over several generations of rulers. Several Russian grand princes took the title Tsar before Ivan IV's coronation as the first official autocrat of Russia in 1547. A study of the Muscovite royal women before this date can help destabilize commonly held assumptions about the oppressive nature of the Muscovite autocracy's impact on the role of women.[6] The role of the tsaritsa, like that of her husband, cannot be understood unless we take into account the impact of the demise of the Byzantine state in 1453 on Muscovite ideas of government. If in the early fifteenth century an all-powerful Byzantine monarch still put Vasilii I in his place, Vasilii's grandson Ivan III actively pursued the acquisition of an imperial aura by marrying Sofiia Paleolog, a niece of the last Byzantine emperor.[7] Sofiia herself, sensitive to the difference between her own imperial status expressed in her Russian title Tsarevna and her husband's lesser title Grand Prince, played an active part in the creation of the notion that her son Vasilii III ruled by divine grace. In order to further her goals regarding Vasilii III, Sofiia Paleolog engaged in the politics of religious symbolism, a highly developed Byzantine skill to which the great *sakkos* already attests. To begin a study of the royal women of Muscovy with the date of the coronation of the first official tsar thus would obscure some of the larger political and cultural issues that historically conditioned the image and position of the tsar's wife.

An examination of the conceptualization of the role of the Muscovite ruler's wife in medieval Russian politics, society, and culture seems to be appropriate considering the recent resurgence of interest in the concept of queenship among scholars of medieval and early modern Europe.[8] While much has been gained from the new focus on the semiotics of queenship, evident in myths and rituals surrounding the person of the king's wife, experts have found it difficult to escape traditional assumptions about the power of royal women. A modern desire to search for evidence of the equality of the sexes in historical texts in order to validate contemporary social agendas, a ready acceptance of a social model that sharply divides the official domain (identified with male action) from the private sphere (dominated by women and the family), and a tendency to equate the king as lawgiver with culture and his wife with nurture have to a certain extent obscured an appreciation of medieval and early modern queens' political and cultural significance.[9] In view of these paradigms it is not surprising that the queen's role is perceived as secondary, unofficial, intuitive, emotional, and subject to the male social order. Scholars often stress the association of queens with extraordinary times in the history of a realm when male power is eclipsed, such as in periods of a king's absence or untimely death. In spite of the sensitivity of these studies to anthropological concepts, their negative interpretation of the intercessory aspect of a queen's power is striking.[10] One cannot help detect a tone of disappointment in many of the recent studies on European queenship, in spite of their celebration of royal women who against all odds occupied the royal throne from time to time.

In spite of the complications in the assessment of the position of Western medieval and early modern queens, a comparative framework can further our understanding of the role and image of the Muscovite royal women. In particular, the historian is struck by the analogous situation of the spouses of early medieval kings and of the Muscovite rulers' wives, the tsaritsy. Although the mature Muscovite period, characterized by the institution of tsardom, coincides with the sixteenth and seventeenth centuries, its political and religious culture resembles more closely that of the early medieval West than that of early modern Europe. Daniel Rowland, who recently pointed out the similarities of Muscovite Russia and Carolingian Europe with regard to their size and administrative and cultural challenges, in particular stresses the religious conceptualization of the ruler in both political entities.[11] While royal authority was sanctioned by the divine, the absence of an elaborate bureaucracy in early medieval Europe and Muscovy also cast ruler-subject relations in more personal terms.[12] The spiritual and personal aspects of royal power profoundly influenced the definition of the image and the role of early medieval queens. In the absence of a secular political discourse, which in the West did not arise before the eleventh century, the queens' position was cast in religious, often biblical language.[13] At the same time the personal nature of royal government, notably its reliance on the family principle, gave royal women in the Carolingian Empire and in Ottonian Germany a much wider range of opportunities to exert political power than from the High Middle Ages on.[14] The situation was much the same in Muscovite Russia, where royal women were considered to be spiritual intercessors for their husbands and subjects and helpmates to the tsars in affairs of the realm.

Although the present study has undoubtedly benefited from the recent investigation of the ramifications of queenship in the early medieval West (and in preindustrial Europe at large), it takes a different approach to the conceptualization of the tsaritsa's power in Muscovite Russia. This study does not deny the existence of misogyny in medieval Russia (the vast literary evidence for religiously and socially sanctioned misogyny in Muscovite Russia speaks for itself), but it investigates the question of female royal authority strictly within the parameters of the Muscovite political, social, and cultural environment. Rather than working from any theoretical assumptions about male-female relations and the nature of sovereign power, this book explores the development of the image and role of Muscovite royal women in the evolution of the ideology of centralized government in Muscovy and the role of the church and women in this process. This makes sense considering that in Muscovite Russia extraordinary circumstances such as regencies, dynastic transitions, or the absence of rulers from the capital were more the norm than the exception. Under these circumstances the role of royal women became naturally integrated into the concept of government. To come to a true understanding of Muscovites' view of their rulers' wives, we need to explore the Muscovite discourse of gender and power. At the same time we must also be sensitive to the circumstance that the medieval Russian language of gender and power carried connotations that cannot easily be transferred to a modern environment. Much of this book therefore deals with the production of meaning as it applied to the wives of Muscovite rulers and with the agents in that production, the Muscovite government, the Orthodox church, and the royal women themselves. At the same time the perceptions of a grand princess's or tsaritsa's power were rooted in specific legal, social, and economic traditions. For this reason it is necessary to compare royal women's legal rights, social prestige, and economic status with their ideological value relative to their various historical environments. This approach renders a complex picture of the function of Muscovite royal women in their society and government, which impresses even the modern reader with its scenarios of traditionally masculine institutions embracing feminine notions of power and of royal women achieving a degree of visibility usually reserved for their male counterparts.

A study of the image and role of the medieval Russian royal women faces a variety of challenges. Some of them, for example an appreciation of the complexity of terms such as the status of women, are familiar problems to experts in women's history. Whenever possible, this work compares the image of the grand princesses and tsaritsy to their roles in the Muscovite government and the Russian realm at large. Specific judicial and economic activities of these women are investigated as far as they have a bearing on their political and dynastic significance. Other problems arise out of the peculiarities of the medieval Russian field. With few exceptions the royal women of Russia before the end of the seventeenth century left no written records of themselves. When tsaritsy engaged in correspondence or issued charters, they (like their male counterparts) employed official scribes. As a result we possess no firsthand accounts of their intellectual and emotional lives, no direct evidence of their expressed hopes and desires, and no self-reflective statements on their position in Russian society. The stereotypical nature of medieval Russian sources often requires that the researcher deals creatively with the available material. This involves the reading of sources against the grain. We may, for example, derive new insights about the cultural role of a tsaritsa by mining official court records regarding customary day-to-day activities for the religious implications of her role. Such an approach requires constant vigilance, since it is tempting to assign too much value to what is written between the lines. On the other hand, our understanding of the challenges and actions of medieval Russian royal women is tremendously enriched if we heed Elaine Pagels's observation that historical imagination can breathe new life into known texts.[15]

Still other problems in uncovering the history of medieval Russian royal women pertain to the preconceived notions of Russian and Western scholars. With few exceptions, existing studies adhere to nineteenth-century Russian notions that Muscovite women were kept out of the public sphere.[16] Russian works in particular often do not evaluate dispassionately the actions of outstanding women in Muscovy. Already Lindsey Hughes has remarked on the misogynous bias that pervades the scholarship on Sofiia Alekseevna.[17] Even as acclaimed a scholar as A. A. Zimin, who generally acknowledges women's contributions in medieval Russian history, could not extricate himself from the framework provided by ecclesiastic didactic sources, which see women as weak or evil. Echoing the concern of these sources that evil women subvert the traditional social order, Zimin calls Sofiia Vitovtovna, who defended the claims of her son, Vasilii II, to the grand-princely throne, a "power-loving" woman.[18] Efforts to compare Christian Muscovite women with their pagan counterparts in the Kievan period also have not been helpful since they categorically branded the Orthodox influence on Russian women as negative.[19] Equally uncritical views by scholars apologetic of Christianity celebrate the ability of this religion to make independent, physically and mentally strong pagan women into sensitive sisters, devoted wives, and caring mothers.[20] While it is easy to see that such preconceptions obscure rather than aid our understanding of medieval Russian women, avoiding such models completely in one's research is no easy task. In the course of my investigation I have therefore tried to interrogate medieval Russian notions of the public and private and the masculine and feminine in their relation to power issues. As a result, this study does not merely represent a narrow investigation of the lives of the Muscovite tsars' wives. Rather it seeks to make a larger contribution to the field of medieval Russian culture and religion. The book's concern with the impact of religious myths and rituals on the social and political role of the royal women of Muscovy necessarily treats only cursorily political issues such as those relating to the rise of the Muscovite state and the creation of the Muscovite autocracy. These issues are mentioned only insofar as they involve the participation of Russian royal women.[21] Although I have tried to expand our current knowledge of individual personages whenever possible, this work is not intended as a compendium of biographies of Russian royal women, nor does it take the description or reconstruction of their environment as its aim. (In this sense the present study seeks to complement rather than replace Ivan Zabelin's work on the everyday life of the tsars' wives in the sixteenth and seventeenth centuries).

By its nature my focus on the role of the Russian Orthodox symbolism in the definition of the tsaritsa's status privileges the discussion of Orthodox royal women. For this reason I only cursorily mention Marina Mniszech, the Catholic wife of the first False Dmitrii. Although her role in the dynastic and social turmoil of the Time of Troubles was undoubtedly significant, Marina's Latin faith prevented her from being accepted as a "pious tsaritsa" in Muscovy. In many ways Marina's bid for power failed precisely because many Muscovites saw her as a threat to the established notion of a divinely blessed Orthodox tsardom. In contrast, foreign women who either were Orthodox or converted to Orthodoxy prior to marrying Muscovite rulers could use the symbolic language of the faith to bolster their legitimacy and increase their prestige in the Russian realm.

Methodologically this book employs the principles of the new cultural history. It does not assume that medieval Russian texts speak for themselves, nor does it seek to bring these texts into line with modern theories. Instead this work proceeds from the assumption that historical texts carry their own meanings, which can be discovered if we pay attention to their social and cultural context. This kind of discovery benefits from insights gained by experts in anthropology and material culture, art history, women's history, and religious studies. Although primarily a historical work, this book therefore follows an interdisciplinary approach.

The methodological ecumenism is required by the wide variety of sources I utilize: documentary, narrative, and literary materials, artifacts, and art. While some of these sources are well known, I have tried to include less accessible materials or materials that so far have received little scholarly attention. Information about the lives of the Muscovite grand princesses and tsaritsy and about Muscovites' perception of these women can be found in the medieval Russian chronicles, royal wills, and charters (some issued by the wives and mothers of Muscovite rulers themselves), hagiographic texts, political tales, foreign travel accounts, letters by members of the tsar's family and ecclesiastics, inscriptions on liturgical gifts commissioned by royal women, and the iconographic program of officially sponsored art. Each type of source poses its own challenges to the historian. In cases where the dating of sources has been disputed, I have relied on the more conservative estimates. Information derived from the chronicles generally is placed in the context of the time and place of its compilation. Whenever appropriate, I have tried to take into consideration the possibility of forgery (and the intention behind it), which represents a common problem for medieval Russianists. Hagiographic tracts have been mined not for their historical facts, which often cannot be ascertained, but for the message they intended to convey to their audience. In the same vein, I have compared information from foreign travel accounts, which sometimes perpetuated foreign stereotypes of Russian culture, with evidence derived from native Russian sources. Since expressions of personal feelings are a rare exception in royal letters, I have examined themes in these letters for their social and cultural implications. With regard to artifacts, I have tried to treat these objects as historical texts. Whenever possible their date and origin have been ascertained. In cases where works of religious art contain inscriptions, text and image have been studied in relation to each other. Realizing that historians often feel uncomfortable extracting meaning from a strictly pictorial source, I have attempted to establish long-term patterns of the use of images in Muscovite Russia. The pictorial evidence then has been juxtaposed with the testimony derived from documentary and literary sources. Close comparison of all these types of materials (while keeping in mind their provenance) allows us to trace the origin and evolution of cultural concepts and customs such as myths and rituals with reasonable certainty. Finally, I have tried to gauge the success of myths and rituals involving Muscovite royal women by studying, whenever possible, not only the mythmakers and their message, but also the reception of these myths by the medieval Russian community. Descriptions of royal receptions and pilgrimages, monastic memorial registers, and stories circulating among the Muscovite subjects all can help illuminate the process that anchored the mythopoeic efforts involving royal women in the communal memory.

The individual chapters of this book are arranged thematically proceeding from the assumption that throughout the Muscovite period, the image and role of the tsaritsa were informed by a pool of similar political, social, and cultural considerations. Nevertheless, in order to convey to the reader the extent of the creativity of Muscovite mythopoeic activities (and of the flexibility in the interpretation of Muscovite myths and rituals involving the tsaritsy), the discussion occasionally traces the evolution of themes relating to the royal women from the sixteenth through the seventeenth century. This approach will enable the reader to see that, in spite of variations, the basic motifs underlying the tsaritsa's image and actions (such as her ability to protect the royal family, to intercede for the tsar and his realm, to assure dynastic continuity, and to appear as a champion of the Orthodox faith) reoccurred in every generation throughout the Muscovite period.

Following a short introduction to the role of the mothers of the grand princes of Moscow in the political conditions that shaped the emerging Muscovite state in the fourteenth and fifteenth centuries, Chapter 1 deals with the mythopoeic activities of the Russian rulers' wives regarding the issue of royal motherhood in the face of the emerging Muscovite autocracy in the sixteenth and seventeenth centuries. The challenges and dangers faced by Muscovite royal women are juxtaposed with the effects of their image-building activities, not only on their own position in government but on the Russian tsardom as a whole. The chapter argues that, with the help of the church, the royal women of Muscovy devised the myth of the blessed womb of the tsaritsa to counter the threat to their social position resulting from their inability to conceive an heir to the throne. The evolution of the image of the barren Solomoniia Saburova, who was forced to take the veil, to that of a popularly venerated saint whose spiritual fertility enabled her to intercede for the Russian ruler and his realm shows that the myth of the tsaritsa's blessed womb transcended its original biological context and ascribed to royal women a larger, political function. The "public" possibilities of royal motherhood also come to the fore in the tsaritsy's efforts to promote the cult of specific protector saints of the royal family. For generations the royal women adhered to the myth of the tsaritsa's blessed womb and acted as patrons of saints who were seen as protectors of the royal family. The discussion therefore follows these phenomena from the late fifteenth century to the time of Peter the Great.

Chapter 2 explores the role of the tsaritsy as spiritual helpmates to their husbands and as intercessors for the autocracy before God. In this context the discussion explores the development of the myth of the pious tsaritsa Anastasiia from its inception in the reign of her husband, Ivan IV, to the end of the seventeenth century. In spite of the different usage of the myth by the Rurikide and early Romanov rulers, the theme of the tsaritsa's commitment to the tsardom and its subjects remains remarkably consistent. In order to show the continued validity of the concept of the tsaritsa's spiritual intercession in the Romanov period, the chapter investigates the application of this theme to Mariia Il'inichna, wife of Aleksei Mikhailovich, in two iconographic compositions from the second part of the seventeenth century.

Chapter 3 investigates the role of religious symbolism in the construction of the concept of the tsaritsa as an independent ruler and the tsaritsa's association with dynastic stability in the late sixteenth and early seventeenth centuries. For this purpose the scant written evidence for Irina Godunova's ability to serve as a link between the dynasty of her husband, Fedor Ivanovich, and the family of her brother, Boris, is compared with the artistic testimony provided by the iconographic program of the tsaritsa's reception chamber, the Golden Palace of the Tsaritsy in the Kremlin. The skilled selection of the images of non-Muscovite pious royal women who were unmarried or widowed in the fresco cycles of the Golden Palace confers the message that the spiritual potential of their Muscovite counterpart, Tsaritsa Irina, empowered her to act as a ruler in her own right in times of political crisis. Chapter 3 then investigates the question of how during the subsequent Time of Troubles, the dynastic, political, and social crisis that beset Russia in the early seventeenth century, two royal women—Mariia Grigor'evna Skuratova-Bel'skaia and Mariia (Marfa) Fedorovna Nagaia—manipulated their motherhood status in order to act as regents and advisers for their sons and to claim a decisive role in Russia's quest for a new legitimate ruler. While Mariia Grigor'evna benefited from the recent propaganda surrounding Irina Godunova's figure and, as a result, managed to uphold the claim of the Godunovs to the throne, her contemporary Mariia Nagaia exploited the fact that she had given birth to a son of Ivan IV (albeit in an uncanonical union) to support the claim of a pretender. Although the royal mothers suffered great hardships in their role as guarantors of dynastic stability, they managed to assert their own importance in the process.

Chapter 4 studies the involvement of the female members of the family of the Romanov tsars in affairs of the realm. Much of the source material discussed here—such as travel accounts and the correspondence of the family of Aleksei Mikhailovich—is in principle known to scholars of the period, but I have presented it in a new way. My argument takes issue with the established view that the wives, daughters, and sisters of the Romanov tsars led a detached and sheltered life in the *terem* (the royal women's quarters). Undoubtedly the lives of these women were subject to a larger degree of ritualization than those of their predecessors, but so were the lives of their male counterparts. Anyone researching the living arrangements of the royal family in the Kremlin in the seventeenth century must be careful to avoid modern assumptions about the meaning of the private sphere and its relation to the public realm. My study of the tsars' treatment of their female family members and royal women's interaction with government officials in the Kremlin and their subjects at large shows them informed about affairs of the realm. Mariia Il'inichna was determined and able to wield authority in the crisis year of 1654–1655 when the plague struck Moscow during the tsar's absence. Particular attention is paid to the ways in which the religious authority of the tsaritsa sanctioned by tradition was expressed in the Romanov period. Finally, my discussion focuses on the similarities of the tasks of the tsars' wives (*tsaritsy*) and the tsars' sisters and daughters (*tsarevny*). First, I seek to demonstrate that the tsarevny's contribution to the affairs of the realm counted in the same way as that of the tsaritsy. Second, the close examination of the accepted activities of the royal daughters of Aleksei Mikhailovich aims at creating a framework that helps us understand better the rise of one of these daughters, Sofiia Alekseevna, to power in 1682.

A reexamination of the position of Sofiia Alekseevna as a regent and ruler of Russia is the subject of the final chapter. Studies of the tsarevna are abundant, so I do not present a comprehensive account of Sofiia's achievements or transgressions. A balanced view of the tsarevna's governmental and cultural activities is provided in Lindsey Hughes, *Sophia, Regent of Russia 1657–1704*. Still, the customary view that Sofiia Alekseevna's reign represented an early, though abortive, attempt to create a modern government in Russia, which Hughes shares in spite of her consideration of the tsarevna's pious image, deserves closer scrutiny. The long-standing Muscovite tradition of enhancing the position of Russian royal women in government and society through their association with powerful religious symbols makes it seem reasonable to look for connections between this tradition and Sofiia Alekseevna's role as regent and ruler. In this context I investigate the mythopoeic efforts at Sofiia's court, evident in the secular panegyric literature and the semi-Western art of the pre-Petrine period. The striking resemblance between the religious metaphors developed as a means to legitimate Sofiia's predominant position in government and the religious constructs relating to sixteenth- and seventeenth-century tsars' wives uncovers an indebtedness of Sofiia's regime to Muscovite definitions of gender and power that has not yet been sufficiently appreciated.

A few further comments may help clarify the perspective of this book. The focus of this study is the empowerment of medieval Russian royal women through religious symbolism. Such an approach by its nature emphasizes the integration of these women into the complicated fabric of social and political obligations and opportunities. If my research treats the potential of Muscovite tsaritsy and tsarevny to participate in affairs of the realm optimistically, this does not imply that I deny the difficulties of their position. The dangers of political persecution, forced tonsure, or exhaustion from childbirth were real for these women, and whenever possible I stress their seriousness. Furthermore, if I speak of the tsaritsy's share in governmental responsibilities, I am fully aware that this share was qualitatively different from that of the male ruler. What motivated this study, however, was a conviction that medieval Russian society and culture offered women opportunities to deal with adversities specific to their gender. Some help came from unexpected corners. In principle suspicious of women with authority, the Orthodox church supplied the religious symbolism that broadened the scope of the tsaritsy's influence.

The findings of this study cannot be easily generalized. In view of their exceptional social status, the experience of Russian royal women may well be different from that of their noble and non-noble counterparts. The roles of religious myths and rituals in the lives of ordinary medieval Russian women still await investigation.

Another caveat concerns the use of myth and ritual in this work. As a cultural historian, I am not concerned with the detection of historical truths behind these phenomena. Rather, I proceed from the assumption that Muscovite Russians accepted the validity of myths and rituals. In evaluating their impact and meaning in medieval Russia, I follow mythographers such as William G. Doty, who defines myth and ritual as tools that bring about social integration and serve as "communicative means through which persons find meaningful systems of symbols for identifying their experiences."[22] Finally, I wish to avoid the impression that mythmaking and the performance of ritual in Muscovite Russia concentrated exclusively on the issue of gender and power. A true appreciation of the importance of Russian royal women to the Muscovite tsardom can only be gained if we appreciate the degree to which mythopoeic endeavors concerning the person of the tsaritsa were part of larger ideological efforts to define the position of the tsar. From this perspective this work should be read in conjunction with the recent works of Michael Flier and Daniel Rowland on the religious imagery relating to the Muscovite tsar.[23]

This work contributes to the discussion of the relation of gender and sovereignty. Historians generally point out that the role gender played in the conceptualization of sovereignty in Western societies was shaped by patriarchal attitudes and sanctioned by cultural, religious traditions. In a world where the survival of the state and the institution of the church in it depended on physical prowess, display of strength, or military muscle, women were less likely to be given the opportunity to take the reins of government. While supporters of the patriarchal order proclaimed women's physical or mental limitations, members of the church resisted the notion of women in power on theological grounds, arguing that women were of weaker moral character than men. The strong, unmitigated language of patriarchy and the church with regard to the subject of gender and sovereignty often has led scholars to assume that both patriarchy and the church were monolithic constructs that in essence were detrimental to women seeking political authority and cultural influence. The case of Muscovite royal women shows that such a view is one-sided. Although both institutions denied royal women equal access to power in principle, they allowed for and even promoted possibilities for these women to claim political and cultural visibility. For the male rulers women's involvement in government was a matter of convenience; able women could be politically active and strengthen the patriarchal system at the same time. The Russian Orthodox church, which was concerned with the salvation of all its members, in the end could not afford to treat women as innately weak vessels. Women's spiritual potential had long been acknowledged in the traditional stories of the female martyrs and saints and the Virgin's capacity to intercede for mankind before God. When Muscovite Russians coined the notion of a tsardom sanctioned by God, they ascribed this kind of spiritual power to the wife of the tsar so that she might engage the support of the supernatural for her royal husband and her realm. In exercising this task, the royal women of Muscovy reversed the inferiority associated with their sex. Traditionally subordinate to their husbands, they used their function as spiritual mediators to assume a prominent position between God and tsar.

1 The Myth of the Tsaritsa's Blessed Womb

ONE OF THE MOST IMPORTANT aspects of the wives of royal figures is their ability to give birth to a male heir to the throne. While the delivery and rearing of healthy children are commonplace, timeless goals, the challenges these tasks present to royal mothers and their response to them lend themselves to historical investigation. In Muscovite Russia motherhood became a crucial element in the definition of the image and role of a grand princess or tsaritsa. From the inception of the Muscovite state, the mothers of the Russian rulers figured prominently in the political, social, and economic way of life that eventually gave rise to an autocratic system of government. When in the sixteenth and seventeenth centuries, the tsars' wives struggled with the problems of infertility and infant mortality, the strong image of the royal mother in Russian political culture enabled these women to strengthen their social position by transcending the narrow biological definition of their motherhood and giving it a larger, religious meaning. The following discussion explores the practical aspects of the maternal role of the Russian rulers' wives during the period of the consolidation of the Muscovite grand principality and the manipulation of the concept of royal motherhood through the creation of myths and rituals in the subsequent tsarist period.

The Muscovite Royal Mother in the Fourteenth and Fifteenth Centuries

In their evaluation of the position of Russian women, scholars in the East and West generally view the fourteenth and fifteenth centuries (the so-called appanage period) as a kind of golden age during which women and especially those associated with ruling families enjoyed extensive economic and legal rights and exercised political power on the basis of their prominent position in their families. During this period women freely bought and sold landed property, inherited estates from their husbands and levied dues from them, acted as litigants and witnesses, and even administered justice in their own territories.[1] In the absence of a unified Russian realm, the notion of the public domain indistinguishably merged with the private sphere of the ruling families in the numerous principalities that dotted the Russian landscape, thus enabling women to play a visible, political role.[2] Experts on medieval Russian women such as Susanne McNally, Alexandre Eck, and Carsten Goehrke stress the large share of properties the grand princes bequeathed to their wives and the administrative competence of the grand princesses, who supervised not only the legal and economic affairs on their estates but also a large staff of servitors. The Muscovite rulers' wives also enjoyed unique discretionary powers in granting away extensive fiscal and judicial immunities.[3] According to received opinion these rights and opportunities were curtailed by the rise of the Muscovite state, culminating in the efforts of Ivan III at the end of the fifteenth century to become the sole ruler of all Russian territories. Scholars tend to argue that women's role in the family became privatized in the subsequent two centuries, reducing women to play the role of helpless wives who could aspire to power only by illegal means.[4]

A close look at the grand princesses of Moscow during the appanage period, which witnessed the gradual formation of the Muscovite state, suggests that this view must be modified. While tsardom undoubtedly changed some of the activities of the wives of the Russian rulers (the evidence for judicial and economic activities of royal women declines significantly for the sixteenth and seventeenth centuries, and they lose their significance as landholders for the Russian state), Moscow's centralizing effort nevertheless proceeded without disturbing basic assumptions about the role of Russian royal women as matriarchs and mothers within the royal family.[5] An understanding of the tsaritsy's role as mothers in the sixteenth and seventeenth centuries thus entails an appreciation of the implications of the grand princesses' position in the royal family for the Muscovite political system.

The grand princes of Moscow faced great challenges from their external and internal political rivals in the fourteenth and fifteenth centuries, a result of the political and economic weakness of the Muscovite ruler and the Russian predilection for the principle of collateral succession. These challenges affected the scope of action of their wives, and decisively so, since they shared the burden of keeping the grand-princely succession in the family.[6] In order to ensure the survival of a unified Muscovite territory, Dmitrii Donskoi not only willed the grand principality to his oldest son, Vasilii, but also made his wife, Evdokiia, the guardian of all his children.[7] Although Vasilii's brothers were to obey him in his father's stead, Donskoi apparently thought it wise to commit all his children to a higher authority within his family, who could watch over the proper transfer of the grand principality to his second son, Iurii, in the case of Vasilii's demise.[8] The interconnectedness of the grand princess's guardianship and the larger political challenges faced by the emerging Muscovite state are also evident in Vasilii I's treatment of his wife, Sofiia Vitovtovna. Although in his second and third will Vasilii entrusted the overall guardianship of his wife and his children to his younger brother and to his Lithuanian father-in-law, Vitovt, he also increased the responsibility of his wife. He committed his successor to the Muscovite throne, Vasilii II, to Sofiia Vitovtovna—with the stipulation that he was to honor her and obey her in the place of his father.[9] Vasilii II in turn followed the precedent of his father when he entrusted his younger children to his wife, Mariia Iaroslavna, with the stipulation that they obey her wishes in his place.[10]

The grand princesses of Moscow played a crucial role in the creation of a strong grand principality as overseers of their sons' inheritances. Since the days of Dmitrii Donskoi, the grand princes issued the command in their wills that their sons obey their mothers' decisions if changes to a will had to be enacted. While the requirement that a son had to respect his mother's decision in inheritance matters had deep roots in the Russian legal tradition, as Carsten Goehrke points out, its strict application to a grand princess in the late fourteenth century served the specific purpose of strengthening the grand-princely rule.[11] Before Dmitrii Donskoi's reign, the Russian grand princes generally stipulated that in case one of their heirs lost some of his inherited territories to the Tatars, the remaining properties were to be redistributed among their sons and wives.[12] This arrangement may have satisfied all parties while all sons shared the grand principality of Vladimir. When Dmitrii Donskoi, however, decided to pass it on in its entirety to his oldest son, he realized the need to appoint an arbiter who stood above the future grand prince and his younger brothers to regulate the economic aspects of the succession. Relying on a mother's instinctual love for all her children, Donskoi bestowed upon his wife the privilege and duty to reallocate patrimonial property if one of their sons died, or if another one was born. Evdokiia also was to see to it that a son who had suffered a territorial loss was compensated with lands from his brothers' patrimonies. If the future grand prince died, her task was to assure that his successor received his patrimony and to redistribute the new ruler's share among his brothers.[13]

The supervisory role Dmitrii Donskoi accorded to his wife in the redistribution of patrimonial lands required that the grand princess's social position in the family be enhanced. For this purpose Donskoi did not appoint a guardian for his wife and included the firm command that his children were to render absolute obedience to their mother.[14] Donskoi went so far as to threaten that he would withhold his parental blessing for anyone opposing his wish. His insistence that his children owed their mother obedience in matters concerning the reallocation of patrimonial lands was not just a formula inserted in his will, but consciously made the grand princess the guardian of family peace and, as a result, political stability.[15] Vasilii II, who in his mature years was the proud father of five male children and one girl, applied his grandfather's provision concerning the redistribution of patrimonial lands among his children in the case of a future emergency to his own wife, Mariia Iaroslavna. Like Donskoi before him, he urged his children in his will to uphold family harmony and render obedience to their mother.[16] To underscore the grand princess's elevated role in the grand-princely inheritance scheme, Vasilii himself respected his own mother's bequests to his younger sons Iurii, Andrei the Elder, and Boris.[17]

The association of the grand princesses with social harmony in the ruling family—and by implication, the realm at large—inevitably led to their participation in the politics of the grand principality. The royal wives and mothers served as a symbolic center for the Muscovite rulers, who were often away from home. When Vasilii II received the grand-princely patent from the Mongol khan during his stay at the Horde in fall 1446, he lost no time to send messengers to his mother and his wife and children in Moscow with the news.[18] By the later fifteenth century, it had become customary for the Russian rulers to announce major political decisions to the matriarch of their family. In 1471 Ivan III shared his plan to move against Novgorod not only with his boyars and with the head of the Russian church, Metropolitan Filip, but also with his mother, Mariia Iaroslavna.[19] The *Novgorod II Chronicle* states that the grand princess interceded with her son on behalf of the Novgorodians and persuaded him to grant letters of security to their leaders for their trip to Moscow.[20]

The Muscovite rulers frequently engaged in consultations with their mothers concerning matters of the realm. Although it goes without saying that the grand princes' political decisions did not depend solely on their mothers' approval, the fact that crucial issues of the realm demanded the grand princesses' input makes clear that their consent was considered vital to the success of the grand principality. The motherly approval expressed the ruling family's undivided support for its champion, the grand prince. In 1425, when Iurii Dmitrievich of Zvenigorod and Galich challenged the claim of his young nephew Vasilii Vasil'evich to the throne, Sofiia Vitovtovna figured prominently in the grand prince's council, next to his uncles Andrei, Peter, and Konstantin, and Metropolitan Fotii. As an adviser to her son, Sofiia was instrumental in working out a truce between the two contenders.[21] When Ivan III saw an opportunity to enhance his prestige as a ruler by marrying Sofiia Paleolog, the niece of the last Byzantine emperor, he sought the consent of his mother, Mariia Iaroslavna, next to that of the metropolitan, his boyars, and his brothers. In 1480, when Khan Akhmet stood at the Ugra river, Ivan III took counsel about his military response with his boyars, Metropolitan Gerontii, his uncle Mikhail Andreevich Vereiskii and his mother. Ivan returned to the Ugra after receiving the blessings of Gerontii and Mariia Iaroslavna.[22]

The central position the grand-princely mother held as an adviser to the Muscovite ruler is closely connected with her function as mediator in the royal family. If we can trust the late-fifteenth-century copy of an agreement between Vasilii Dmitrievich and his brothers Andrei and Peter from ca. 1401–1402, which aimed at affirming the siblings' mutual respect and their united stand against enemies, the document was issued with the blessing of Metropolitan Kiprian and "at the order" of grand princess Evdokiia Donskaia.[23] As A. A. Zimin points out, during her regency for Vasilii II, Sofiia Vitovtovna pursued judicial reforms that limited the power of the grand prince's provincial governor (*namestnik*) to appease the minor princes and keep them from joining Iurii Dmitrievich's camp. According to the so-called *gubnaia zapis'*, which Sofiia had issued shortly after her husband's death, the *namestnik* of the senior prince no longer could pass judgment in crimes that were committed in Moscow and involved the junior princes' subjects without considering the opinion of the junior princes' judges.[24]

The grand princesses' capacity to maintain peace among the members of the Muscovite ruling family is particularly evident in the case of Mariia Iaroslavna, who confronted severe discord among her sons when Ivan III set about curtailing the economic and political privileges of his brothers. Mariia Iaroslavna's handling of the events of the 1470s suggests that the grand princess did not fall victim to Ivan III's policy of creating a centralized Russia, as McNally claims. Rather, Mariia Iaroslavna skillfully utilized her potential as a mediator to reconcile her younger sons to the notion of one unified Russia under the senior prince.[25] When in 1472 Andrei Vasil'evich the Elder and his brother Iurii became nervous about the grand prince's power to interfere in their patrimonial holdings, Mariia Iaroslavna asserted her right to intervene on their behalf. A draft of an agreement Andrei and Ivan may have presented to Mariia while she lay ill in Rostov in fall 1472 states that, at her order and with the metropolitan's blessing, Ivan was to respect their territorial and judicial rights in their inheritances.[26] In view of the recent military cooperation of the brothers with the grand prince against the Mongols, Mariia may have appealed to Ivan to be generous to his immediate siblings, as custom demanded.[27] The death of Iurii Vasil'evich in September 1472, however, rekindled the conflict of interest between the grand prince and his younger brothers. When Ivan decided to take over Iurii's holdings without apportioning to the junior princes their fair share, they called upon their mother to intervene on their behalf. The *Tipografskaia Chronicle* and the *Voskresensk Chronicle* state that, at Mariia's initiative, the grand prince compensated his brothers Boris and Andrei the Younger with the territories of Vyshegorod and Tarusa while the grand princess herself gave Andrei the Elder her city of Romanov.[28]

On the surface Ivan III's unwillingness to accede to his brothers' demands in 1472–1473 and his mother's resulting territorial loss could appear as a defeat for the grand princess, who in her husband's will had been given the right to redistribute patrimonial lands. Vasilii II, however, had put

Mariia Iaroslavna in charge of redividing the patrimonial lands of his sons only if one of them suffered a loss, not if one of them died.[29] Since the latter provision is only attested in the second will of Dmitrii Donskoi, its application to all grand princesses of the fifteenth century is problematic, although Ivan's brothers undoubtedly wished to see it upheld.[30] Under these circumstances Mariia Iaroslavna's involvement in her sons' quarrel and her ability to pressure the grand prince into making any kind of concession at all must be viewed as a sign of her undiminished success as a mediator in the grand-princely family. Moreover, her willingness to part with a minor piece of her own property betrays true diplomatic skill insofar as it made a statement to both parties about her serious commitment to peaceful relations among her kin. From this perspective, the crisis of 1472–1473 only increased the grand princess's stature as a fair arbiter among her children.

The evolution of the Muscovite grand principality in the fourteenth and fifteenth centuries into a large centralized state depended considerably on the success of the grand prince in manipulating the kinship politics of his clan. In the absence of an accepted principle of primogeniture, the territorial integrity of the grand principality could remain intact only if the ambitions of the rightful heirs within the grand-princely family could be curtailed and harnessed to the larger cause of the consolidation of grand-princely power. In this process the wives and mothers of the Muscovite grand princes played a key role. The wills of the Muscovite grand princes show that the Russian rulers relied on their wives to ensure that the redistribution of patrimonial holdings among their sons proceeded smoothly. The royal mothers had the right to the unconditional obedience of all their children, which gave them the authority to intervene in fraternal plots against the future heir to the throne. Whenever the political situation demanded it, the royal mothers could appear as guardians for the future grand princes. The Russian rulers soon realized that the respect their mothers enjoyed in the royal family could be advantageous to their goals. As a result, they increasingly sought out the advice of the grand princesses in matters of state and availed themselves of their diplomatic expertise whenever the unity of the realm was at stake.

The Myth of the Tsaritsa's Blessed Womb

While the Muscovite grand princesses during the appanage period were able to manipulate their maternal role to their own political and social advantage, the royal women of the subsequent tsarist period, who experienced difficulty in producing viable offspring, suffered from the connection of their reproductive function and social status. In Muscovite Russia the inability to give birth, for reasons of infertility or illness, could lead to divorce or forced tonsure of a grand princess or tsaritsa. When Vasilii III was unable to father offspring with his first wife, Solomoniia Saburova, he divorced her and forced her to take the veil in the Suzdal' Pokrov Monastery.[31] Whereas in the sixteenth century Muscovite ruler couples often faced the problem of producing any offspring at all, in the seventeenth century the wives of the Romanov tsars, who gave birth to numerous baby girls, had to be concerned with presenting the realm with a male heir. When Evdokiia Luk'ianovna Streshneva gave birth to a number of female children, rumors circulated that the tsaritsa might be forced to take the veil.[32] According to Samuel Collins her successor, Mariia Il'inichna, barely escaped the same threat.[33]

In medieval Russia women often took recourse to traditional magical remedies that aided against infertility and difficult birth and offered a means to determine the sex of a baby.[34] Once pregnancy was ascertained, Muscovite women often resorted to midwives and folk healers to ensure a successful birth. Grigorii Kotoshikhin, who describes the conditions at the Muscovite court in the early seventeenth century, testifies to the fact that the tsaritsa gave birth to royal children in the bathhouse in the presence of an experienced midwife (*babka*) and a few other women. The bathhouse was taboo and no one else could enter until a priest had performed prayers over the child and the women present at the birth.[35]

In spite of the suspicious attitude of Christian theology toward sex and reproduction, the Christian faith offered the tsaritsy a larger framework to solve the complex issue of their personal security and the realm's stability.[36] The Russian Orthodox church was quite willing to adopt a policy of spiritual care when it dealt with the Muscovite rulers' wives, who struggled with infertility, infant mortality, and the pressure to produce a male heir to the throne. Moreover, the language of Orthodox religion became a powerful tool in the hands of royal women who created a powerful myth that associated their ability to conceive with divine providence. The myth accorded to the tsaritsa the ability to function as a receptacle and a transmitter of divine grace during the conception of the future ruler and thus made her an important factor in the ideology of the Muscovite tsardom.

When Sofiia Paleolog, a niece of the last Byzantine emperor, became Ivan III's wife in 1472, her future as Russian grand princess was by no means assured, since Ivan had a son from his previous marriage to Mariia of Tver'.[37] The death of this son, Ivan Molodoi, in 1490 led to a struggle between Ivan Molodoi's son, Dmitrii, and Ivan III's and Sofiia's first-born son, Vasilii. The *Sophia II Chronicle* states that, during the period of Ivan III's confusion over the choice of his successor, Sofiia tried to promote her son's fortunes to a point where she was even accused of sorcery.[38] Although Ivan III chose Dmitrii as his heir in 1498, Sofiia could claim victory in the following year when Ivan III granted Vasilii the rule over Novgorod and Pskov, which foreboded Dmitrii's eventual removal from power in 1502.[39]

Sofiia's support for her son cannot be explained simply as an act of motherly love; Dmitrii's survival would have meant the loss of her role as a matriarch of the royal line. Sofiia's recognition that her fate was inextricably linked with that of her son (and her consequent resolve to do everything possible to assure his success) is evident in the inscription of a tapestry she

2. Tapestry of Sofiia Paleolog from 1499 (Historical Museum of the Trinity-Sergius Monastery, inventory no. 413). The tapestry associates Vasilii III (represented by his name saints, Archangel Gabriel and Basil of Parion) with the iconographic theme *The Descent of the Holy Spirit.* It thus promotes his claim to be the rightful, divinely blessed heir to the Muscovite throne.

donated to Saint Sergius in 1499, which not only names Vasilii Ivanovich but also proclaims Sofiia as the sole designer of the embroidery. Moreover, the tapestry advertises Sofiia's imperial background and her acceptance of Saint Sergius as a holy intercessor for the Russian ruler's family (see Figure 2).[40]

Sofiia's intention to use the liturgical embroidery to proclaim her son Vasilii's rightful status as heir to the throne and his supernatural approval as future ruler of Muscovy can also be seen in the iconography of the tapestry.[41] The images of the tapestry are grouped around a central axis defined by the depictions of the Old Testament Trinity and the Appearance of the Virgin to Saint Sergius. Both themes not only invoke an association with the Trinity-Sergius Monastery, to which the tapestry was donated, but represent incidents of man's visitation by the divine. The images to the right of the axis all express an eschatological theme. The death of John the Baptist, who is called the Forerunner in the Orthodox tradition, points to the arrival of the Kingdom of Heaven. The prophesied union of Christ and his father is manifest in the image of God Father Enthroned. The Descent of the Holy Spirit demonstrates man's participation in the Kingdom of Heaven. The location of one of Ivan's name saints, Timothy, next to John the Baptist closely connects the eschatological theme with Ivan III.[42] The choice of the iconographic composition of the Descent of the Holy Spirit elucidates the purpose of the association of the Muscovite ruler with the Kingdom of the Spirit.[43] The implicit meaning of the outpouring of divine grace on the royal figure in the composition, who is often associated with King David, is clarified by the appearance of Vasilii III's name saints, the archangel Gabriel and Saint Basil of Parion, immediately below the image of the Descent of the Holy Spirit.[44] By making her son Vasilii the receiver of divine grace and associating him with the king figure of the Pentecost image, Sofiia stated the claim that Vasilii was the rightful, divinely blessed successor to the grand-princely throne. The eschatological scheme on Sofiia's tapestry thus represents one of the earliest manifestations of the Muscovite theory of the divine origin of the Russian ruler's power, which Iosif Volotskii officially formulated in the 1510s.[45]

The notion of Vasilii's spiritual approval as heir to the throne is reinforced by the intercessory scheme to the left of the tapestry's iconographic axis. Here we find the Virgin Bogoliubskaia petitioning Christ. The image of the Annunciation, which shows the archangel Gabriel bringing the Virgin the news of her conception, refers to the Mother of God as a bridge between the divine and human spheres. The intermediary position of the Virgin is also stressed in the iconography of the Ascension, which shows the Mother of God remaining behind with the Apostles in the physical world, while Christ is carried up to heaven by two angels. The intended beneficiary of the Virgin's intercession is represented by the figure of John Chrysostom, who is also one of Ivan III's name saints.[46] Sofiia Paleolog's effort to connect the theme of spiritual intercession with the Muscovite grand prince is further underscored by the depiction of the Russian metropolitan saints Peter (1308–1326) and Aleksii (1354–1378) on the left side of the tapestry. As Günther Stökl points out, the practice of the Muscovite rulers to petition these two Russian miracle-workers along with the Virgin for political success had become regularized since the 1470s.[47]

Sofiia's selection of saintly supporters for her cause displays both her political shrewdness and her sense for the power of religious symbols in Muscovite Russia. Undoubtedly she was aware of Saint Sergius's reputation as an intercessor for the Muscovite dynasty. Her inclusion of Saints Peter and Aleksii in the tapestry of 1499 shows her ability to manipulate a recently established religious tradition to advance her dynastic claim. If Sofiia wanted to assure the continuity of her own line, she needed only to emphasize the special relationship between Vasilii and the dynasty's protector saints. The notion that Vasilii's selection as heir to the Russian throne was sanctioned by divine providence strengthened his political position, in particular since he lacked the legitimizing force of a coronation ceremony, as enjoyed by his rival, Dmitrii.[48]

In crafting the message on her tapestry, Sofiia Paleolog may also have been inspired by the tale of Vasilii II's birth found in the *Moscow Chronicle Compilation of 1497*. According to the chronicle, on March 15, 1415, Vasilii I's wife, Sofiia Vitovtovna, experienced difficulties delivering the child. When the grand prince asked a monk from the Monastery of Saint John the Baptist Below the Pines to pray for her, the monk ordered him to pray and promised him that the princess would give birth to a son that evening. At the moment of the child's delivery, Vasilii's spiritual father was saying his regular prayers in his cell in the Monastery of the Transfiguration. Suddenly a man appeared to him and told him to go and pray for the princess and her newborn son. The priest obeyed and paid a visit to the princely family, but nobody there knew who had sent for him.[49] The story uses a divine prophecy of the birth of the princely child as a means to heighten his reputation as a legitimate ruler. The major actors are the grand prince himself and his spiritual adviser through whom the divine will speaks. Grand Princess Sofiia plays a largely passive role, depending on the physical support of her servants and the spiritual support of her husband and the clergy, who are charged with the responsibility of praying for her. The theme of this episode, God's goodwill regarding the Muscovite ruling house, could have easily been appropriated by Sofiia Paleolog to stress her son's right to the throne.[50]

The close association of Saint Sergius with the heir to the Russian throne, promoted by Sofiia Paleolog in the tapestry of 1499, also appealed to her daughter-in-law Solomoniia Saburova, who in the 1520s was struggling with a dynastic crisis of a different kind. When after twenty years of marriage her childlessness threatened to lead to divorce, Solomoniia sought every means available to "loosen the knot of her womb."[51] During an inquest on November 23, 1524, her brother Ivan Iur'evich admitted that she had engaged many sorceresses and sorcerers to cure her infertility with love magic. One year before her husband divorced her because of her infertility, Solomoniia participated in a pilgrimage to Volokolamsk and Mozhaisk, presumably to implore the local saints to grant her offspring.[52] Solomoniia then seems to have made a last effort to avert her fate by donating a tapestry as a liturgical gift to Saint Sergius (see Figure 3).

The compositional alterations of Solomoniia's embroidery, which in iconographic detail is modeled after the tapestry of 1499, reflect a conscious shift from Sofiia's theme (of the divinely approved heir to the Russian throne) to the notion of the blessed womb of the tsaritsa.[53] Solomoniia's hope to engage the help of the divine is evident in the plea contained in the tapestry's inscription that the Lord have mercy on the royal couple and their realm and grant them a child. Pictorially the tapestry privileges the connection between the royal mother and the divine blessing of the future ruler over the relationship of the Muscovite rulers to the divine. All of its corner images (the Annunciation; the Birth of Christ; the

3. Tapestry of Solomoniia Saburova (1525) expressing her wish to conceive an heir to the Muscovite throne (Historical Museum of the Trinity-Sergius Monastery, inventory no. 409). The tapestry associates examples of biblical miraculous conceptions or births in the corners with the name saints of Vasilii III and his wife Solomoniia, i.e. the archangel Gabriel and the mother of the Maccabees.

Birth of the Virgin and the Encounter of Joachim and Anna at the Golden Gate; the Encounter of Zakhary and Elizabeth and the Birth of John the Baptist) depict a biblical example of a miraculous conception or a miraculous birth. The association of the myth of divinely inspired birth with the donors of the tapestry is established by the depiction of Vasilii III's and Solomoniia's name saints, the archangel Gabriel and the mother of the Maccabees.[54] The tapestry further includes depictions of Saints Peter, Aleksii, and Leontii, who as the protectors of the Muscovite ruling family could guarantee the continued survival of its bloodline.[55]

Although Solomoniia's plea to Saint Sergius for offspring remained unanswered and Vasilii III condemned her to end her life as a nun in the Suzdal' Pokrov Monastery, the grand princess's fertility myth was not forgotten. In order to sanction its approval of Vasilii's divorce, soon after 1525 the church sought to emphasize Solomoniia's consent in the matter in the tale *"O postrizanii blagovernyia velikiia kniainy Solomanidy"* ("Tale of the Tonsure of the Pious Grand Princess Solomoniia"), which appears in the *Pafnut'ev Borovskii Chronicle* and the Synodal copy of the *Tipografskaia Chronicle*.[56] The tale sidesteps the issue of Solomoniia's incapacity to bear offspring by comparing the grand princess with Sarah, who renounced her conjugal rights for the sake of the continuity of Abraham's dynasty, and by introducing the claim that Solomoniia had been destined by the divine spirit for spiritual—rather than physical—motherhood.[57] With its assertion that "the Holy Spirit had sown a seed of wheat in her heart that the fruit of virtue might grow," the tale equates Solomoniia's monastic calling with a miraculous conception. In spite of her physical infertility, Solomoniia was still considered "fruitful." The version of the tale found in the *Pafnut'ev Borovskii Chronicle* emphasized Solomoniia's spiritual fertility to the point that it retracted the previous comparison of the grand princess with Sarah, who after all had been so chagrined by her infertility that she urged Abraham to have intercourse with his slave Hagar. Instead, the *Pafnut'ev Borovskii Chronicle* claimed that Solomoniia imitated Anna, the mother of the Virgin, who "untied the knot of her infertility through fasting and prayer, and conceived the Virgin Mary in her womb, and by this act gave birth to the immaterial light, the queen."[58]

Under Metropolitan Makarii (1542–1563) Muscovite ecclesiastics further developed the theme of the tsaritsy's blessed womb in the *Stepennaia kniga (Book of Steps)* to underscore the divinely inspired position of the Russian ruler, a notion designed to bolster the tsar's claim to the leadership of the Orthodox world after the fall of Constantinople in 1453.[59] This chronicle linked the hagiographic *topos* of miraculous birth with the Muscovite tsaritsy, starting with Sofiia Paleolog. According to the chronicle, Sofiia gave birth to Vasilii III with the help of Saint Sergius of Radonezh after producing only daughters for many years.[60] During a pilgrimage, which Sofiia undertook on foot to the Trinity-Sergius Monastery to implore the saint for male offspring, she suddenly encountered Saint Sergius. The saint, who held a baby boy in his arms, hurled the infant into Sofiia's lap and disappeared. The bewildered princess searched for the baby in the folds of her gown, but to no avail. Sofiia continued her pilgrimage and prayed at the shrine of Saint Sergius, fully confident that the saint had listened to her plea. From that time on her womb was blessed. She eventually gave birth to the future heir to the throne on March 25, the very day of the Annunciation.[61]

The tale not only reflects Sofiia's notion of her son's divinely approved succession to the throne, as the tapestry of 1499 did, but also seeks to portray her as a vessel of the divine. By focusing on Sofiia rather than on her child, the story allots to the royal mother a crucial role in the issue of succession. As the episode points out, not only was Sofiia concerned about her inability to produce male offspring but her dynastic significance was in question since the previous wife of Ivan III already had given birth to a son. By claiming that the conception of Vasilii was divinely inspired and revealed to Sofiia by Saint Sergius, the chronicle ascribed to her the uncontested prestige of a legitimate royal mother. The heightening of Sofiia's prestige through the myth of miraculous conception is also evident in the story's emphasis on her giving birth to Vasilii on the feast of the Annunciation, which contrasts with the simple references in earlier chronicles to Vasilii's birth date and the feast day of his patron saint Gabriel.[62] Thus Sofiia's experience of miraculous conception is equalled to that of the Virgin.

The *Stepennaia kniga* also connects the theme of miraculous birth with Ivan IV's mother, Elena Glinskaia, who during the first four years of her marriage did not conceive. Glinskaia accompanied her husband on arduous pilgrimages to distant monasteries to beseech the saints to help reverse her barrenness. In 1528 Vasilii and Elena journeyed to Vologda, Beloozero, Kirillov, and the Ferapontov Monastery.[63] The *Stepennaia kniga* compared the eventual delivery of Ivan IV to the miraculous birth of famous biblical figures such as Isaac, the prophet Samuel, Samson, John the Baptist, and the Virgin Mary.[64] In another episode Elena Glinskaia receives the prediction from a holy fool that she would give birth to "Titus, a large mind."[65] The very existence of such stories contributed to the development of a myth that linked the revelation of the divine will and the mystery of childbirth in the figure of the royal mother, who thus became a key factor in the development of the ruler mystique of her son.

Once the myth of the divinely inspired conception of the Russian rulers had been created, it could serve as an effective tool to shield the royal wives temporarily from the pressures of having to produce male offspring. The value of such a socioreligious mechanism is significant in light of the fact that the tsaritsy struggled with the enormous problem of infant mortality.[66] Even a fertile royal mother could never be sure of actually seeing one of her sons succeed to the throne. In the periods between pregnancies, when the fate of a childless tsaritsa and that of the realm hung in the balance, the myth of royal miraculous birth provided a reprieve for the tsaritsa since it maintained the hope that God and the saints could still grant her offspring. This hope in turn could inspire her to regain control over her life by engaging in pious activities, such as almsgiving and pilgrimages, in order to assure the support of the supernatural.

The value of the myth of the tsaritsa's blessed womb is evident in the case of Ivan IV's first two wives, Anastasiia Romanovna and Mariia Temriukovna. Anastasiia's failure to produce children in the first two years after her marriage to Ivan IV on February 3, 1547, caused her to undertake numerous pilgrimages to the shrine of Saint Sergius to petition him for offspring.[67] The events surrounding the birth of Ivan's and Anastasiia's first child on August 10, 1549, reveal that the royal couple had entertained the hope for a miraculous conception. Shortly after the delivery of a baby girl, Ivan founded a chapel in the names of Joachim and Anna, the parents of the Virgin, at the Novodevichii Monastery and baptized his daughter there with the name Anna.[68] This ceremonial act clearly compares the delivery of the royal baby girl to Saint Anna's miraculous conception of the Virgin. The royal couple's interest in the miraculous birth theme again surfaced after the death of their first son, Dmitrii.[69] According to Chapter 19 of the *vita* of Saint Nikita of Pereslavl', the royal spouses came to Rostov to implore Saint Leontii for more children.[70] Chapter 20 of the *vita* notes that the royal couple prayed to Saints Peter, Aleksii, Iona, Sergius of Radonezh, and Nikita of Pereslavl' during this pilgrimage.[71] Anastasiia's eventual pregnancy was attributed to Saint Nikita of Pereslavl', at whose shrine the tsar and tsaritsa had prayed for offspring. Saint Nikita also attracted the attention of Ivan IV's second wife, Mariia Temriukovna, who also suffered from infertility. In March 1563, two years after her marriage, Mariia finally gave birth to a baby boy named Vasilii, but the child died within two months.[72] During a trip to the monastery of Saint Nikita of Pereslavl' in the following year, Mariia Temriukovna asked the abbot to implore Saint Nikita for "the fruit of the womb for the succession of our realm."[73] Mariia's belief in the notion that Saint Nikita could bring about the miraculous conception of royal offspring may well have been inspired by her spiritual adviser, Metropolitan Afanasii, who accompanied the royal family on the trip to Pereslavl'.[74]

The myth of the tsaritsa's blessed womb continued to find supporters among the Muscovite clergy after Ivan the Terrible's death in 1584. Conceivably the violent death of Tsarevich Ivan and the physical and mental frailty of his brother Fedor, who succeeded his father to the throne, induced ecclesiastics to recall the auspicious beginnings of the tsardom marked by Ivan IV's own miraculous birth. In 1584 Bishop Leonid of Riazan' testified to the veracity of the claim that Saint Pafnutii Borovskii had inspired Ivan's conception.[75] The monk Nafanail, who composed the *vita* of Kornilii Komel'skii in 1589, used Vasilii III's and Elena Glinskaia's pilgrimage to the Kirillov monastery in 1528 as a backdrop for another story of the royal blessed womb.[76] According to Nafanail, Vasilii and Elena intended to implore Saint Kirill for an heir. On his return trip from Beloozero, the grand prince met Saint Kornilii and asked him to pray for royal offspring. After receiving a rich reward, the saint complied. When Elena successfully delivered the future Ivan IV, Vasilii III acknowledged the saint as the supernatural agent responsible for his birth.[77]

Faced with the specter of childlessness (a result of the poor constitution of Tsar Fedor), his wife, Irina, followed the custom of her predecessors and took recourse to the myth of miraculous royal birth to convey a sense of confidence that a successful pregnancy was still possible. In July 1585 Fedor Ivanovich urged his wife to attend the translation of Saint Sergius's relics to a new shrine and to pray to the saint for children. Irina willingly consented and undertook the pilgrimage to the Trinity-Sergius Monastery on foot. According to Giles Fletcher, Irina visited Saint Sergius's shrine yearly to implore the saint to bless her womb since he had "a special gift and faculty that way."[78]

Irina's childlessness seems to have inspired the major monastic centers in Russia to engage the help of their miracle-working founders to avert the extinction of the Rurikide house. The inscription on an icon depicting the Appearance of the Virgin to Saint Sergius—painted by the cellarer of the Trinity-Sergius Monastery, Evstafii Golovkin, in 1588—contains a prayer for the health and fertility of the royal couple. Another icon by Golovkin from 1591 with Saint Sergius's image contains a similar request to the saint.[79] A miracle-story involving Saint Antonii Siiskii notes the intercession of Saints Sergius of Radonezh, Kirill of Beloozero, Zosima and Savatii of Solovki, and Antonii Siiskii for Irina's fertility. The tale relates that one night in 1585, the monk Nifont of the Antonievo-Siiskii Monastery saw a candle light up near the shrine while he was praying at Saint Antonii's tomb. In the semi-dark room the monk observed a beautiful woman kneeling and silently praying at the tomb. Thinking that he was experiencing a demonic illusion of a prostitute, Nifont left the site terrified and angrily vowed not to return to the saint's tomb. Saint Antonii, however, appeared to the monk in his sleep and convinced him that he had not seen the apparition of a temptress but, rather, the angel of Tsaritsa Irina, who had taken on her earthly image. The angel had been visiting the monastic establishments of Saints Sergius, Kirill, Zosima and Savatii and had made a final stop at Saint Antonii's tomb to pray for Irina's ability to conceive offspring.[80] The miracle story shows that, in her struggle to conceive an heir to the throne, Irina was thought to command the spiritual support of the major Russian miracle-workers, whose mediating skills were unquestioned. Irina's close relationship with the saints strengthened her position in the royal family and instilled in her and her subjects the confidence that an heir to the throne might yet arrive.

The Muscovite belief in the power of the myth of the tsaritsa's blessed womb is also evident in Patriarch Iov's letter to Irina Godunova regarding the premature death of her only child, the infant Feodosiia.[81] In the letter Iov insisted that Irina's womb could be blessed again if she lived a God-pleasing life and engaged in prayer with a contrite heart like Anna, the mother of the Virgin Mary, who lamented her infertility under a laurel tree and then received the prophecy that God had granted her to bear a child.[82] Patriarch Iov also encouraged Irina to put her faith in the Virgin Mary, who was known to help women with fertility problems and could intercede with Christ on Irina's behalf.[83] Moreover, the all-Russian saints, notably Saints Peter, Aleksii, and Iona, were able to come to Irina's help. The patriarch suggested that Irina emulate Hannah, the mother of the prophet Samuel, who conceived miraculously as a result of steadfast prayers.[84]

During Fedor Ivanovich's reign, non-Russian leaders of the Orthodox church as well played an important role in the royal couple's battle against infertility. In 1585 Fedor Ivanovich confirmed his father's gift of a house to the Hilandar Monastery on Mount Athos in return for prayers that his wife might give birth to a child.[85] Four years later, the tsar sent one thousand rubles to the patriarch of Jerusalem with the request that the patriarch pray for his and Irina's health and her ability to conceive.[86] According to Arsenios Elassonis, who in 1589 participated in a meeting between the patriarch of Constantinople and Irina Godunova in the newly built reception room of the tsaritsa, the Golden Palace of the Tsaritsy, Irina presented gifts to the patriarch of Constantinople. She personally appealed to the patriarch to pray to God "for the king and for me, the tiniest of your daughters, that he will fulfill the wishes of our subjects and finally grant a child to me, and an heir to this realm of Vladimir, Moscow, and all Russia."[87]

Patriarch Jeremiah's response to Irina's request betrays his familiarity with the myth of the blessed womb of the tsaritsa. In his address to Irina, he expressed the hope that she would conceive by divine inspiration, just as the Virgin had been blessed by God during the Annunciation:

> the same God who dispatched the archangel Gabriel to announce the mystery of the Incarnation to the most holy immaculate Virgin, who is full of the grace of God and is justly called the vessel containing the manna, the sacred mountain, the bush that does not burn . . .—the same God will not cause to oppress you with so much pain and anguish that he will not grant you to be pregnant and not pour out over you, o queen, a more abundant effusion of his grace.[88]

Although the Russian realm and the royal court undoubtedly placed the burden of responsibility for the continuation of the ruling dynasty on Irina Godunova's shoulders, she was not left to her own devices to confront the precarious situation she faced on account of her failure to produce royal  offspring. Arsenios's account shows that the Orthodox church endorsed the development of an elaborate ritual of gift-giving with which the tsaritsa could oblige the clergy to present her case before God. By ritually humiliating herself, she emphasized the significance of her position in the continuum of the dynasty. Irina's appeals for spiritual intercession did not merely denote a personal wish for motherhood but represented the interest of the realm at large. In this sense the tsaritsa not only found a way to gain control over the threat of infertility in her life but was able to take on an active role by appearing herself as a petitioner for the success of the tsar and the Russian realm.

In the seventeenth century, the myth of the miraculous conception of the tsaritsy enjoyed great popularity. As in the previous century, the Russian ecclesiastical establishment during the Romanov period regularly performed prayers to incline God and his saints to grant the realm royal offspring.[89] Supporters of the Romanov dynasty used the myth of the tsaritsa's blessed womb to bolster their claims that Filaret's son mounted the Russian throne with divine approval. In his description of Mikhail Fedorovich's coronation in 1613, Avraamii Palitsyn noted that God had selected the

Russian ruler before his birth and anointed him in the womb of his mother.[90] In his *Istoriia o tsariakh i velikikh kniaziakh zemli russkoi (History of the Tsars and Grand Princes of the Russian Land),* composed in the second part of the seventeenth century, Fedor Griboedov made a similar claim regarding Aleksei Mikhailovich.[91] When Patriarch Filaret blessed his son's marriage with Evdokiia Luk'ianovna Streshneva in 1626, he wishfully compared his son and his bride with the biblical couple Abraham and Sarah and with the couple Elkanah and Hannah, whose sons Isaac and Samuel had been miraculously conceived.[92] The connection between biblical miraculous conceptions and the royal couple's fertility was also maintained in the wedding ritual of 1626. According to the wedding roster, the marital chamber of the royal couple was decorated with icons depicting the Birth of Christ and the Birth of the Virgin Mary. The images, placed at the head of the bed, clearly were intended to serve as a model for the newlyweds during their first conjugal intercourse.[93]

The Romanov women seem to have been well aware that certain saints had the power to bless the royal womb. According to Zabelin, on February 21, 1628, during her pregnancy with Tsarevna Pelagiia, Evdokiia Luk'ianovna Streshneva went to the village Rubtsovo-Pokrovskoe in order to pray. In her customary gifts the tsaritsa included a generous donation to the local chapel of Saint Sergius. On June 16, 1629, Evdokiia undertook a pilgrimage on foot to the Trinity-Sergius Monastery to give thanks for the birth of her first son, Aleksei, the heir to the throne.[94]

The wide dissemination of the myth of the tsaritsa's blessed womb in the seventeenth century can be gleaned from the treatment contemporary literature and art gave the story of Sofiia Paleolog's miraculous conception on the way to the Trinity-Sergius Monastery (found in the *Stepennaia kniga).* The *Piskarev Chronicle* modified the story by ascribing the incident to Elena Glinskaia, who was so frightened by the experience of having an infant hurled at her by Saint Sergius that she fell to the ground. Her husband, who was with her, had her carried to the Trinity Church in the monastery where she lay speechless for a long time. Upon her return to Moscow, she conceived Ivan IV.[95] The changes in the story shift the focus away from the royal mother to the Muscovite ruler who both initiated the trip and rescued his wife, but the actual act of the miraculous conception still involves exclusively the saint and the grand princess. The episode of Sofiia Paleolog's miraculous conception in the *Stepennaia kniga* was also included in the new account of Saint Sergius's miracles compiled by the cellarer of the Trinity-Sergius Monastery, Simon Azar'in, and published for the first time in 1646 at the order of Aleksei Mikhailovich.[96] Moreover, the story of Sofiia Paleolog's fateful pilgrimage to the Trinity-Sergius monastery was also worked into the composition of an icon of Saint Sergius and his *life,* attributed to one of the Iaroslavl' masters in the middle of the seventeenth century.[97] The icon shows Sofiia Paleolog's encounter with the saint in two scenes in the upper left corner of the center panel. Sofiia and several servant women appear in a stylized landscape of hills and trees. Judging from the movement of the folds of their gowns, the women have come to a sudden stop. Sofiia's gazes at the nimbed figure of Saint Sergius, who holds a child in white swaddling clothes up to her. The women seem stunned by the incident. Further below, the servant women are seen clustering around their mistress, who is seated with her cape thrown back and her left hand shoved into a fold of her gown. An inscription links the illustrations to their source, the miracles of Simon Azar'in's 1646 edition.[98]

The myth of the blessed womb of the tsaritsa not only flourished in the religious atmosphere of Muscovite Russia but survived in the secular setting of the Russian court culture of the eighteenth century. P. N. Krekshin's description of Peter the Great's deeds from the 1730s includes a segment entitled "The Conception and Birth of the Great Tsar and Emperor Peter I, Autocrat of All Russia." Designed in essence to impress upon the reader the extraordinary position of this ruler in Russian history, the composition abounds in stories about celestial portents announcing Peter's conception, prophesies about his future military might, and stories about his difficult birth and divinely chosen name. While most of these tales seek to emphasize Peter's greatness from a secular—though mystical—perspective, one story recounts a supernatural blessing of the womb of Peter's mother, Natal'ia Kirillovna Naryshkina. On September 1, 1672, a holy man reportedly entered the tsaritsa's chambers and insisted on kissing her abdomen. When, at the tsaritsa's urging, Aleksei Mikhailovich arrived at the scene and granted his request, the man announced that a great lord was located in the tsaritsa's womb who would be a formidable ruler and exceed even his father's reputation.[99] That the theme of Natal'ia's divinely blessed womb still served a useful purpose in the secular court setting of the eighteenth century is also evident in the panegyrical works of A. P. Sumarokov. An ode he composed in honor of a victory of Peter the Great notes that the womb through which Peter was introduced to the world was blessed. In another panegyrical piece composed for Paul I's birthday in 1761, Sumarokov compares the moment his mother, Catherine II, conceived him to the archangel Gabriel's encounter with the Virgin Mary during the Annunciation. As B. A. Uspenskii has pointed out, the poet addresses the empress in an adaptation of the archangel Gabriel's words in Luke 1:28: "Rejoice, Catherine, you are blessed amongst women, and the fruit of your womb is blessed."[100] Since Sumarokov's works were written in the new literary style of his age, which was oriented on the classics, the inclusion of the miraculous birth motif suggests that, by the middle of the eighteenth century, the myth of the tsaritsa's blessed womb had become a standard part of Russian court culture. Divorced from its religious connotation, it found a new applicability in an age where males ascending to the Russian throne derived their dynastic status from strong female Russian rulers.

The appearance of the myth of the blessed royal womb in Muscovite Russia is closely connected with the precarious dynastic position of the tsars' wives, which was dependent on their reproductive ability. To achieve greater social stability, the tsaritsy in the sixteenth century sought to shift the attention from the child as the desired product to their own bodies where the mystery of childbirth and the will of the divine were revealed. By emphasizing a special relationship between the royal mother and the supernatural, the tsaritsy fostered a mystique that elevated the prestige of both the royal mother and the future ruler. In the process the tsaritsy exploited the flexibility of the myth with regard to the agent of their miraculous conception. In their hopes to produce an heir to the throne, they compared themselves to biblical women who had experienced a miraculous conception. As in the medieval West, some of these figures, such as Saint Anna or the Virgin Mary, became known for their ability to bless the womb of royal women.[101] Moreover, the royal wives (with the help of their spiritual advisers) expanded the cult of the miracle-working protector saints of the Muscovite grand princes by adding a new specialization, the blessing of the royal womb, to their repertoire of powers. In addition to their traditional role as supporters of the tsar's political success, these saints were now appreciated for assuring the continuity of the ruling dynasty. The affirmation of a holy man's capacity to inspire miraculous births by the tsaritsy added a new, gender-specific dimension to his cult. By manipulating the religious concept of sainthood and its manifestation in ritual, these women were able to expand their ability to live a meaningful life within a restrictive social environment.

The myth of the tsaritsa's ability to conceive miraculously appealed particularly to leaders of the Orthodox faith in Russia and abroad who sought to portray the Russian ruler as a divinely blessed leader of the Orthodox world. Leading Muscovite ecclesiastics who provided spiritual instruction to the tsar's family and thus had an opportunity to become acquainted with the Muscovite tsaritsy's idea of miraculous conception became the primary promoters of the spiritualization of the tsaritsa's role. The literary expression of the notion of the tsaritsa's blessed womb in chronicles and tales by members of the religious hierarchy helped anchor the myth in the cultural consciousness of the Muscovite elite and thus reinforced the notion that the tsaritsa played an integral part in the definition of the Muscovite ruler.

Biological Motherhood Transcended *Solomoniia Saburova*

A close examination of the perceived role of the Muscovite royal mothers has shown that the wives of the Russian rulers shared in the prestige of their husbands and were believed to play an integral part in the socioreligious destiny of the Muscovite state. The influence of political considerations and the shaping force of religion on the perception of the Russian ruler's wife can also be observed in the development of the image of Solomoniia Saburova as a holy intercessor for the Muscovite realm.

Through the vehicle of myth, Vasilii III's first wife came to be revered as a royal woman saint in spite of her failure to produce offspring. Even though motherhood eluded her, she continued to be regarded as a valuable asset to the Muscovite ruler and his realm. In the mind of the Muscovite elite, the spiritual disposition of Solomoniia could assure God's continued favor for the Russian tsardom.

At first glance Solomoniia Saburova seems a very unlikely candidate for sainthood. She was married to Vasilii III for twenty years, but since she was unable to give birth to an heir Vasilii divorced her in 1525. Contemporary sources for Solomoniia's divorce and tonsure portray the events of 1525–1526 in a very somber light. Sigismund von Herberstein, who visited Moscow in the early sixteenth century on a diplomatic mission, reports that the grand princess opposed the divorce and was tonsured under duress. According to Herberstein, Solomoniia stamped upon the monastic hood during the act of tonsure, causing one of the grand prince's councilors to beat her. Even then she declared her opposition to becoming a nun and "invoked the vengeance of God on her behalf for so great an injury."[102] Solomoniia's forceful removal from the Kremlin is also acknowledged in sixteenth-century chronicles that were produced outside the tsar's and the metropolitan's court. The *Vologodsko-Permskaia Chronicle* presents the incident as an act in the best interest of the state. The *Pskov I Chronicle* is particularly insensitive toward Solomoniia, likening her to an unfruitful fig tree that had to be "cut down and removed from the vineyard."[103]

Solomoniia never seems to have given up the hope that she could still become a mother. Before her monastic confinement, she regularly enlisted her brother Ivan Iur'evich's help in procuring sorceresses, who treated her with potions and magic ointments. Her refusal to accept her fate may well have given her a notorious reputation. According to Herberstein, a rumor that she had given birth to a son in the Suzdal' Pokrov Monastery circulated in Moscow shortly after her tonsure.[104] Moreover, the wives of two of Vasilii III's chief councilors claimed that they had heard the grand princess confirm her pregnancy before her tonsure. Solomoniia herself is said to have exploited the rumor for her own purposes. Although she refused to let anyone see him, she insisted that she was the mother of a son who had a legitimate claim to the throne. At least initially Vasilii seems to have taken the rumor seriously; he ordered that the two councilors and their wives be investigated.[105]

The depiction of Solomoniia as a desperate woman who tried to preserve her royal status at any cost undoubtedly was embarrassing to Muscovite chroniclers who endeavored to glorify the ruling dynasty. In order to justify its sanction of the divorce, the church was particularly eager to emphasize Solomoniia's consent in this matter. According to the "Tale of the Tonsure of the Pious Grand Princess Solomoniia" in the *Tipografskaia Chronicle*, Solomoniia, "upon seeing the infertility of her womb, as the Sarah of old" implored her husband to let her enter a monastery. When the grand prince refused to break God's law, she managed to persuade him with the help of Metropolitan Daniil.[106] According to the *Pafnut'ev Borovskii Chronicle,* Solomoniia implored the grand prince to let her leave Moscow where "great men, relatives, princesses, and boyar women" distracted her from living a God-pleasing life. The attempts of the story to whitewash the unseemly role of the grand prince and the church in Solomoniia's tonsure led to a completely new interpretation of her figure. The tale completely ignored Solomoniia's concern about fertility and instead ascribed to her the desire to live an ascetic life. As a result, Solomoniia's person acquired an air of piety that commanded respect. The *Pafnut'ev Borovskii Chronicle* in particular emphasized her fasting, prayer, and betrothal to Christ, acts that were respected monastic accomplishments.[107] Moreover, the tale's comparison of Vasilii's first wife with Sarah, who renounced her conjugal rights for the sake of the continuity of Abraham's line, placed Solomoniia on an equal footing with biblical holy women.

It is striking that, in their efforts to present Solomoniia's tonsure as the voluntary act of a religious person, the composers of the "Tale of the Tonsure of the Pious Grand Princess Solomoniia" did not attempt to privatize her image, but rather related it to the greater cause of a prosperous Russia. The story makes clear that through her betrothal to Christ, Solomoniia performed a final valuable service to her royal husband and his realm. As the nun Sofiia, she is said to have defined the purpose of her monastic life as her unceasing intercession with God for the well-being of the Russian ruler and his realm.[108] In spite of her removal to a monastery, Solomoniia thus never lost her role as grand princess. Whether married to Vasilii in the flesh or to Christ in the spirit, Solomoniia was expected to work for the good of the realm.

The "Tale of the Tonsure of the Pious Grand Princess Solomoniia" represents an early example of the transformation of the image and role of the tsaritsa in Muscovite Russia with the help of religious myth. In spite of her inability to produce an heir to the throne, Solomoniia counted in the struggle for the well-being of the Russian tsar and the tsardom. Instead of acting as a caretaker for the royal family, the nun Sofiia could use her newly won spiritual fecundity to intercede in a saintlike manner for the Russian ruler and his realm.

The Muscovite chronicle compilations of the mid–sixteenth century, which tried to embellish the position of the first Russian tsar and that of his mother, Elena Glinskaia, understandably displayed little interest in Vasilii III's first wife. The *Voskresensk Chronicle* and the *Nikon Chronicle* both maintained that Solomoniia consented to her divorce, but they showed little interest in Solomoniia's "holy" aspects. Instead, these chronicles claim that the grand princess renounced the throne because of "the burden and illness of infertility." The *Stepennaia kniga,* which aimed at underscoring the illustrious origin of the Muscovite dynasty and therefore stressed the notion of the blessed womb of the tsaritsa, left out any reference to

Solomoniia's divorce and simply mentioned her tonsure.[109]

In spite of the efforts of the official Muscovite chroniclers in the later sixteenth century to play down the impact of Solomoniia Saburova's taking the veil, the memory of her spiritual life persisted. Solomoniia's reputation for her piety was perpetuated by the inclusion of the tale of her tonsure into the *"Povest' o vtorom brake Vasiliia III"* ("Tale of Vasilii III's Second Marriage"), which enjoyed great popularity in the seventeenth century.[110] The view that Solomoniia took the habit out of personal conviction and lived an austere, ascetic life was perpetuated by the *Postnikov Chronicle*. The chronicle states that after her tonsure the grand prince had Solomoniia removed to a walled cell in the forest in the Kargopol' region before her final transfer to the Suzdal' Pokrov Monastery five years later.[111] The reference to Solomoniia's disgrace and her forced departure to a remote and inhospitable place seems to reflect a wide-spread empathy for the abandoned royal wife. In a similar manner Kurbskii's *Istoriia o velikom kniaze Moskovskom (History of the Grand Prince of Moscow)* emphasizes the grand princess's outright resistance to a monastic life, her forced confinement in the distant Kargopol', and her prisonlike existence there. The *History* calls Solomoniia a holy and innocent woman and stresses her unjust suffering.[112]

Solomoniia's image of a royal woman who chose to live for the faith and simultaneously for her realm played an important role in the revival of her memory and in the establishment of the cult of her relics in the seventeenth century. According to the 1597 inventory of the Suzdal' Pokrov Monastery, Irina Godunova donated a shroud decorated with a cross for the tomb of the grand princess.[113] In 1606 Tsar Vasilii Ivanovich Shuiskii granted the Suzdal' Pokrov Monastery economic and legal privileges on behalf of his relatives and Solomoniia Saburova and ordered the office for the dead and prayers performed for her.[114] The inmates of the monastery had no doubts as to the pious nature of Vasilii III's ex-wife and came to revere her locally as a saint. The relics of the royal nun were kept hidden, but later a shrine was erected over them and covered with a shroud depicting Sofiia's image.[115] Solomoniia's miracle-working activity apparently was discovered in 1602 when she healed a blind woman servant of Princess Aleksandra Nogteeva at her grave site on her name day, August 1. During the Polish-Lithuanian invasion of Suzdal' in 1609, Solomoniia was credited with saving her monastery and the town of Suzdal' from the attack of a rapacious Lithuanian lord. The grand princess was said to have appeared to the man as a terrible vision and to have singed him with a candle, which paralyzed his right hand. Terrified, the Lithuanian persuaded his men not to destroy the town of Suzdal'. Other "pagan" lords were "struck by an ailment and swept from their horses to the ground."[116]

The circumstances in Suzdal' in the early seventeenth century shed light on the value of Solomoniia as a protector of the Pokrov Monastery. In 1608 Suzdal' was divided between Vasilii Shuiskii and the False Dmitrii. While Shuiskii was beleaguered in Moscow, a supporter of Dmitrii appeared in

Suzdal' and declared him a false tsar. In the following two years, Suzdal' became a bastion of support for the pretender. During this period the Suzdal' Pokrov Monastery, which housed many members of the Shuiskii family, suffered from the heavy hand of the Polish occupiers. A letter from Abbess Ol'ga to the leaders of the government in Moscow in 1612 notes that the Poles had destroyed monastic lands, plundered the monastic complex, and forced the inhabitants of the monastery to live in town.[117] In the face of these traumatic events, Solomoniia acquired the role of a patron saint who looked out for the well-being of her monastery.

Once the threat of the foreign invasion had passed, the perception of the local saint focused again on her personal spiritual qualities and her healing power. The *kondakion* composed in Sofiia's honor no longer mentions her support against the Poles and instead concentrates on her personal piety, fasting, prayer, and chastity, through which she attained angel-like status. The *kondakion's* plea to Sofiia to help the ill and unfortunate manifests the new focus on the grand princess's austere life: "you chased the unclean spirits away from people, and you give all sorts of healing and deliver [us] from many a misery and evil. Blessed Sofiia, pray for the salvation of our souls."[118]

With the establishment of the local veneration of the royal nun in Suzdal' in the middle of the seventeenth century, Solomoniia's role vis-à-vis her realm and subjects became more narrowly defined. The epidemics ravaging Suzdal' in the middle of the seventeenth century may have heightened the need for a local miraculous healer.[119] From 1627 onward Solomoniia solely performed healing miracles. Her clientele (mostly women) consisted primarily of nuns and servants of the Suzdal' Pokrov Monastery, peasants, and petty nobles from the immediate surroundings. In 1650 Solomoniia's miracle-working quality induced Serapion, the archbishop of Suzdal', to verify the relics that lay buried under the cathedral church of the Pokrov Monastery and to send a report to Moscow. Patriarch Iosif approved the verification but rejected Solomoniia's veneration as an all-Russian saint. He ordered the archbishop to have a shroud placed on her shrine and to have prayers and the office for the dead sung for her, but he discouraged a translation ceremony for her remains.[120]

Although only memorial services were held for the grand princess during the nineteenth century, the notion of Solomoniia's saintly status persisted. An oral tradition developed that Solomoniia created a fountain in the Suzdal' Pokrov Monastery when she once dug for water with her own hands. Pious visitors to the monastery considered the water holy.[121] In Imperial Russia the royal nun's reputation for performing healing miracles inextricably became linked with her role as protector of Suzdal' and spiritual intercessor for the Russian ruler. A nineteenth-century copy of Serapion's service for Solomoniia/Sofiia addresses the grand princess as a blessed mother who with her prayers could stand up for her town, assure Tsar Nicholas I health and victory over his enemies, and give peace and kindness to believers visiting her relics. The text associates Sofiia's success with her ability to function as a "vessel of the Holy Spirit" and notes that God had granted her the gift of miracles because of her virtuous, chaste life.[122]

The story of Solomoniia Saburova shows that childlessness did not prevent royal women from participating in Muscovite Russia's political and spiritual leadership. Social isolation, whether associated with the dissolution of the marital bond or the otherworldliness of monastic life, did not eliminate a tsaritsa's responsibilities associated with her royal rank. Once she was married to a Muscovite ruler, she was perpetually involved in issues concerning the continuity of the ruling dynasty and the prosperity of the realm. Although Solomoniia's failure to produce an heir to the throne undoubtedly affected her personal life negatively, it did not lead to the degradation of her role as tsaritsa. Faced with the need to whitewash the unsavory treatment of a royal woman, the spin doctors of the tsarist period deemphasized the significance of her biological motherhood and instead proclaimed her spiritual fecundity, which enabled her to become a saintly protector of and intercessor for the Russian ruler and his realm. In this manner the myth of the tsaritsa's miraculous womb received yet another interpretation. In Solomoniia's case, the grand princess's ability to transmit the grace of God to the next ruler during the act of conception was replaced by her spiritual union with Christ, which assured the divine blessing of the Russian ruler and his subjects for generations to come.

The Tsaritsy and the Cult of the Protector Saints of Royal Children

In Muscovite Russia the issues of miraculous birth and the protection of the health of royal children were closely intertwined. Although the royal family doubtless welcomed the successful delivery of a child with a sigh of relief, the burden of the responsibility to produce an heir to the throne was by no means lifted from the mother. Illness (often ascribed to witchcraft) and accidents contributed to a high rate of infant mortality, which could endanger the royal succession.[123] Although the tsaritsy's options in the absence of effective medical care were limited, they did not face the task of rearing their offspring alone. The Muscovite church hierarchy empathized with the royal women's position and encouraged them to seek support from God. Realizing the potential of the supernatural, the tsaritsy not only promoted the cult of saints who could inspire the production of royal offspring but also fostered the veneration of holy figures who had the power to guarantee the safety and health of their children. In this way the tsaritsy played a vital role in assuring the continuity of the tsardom in Muscovite Russia.

The few details that are known about the upbringing of royal children at the Muscovite court suggest that infant care was accorded a high priority. The tsar's children were looked after by a number of nursemaids under the supervision of a nanny (*mamka*), a prestigious, often influential, old boyar woman or widow, who was well paid but who carried a heavy responsibility for the life and health of the child assigned to her.[124] If a royal child died early, his nanny was often forced to take the veil.[125] The royal mother was also intimately involved in the supervision of the health of her children. Several extant letters attributed to Vasilii III show that the grand prince held his wife responsible for the well-being of his children and expected her to keep him informed about any changes in their health and behavior.[126] When little Ivan developed a cyst on his neck soon after his birth, Vasilii, who at that time was absent from Moscow, impatiently rebuked his wife for not relating the development of Ivan's sickness to him in the minutest details. Elena was also expected to seek out every help and advice possible to combat any incidence of sickness. Vasilii ordered her to discuss Ivan's affliction with her female servitors to find out the cause of the cyst, the frequency of such an occurrence in children, and its long-term effects on the health of the tsarevich. Elena was charged with monitoring not only serious illnesses, but also any psychological dysfunction of the royal children, which was generally seen as some form of possession. When Vasilii's second son, Iurii, seemed to suffer from a "dark mood," Elena ordered a steam bath with rose hip. Most of all, however, the grand princess was expected to supervise the nutrition and eating habits of her children, which she was required to relate to her husband in detail. The responsibility for the physical welfare of the royal offspring must have weighed heavily on the royal mothers, who could do little more than pray for the survival of their children. Vasilii III seems to have been aware of Elena's difficulty to live up to her obligations; at one time in his letters he encouraged her not to lose her head and to put her hope in God.[127]

The tsaritsy received the same advice from their spiritual fathers, members of the Russian Orthodox church who occasionally provided grief-counseling to noble mothers who had lost their children.[128] In a letter to Tsar Fedor Ivanovich's wife, Irina Godunova, regarding the premature death of her only child, the infant Feodosiia, Patriarch Iov offered the tsaritsa alternatives to overcome her grief and to calm her concerns about producing an heir for the realm. Resorting to examples from the teachings of the Christian church, the patriarch attempted to provide Irina with an explanation of her grief along with concrete suggestions on how to deal with her sorrow. He insisted that Irina stop crying and put her faith in God who determined fate. With regard to the premature death of Irina's daughter, the patriarch cited writings ascribed to Athanasius the Great and John Chrysostom that proclaim the automatic salvation of infants who die soon after birth without baptism since they never had an opportunity to sin.[129] Since divine providence placed such children among the Wise Virgins, the tsaritsa should be grateful to the Lord for accepting the fruit of her womb. Her worries about producing an heir to the throne were ultimately of secondary importance: already Saint Chrysostom had pointed out that man's eternal well-being was more important than his earthly concerns.[130]

Patriarch Iov's counsel offered meaning to an inexplicable phenomenon and thus provided Irina with a means to gain back control over her life. It is hardly accidental that Iov espoused Saint Chrysostom's notion that a person should praise the Lord instead of crying for the dead. While mourning focuses men and women on their inner selves, the act of rejoicing in the Lord reintegrates them into the Christian community and thus is by its nature life-asserting. Iov was interested in Irina's speedy return to a normal life. Citing Saint Chrysostom's view that if somebody suffers grief with gratitude he will be forgiven sooner, the patriarch reminded Irina that her suffering was not without purpose and could still lead to eternal joy and the fruit of childbirth for generations to come.[131]

The church's call for life-asserting action on the part of royal mothers seems to have fallen on attentive ears. If the royal women took refuge in the supernatural to ensure that they produced offspring, it was only a small step to engage the help of the saints to keep their children safe and healthy and to lessen the royal mothers' burden of responsibility. By promoting the cult of saints who were considered protectors of the royal children (that is, interceding with the saints for the well-being of the future ruler), the tsaritsy not only gained the support of powerful spiritual helpmates in their daily tasks but also commuted their reproductive role into a socioreligious one.

The idea that the wives of the Muscovite rulers could seek out the saints' protection for the royal family was completely acceptable to Muscovite society. The notion that specific saints could protect the health of royal children was put forth in the *vita* of Metropolitan Iona (composed in the 1540s), which notes that Vasilii II and his wife, Mariia, took their sick daughter Anna to the saint and implored him to save the child. Iona interceded for the girl before God and saved her life.[132]

Saint Sergius seems to have been a particularly popular protector saint for the children of the Muscovite ruling house. After Sofiia Paleolog gave birth to Vasilii III in 1479, his father, Ivan, is said to have baptized him at the saint's shrine in the Church of the Trinity at the Trinity-Sergius Monastery.[133] This act seems to have been intended as a form of thanksgiving to the saint for his intercession for offspring, but also expressed the parents' faith in the saint's protective powers with regard to the future of the child. When his second wife, Elena, finally bore him a son, Vasilii III emulated his father in having the baptism performed at the shrine of Saint Sergius. During the ceremony Vasilii implored Saint Sergius to keep little Ivan "unharmed from any kind of visible enemy attack" and to protect him with his prayers.[134] In order to assure the continued protection of the saint, the Muscovite rulers and their families undertook numerous pilgrimages to the shrine of Saint Sergius.[135] Conscious that both he and his father had been raised under the protection of Saint Sergius, Ivan IV had his first son, Dmitrii, baptized at the shrine of Saint Sergius in the Trinity-Sergius Monastery.[136] The traditional pilgrimages continued under Tsar Fedor and his wife, Irina, and (after the Time of Troubles) in the Romanov period.[137]

The concern for the survival of the future heir to the throne was also apparent in the royal patronage of the cult of Saint Nikita of Pereslavl'. The miraculous conception of Ivan IV's son Ivan marked the first step in the development of the cult of Saint Nikita as a protector of the tsar's offspring. Chapter 19 of the saint's *vita* maintains that the association of Saint Nikita with the protection of royal children developed in the living quarters *(terem)* of Anastasiia Romanovna where Ivan Ivanovich grew up surrounded by nannies and wet nurses. According to the *vita*, one day a wet nurse who was holding the tsarevich was startled by the sound of water boiling in a pewter vessel behind the bench on which she was sitting. The tsarevich's nanny, the boyar woman Fotiniia, immediately took the child from her, picked up the vessel, and found that it contained water from the well of Saint Nikita of Pereslavl'. Realizing that the boiling water was a sign from God, she anointed the head and face of the tsarevich with it and prayed that the tsarevich, his parents, and his realm would be blessed with long life, health, and joy. Anastasiia, who awoke from the commotion, touched the vessel with Saint Nikita's water and anointed herself and the tsarevich with it.[138]

The story, which combines folk elements such as the belief in the healing qualities of the life-giving water with the Christian cult of contact relics, reflects the heightened concern about the future of the royal family after the death of Tsarevich Dmitrii. In order to assure little Ivan's wellbeing, water from Saint Nikita's monastery apparently had been brought to Moscow and placed in the women's quarters, an act that presumed the faith of the members of the royal *terem* in Saint Nikita's protective powers. The fact that the nanny interpreted the boiling water as a sign of God's grace suggests that the women in the *terem* consciously used the mechanism of protective Christian magic to alleviate their insecurity about the tsarevich's future. The ointment that the nanny applied to Ivan Ivanovich was to guarantee the tsarevich's survival and his eventual succession to the throne, and thus indirectly also the position of the child's caretakers. The need of the women at court to reassure the stability of their position is also evident in the behavior of Tsaritsa Anastasiia when she learned about the miraculous occurrence. She accepted without question the notion of the healing powers of Saint Nikita's water. By applying the liquid to her son and to herself, not only did she put her fate into Saint Nikita's hands as she had done earlier when she prayed at his shrine for the birth of an heir, but she also linked her fate with that of her son. As a result, any effort on her part in the promotion of the cult of Saint Nikita would not only be perceived as a means to assure her child's future but also would make her appear as a decisive agent in this process.

The connection between the royal *terem* and the cult of Saint Nikita can be seen in another incident in which the saint saved the tsarevich from a serious illness. According to Chapter 20 of the saint's *vita*, Ivan Ivanovich fell ill one year after his birth. When official prayers achieved no result, the tsar ordered mass sung for Saint Nikita in his son's bedroom in the presence of the saint's life-giving water and his crosses and chains, which were regarded as venerable relics. The tsar and his wife prayed for the aversion of the sickness from their child while their close friends and advisers looked on helplessly. When Ivan's nanny held the child over the saint's relics, the tsarevich suddenly reached out for the vessel with the blessed water. The water started to boil again, "as once the horn with oil boiled up in the hands of the prophet Samuel, who held it for the anointment of the Jewish king Saul, the son of Kish, or for the anointment of the son of Jesse, the king and prophet David."[139] Witnessing this, Ivan IV had the liquid applied to his son's body and placed into his mouth. The illness quickly subsided, and Tsarevich Ivan recovered.[140]

The incident shows that the health of the future successor to the Muscovite throne was the responsibility of his mother and nurses, who deliberately manipulated the power of the supernatural to assure their success. The healing liquid was tied to the expectation that the sick child would eventually succeed to the throne. The ceremony of the saint's veneration and the healing miracle occurred in the *terem* quarters in the presence of the royal mother and her female servants. The child's nanny, who again initiated the tsarevich's contact with the healing substance, was instrumental in bringing on the miracle. The connection between the health of the tsarevich and the desire for stability among the women of the *terem* is sustained in this episode as well.

Anastasiia seems to have been the driving force behind her husband's support of the cult of the tsarevich's saintly protector. According to the *vita* of Saint Nikita, she encouraged Ivan, who took counsel with her after the miraculous healing, to thank the saint by introducing the cenobitic rule in his monastery. After approximately one year, during which the healing power of Saint Nikita's water proved itself several times more, the royal couple undertook a trip to Pereslavl' with the tsarevich to realize their intention.[141] During the royal couple's stay at the monastery of Saint Nikita, Anastasiia donated numerous liturgical vestments, which she herself had made, to his shrine. The most valuable among those gifts was a tapestry decorated with pearls and edged in gold with the image of Saint Nikita.[142] According to the *vita*, Anastasiia's purpose for donating this precious embroidery was to thank the saint for removing the grief from her heart and to implore the saint to grant the child more years so that he might assume the throne and perpetuate the royal line.[143]

The effects of Anastasiia's personal engagement of Saint Nikita as a protector saint for the tsarevich outlasted the tsaritsa. In his *Vremennik,* Timofeev asserts that the healing of the tsarevich by Saint Nikita caused the royal family to modify its customary pilgrimage pattern by adding a trip to the saint's shrine in Pereslavl' whenever the tsar and his family undertook one of the customary pilgrimages to the Trinity-Sergius Monastery.[144]

When after Anastasiia's death in 1560 her husband ordered the construction of new living quarters for his sons, he specified that a chapel in the name of Saint Nikita of Pereslavl' be included in the complex.[145] Clearly Ivan accepted Saint Nikita as the protector saint for his two sons. His second wife, Mariia Temriukovna, who inherited the difficult task of assuring the welfare of the tsarevichi Ivan and Fedor, readily invoked the help of the traditional miracle-workers who could share the responsibility. During her stay in the monastery of Saint Nikita in 1564, Mariia asked the local monks to direct their prayers to Saint Nikita of Pereslavl' (and Saints Peter, Aleksii, Iona, Sergius, and Nikon) for the health of the tsar and his children and that of her own.[146] Mariia Temriukovna's petition shows clearly that a tsaritsa's task not only extended to producing a son but also included the obligation of looking after the future heir to the throne, even if she was not his biological mother.

The role of the royal mother as caretaker of the tsar's offspring was considered crucial in the early years of the Romanov dynasty, when the newly elected sovereign, Mikhail Fedorovich Romanov, was still an adolescent. Mikhail's mother, Marfa Ivanovna Shestova, whom Boris Godunov had forced to take the veil, sought every means to assert her position in the royal family in her capacity as the mother of the tsar. She repeatedly stressed her maternal status in letters to Patriarch Filaret, who before his tonsure had been married to her.[147] In her daily activities Marfa assumed all the responsibilities of a royal mother. She monitored the physical condition of young Mikhail closely and reported it to the patriarch. During her numerous pilgrimages with her son, she customarily sent written updates to Moscow concerning the child's health. When the child experienced any kind of discomfort, Marfa described the affliction in great detail.[148]

Like her Rurikide predecessors, Marfa did not merely acquiesce in performing her routine maternal duties but sought to procure divine support in her struggle to maintain the tsar's well-being. In her correspondence with Filaret, Marfa repeatedly addressed him in his official position as patriarch of Russia with requests for intercessory prayers for Mikhail's health. In addition, Marfa accompanied her son on numerous pilgrimages, especially to the Trinity-Sergius Monastery and to Pereslavl', to implore the local saints to intercede for the well-being of the tsar and his realm.[149]

The conscious patronage of saints who were thought to protect royal children can also be observed in the case of Marfa's daughter-in-law Evdokiia Luk'ianovna Streshneva, who seemed to be haunted by the ghost of infant mortality. Ivan Zabelin's reconstruction of the tsaritsa's pious activities on the basis of her expense records reveals Evdokiia's patronage of a number of saints who were renowned for their healing of children. When in 1627 a chapel in the name of Saint Catherine was erected in the Terem Palace for the private use of the tsaritsy, the royal family had a special altar set up in honor of Saint Onufrius the Great, who was credited with protecting newborn children against sudden infant death. After the difficult birth of her daughter Pelagiia in the following year, Evdokiia repeatedly sought to enlist Saint Onufrius's help by having the sickly child receive communion at his altar.[150] When the birth of the tsarevny Pelagiia and Anna resulted in complications, Evdokiia ordered prayers at the shrine of Saint Nikita the Martyr in the church of Saint Nikita beyond the Iauza. Tsarevna Marfa received communion there before her death in 1632. When the health of her second son, Ivan Mikhailovich, did not improve after another difficult delivery, the tsaritsa undertook a pilgrimage to the shrine of Saint Nikita of Pereslavl', who had proved his protective powers in the case of Ivan Ivanovich.[151]

Marfa Ivanovna's and Evdokiia Luk'ianovna's ritual activities demonstrate how the women of the early Romanovs used a basic Christian institution, the cult of the saints, to make their difficult task of maintaining the health of the royal family and nurturing an heir to the throne more manageable. By the early seventeenth century, the arsenal of saints who could perform this task had increased significantly. Whereas the royal women of the Rurikide dynasty in the sixteenth century had sought recourse only to major Russian saints such as the metropolitan saints and Saints Sergius and Nikita of Pereslavl', the Romanov women engaged the additional help of holy figures who specialized in the cure of certain childhood afflictions. As a result the religious activity and, along with it, the visibility of the tsaritsy increased in the Romanov period.

. . .

A close examination of the Muscovite grand princesses' and tsaritsy's role as mothers refutes the pervasive opinion that the royal women of Muscovy suffered continuous oppression and discrimination from the socioreligious system surrounding them, which led to their complete political insignificance. We gain a better understanding of the status of the Muscovite tsaritsy if we inquire into the meaning of their existence, and how this meaning was constructed. Since the early beginnings of the Muscovite state during the appanage period, the mothers of the Muscovite grand princes were intricately bound up with the prosperity of their realm. The situation did not change in the sixteenth and seventeenth centuries when the social position of Muscovite royal women was endangered by infertility and the political demands for an heir. The wives of the tsars recognized and seized opportunities offered by their cultural environment to develop methods of coping with their task of producing and raising heirs to the throne. As the examples of Metropolitan Afanasii and Patriarch Iov show, the Muscovite church was sympathetic to the tsaritsy's fertility problems and their struggle with infant mortality. These hierarchs even went so far as to support the creation of a powerful myth that presented the wives of the Muscovite rulers as vessels of divine grace. The tsaritsy on their part continually sought out new opportunities to anchor this myth in ritual acts, such as pilgrimages and donations to shrines of saints who were known specifically for their sensitivity toward the tsaritsy's concerns. The promotion of the cult of these saints provided an effective means for the Muscovite royal women to gain control over social expectations. Careful examination of the patronage of these saints, however, reveals that the tsaritsy did not content themselves merely with coping with their endangered position but instead sought ways to improve the conditions of their existence. By assuming the responsibility for the well-being of the future heir to the throne, an act that was ritually expressed in their patronage of protector saints of royal children, they extended their role as mothers of the royal family to that of mothers of the realm. This enhanced their own dynastic legitimacy and image. In this context the ritual of the tsaritsy's patronage of certain miracle-workers (in Kay F. Turner's sense) not only repeated the customary pattern of the veneration of saintly intercessors but also presented a way for women's self-definition.[152]

2 Helpmate to the Tsar and Intercessor for the Realm

THE RISE OF THE MUSCOVITE tsardom in the middle of the sixteenth century was accompanied by changes in the perception of the Russian ruler's power. According to Michael Cherniavsky, Muscovite Russia during this period turned away from the concept of the saintly ruler-prince and looked instead to pious rulers of ancient Rome, Byzantium and Kiev for models of the Muscovite tsar. While Cherniavsky correctly points out the ambition of the Muscovite elite in the middle of the sixteenth century to forge mythical dynastic links with Kiev and Byzantium and thereby strengthen the power of the ruler and the state, the interpretation of this phenomenon as an exclusively political move must be treated with caution. Recently Daniel Rowland has noted the significance of biblical military images in the Muscovite ideology of the tsar. Muscovite circles that were responsible for developing the official ideology of the tsar liked to compare Ivan IV to King David or the Byzantine ruler saint Constantine the Great.[1] New Muscovite court rituals such as the Palm Sunday Ritual and the Epiphany ceremony ascribed to the Russian ruler a pious disposition that enabled him to serve as a link between God and the Russian people. As a result the tsar played a crucial role in the Muscovite concept of the "economy of salvation."[2]

While historians have come to accept the religious overtone of the tsar's persona, little attention has yet been paid to the religious aspects of the tsaritsa's position. If religious symbolism enhanced the prestige of the tsar, to what extent did the tsar's wife share in this kind of image enhancement? The myth of the blessed womb of the tsaritsa and the tsaritsa's patronage of royal protector saints show that royal wives (with the blessing of the church hierarchy) were able to manipulate the religious language and ritual of the

Orthodox belief to improve their standing within the royal family. While the religious connotation of royal motherhood in Muscovy made the tsaritsa appear as a personal mediator between the tsar or his family and the divine, the application of other Christian symbolisms to Russian royal women suggests that the tsars' wives were not only expected to play a vital role within their family unit. They also were counted on to buttress the Russian state with their pious deeds, just as their husbands were. The following examination of the Muscovites' perception of the role of their first official tsaritsa, Anastasiia Romanovna, shows that the Russian royal wives functioned as spiritual helpmates to their husbands and interceded before God for their salvation and for that of their realm. In the seventeenth century the wife of the Romanov tsar Aleksei Mikhailovich was credited with the same capacity.

Anastasiia—Spiritual Helpmate to the Tsar

One of the earliest manifestations of the concept of the role of the tsaritsa survives in the instructions of Metropolitan Makarii to Ivan IV and his wife Anastasiia on their wedding day in 1547. In his instructions, designed to familiarize the newlyweds with the duties associated with their royal status, Makarii carefully included the tsaritsa alongside her husband.[3] Makarii's apparent view that both members of the ruling couple shared in the dignity of the Muscovite tsardom can be gleaned from his own interpretation of the notion developed by Iosif Volotskii in the first decade of the sixteenth century that the Russian tsar ruled by divine grace.[4] Makarii referred to both Ivan and Anastasiia as shepherds of "the spiritual sheep of Christ's flock," which had been entrusted to them by God.[5]

Sharing in the epithets of her husband, the tsaritsa was expected to participate in the privileges and duties of the Russian ruler. Moreover, in Makarii's view the royal wedding itself signified both Ivan's and Anastasiia's inclusion into the family of previous saintly royal men and women. In particular, Ivan and Anastasiia were to heed the fact that all members of the family of saints, the patriarchs and apostles of the Bible, and the saintly rulers of the postbiblical era (notably Constantine the Great and his mother, Helena) had been lawfully married.[6]

The Russian ruling couple seems to have taken seriously the metropolitan's concept of the family of Christian saints. The notion was worked into the composition of a liturgical curtain *(katapetasma)* that Ivan and Anastasiia donated to the Church of the Presentation of the Virgin in the Temple in the Hilandar Monastery on Mount Athos on November 20, 1555. The *katapetasma*, which is ascribed to Anastasiia Romanovna's embroidery workshop, shows a coronation portrait of Ivan IV in the central panel. Medallions lining the top, left, and right borders of the curtain feature the Old Testament figures David, Solomon, Isaiah, Elijah, Zachary, and Daniel, along with the New Testament figures Peter and Paul and a collection of Early Christian, Byzantine, Serbian, and Russian saints including Constantine the Great and

Vladimir of Kiev. In the bottom row, the images of Saint Helena and of Anastasiia Romanovna's patron saint, the martyr Anastasia, are juxtaposed as if to underscore the tsaritsa's spiritual equality with the Byzantine empress.[7]

The inclusion of Anastasiia in the family of saints, evident in the comparison of the tsaritsa with Saint Helena, makes clear that the role of the Muscovite ruler's wife was not restricted to private, domestic duties. The attribution of saintly status resulted in the elevation of the tsaritsa's status. As with all holy individuals, her actions not only determined her personal fortunes in this world and her own salvation in the hereafter but affected the well-being of her entire realm.[8]

In order to assure the prosperity of the Muscovite realm under God's protection, the tsar and his wife had to live according to God's commandments, to honor the Lord, the Virgin, and the miracle-workers, and to observe the ritual of the church. They were required to foster good relations with the church by visiting the houses of God and supporting monastic institutions. In accordance with their mandate from God, the tsar and his wife were expected to display justice and mercy and deal fairly with their relatives and members of the nobility, both male and female, and with all their Christian subjects. Moreover, in accordance with its attributed saintly status, the royal couple was expected to devote itself to pious deeds. Makarii insisted that by feeding the poor, protecting the orphans and widows, and visiting the incarcerated in prison, Ivan and Anastasiia could curry favor with God.[9]

The royal duties Makarii outlined in his instructions to the illustrious couple were to be carried out by both the tsar and the tsaritsa. This, however, did not mean that Anastasiia shared equally in Ivan's position. However elevated her status as a member of the ruler team, her role as wife placed her under the authority of her husband. In order to reconcile the tension between the two roles, Makarii invoked the pseudo-Pauline notion of the sanctified household, which called on husbands to love and respect their wives and on wives to submit to their spouses. In particular the metropolitan referred to Eph. 5:22–23, which requires a wife's submission to her husband based on the assumption that just as Christ is the head of the church, the husband is the superior of his wife. The hierarchical structure of the husband-wife relationship, however, did not imply a one-sided dependency of the wife on the spouse. After all, although Christ was considered the head of the church, his message could only be realized within the confines of the church. Thus Makarii invoked the principles of partnership and mutual loyalty of the married couple by quoting Eph. 5:28–30:

> So husbands shall love their wives, as they love their own bodies; for by loving his wife he loves himself. For nobody then hates his flesh, but nurtures and cherishes it as the Lord the church. The husband shall give his wife the due love, and in the same way the wife [shall give love] to her husband, [for as] the wife does not own her body, but the husband, so the husband does not own his body, but the wife.[10]

Metropolitan Makarii carefully chose the pseudo-Pauline passage to reconcile the traditional Christian notion of the subordinate role of the wife in marriage with the contemporary Muscovite idea of the royal couple deriving its power to rule from God. Peter Brown has pointed out that Eph. 5:22–23 presents a corrective to 1 Cor. 11:3, which stresses the subordination of the wife to her husband without qualification.[11] For Anastasiia this meant that even though she did not enjoy social equality as a married woman, she was expected to share in her husband's duties with regard to God and the realm.

In practice the participation of the subordinate wife in her husband's duties translated into her functioning as a helpmate to the tsar in all matters concerning the spiritual welfare of the realm. The ramifications of this new role are evident in Ivan IV's farewell speech to Anastasiia before his departure on his campaign against the Tatars of Kazan' in 1552. While the tsar stated his readiness to die in battle for the true faith, as "the martyrs, the apostles, the previous pious tsars, and our kinsmen," he expected his wife to lend him spiritual support:

> I order you, my wife, not to grieve about my leaving, but to persist in great spiritual deeds, and to go often to the holy churches of God, and to say many prayers for me and yourself, and to give alms to the poor. I command you to release many of the unfortunate [who live] in royal disgrace. Give orders to free those who are incarcerated in prison that we will receive double recompense from God, I for prowess, and you for good deeds.[12]

The passage interprets the role of the Muscovite tsar and tsaritsa in the struggle with the Tatars of Kazan' within a larger cosmological framework. As one of the key figures in the struggle between good and evil, the tsar carried the heavy responsibility to lead his people into battle in defense of the true faith. In order to win this battle, he must not only display military prowess but also be ready to die for his cause. His task is likened to that of the apostles, the Early Christian martyrs, and other pious rulers before him.[13] The two distinguishing features in a tsar, however (military prowess on the one hand and the pious, humble disposition of a martyr on the other), were hard to reconcile in one person. The first was intrinsically associated with a secular ruler. In order to develop the second quality, the tsar was dependent on the spiritual support from members of his realm. Although the clergy was expected to pray for the general well-being of the Muscovite tsar, it was considered the tsaritsa's task to monitor the pious behavior of her husband and to assure that the grace of God fell on him and his realm.[14] Ivan IV asked his wife not merely for private prayers but for great spiritual deeds, which would strengthen his own position in the cosmological struggle against evil. By carrying out this assignment, the tsaritsa participated in the realization of the public goal of the salvation of the Russian realm and acquired the role of a saintly mediator in the process. In essence Anastasiia Romanovna was credited with being able to influence the fate of the Russian realm because of her special relationship to the divine.

Anastasiia's role as helpmate to the tsar in spiritual matters entailed the promotion and defense of the Orthodox faith in her realm. In the preparatory stage of Ivan IV's campaign against the infidel Tatars, Anastasiia accompanied her husband on pilgrimages to the Trinity-Sergius Monastery that were meant to win the saint's support. It is not surprising that Ivan sent the first messengers carrying the news of his victory over the Tatars in 1552 not only to his brother but also to his spiritual intercessors, Metropolitan Makarii and Tsaritsa Anastasiia. The tsaritsa's connection with the maintenance of the faith in Russia can also be seen in Anastasiia's participation in the dedication of seven churches in the Cathedral of the Intercession of the Virgin on the Moat, which Ivan erected in honor of his victory over Kazan'.[15]

Anastasiia's function as helpmate to the tsar in the spiritual matters of the realm is particularly evident in her participation in the processions of icons. In medieval Russia, the processions and translations of images were intended to secure the intercessory and protective powers of the holy figures depicted in the icons.[16] Already in the late fifteenth century, women of the ruling family seem to have participated in the Palm Sunday procession, as can be seen in the tapestry of Elena Voloshanka. The tapestry, commissioned by this daughter-in-law of Ivan III in 1502, portrays the grand prince's family, Metropolitan Simon, his clergy, and other high-ranking members of the Muscovite secular and ecclesiastical hierarchies worshiping an icon of the Virgin Hodegetria.[17] In the mid–sixteenth century, Anastasiia Romanovna participated in the promotion of the cult of several icons that were brought to Moscow so that they might dispense their blessing on the Russian ruler and his realm. On August 3, 1556, the tsaritsa attended the liturgy with her family at the Church of the Virgin on the Moat in honor of the icon of Saint Nikola Velikoretskii, which had been brought from Viat'ka to Moscow in 1554 for restoration purposes. After the liturgy, Ivan IV with his wife and children escorted the icon out of Moscow on its way to Ustiug. A year later, on August 9, 1557, an icon of the Virgin Hodegetria and another image depicting Nicholas the Miracle-Worker, Basil the Great, and Kosmas and Damian were translated from Narva to Moscow. The ceremonious reception of these icons in the capital shows the special position of the royal women in matters of the divine. The tsar, his son Ivan, and his brother, Iurii, the metropolitan, the holy synod, and the people of Moscow first welcomed the icons at the Church of Paraskeva Piatnitsa Rzhevskaia. After the metropolitan performed the liturgy, the images were escorted to the Kremlin where a group of noble women headed by Anastasiia Romanovna and her sister-in-law Uliana, wife of Prince Iurii Vasil'evich, met them at the Rizpolozhenskii Gate. The women crossed themselves before the icons and received blessings from the metropolitan, and then joined the procession of the icons to the Cathedral of the Dormition.[18]

Some scholars may regard the separation of the sexes in the religious ritual on this occasion as evidence for the contraction of the public role of royal women in sixteenth-century Muscovy. Such an interpretation does not address a number of considerations, however.[19] If the Muscovite tsaritsy were expected to devote themselves only to a privatized role in the social and religious life of Muscovy, there was no reason why they should have participated in a ceremony of this kind. The fact that they participated at all in this event, which ranked as high as an official state reception, belies the assumption that there was a systematic effort to exclude royal women from the public sphere. The separation of the sexes in the ceremonial procession of icons in 1557 was only partially achieved, since the women and men walked together on the last stretch of the procession. The manner in which the ritual of meeting the icons unfolded actually emphasized the superior spiritual position of the royal women. Strikingly, the initial encounter with the images at the Church of Paraskeva-Piatnitsa Rzhevskaia involved members of all ranks, regardless of their social position. Contemporaries must have seen the tsar's departure from the Kremlin to join his subjects in paying his respects to the icons as a sign of his special humility toward the holy figures they depicted. According to the protocol of royal receptions in sixteenth-century Muscovy, a prominent guest visiting the tsar's court was received by several detachments of royal dignitaries on his way to the capital.[20] As he neared Moscow, the rank and influence of these dignitaries at court increased. The same principle seems to have been applied in the case of the icons that had been brought from Narva to Moscow. The images were met in stages on their way to their final destination, the Cathedral of the Dormition of the Virgin in the Kremlin, the spiritual center of the medieval Russian Orthodox community. It stands to reason that the encounter closest to the cathedral would involve the tsaritsa and other prominent women at court, who were considered responsible for the collective salvation of the Russian realm. Their appearance in the ritual of the meeting of the icons after the tsar and other representatives of the realm demonstrates their intercessory position vis-à-vis the holy.

Information derived from contemporary sources about the wife of the first Russian tsar, Anastasiia Romanovna, shows that to a large degree the recently developed concept of the tsaritsa defined Anastasiia's actual role. Although Muscovy continued to uphold the traditional notion that a woman was subordinate to her husband, the tsaritsa's saintlike status—transforming her subsidiary function into that of a spiritual helpmate to her royal husband and intercessor for the Russian realm—overcame this limitation. Since saints were generally expected to display humility and to intercede for their community, the saintly element could eliminate the tension between the tsaritsa's private obligation to be obedient and her public duty to her realm. Thus, whether we study the ideal of the Muscovite tsaritsa or her actual activities in sixteenth-century Muscovy, we find both traits traditionally perceived as feminine (private, complementary) such as spiritual purity, mercy, and charity and traits commonly associated with masculine (public, independent) functions such as fighting the infidel and maintaining the Christian order in the realm.

The Myth of the "Pious Tsaritsa Anastasiia"

The theme of the spiritual value of a royal wife to the Muscovite ruler and his realm also occurs in Muscovite mythopoeic efforts that defined the image of Russia's first tsaritsa in the later sixteenth and seventeenth centuries. While the importance of Anastasiia Romanovna, the great aunt of Mikhail Fedorovich, for the Romanov dynasty, which acceded to the throne in 1613, is generally acknowledged, scholars have yet paid relatively little attention to the process through which Anastasiia's figure was mythologized. A close study of the Muscovites' perception of their first tsaritsa from the time of her and her husband's accession to the throne suggests that her persona already became the subject of mythopoeic efforts during her lifetime and immediately after her death. In their early interpretations of Tsaritsa Anastasiia, Muscovites stressed her spiritual role, which was considered crucial to the success of the Rurikide dynasty. In the aftermath of the Time of Troubles, the emerging Romanov dynasty skillfully drew on the spiritual and dynastic dimensions of the already existing Anastasiia myth to strengthen its claim to the throne.

As is the case with most of the wives of sixteenth-century Russian rulers, we possess very little personal information about Anastasiia, daughter of Roman Iur'evich Zakhar'in-Iur'ev, who was married to the first official Muscovite tsar, Ivan IV, shortly after his coronation in 1547. Virtually nothing is known about her youth, and even during her marriage to Ivan, apart from a number of embroideries, she left few records of herself. From the time the royal bride appeared at the tsar's court, she became a favorite subject of ideologues under the leadership of Metropolitan Makarii, who strove to elevate the Russian tsardom by attributing to it a religious connotation. The tsaritsa herself engaged in mythopoeic activities that focused on her personal condition, notably her struggle to conceive and raise royal offspring.

The association of Anastasiia with saintlike qualities during her lifetime laid the ground for her survival after her death as a spiritual icon in the consciousness of the Muscovite populace and the elite. The Muscovite subjects' fondness for their pious tsaritsa is expressed in the emotional outpouring of the masses during her funeral in August 1560. The *Lebedev Chronicle* notes that "all the poor and needy from the whole city came to the burial, not for charity, but they accompanied her with much crying and sobbing, and they barely managed to carry her body into the monastery because of the multitude of people in the streets."[21] The continued remembrance of Anastasiia Romanovna, however, did not rest with the populace alone; the ultimate initiative in fostering the image of the pious tsaritsa has to be sought with Ivan IV himself. The grieving tsar widower spent large sums for the commemoration of his wife. For example, the donation records of the Trinity-Sergius Monastery note that Ivan gave one thousand rubles on August 21, 1562, for Anastasiia's commemoration. The sum, which equals Ivan's commemoration gift for his brother, Iurii, the following year, starkly contrasts with the two hundred rubles the tsar expended earlier on his daughters, Anna and Mariia.[22] Nine years later, Ivan sent one hundred rubles to Mount Sinai for liturgical prayers for his first wife, twice the amount sent then for prayers for his brother.[23]

Ivan IV's lavish expenditure on his first wife's commemoration a decade after her death, when he had already remarried, suggests that personal devotion may not have been his main motivating factor. The imagery on a gilded Gospel cover, which the tsar donated to the Cathedral of the Annunciation in the Kremlin in February 1568, leads one to conclude that, even after Anastasiia's death, the Muscovite ruler continued to adhere to Metropolitan Makarii's notion that his tsardom was a religious responsibility, which could be alleviated by the intercession of his wife (see Figure 4).[24] The idea of tsardom by divine grace is expressed by the central composition *The Queen Stands to Your Right* in which the Virgin (on the left) and John the Baptist (Ivan's name saint) raise their hands in a petitionary pose to a blessing Christ figure seated on a large round throne.[25] The gender-specific roles of the ruling couple are expressed in the medallion featuring "Tsar Constantine

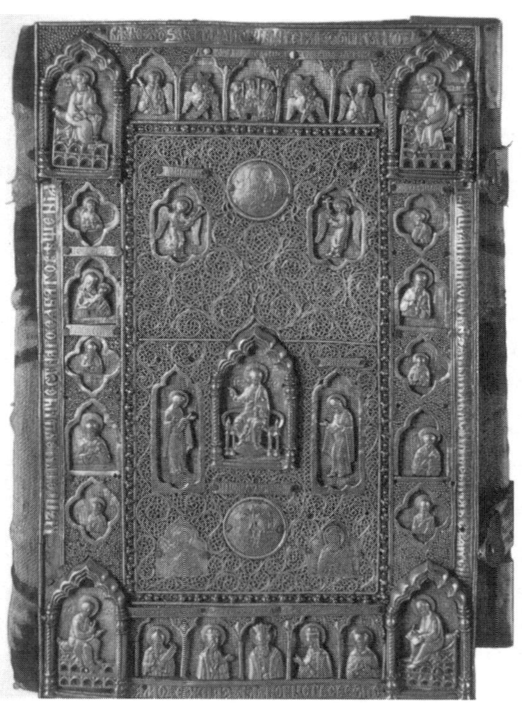

4. The Gospel cover donated by Ivan IV to the Cathedral of the Annunciation in the Kremlin in 1568 (Kremlin Museums, inventory no. KN-33; 316 Bl. s.; 711 sob). The row of royal protector saints in the lower border include Anastasiia Romanovna's name saint (Saint Anastasia of Rome) and Saint Nikita of Pereslavl', whom Anastasiia credited with the capacity to protect royal fertility and offspring.

and Tsaritsa Helena" holding the Orthodox cross. The Constantine-Helena typology referred to the instrumental role of the Byzantine empress in bringing the symbol of the Orthodox faith, the Life-Giving Cross of Christ, from Jerusalem to Constantinople. The supportive role of the empress vis-à-vis her son was already recognized by Metropolitan Makarii in his wedding sermon for Ivan IV and Anastasiia in 1547. The Muscovite hierarch held up Helena as a model to Russia's first tsaritsa in the hope that she could facilitate Russia's attainment of the happy Jerusalem.[26] Constantine and Helena also appear in the border medallions of the *katapetasma* of 1555 in the hierarchy of saints who protect and intercede for the tsar. The liturgical curtain juxtaposes Constantine with the first Orthodox ruler of Russia, Saint Vladimir, and Helena with the tsaritsa's name saint, Anastasia.[27]

The continued significance of Russia's first tsaritsa for the spiritual well-being of the tsar and his realm is also evident in the inclusion of Anastasiia's name saint among the protector saints of the Muscovite ruler in the lower border of the Gospel cover. The inscriptions above their heads identify, from left to right, Saint Nikita of Pereslavl', Saint Boris, "the holy prince Vladimir", Saint Gleb, and Saint Anastasia of Rome. The three figures in the middle represent saintly princes of the Rurikide house whose duty it was according to tradition to pray for their relative on the Muscovite throne. They also appear in the border medallions of the *katapetasma* of 1555. The combination of Boris, Gleb, and Vladimir is commonly found in Russian iconography since its occurrence in the pall of Grand Princess Mariia, wife of Simeon the Proud, in 1389, but the depiction of Saint Nikita of Pereslavl' is exceedingly rare.[28] The saint played no significant role as a protector of the Muscovite ruling dynasty before Ivan IV's and Anastasiia's visit to his shrine in Pereslavl' after the unfortunate death of the royal infant Dmitrii in 1553, which led to the saint's association with the successful birth of Tsarevich Ivan. During the 1550s Anastasiia and her female staff in the *terem* fostered the cult of this saint to whom they ascribed the ability to keep the royal children from harm.

The juxtaposition of Anastasiia Romanovna's name saint and Saint Nikita suggests that the donor of the Gospel cover, Ivan IV, tried to show his appreciation for his wife's spiritual deeds for the sake of the autocracy. Flanking Boris and Gleb, the traditional protectors of the Russian realm, Saint Nikita and the tsaritsa herself join the ranks of the tsar's personal spiritual intercessors, who safeguard his divinely sanctioned position so vividly expressed in the central panel. As in the *katapetasma* of 1555, Saint Helena and (as implied) Anastasiia are the only women who appear in the Gospel cover. While the *katapetasma*, however, stresses the role of both women vis-à-vis the rulers of their respective country, the Gospel cover of 1568 elevates the tsaritsa to the status of saintly intercessor after her physical death. No longer serving as a mere helpmate to the tsar in matters of the spirit, Anastasiia appears as a permanent saintlike intercessor for the Russian ruler and his realm.

The success of the tsar's mythopoeic effort ultimately hinged on his acceptance of Anastasiia's family as an integral part of the royal dynasty. Ivan IV's preferential treatment of Anastasiia's natal kin and his equation of Anastasiia with one of his ancestors (thought to support the Rurikide ruling house even after their deaths) can also be seen in Ivan IV's extant testament, which dates from between June and August 1572.[29] Ivan's testament makes clear that the tsar continued to cherish the kin of his deceased first wife and gave it preferential treatment over the relations of his fourth wife, Anna Koltovskaia. While Ivan set aside lands for Anna in Rostov, Iaroslavl', and near Moscow, he made no provisions for her siblings. In contrast, the will of 1572 reveals that Ivan had already given property to Anastasiia's mother, Iuliniia Fedorovna, and brother, Nikita Romanovich, and tried to assure that the Romanovs could hold these lands outright after his death without any interference from the future ruler.[30] If the tsar had merely intended to provide for his aging ex-mother-in-law, he could have assigned her property in usufruct for her lifetime.[31] The tsar's primary concern, however, seems to have been the exemption of his first wife's mother, her son Nikita, and their future offspring from the legal and economic obligations to members of the ruling house. In essence, Ivan IV valued Anastasiia's mother as a matriarch of an honored line, distinguished in its integrity toward the autocracy, that continued to thrive in his own successors, the tsarevichi Ivan and Fedor. She seems to have enjoyed this prestigious position throughout her remaining years; after her death in 1579 the tsar had her buried in the traditional resting place of the Muscovite grand princesses, the Monastery of the Ascension in the Kremlin.[32]

The generous treatment of the Romanovs in Ivan IV's will reflected the tsar's pious devotion to his first wife and his faith that she could protect the Muscovite dynasty through her mediating presence before God's throne. The tsar's need for spiritual intercession is evident in the gloomy tone of the will, which makes reference to the *oprichnina*. The phrase "having passed from the Jerusalem of God's commandments to the passions of Jericho" and the exclamation "But what then shall I do, for Abraham will not know us, Isaac will not be cognizant of us, and Israel will not recognize us" suggest that the tsar was aware that the turbulence of the previous decade of his reign threatened to undermine the ideological basis of the Russian tsardom expressed in the notion that Moscow followed in the footsteps of the Heavenly Jerusalem. In order to avoid the impending loss of Jerusalem and the concomitant doom of his realm, Ivan petitioned the traditional protector saints of the Muscovite realm to stand by his sons forever. Among the holy figures, Ivan in particular invoked the blessings of his own mother, Elena Glinskaia, and of his wife Anastasiia, the mother of his two sons.[33]

Ivan's will clearly treats Anastasiia as an integral member of the royal family. Through her motherhood, assured by the supernatural intervention of Saint Nikita of Pereslavl' (the will includes this saint in the group of royal protector saints), the tsaritsa transcended the barrier between her own bloodline and that of the Rurikides. In this capacity Anastasiia stands in clear contrast to the tsar's second and third wives, Mariia Temriukovna and Marfa Sobakina, whom Ivan considered worthy of compassionate commemoration but did not credit with a special intercessory ability.[34] Like the Gospel cover of 1568, Ivan's testament linked the success of the Muscovite autocracy to Anastasiia Romanovna's extraordinary spiritual disposition.

The memory of Russia's first tsaritsa did not fade under Ivan IV's successor. Fedor Ivanovich regularly ordered prayers for his mother and even sent gifts to monastic institutions abroad to assure her commemoration. According to Arsenios Elassonis, who accompanied Patriarch Jeremiah on his trip to Moscow in 1589, Fedor Ivanovich's reign was blessed with peace to a large extent because of his subjects' respect for his mother.[35] The *vita* of the Russian saint Gennadii Kostromskii i Liubimogradskii (composed by Aleksei, *hegumen* of the Spaso-Gennadiev Monastery, around 1584–1586) espoused the idea that Anastasiia's kinship ties to Tsar Ivan were sanctioned by God and furthered the prestige of the Russian tsardom. In one of the miracle stories in the *vita*, Anastasiia's mother received Saint Gennadii in her home during his stay in Moscow in 1546 to have him bless her sons Daniil and Nikita and her still unmarried daughter. To her surprise the saint, who willingly complied with her wishes, prophesied that Anastasiia, "a beautiful vine and a fertile branch," would become a "pious mistress and tsaritsa to all the world."[36] When in the following year Anastasiia became the tsar's wife, she remembered the miracle-worker's prophesy and sent icons and liturgical vestments to his monastery as a sign of her faith in him.[37]

The themes of Anastasiia's supernaturally attested fertility and her pious disposition attest to the continued respect enjoyed by her kin. At the same time the prophesy that Anastasiia would become the royal mistress of the entire world suggests that during her son's reign she continued to be esteemed for her contributions to the cause of the autocracy.

In the late sixteenth century, Anastasiia Romanovna's reputation for her piety also spread among monastic and ecclesiastical dignitaries abroad. In 1585 the patriarch of Alexandria, Silvester, in a letter to Irina Godunova tried to persuade the tsaritsa to work jointly with her husband for the protection of Alexandria. In order to provide an incentive for Irina, the patriarch urged her that she should always remember her mother-in-law, the blessed tsaritsa Anastasiia, who had distinguished herself through her virtues and who had always guided her husband, Ivan, to undertake God-pleasing deeds.[38]

Patriarch Silvester's letter gives evidence of two new elements in the myth of the "pious tsaritsa Anastasiia." It is one of the earliest sources that document the notion popular among many modern historians that through her kind disposition the tsaritsa was able to influence the unruly behavior of her husband.[39] Whereas Russian sources from the time of Ivan IV's reign had characterized the tsaritsa as a helpmate and intercessor who performed spiritual deeds to support her husband in his political tasks, the foreign author of the letter attributed to her the ability to influence his actions directly. The patriarch's notion clearly grew out of his understanding of the new dynamic between Tsar Fedor and his wife, Irina, which was the result of the Muscovite ruler's physical and mental fragility. One must speculate whether his view was representative of broad Muscovite attitudes, but at the very least it made an ideological contribution by presenting the pious Anastasiia as a model to other Russian tsaritsy. The ideas that Anastasiia exerted a positive influence on Ivan and could be a role model for future royal women were both incorporated in the Romanovs' approach to their matriarch after their accession to power in 1613.

In the face of the dynastic confusion Russia experienced during the Time of Troubles, it was only natural that the selection of Mikhail Fedorovich as the next ruler of Muscovy by the Assembly of the Land was influenced by considerations concerning his legitimate right to the throne. In their efforts to make their case that Mikhail Fedorovich was the logical successor to the vacant royal seat, the supporters of the Romanov government shaped the already existing Anastasiia myth to accommodate their claims. In the early years after the establishment of the Romanov regime, the dynastic aspects of the Anastasiia myth became increasingly important. As a result the myth of the "pious tsaritsa Anastasiia" deemphasized the tsaritsa's role as an active spiritual helpmate to the tsar and instead treated her as a deeply religious figure through whom God worked his grace on the ruling dynasty.

The indebtedness of the Romanov supporters to Ivan IV's conviction that in Anastasiia's children the bloodlines of the Rurikide and Romanov families had merged into a new Muscovite royal dynasty can be observed in their construction of Mikhail Fedorovich's legitimacy. According to the *Gosudarstvennaia kniga (Book of State),* the Assembly of the Land chose Mikhail as the next ruler in 1613 because he was a relative of the last Rurikide tsar, Fedor Ivanovich, and because he was "the son of Fedor Nikitich Romanov Iur'ev, the natal nephew of Tsaritsa and Grand Princess Anastasiia Romanovna Iur'eva, the wife of the great lord tsar and grand prince Ivan Vasil'evich of blessed memory."[40] Anastasiia's key role in bridging the gap between the last Rurikide and the first Romanov ruler is expressed in the charter confirming the election of Mikhail Fedorovich, which lists Anastasiia Romanovna, mother of Fedor Ivanovich, as the first woman in the opening genealogy of Russian rulers. The document stresses that the tsaritsa was Ivan IV's legitimate wife.[41]

The elevation of Ivan IV's first wife to the status of the matriarch of the new Romanov line in the early seventeenth century was also connected with a perceived need for dynastic stability. Those who engaged in shaping the myth of the "pious tsaritsa Anastasiia" used it to combat the difficult circumstances the dynasty faced as a direct result of the Time of Troubles. In his *Vremennik,* Ivan Timofeev takes pains to point out that Anastasiia had been a native Russian girl who had distinguished herself through great spiritual and physical nobility and fertility.[42] This fortuitous image represented a stark contrast to the recent Russian quest for an heir to the throne, which had brought foreign pretenders to Moscow. The myth of the "pious tsaritsa

Anastasiia" served to neutralize the Romanovs' awkward position vis-à-vis the late tsarevich Dmitrii Ivanovich, the last son of Ivan IV. By insisting on the transfer of royal legitimacy from Ivan IV to their own line through Anastasiia, the Romanovs also declared Tsarevich Dmitrii, who had attained the status of an all-Russian royal martyr saint, not throne-worthy since he descended from a different mother.[43] The author of the *Inoe skazanie* acknowledged the royal background of both of the "two most noble offshoots" of Ivan IV, Fedor and Dmitrii. At the same time, he sought to explain Fedor Ivanovich's precedence over his younger brother by pointing to the different spiritual status of their respective mothers. In contrast to Dmitrii's mother, Mariia Nagaia, whom he merely acknowledged as a royal mother, he called Anastasiia "a tsaritsa who was pious and wise in God."[44] By appealing to the superior spiritual position of Anastasiia Romanovna, the *Inoe skazanie* avoided a direct comparison between Fedor Ivanovich, whose kinship ties with Mikhail Fedorovich the Romanovs stressed, and Tsarevich Dmitrii.

The need to transcend the gap between the two royal brothers is also evident in a contemporary icon from Ustiug. In the image, which features the Virgin Bogoliubskaia, Anastasiia's name saint stands next to the Byzantine ruler saint Theodora and Saint Dmitrii of Uglich.[45] The appearance of Anastasiia in the place of Mariia Nagaia suggests that the icon proclaimed Anastasiia as the one tsaritsa who legitimately carried on the continuity of the royal dynasty. At the same time, by grouping Saint Dmitrii with Saint Anastasia rather than Mariia Nagaia's name saint, the icon created the impression that the saintly tsarevich was co-opted by the new dynasty.

In order to press their dynastic claims, the Romanovs were ready to exaggerate the genealogical significance of Anastasiia Romanovna. Already the charter confirming the election of Mikhail Fedorovich from May 1613 attributed to Anastasiia's kin a fictitious royal descent. The opening genealogical section presents Anastasiia as a distant offshoot of the illustrious Caesar Augustus. The same claim appears in the speech of Feodorit, the archbishop of Riazan', before Mikhail Fedorovich in Kostroma in 1613, which aimed at securing Mikhail's acceptance of the Russian throne, and in *d'iak* Fedor Ioakimovich Griboedov's *History of the Tsars and Grand Princes of the Russian Land*.[46] The *History* traces the family tree of Anastasiia Romanovna, mother of Tsar Fedor Ivanovich, to an Andrei Ivanovich Romanov from Prussia, whose family was said to be related to "Augustus, Caesar of Rome, who ruled over the entire universe." The following fictitious genealogy is highly selective in the choice of the ancestors of the Romanov regime to highlight Anastasiia's dynastic key role.[47]

The Romanovs made Anastasiia's memory an integral part of their official ideology of government by incorporating it into their court ritual. When in 1616 Mikhail Fedorovich's first bride, Mariia Ivanovna Khlopova, was moved to the royal women's quarters in the Moscow Kremlin and groomed for her future role as tsaritsa, the Romanovs renamed her Anastasiia in honor of their illustrious ancestor.[48] The act evidently was designed to uphold the Romanov matriarch as a model for the new royal wife and mother. When the Khlopova match failed, the court became more cautious and withheld the title Anastasiia from Mikhail Fedorovich's future brides to avoid compromising its own position.[49]

A comparison of the interpretation of Anastasiia Romanovna's figure during the reign of Ivan IV with her image in the period of the first two Romanov tsars reveals a noticeable shift from her perception as a spiritual intercessor for the Muscovite ruler to her appreciation as a crucial dynastic link. This new approach to the tsaritsa, however, by no means eclipsed the notion of Anastasiia's piety. A closer look at the development of the image of the pious tsaritsa in the official mythopoeic efforts of this period suggests that, within the Romanov context, the concept of the interceding tsaritsa was consciously domesticated to avoid any impression of the new dynasty's weakness. Anastasiia's piety came to be seen as an esteemed personal trait that enhanced her position as matriarch of the new royal line. In the later seventeenth century, this process led to the personalization of Anastasiia's piety, which is attested by the tsaritsa's inclusion in hagiographic works of the period.

One of the earliest examples of the Romanovs' appreciation of Anastasiia's piety comes from the *1617 Khronograf*. The elaborate eulogy to Ivan's wife betrays the familiarity of this work with the interpretation of the role of this tsaritsa in the reigns of Ivan IV and his son Fedor:

> For he [Ivan IV] found a very handsome treasure, like a shining pearl or ruby, a precious jewel, a pious maiden, blessed amongst the women, Anastasiia, the daughter of a strongman by the name Roman. She led a God-pleasing life, not only in her maidenhood, but also in marriage, without being proud of her crown. She did not regard the glory of this vain world as a merit, but decorated herself eternally with humble wisdom, and she always devoted herself to extreme abstinence, engaged in prayer, and extended her hands in a deep love of the poor. Not only that, but she urged on and led her honorable and noble husband, the tsar and grand prince Ivan Vasil'evich of all Russia, to virtue of any kind.[50]

The *1617 Khronograf's* reference to Anastasiia's disposition toward prayer and her love of the poor faintly recalls the notion developed at the Russian court in the late 1540s and 1550s that, by devoting herself to spiritual tasks, the tsaritsa aided her husband in assuring the success of the autocracy. The public aspects of her piety, however, are remarkably toned down in the seventeenth-century source. The author of the *Khronograf* clearly preferred the notion espoused by the patriarch of Alexandria in his letter to Irina Godunova in 1585 that Anastasiia exerted a personal influence on her husband's behavior. Anastasiia's traits in the *Khronograf*—humility, the absence of pride, and abstinence—represent qualities usually associated with a person who devotes his or her life to God rather than assuming the responsibilities associated with governing. By ascribing these virtues to Anastasiia, the *Khronograf* likened the Romanov matriarch to a saint who with her God-pleasing ways gave religious sanction to her kin's right to the throne. The same approach to the tsaritsa can be observed in Ivan Timofeev's *Vremennik*, which celebrates the tsaritsa's spiritual virtues alongside her physical nobility. It can also be found in the memoirs of Archbishop Arsenios, who called the first Romanov tsar "smart, humble, and reasonable" and likened him in his character to his great aunt Anastasiia.[51]

With their portrayal of Anastasiia as a saintly tsaritsa, the chroniclers and authors of historical tales during the period following the Time of Troubles sought approval for the new dynasty. At least in one instance, however, we possess evidence of the difficulty of this undertaking. In 1616, three years after Mikhail Fedorovich's accession to the throne, a number of men from the town of Lukh were accused of having used the name of the pious tsaritsa to cast dispersions on the present ruling house. During a visit to a tavern, one of the men, Veseloi Pifanko, sang a song about Anastasiia Romanovna that prompted a number of his companions to reminisce about the tsaritsa's piety. They recalled a popular legend according to which, on one of her pilgrimages to the Trinity-Sergius Monastery, Anastasiia already saw the saint's institution from the site of a cross that was located three miles away. In the course of the discussion of the miracle, the peasant Miliutka Kuznets allegedly unfavorably compared the present ruler with the saintly Anastasiia. The peasant was supposed to have regretted that similar stories were not circulating about Mikhail Fedorovich.[52]

Although the actual events in the tavern in Lukh will never be known, the incident illuminates both the potential and the limitations of the myth of the "pious tsaritsa Anastasiia" in aiding the Romanov regime's quest for legitimacy. On one hand it attests to the popular acceptance of Anastasiia's extraordinary spiritual disposition. When questioned, all the eyewitnesses concurred that Veseloi Pifanko's singing had caused the discussion of the spiritual fitness of the Russian rulers. The fact that common subjects sang songs about the first Muscovite tsaritsa and wove her person into miraculous tales suggests that by the early seventeenth century she had become an integral part of Russian folklore. The myth of the pious Anastasiia, however, had to be pruned carefully to avoid any direct comparison between the illustrious tsaritsa and the present ruler. Whether Miliutka Kuznets uttered the fateful words about the lack of Mikhail Fedorovich's charisma in the tavern in Lukh or not, the court's interest in the episode suggests it was concerned about such a possibility. This may explain Anastasiia's domesticated image in the *1617 Khronograf,* which deemphasized her role of intercessor for the tsar and his realm and instead heightened her personal sanctity.

The emphasis on Anastasiia's personal religious devotion, which was designed to give the Romanov dynasty much needed charisma, persisted in the reign of Aleksei Mikhailovich. The perceived need to celebrate the tsaritsa's saintly qualities is evident in Griboedov's *History of the Tsars and*

Grand Princes of the Russian Land. While the original version of the work made only passing reference to Anastasiia Romanovna as the wife of Ivan IV, the redacted version Griboedov presented to the tsar in 1669 inserted verbatim the description of Anastasiia found in the *1617 Khronograf.* The passage particularly stands out since Griboedov paid only cursory attention to Russian royal women in his work.[53]

The process of the sanctification of Anastasiia Romanovna's image evident in the records and literature of the court also found reflection in the hagiography of the later seventeenth century. The underlying connection between Anastasiia's religious devotion and the glorification of her dynasty is particularly evident in the first part of the *"Skazanie o Khristoforovoi pustyni"* ("Tale of Khristofor's Hermitage").[54] Vaguely familiar with Anastasiia's health, fertility, and infant mortality problems that led to her patronage of the cult of Saint Nikita of Pereslavl', the anonymous author of the tale recalls her fateful pilgrimage with the tsar to the Kirillov Monastery in 1555, which resulted in Tsarevich Dmitrii's death. The tale contrasts the trip to Kirillov (which the royal couple undertook to pray for peace and order in the realm) with Anastasiia's personal distress after her return.[55] After spending many days in prayer, the tsaritsa one night dreamed of a beautiful woman, who turned out to be the Mother of God. The Virgin told her that in order to receive relief she should request holy water from a rock in the hermitage of Saint Khristofor where an icon of the Virgin Hodegetria was located. The next morning Anastasiia shared her dream with her husband, who sent out messengers to the hermitage. Before they even reached their destination, Saint Khristofor set out for Moscow with holy water and a life-giving cross to visit the royal couple. The Virgin herself announced his arrival to Anastasiia in a second vision. After the reception of the saint in the tsar's chambers, the royal couple during a liturgical service prayed to Christ and the Virgin for their realm and their spiritual and physical health. Then Ivan IV crossed himself with the saint's cross, sprinkled himself with the holy water from the hermitage, and ordered his wife to do the same. She eventually recovered completely from her affliction after imbibing the holy liquid. At the tsaritsa's urging, Ivan endowed the hermitage generously.[56]

The "Tale of Khristofor's Hermitage" demonstrates that in the later seventeenth century Anastasiia Romanovna was perceived as a devout royal woman who on a personal level entertained a special relationship with the divine. The tsaritsa does not play a role with regard to matters of state but appears as a petitioner for the reversal of her own personal affliction. As if to underscore the personal nature of her condition, the "Tale of Khristofor's Hermitage" associates her recovery with private visions. Anastasiia also appears passive with regard to the performance of pious deeds. When the saint arrived in the Kremlin, it was not Anastasiia but her husband who took the initiative in her eventual cure and rewarded the saint's monastery. All in all, the tsaritsa appears as a laudable but inactive figure, who decorated the autocracy with her religious devotion.

The complexity of Anastasiia Romanovna's image in medieval Russia is still evident in her representation in modern folklore. The efforts of ideologues at the court of the early Romanovs to structure Anastasiia Romanovna's piety in more personal terms seem to have left a lasting impression on the perception of the tsaritsa in Russian folklore. Modern folk songs emphasize the personal saintly goodness with which she propelled her husband to be kind to his subjects. For example, in *"Smert' tsaritsy"* ("The Death of the Tsaritsa"), Anastasiia on her deathbed pleads with Ivan IV to control his temper and to show mercy to his family, the boyars, peasants, and widows in his realm.[57] Still, in view of the apparent existence of a tradition of folk songs about Russia's first tsaritsa in the early seventeenth century it is not surprising that in the lore of the people the theme of Anastasiia's pious service to the country and its people was not entirely eclipsed. As Norman Ingham has pointed out, several versions of "The Death of the Tsaritsa" represent Anastasiia's death as a threat to the Orthodox faith in Russia.[58] The evidence derived from this song suggests that, within the medium of folklore, sixteenth- and seventeenth-century notions of Anastasiia Romanovna survived side by side into the modern period. While folk songs cannot illuminate the medieval contexts of the myth of the "pious tsaritsa Anastasiia," they attest to the multiple roots of the myth, which were responsible for its continued vitality.

The image of the first Russian tsaritsa played an important role in the conceptualization of the Russian tsardom from the time of the official inception of the autocracy in the mid–sixteenth century to the end of the Muscovite period. The myth of the "pious tsaritsa Anastasiia" already took shape during her lifetime, because of the mythopoeic activities of the church hierarchy. In his wedding sermon to Ivan and his first wife, Metropolitan Makarii defined the position of the tsaritsa as a spiritual helpmate to the tsar. This view emphasized the tsaritsa's ability to support her husband's commitment to the maintenance of the Orthodox realm by taking over liturgical and charitable duties. By carrying out these responsibilities, Anastasiia herself contributed to the well-being of her subjects. Tsar Ivan promoted this notion further in the Gospel cover of 1568, which cast the late tsaritsa as a saintly intercessor for the realm. During the later part of Ivan's reign, the same idea led to an increased emphasis on Anastasiia's positive effect on the fate of the autocracy in her capacity as royal mother. The appreciation of the dynastic aspects of the tsaritsa's role is evident in Ivan IV's testament of 1572, which accorded the Romanovs preferential status.

After the death of Ivan IV, the myth of the pious Anastasiia underwent substantial changes. In the reign of Fedor Ivanovich, the divine approval of his mother's line was stressed. At the same time Anastasiia was held up as a model for other royal wives. This concept, which was largely supported by high-level non-Russian religious leaders who had to deal with a frail tsar, led to the development of the notion that through her piety Anastasiia had steered her husband away from harmful deeds. The most profound change in the interpretation of Anastasiia Romanovna's figure, however, occurred in the seventeenth century. Overshadowed by questions of legitimacy and the threat of pretense, a legacy of the Time of Troubles, the new Romanov regime reinvented the myth of the "pious tsaritsa Anastasiia" to bolster the regime's claim to the throne and to eliminate competition. The heightened interest in Anastasiia's position as the matriarch of the Romanov dynasty in time eclipsed the notion of a spiritual helpmate to the tsar and an intercessor for the realm, although Anastasiia continued to be held up as an exemplary tsaritsa to the Romanov wives. The conscious reconceptualization of the myth to accommodate the need for dynastic legitimization is evident also in the emerging notion of the extraordinary spiritual disposition of the Romanov matriarch in the court literature and hagiography of the period. By the end of the seventeenth century, the image of Tsaritsa Anastasiia as a ruler's wife who engaged in pious deeds for the sake of the realm had become transformed. The new image presented her as a saintlike, suffering woman who was largely removed from affairs of state, who indulged in private visions, and who acted as a moral force on her husband.

The Image of Mariia Il'inichna

Scholars have often argued that the western influence in Muscovite iconography during the seventeenth century led to a loss of the spiritual content of the icon in Russia.[59] While the emerging new style of icon painting was less concerned with theological than political statements, it would be false to assume that the new icons were devoid of religious content. This is especially true for images featuring members of the secular and ecclesiastical hierarchies, which were produced during the reign of Aleksei Mikhailovich. An early example of this type of image is found on a great bell that was cast in 1653 and later dedicated in honor of the tsar's return from his Smolensk campaign. According to a sketch based on Augustin Meyerberg's memory, the front of the bell shows Christ blessing Aleksei Mikhailovich and his wife Mariia Il'inichna. Paul of Aleppo, who witnessed the casting, notes that the back of the bell showed Patriarch Nikon with a crown and a crozier.[60] The efforts of Soviet scholars to interpret images of this type as early examples of "secular realist" portrait art have obscured not only the perceived socioreligious status of the secular and religious leaders portrayed in these images, such as the tsar and the patriarch, but also that of the tsaritsa, who is depicted alongside her husband.[61] An examination of the tsaritsa's position and function in two compositions that are products of the new artistic style, *The Veneration of the Cross* and *The Tree of the Russian Realm,* shows that the notion of the tsaritsa's elevated spiritual prestige persisted in the later seventeenth century. In particular, these icons express the idea that the Russian tsaritsa could serve as an intercessor for the tsar and his realm in times of crisis.

The overall composition of *The Veneration of the Cross* features five

5. *The Veneration of the Cross.* Seventeenth-century icon in Patriarchal Palace, Kremlin Museums. The image shows the Byzantine emperor Constantine and his mother, Helena (standing), Aleksei Mikhailovich and his wife Mariia Il'inichna (bowing), and Patriarch Nikon (kneeling) in the act of venerating a large reliquary cross. The cross separates the male from the female figures. The scrolls in their hands underscore the gender-specific roles of the rulers and their wives.

crowned figures—three males and two females—holding scrolls in their hands and flanking a large seven-ended reliquary cross (see Figure 5).[62] The man in upright position on the left is referred to as "the holy pious tsar Constantine," while the figure below him, performing a bow, is identified as "the lord tsar and grand prince Aleksei Mikhailovich." Below Aleksei, "the most holy Nikon, Patriarch of Moscow" is kneeling on the ground.[63] To the left of the cross, opposite Constantine, stands a female figure who is identified as Constantine's mother, "the holy pious tsaritsa Elena." Immediately below her and across from Aleksei Mikhailovich, his wife, "the mistress tsaritsa and grand princess Mariia Il'inichna," performs a graceful bow.[64]

The peculiar nature of the cross in *The Veneration of the Cross* suggests that the composition was originally commissioned at the behest of Patriarch Nikon, who was devoted to the cult of the True Cross. In 1657 Patriarch Nikon sent such a cross, containing approximately one hundred relics, to the Monastery of the Cross on the island of Kii in the White Sea. The incident is commemorated in the composition itself, either in an inscription on the bottom frame or in two medallions to the left and right of the top crossbar of the cross that contain eulogies of the True Cross.[65]

Although the conception of *The Veneration of the Cross* was a result of Nikon's initiative, the composition also appealed to the Russian ruler.

Kapterev points out that both Mikhail Fedorovich and Aleksei Mikhailovich displayed a vivid interest in relics of the True Cross because of its connection with the victorious emperor Constantine. The image that Saltanov painted in 1678 was commissioned by the tsar.[66] The omission of the two oval medallions above the cross and the plaque with inscriptions under the crossbar in the Kremlin icon points out that, in contrast to Nikon, Aleksei Mikhailovich was not primarily interested in the promotion of the cult of the True Cross through commemorations and devotional hymns. Given that the icon was displayed in a *terem* church, the image seems to have served as a propaganda piece expressing the position of the royal family in relationship to the divine. Within this context, the reference to Nikon's involvement in the cult of the True Cross represented a distraction. The emphasis on the spiritual status of the Russian royal couple in the Kremlin copy also explains the absence of the cross scepters in Constantine's and Helena's hands, which appear in other copies of *The Veneration of the Cross.* The royal patron was less interested in the imperial status of the two Byzantine figures (recognized as such by their regalia) than in their aura of piety, expressed in the accompanying inscriptions.[67] *The Veneration of the Cross* therefore expresses the piety of the royal family and the patriarch in the act of worshiping the cross and their aspiration to be equal with the ideal Christian rulers in their imitation of Constantine and Helena.[68]

The spiritual status of Aleksei Mikhailovich and his wife Mariia is expressed in their close affiliation with the ruler saints Constantine and Helena. The garments of the tsar and tsaritsa replicate the patterns found on those worn by Constantine and Helena. The symbolic association of Aleksei Mikhailovich and his wife Mariia Il'inichna with Constantine and Helena stands in a long tradition that equates tsars and tsaritsy with the illustrious Byzantine ruler saints. The comparison of the tsar and his wife with Constantine and Helena recalls Metropolitan Makarii's statement a century earlier that the royal family had the potential to become part of the family of saints. Aleksei Mikhailovich was often eulogized as a second Constantine in contemporary court poetry.[69] A letter from Theophanes, Patriarch of Jerusalem, to Evdokiia Luk'ianovna from 1629, in which the hierarch thanked her for her generous alms, compares her to Empress Helena, who built churches and restored the Church of the Resurrection in Jerusalem. Twenty years later, another patriarch of Jerusalem, Paisius, ascribed to Mariia Il'inichna the same pious disposition as had been displayed by the holy Helena. In his correspondence Paisius expressed the hope that Mariia would see a son on the throne, just as Saint Helena had witnessed the investiture of Constantine by God. In another letter that dates from December 1652, he lauded Mariia Il'inichna for her generosity and assured her that like Saint Helena, she would always be commemorated. Paisius called her a "second holy new Helena, who beautifies the most holy altar of the mother of churches." Two years later, the Russian priest Ivan Neronov addressed the tsaritsa as "a new Helena" in a petition in which he asked her to intercede with the tsar for the cause of the Old Believers.[70]

While the Russian tsar and tsaritsa followed in the footsteps of Constantine and Helena, they still did not possess the sanctity of the imperial couple. In the icon the royal couple is carefully distinguished from the two Byzantine figures by the absence of haloes, the placement of Aleksei and Mariia below their Byzantine counterparts, and by their slight body movement which, according to B. A. Uspenskii, denotes lesser spiritual importance.[71] The icon thus proclaims the spiritual resemblance of the Russian ruler and his wife to the ruler saints Constantine and Helena and their potential to join the family of ruler saints.

The figures depicted in the icon *The Veneration of the Cross* are differentiated by their spiritual potential and also by their gender. The cross separates the male and female figures into two distinct hierarchies. The icon's sensitivity to the gender-specific approach of each category to the worship of the cross is also expressed in the inscriptions on the scrolls of the figures.

The two male rulers in the icon seem to be concerned foremost with the protection of their respective realms from outside enemies. In his eulogy of the True Cross, Constantine refers to his victory over Maxentius at the Milvian bridge, which, according to Christian legend, the emperor achieved after experiencing a vision of a Christian cross: "O honorable Cross of Christ, I saw you in the sky and entered into the faith of Christ. Your evil enemy Maxentius, who did not believe in Christ, the Son of God, was defeated by you. I saw you in the water during baptism."[72] Constantine's special spiritual status is marked by the reference to two visionary experiences, one before his battle with Maxentius, the other during his baptism. According to his scroll his visionary enlightenment, faith, and victory were closely linked. His vision led to faith in the power of the cross, which in turn brought victory and spiritual enlightenment. The connection of religious experience and victory is also acknowledged in the scroll of Aleksei Mikhailovich: "O honorable cross, you are the divine victory; you bring about our salvation; you overcome our enemies; you are the divine kingdom, protect those who beseech you!"[73]

In spite of Aleksei Mikhailovich's evident desire to follow in Constantine's footsteps, the supplicatory aspect of his invocation stands in sharp contrast to that of Constantine the Great, who had already experienced victory. Possibly the tsar's plea for protection reflects his concern for his country's fortunes in the war with Catholic Poland, which lasted from 1654 to 1667. In contrast to Constantine's scroll, that of the tsar makes no mention of any divine prophesies concerning his future. Since the tsar did not connect with the supernatural through visions and auditions, he was left in the role of a supplicant who must plead for the divine intervention of the cross on his behalf.

In contrast to the male rulers on the left, who see in the cross of Christ an opportunity for victory, the royal women on the right perceive the cross primarily as an object of liturgical worship. Saint Helena's scroll points out that the cult of the True Cross originated with a woman: "O honorable cross of Christ, I recognized you through the divine light during the conception of my son, and I raised you with my own hands from the womb of the earth at the advice of my son Constantine."[74]

The words on Saint Helena's scroll illuminate the Muscovite perception of the ideal ruler couple in seventeenth-century Russia. As in the case of her son Constantine, Helena's saintly status is expressed by her experience of a divine vision. Nevertheless, in contrast to Constantine, who displayed faith in a supernatural sign but recognized Christ only in the sacrament of baptism after his victory over Maxentius, Helena experienced spiritual enlightenment immediately during the act of the conception of her illustrious son. This curious reference to the intervention of the divine in Constantine's conception reflects an old tradition shedding doubt on Constantine's legitimacy. As Drijvers points out, sources from the mid–fourth century onward refer to Constantine as the product of illegal intercourse with a lowborn woman.[75] In the seventh century, a legend arose that presented the encounter of Constantine's parents, Emperor Constantius and Helena, in a better light. According to an embellished version of this legend, which appears in the fourteenth-century church history of Kallistos Xantophulos, during one of his campaigns in the eastern part of the Roman Empire Constantius spent a night with an innkeeper's daughter.[76] In a dream Constantius experienced that night he saw the sun rising in the west. Mindful of the omen, he rewarded Helena with a purple cloak, which years later identified her as the mother of Emperor Constantius's heir.[77] While the legend surrounding Constantine's birth depicts Constantius as the recipient of the prophetic vision that announces the greatness of his future son, the Russian icon *The Veneration of the Cross* focuses on Helena's spiritual enlightenment during the conception of Constantine in her womb. The appearance of the theme of miraculous conception in conjunction with the saintly Byzantine empress reflects the Muscovite perception that the wives and mothers of Orthodox rulers had a special propensity to function as receptacles of the divine. The inscription on Helena's scroll makes clear that this capacity of royal women was not limited to intermittent periods of pregnancy but, rather, extended to their whole lives. The reference to Helena raising the cross of Christ "from the womb of the earth" implies her conscious liturgical reenactment of the birth experience, which symbolizes the awakening of the spirit in man. In a sense Helena's devotional deed—a result of her intimate contact with the supernatural—reinforces her son's spiritual strength and acts as an additional guarantee for his success against his enemies. The imperial mother's role is defined as that of a helpmate to the ruler in matters of the faith. The remark that Helena set out to find the cross at the advice of her son Constantine underscores the perception that the royal women's involvement in religious ritual was important to the ruler and his realm.

The example of Saint Helena assuring supernatural support for her son demonstrates the value of the divine gift of enlightenment in matters of the realm. In the case of Aleksei Mikhailovich, who appears as a supplicant before the True Cross, the need for divine intervention seems to be particularly urgent. The tsar himself is not personally enlightened by the divine, as was Constantine, who received a vision of the cross before the battle against Maxentius. Therefore, in his petition for protection, Aleksei Mikhailovich must rely on the support of intermediaries who labor for spiritual enlightenment on his behalf. As Mariia Il'inichna's scroll shows, his wife fulfilled this function: "We are bowing to the cross for the salvation of the faithful, and we kiss it affectionately; and embracing you, blessed wood of Christ, I pray that you enlighten my soul and mind."[78]

Like Saint Helena, Mariia Il'inichna is closely associated with the performance of a liturgical role, identified by the individual acts of bowing to, kissing, and embracing the holy relic. Through this liturgical activity the tsaritsa is able to procure spiritual enlightenment. Whereas in most of the icons featuring *The Veneration of the Cross* the inscriptions note that Mariia prays for her own enlightenment, the Kremlin copy omits the pronoun "my."[79] As a result, the tsaritsa's plea gains an altruistic connotation. Just as Saint Helena supported her son's cause and petitioned for the spiritual welfare of the believers, Mariia Il'inichna appears as her husband's helpmate in matters that require faith and spiritual strength. By executing the required religious ritual, she also plays the role of an intercessor for the realm.

Mariia Il'inichna's intercessory function depicted in *The Veneration of the Cross* associates the tsaritsa with the representatives of the ecclesiastical hierarchy, who traditionally were considered intercessors for the tsar. This role of the church dignitaries is captured in the kneeling posture of Patriarch Nikon. The analogous religious function of the patriarch and the tsaritsa is expressed in the similarity of their crowns and in the close resemblance of the inscription on Nikon's scroll to that of the tsaritsa: "We fall to our knees and appeal to you, who are full of life, my most holy cross; enlighten my mind and soul, ears, lips and tongue, and my breath."[80]

The association of the patriarch, the spiritual leader of the Orthodox flock, with liturgical acts—such as falling to one's knees and praying for spiritual enlightenment—seems commonplace. Nevertheless, the patriarch does not appear as an intercessor for his religious community but, rather, as a petitioner on his own behalf. Nikon does not pray for the people entrusted to him but for his own spiritual enlightenment. This explains his alignment with Aleksei Mikhailovich, who himself appears as a supplicant.

The Veneration of the Cross bears witness to the continuing influence of the Muscovite ecclesiastical leadership in the construction of the tsaritsa's image in the seventeenth century. Already the earliest example of the image, the Golgotha composition, accords to Mariia Il'inichna the role of an imitator of Saint Helena and a petitioner for the salvation of the faithful. The ecclesiastic commissioner of the Golgotha panels even acknowledged that in the liturgical act of worshiping the Holy Cross, Saint Helena, Mariia Il'inichna, and Patriarch Nikon played a similar role. The words "kneeling" or "bowing" and "embracing" are shared by all three figures. The saintly status and the liturgical role attached to the tsaritsa are also expressed in the remaining copies of this icon. The changes in the Saltanov image, which was executed for a secular patron, merely heighten these aspects by removing the imperial staffs and having the tsaritsa pray for mankind's enlightenment.

Rather than depicting the relationship of the secular and ecclesiastical hierarchies of mid–seventeenth century Muscovy as Vernadskii claims, *The Veneration of the Cross* places both categories into the larger framework of the Russian Orthodox spiritual hierarchy. All the figures are credited either with sainthood or with the potential to achieve a higher spiritual status. The fulfillment of this potential, however, did not depend on a person's rank in the world. In spite of his high ecclesiastical status, the patriarch appears before Christ as a petitioner. Similarly, the tsar must rely on intercessors to assure his success as a ruler. In order to make explicit the distinction between petitioners and intercessors, the icon divides the spiritual hierarchy along gender lines. The male leaders of the world on the left contrast sharply with the women on the right, who are accorded a mere helpmate status. Nevertheless, within the framework of Christian salvation history, the male figures are dependent on the religious conduct of their female counterparts. The key role in this process was played by the tsaritsa, whose faithful imitation of the Byzantine ruler saint Helena earned her the privilege to be able to intercede before God for the most powerful figures in the country. In the Kremlin icon, Aleksei Mikhailovich and Nikon pray for themselves. In contrast, the tsaritsa performs her liturgical prayers for all members of the Orthodox community, including the patriarch and her husband, the tsar. From a religious perspective, her subordinate role as helpmate is suspended in the act of intercession. Pictorially this is expressed by her bowing posture and the absence of a kneeling figure below her.

The depiction of the respective roles of the tsar and tsaritsa as petitioner and intercessor before God occurred in other seventeenth-century images with a complex ideological content. In their most refined form, these roles were expressed in an icon executed by Simon Ushakov in 1668, which came to be known as *The Tree of the Russian Realm, The Virgin of Vladimir,* and *The Praise of the Virgin of Vladimir* (see Figure 6). The icon, now located in the Tret'iakov Gallery, features a view of the Kremlin walls from the Spasskii Gate on the left to the Nikol'skii Gate on the right.[81] Behind the walls, to the left of the Spasskii Gate, stands Tsar Aleksei Mikhailovich, wearing a red caftan with golden trim and a jewel-encrusted crown. Immediately to the left of the Nikol'skii Gate, one sees Aleksei Mikhailovich's first wife, Mariia Il'inichna, adorned by a crown and a red-and-golden gown. In front of Mariia, the tsarevichi Aleksei and Fedor—Aleksei dressed in a red caftan and Fedor in a green caftan—raise their hands in prayer. All royal figures are identified by inscriptions. Mariia and Aleksei Mikhailovich both hold a scroll in their right hands. In the center of the image, we see the Cathedral of the Dormition of the Virgin in the Kremlin with its five gold-plated cupolas. Three branches of a large tree, which covers more than half the entire image, grow out of the cathedral. On the right "the blessed prince Ivan Danilovich"—dressed in an ornate garb, a red overcoat and a princely fur hat—is planting the tree. On the left "the holy metropolitan Peter," who transferred the Russian metropolitanate from Vladimir to Moscow, is watering the tree with a golden vessel.[82] The branches of the tree are covered with

6. *The Tree of the Russian Realm* (GTG no. 28598). Icon painted by Simon Ushakov in 1668. The image expresses the themes of fertility (the leaves, grapes, and roses on the tree) and motherhood (the medallion of the Virgin and Child and Mariia Il'inichna with her sons Aleksei and Fedor). The saints in the medallions in the tree are divided into two hierarchies—the masculine hierarchy on the left characterized by its petitionary role (the tsar, Metropolitan Peter, Ivan Kalita, ecclesiastical saints, Jesus Christ) and a feminine intercessory hierarchy (Mariia Il'inichna, monastic saints, holy fools, and the Virgin).

leaves, grapes, roses, and medallions that feature major Muscovite saints. The figures are chronologically arranged; the more recent figures occupy a place in the upper register. On the left branch we see (from the bottom up) the images of the Muscovite metropolitans Aleksii, Kiprian, Iona, Fotii and Filip, the patriarchs Iov and Filaret, the "blessed prince" Mikhail, and two sons of Ivan IV, Tsar Fedor and Tsarevich Dmitrii of Uglich. Although one cannot exclude the possibility that the "blessed prince" refers to Prince Mikhail of Chernigov, who was venerated as a martyr saint, his placement close to Filaret points to his identity with the first Romanov tsar.[83] The medallions on the right (from the bottom up) feature the monastic saints Prince Aleksandr Nevskii, Nikon and Sergius of Radonezh, Savva

Storozhevskii, Pafnutii Borovskii, Simon and Andronnik, and the fools-in-Christ Maksim, Basil the Blessed, and Ioann Kolpak.[84] The medallions are arranged in such a fashion that the metropolitans stand close to the first Muscovite hierarch, Peter. Similarly, the royal Rurikide ancestor, Aleksandr Nevskii, is found in the vicinity of his grandson Ivan Kalita. The central branch of the tree features a large medallion with an image of the Virgin of Vladimir, which is decorated with numerous roses. Immediately above this medallion, we see Christ in a red tunic, surrounded by a band of clouds. In his right hand he holds a crown and with his left he lowers a red robe down to two "angels of the Lord," who hold the fabric suspended in mid-air.[85]

The image *The Tree of the Russian Realm* has received ample attention in the scholarly literature. Soviet art historians have traditionally contended that the icon expresses the triumph of the autocracy in seventeenth-century Russia. Proponents of this view, such as I. E. Danilova and N. E. Mneva, claim that the figures depicted in the lower register of the icon and in the medallions portray significant statesmen who strengthened the Muscovite state. They assume that the icon was commissioned by Tsar Aleksei Mikhailovich, who wanted to stress the connection of his dynasty with the gatherers of the Russian land.[86] In A. I. Nekrasov's view, the icon represents the notion that the Romanov dynasty inherited the power to rule from the Rurikides. Recent discussions of the icon's ideological content by Western and Russian scholars have been more cautious with regard to statements about the political symbolism of the composition. Kämpfer, who points out that *The Tree of the Russian Realm* was part of a church built by a merchant family, contends that the icon expresses the patriotism of the merchant class. Thinking that all the saints in the medallions were specifically associated with the city of Moscow, he argues that the icon expresses the glorification of the city (also alluded to by the Kremlin walls). In the most recent treatment of the image *The Tree of the Russian Realm,* V. G. Chubinskaia, who for the first time considered the relevance of the inscriptions, focused again on the figure of Aleksei Mikhailovich. Chubinskaia stressed the tsar's role as caretaker of the Russian realm and victor from a religious rather than political perspective. In her view, the icon represents a symbolic, allegorical construction, which combines traditional elements of Christian iconography with a new secular ideology.[87]

None of the theories about the ideological content of *The Tree of the Russian Realm* is based on a comprehensive study of both the compositional structure and the complex imagery of the icon in relation to its inscriptions. The traditional Soviet view that the icon celebrates the Muscovite autocracy is suspect, since only few of the figures depicted in the medallions can be considered Muscovite statesmen. Even if one stretches the term to include the metropolitans, at least half of the saints are monastic figures or fools-in-Christ, who distinguish themselves solely by their spiritual charisma. The same theory also does not account for the presence of Mariia Il'inichna and her sons Aleksei and Fedor in the image. Serious objections must also be raised against Nekrasov's view that the image advances the idea of the dynastic continuity from the Rurikide to the Romanov dynasty. Although the motif of the Tree of Jesse, which served as an iconographic model for *The Tree of the Russian Realm,* originally bore a genealogical connotation, Ushakov's rendition of the tree places less emphasis on dynastic than on spiritual succession.[88] The figures depicted in the medallions are all noted intercessors for the Muscovite realm; in addition to Ivan Kalita at the foot of the tree, only Fedor Ivanovich and Dmitrii of Uglich belong to the Rurikide dynasty. Clearly Fedor, the weak-minded son of Ivan IV, and Dmitrii, who stemmed from an uncanonical marriage and died young, were not outstanding examples of illustrious Rurikide rulers. It is more likely that both appear in the image because they were regarded as saints after their deaths. One may even argue that Ushakov's treatment of the Tree of Jesse motif was designed to counter concerns about the Romanov dynasty's claim to be related to the Rurikides. One of the models for Ushakov's composition was the frontispiece of the *Mech dukhovnyi (Spiritual Sword),* a panegyrical work by Lazar Baranovich published in Kiev in 1666 that contained a genealogical tree of Aleksei Mikhailovich, his wife Mariia, and three of their sons, extending out of the body of Grand Prince Vladimir of Kiev.[89] According to a letter from Lazar Baranovich to Patriarch Nikon, the patriarch objected to the genealogical connection of the Romanovs with the Rurikides in the *Spiritual Sword,* insisting that "this tree does not signify the ancestry, but the realm of the tsardom."[90] Thus the absence of the dynastic element (notably the figure of Vladimir) in Ushakov's image may have been a conscious move to avoid a controversial depiction of the tsar.[91] Questions must also be raised about Kämpfer's view that the icon expresses the political attitudes of the Muscovite merchant class since Simon Ushakov belonged to the masters of the Armoury, who executed works commissioned primarily by the tsar.[92] Moreover, not all the saints depicted in the medallions relate to the city of Moscow. Out of all the monastic saints, only Simon and Andronnik are directly associated with the capital of Muscovy. The significance of Saints Nikon and Sergius of Radonezh, Savva Storozhevskii, and Pafnutii Borovskii lies in their function as protectors of the Russian tsars and their families, who regularly made pilgrimages to their monasteries.[93] Chubinskaia, who focuses on the tsar's role as "the steward of the vineyard," also overlooks the function of the saints with regard to the royal figures.[94]

A comparison of the structural elements of *The Tree of the Russian Realm* and the inscriptions accompanying them reveals that the overall symbolic framework of the icon is eschatological in nature. This is evident in the words in Aleksei Mikhailovich's scroll: "Save, Lord, your people, and bless your heritage."[95] As if to bolster Aleksei Mikhailovich's plea for salvation, Metropolitan Peter and Grand Prince Ivan Kalita extend a prayer to the Lord in which they ask not only for Christ's intervention on behalf of his heritage but for his immediate visit: "Lord, look down from heaven and see. And visit this vineyard and complete it which your right hand has planted."[96] The concern of the icon with the salvation of man on the Final Day, when the Lord sits in judgment, is expressed particularly in the upper register. The iconography of the Christ figure holding a crown and the two archangels hovering over the scene recalls the coronation portraits of Byzantine and South Slavic rulers.[97] The unusual combination of regalia (crown and gown) represents a clear reference to the Apocalypse, which connects both objects with the achievement of eternal life. The inscriptions on both sides of the Christ figure, which refer to Rev. 2:10 and 3:5 respectively, confirm this connotation: "Be faithful to me until death, and I will give you the crown of life. He who is victorious will be dressed in a white shirt, and his name will not be erased from the book of life."[98]

Formally the left side of Ushakov's icon depicts a dialogue between the earthly tsar below and the heavenly tsar above. While the Russian ruler's plea for earthly victory is limited in scope, Christ's answer implies that Aleksei's eternal salvation is at stake. Although in principle the heavenly tsar was willing to invest his earthly counterpart with the regalia of eternal, spiritual rule, the realization of this act depended ultimately on the tsar's faith in God. The fate of the Russian ruler and that of his realm were thus intrinsically linked.

The cosmological perspective of the icon can also be gleaned from the layout of the tree motif, which depicts the Christian salvation drama in terms of the spiritualization of man. In the bottom register, under the branches of the tree, stand the members of the royal family, who in their earthly existence embody the present. Grand Prince Ivan Kalita and Metropolitan Peter, traditional intercessors for the tsar, are located more closely to the trunk of the tree because of their proven saintly deeds.[99] The spiritual status of each figure in the tree is reflected in its position within the branches. The martyr saints and the fools-in-Christ are placed higher than their counterparts from the ecclesiastical and monastic ranks because they enjoy greater charisma. The Virgin Mary, who is considered the intercessor for the entire human race, is located immediately below the angels and the Christ figure. All figures are nimbed, including the royal couple and its two sons.[100] Rather than emphasizing the descending order of a dynastic chart, Ushakov's tree focuses on ascendancy and the spiritualization of man.

In addition to its sensitivity to the hierarchy of charismatic figures, *The Tree of the Russian Realm,* like *The Veneration of the Cross,* displays a concept of sanctity that is gender-specific. Both the inscriptions and the overall compositional structure of the image point to the existence of two spiritual hierarchies—one masculine and one feminine—that are intricately linked in the cosmological struggle for salvation. The bottom rung of the masculine hierarchy (on the left) is occupied by Aleksei Mikhailovich. The inscription on his scroll, which reflects the words of a common priestly prayer during the Orthodox liturgy, alludes to his saintly potential.[101] Nevertheless, in spite of Aleksei Mikhailovich's proclaimed spiritual status, the tsar's plea for salvation makes him appear as a petitioner who is in need of the prayers of his distant ancestor Ivan Kalita and of Metropolitan Peter. The close connection between the tsar and his two symbolic intercessors is underscored by the common form of their accompanying inscriptions. In both cases the words state a request directed to Christ and represent verses from the Psalms. The importance of Metropolitan Peter and Ivan Kalita for the success of Aleksei Mikhailovich's plea lies in their ability to invoke the further support of the ranks of saintly metropolitans and rulers to which they belong. These ranks are represented in the medallions on the left branch of the tree, which feature previous Muscovite metropolitans, patriarchs, and pious rulers. The arrangement of these figures in an upward-reaching vine immediately above the tsar expresses the generally recognized role of Muscovite ecclesiastics as the official intercessors for the tsar and his realm. The inscriptions around the Christ figure suggest that the intercession on behalf of the tsar was successful. Christ, who looks down at Aleksei Mikhailovich, extends to the tsar the promise of victory and eternal life and thus answers the tsar's petition in the affirmative.

The introduction of a separate feminine hierarchy, which takes up the right side and the central part of the image, intensifies the intercessory theme in *The Tree of the Russian Realm*. In contrast to her husband, Tsaritsa Mariia Il'inichna does not direct prayers to Christ. Instead, her scroll contains a praise to the Virgin Mary, who is located in the large medallion in the branches of the tree: "Rejoice, tsaritsa, glory to mothers and maidens."[102]

The idea of an intimate relationship between the earthly royal mother Mariia Il'inichna and the heavenly mother, who is her namesake, was already contained in Lazar Baranovich's *Spiritual Sword*, which proclaimed: "The earthly tsaritsa Mariia with all her shining blessedness [together] with the pious lord, Tsarevich and Grand Prince Aleksei Alekseevich . . . looks at the heavenly tsaritsa Mariia."[103] In his funeral lament for Mariia Il'inichna in 1669, one year after the dedication of Ushakov's icon, the court poet Simeon Polotskii stressed that the tsaritsa always had praised the Virgin, hoping for her help.[104] The inscription in the Ushakov icon suggests that the tsaritsa based her devotion to the Virgin on their common experience as women and mothers. Compositionally this experience is expressed by the presence of children close to the two women. While the Virgin is cradling the Christ child in her arms, Mariia Il'inichna stands close to her eldest son, Aleksei, and the little Fedor, who is brushing against her right sleeve.

In spite of the reference to Mariia Il'inichna's physical motherhood, her role in the image is not primarily a biological, dynastic one. Rather, the tsaritsa's praise of the Virgin hints at a larger liturgical function. A glance at the scrolls of the saints in the tree shows that Mariia does not stand alone in her worship of the Mother of God. The inscriptions in the medallions represent verses that are, as in Mariia's case, devoted to the Virgin. The verses, which all are structurally identical and begin with the word "Rejoice," stem from traditional mariological hymns; some of them are borrowed from the Akathistos hymn, which is thought to have been composed to honor the Virgin for saving Constantinople in the seventh century.[105]

The careful choice of epithets ascribed to the Virgin in the individual verses underscores the notion expressed in Mariia Il'inichna's scroll that the earthly tsaritsa and the heavenly queen were linked through their maternal status. Most of the epithets ascribed to the Virgin celebrate the fertility associated with Creation. Birth symbolism is evident in the scrolls of Saint Maksim the Blessed ("Rejoice, branch that has born the grape of life"), of Saint Ioann Kolpak ("Rejoice, secret vineyard from which life has grown"), of Tsar Fedor ("Rejoice, rod that sprouts the secret unwilting flower"), of Prince Aleksandr ("Rejoice, as you sprout forth as the sweet paradise"), and of Metropolitan Fotii ("Rejoice, well-sown leafy tree with which many cover themselves"). The celebration of things born or created is evident in the verses of the blessed Nikon ("Rejoice, root of the Orthodox faith and immortal fruit") and of Metropolitan Iona ("Rejoice, true vine that has grown the fruit of life"). The life-giving property of food, essential to Creation, is pointed out in the scrolls of Saint Andronnik ("Rejoice, secret grape from which wine flows which makes the faithful merry") and of Patriarch Filaret ("Rejoice, fruitful tree on which the faithful feed").

Many of the verses make reference to the pleasurable aspects of Creation that appeal to the senses, notably sight and smell. The association of the Virgin with physical beauty is maintained in the verses of Tsarevich Dmitrii ("Rejoice, beautiful and animated paradise"), of Saint Savva ("Rejoice, beautiful leaf from the tree of the living Christ"), and of Simon ("Rejoice, beautiful lily that never wilts"). Several scrolls refer to olfactory pleasures: that of Saint Sergius of Radonezh ("Rejoice, fragrant apple that is beautiful to look at"), of Saint Pafnutii ("Rejoice, sea exuding the fragrance of immortality"), of Saint Basil the Blessed ("Rejoice, fragrant aroma that has filled the hearts of the faithful"), of Patriarch Iov ("Rejoice, fragrance of the one tsar Christ"), and of Metropolitan Aleksii ("Rejoice, eternally flowering vine and pomegranate of immortal fragrance"). The exuberance of Creation associated with the Mother of God is expressed in the numerous tree, fruit, flower, and vine motifs in the medallions. While the epithets ascribed to the Mother of God celebrate Creation in its stage of physical maturity, they also attribute to the heavenly queen the ability to transcend the transitory aspect of earthly existence. The hymnal addresses of Metropolitan Filip ("Rejoice, sealed vineyard and flower of eternity") and Metropolitan Kiprian ("Rejoice, secret vineyard that was planted by God and that grew the ripe grape of eternity") refer to the Virgin's ability to guarantee the salvation of all created beings and to assure them that they can reach the "heavenly vineyard" (Aleksei Mikhailovich) and the "sweet paradise" (Aleksandr Nevskii).

The gendered language of the medallions in *The Tree of the Russian Realm*, associating the Virgin's motherhood with the immortality of cosmic creation, hinges on Tsaritsa Mariia Il'inichna's recognition of the potential that lies inherent in the position of the Mother of God. With her liturgical celebration of the Virgin, the tsaritsa imitates the appeal of all the traditional intercessors of the tsar to the heavenly queen that she petition her son to grant the tsar's plea for help and salvation. She who is credited with growing the "fruit of life" (Metropolitan Iona) and the "grape of life" (Maksim the Blessed) also has the ability to persuade Christ to grant the tsar the "crown of life," which is visible in the upper register of the icon.

While the close association of the tsaritsa's activity with that of the saints thematically and conceptually emphasizes her own saintlike intercessory status, the peculiar arrangement of figures suggests that the link between gender and intercession was crucial to the success of Aleksei Mikhailovich's petition. The mariological hymnal verses provide a balance to the petitionary Psalm verses directed by the ranks of the masculine secular and ecclesiastical hierarchy to Christ. The members of this hierarchy, which moves its petition for salvation through the traditional channels of intercession until it receives the attention of the Lord of Creation, is juxtaposed with another saintly hierarchy, which consists of women, children, and saints without earthly rank, such as monks and fools-in-Christ. (The imagery of the inscription on Aleksei Alekseevich's scroll demonstrates the close affiliation of the children with their mother: "We bring you this cluster of grapes and these flowers, O vine of the heavenly vineyard.") In contrast to its masculine counterpart, the feminine hierarchy does not seek the granting of wishes from the Creator directly. Its focus is entirely on the Mother of God, whom Muscovite Russians regarded as the most powerful intercessor for the human race.[106]

The members of the two spiritual hierarchies represent qualitatively different values and perform functions specific to their gender. As the ruler of Russia, Aleksei Mikhailovich carried the primary responsibility for peace and prosperity in his realm and for the protection of his subjects. The inscriptions on the icons *The Veneration of the Cross* and *The Tree of the Russian Realm* both associate the tsar with victory, protection, and the final salvation of the realm. Aleksei's scroll in *The Veneration of the Cross* specifically refers to the divine victory, salvation, and the heavenly kingdom. In Ushakov's icon the tsar asks for the salvation and divine blessing of his realm while Christ extends the promise of the robe of the victor and the crown of eternal life. The tasks of the Russian ruler, however, were perceived to be so great that he was forced to enlist the help of intercessors to assure the goodwill and support of the divine. His elevated position as a head of state notwithstanding, the tsar was dependent on mediators to guarantee divine intervention on his behalf. In order to achieve his aim, Aleksei Mikhailovich addressed his traditional intercessors, the saintly princes and metropolitans. Although the intercessory prayers of this group counted for much, they alone were not sufficient to achieve the tsar's goal. The words "Be faithful to me" and "he who conquers" in Christ's scroll show that the divine support for the Russian ruler was conditional and depended to a large degree on his inner disposition and his readiness to defend the faith. If Aleksei Mikhailovich was to succeed in this respect, he needed assistance of a more intimate, personal kind, which could strengthen his faith and advance his cause through God-pleasing deeds. The members of the feminine hierarchy on the right extended this type of support. With her praise of the Virgin Mary, Mariia Il'inichna effectively displayed the faith her husband needed to succeed as a ruler. As in *The Veneration of the Cross,* the tsaritsa helped to promote the cause of her spouse through her liturgical acts.

The tsaritsa's role as helpmate to her husband in spiritual matters expressed in *The Tree of the Russian Realm* was not limited to supplementing the tsar's faith in God. A comparison of Aleksei Mikhailovich's and Mariia Il'inichna's position in the icon shows that, although Mariia was depicted on the same level as her husband, her relationship with the spiritual hierarchy in the upper part of the image was much closer than that of Aleksei Mikhailovich. While the tsar is engaging the help of Ivan Kalita and Metropolitan Peter at the foot of the tree, the hymn to the Virgin connects Mariia directly with the saintly intercessors in the tree above her. By joining in the eulogy of the Virgin, Mariia takes her own place in the hierarchy of intermediaries who pray for the tsar's success.

The significance of the tsaritsa's function vis-à-vis the tsar becomes apparent if one considers the preponderance of the mariological motif in Ushakov's icon. The small proportions of the royal figures on the bottom and Christ and the angels at the top of the image stand in stark contrast with the size of the tree and the image of the Virgin in its branches.[107] The focal point of the icon is the medallion featuring *The Virgin of Vladimir,* one of the most famous and charismatic icons in medieval Russia. The tree with its vines, roses, and grapes provides an illustration of the metaphors for the Virgin contained in the hymns of the saints in the branches. The unifying force of the tree also affects the male and female hierarchies of saints. In spite of their varying degrees of charisma as royal, ecclesiastical, and monastic saints and holy fools, they are united in their devotion to the Mother of God, who alone can act as the intercessor for the entire realm. Under these circumstances, Mariia Il'inichna's position at the bottom of the feminine hierarchy represents the first direct link to the most powerful Virgin, who is able to present Aleksei Mikhailovich's petition before Christ.

Ushakov's icon *The Tree of the Russian Realm* represents the culmination of a Muscovite tradition that regarded the tsar and tsaritsa as members of the family of saints. Within the saintly ranks, the tsar and his wife played distinct roles determined to a large degree by their gender. Whereas the Russian ruler was expected to look out for the welfare of his realm and people, it was considered the tsaritsa's task to further his undertaking with God-pleasing acts. In Ushakov's icon the different responsibilities of tsar and tsaritsa are expressed by the juxtaposition of the masculine and feminine hierarchies; their common cause is illustrated by the united action of the saints in the tree. Although as a member of the female hierarchy the royal wife and mother lacks the official recognition of the traditional petitioners for the tsar before God, she becomes an indispensable spiritual intercessor for the Russian ruler by allying herself with the Mother of God.

. . .

The myths developing around two prominent Muscovite royal women in sixteenth- and seventeenth-century Russia—Anastasiia Romanovna and Mariia Il'inichna—demonstrate the ideological contribution made by the tsaritsy to the medieval Russian tsardom. In spite of their different personal circumstances and historical experiences, these women had a similar part to play in the definition of the role of the Russian ruler. Through the mythopoeic efforts of the Muscovite court, ecclesiastical and monastic circles, and (to a limited extent) the populace at large, Anastasiia Romanovna posthumously continued to be cherished as a pious tsaritsa. Originally considered a spiritual intercessor for Ivan IV and a guarantor of the salvation of the Russian realm, Anastasiia was later esteemed for her ability to contain her husband's unruly behavior. As a result, she was held up as a role model for the wives of rulers who followed the turbulent reign of Ivan IV. During the dynastic crisis of the Time of Troubles, Anastasiia Romanovna, the grandaunt of Tsar Mikhail Fedorovich Romanov, was celebrated as a dynastic cornerstone upon which the legitimacy of the Romanov house rested. The new image of the Rurikide tsaritsa ultimately was based on her reputation as a pious tsaritsa who had distinguished herself through her personal religious devotion. Although Anastasiia lost the epithet "spiritual intercessor" in favor of a more generic saintly or pious quality, the notion of the tsaritsy's ability to mediate between God and the tsar was retained during the reign of the first two Romanov rulers.

Evidence derived from new iconographic compositions, such as *The Veneration of the Cross* and *The Tree of the Russian Realm,* proves that Aleksei Mikhailovich's wife Mariia Il'inichna enjoyed the same spiritual status as was credited to Anastasiia Romanovna during Ivan IV's Kazan' campaign in 1552. Like Anastasiia before her, Mariia Il'inichna was linked with the political success of her husband by means of her spiritual capacity to intercede with the divine. While the images in question ascribe saintly status to both Aleksei Mikhailovich and Mariia Il'inichna, the tsar alone appears as a petitioner before Christ or his cross. Mariia assures the success of her husband's petition by faithfully performing her religious duties. In *The Veneration of the Cross,* where Aleksei Mikhailovich is praying for salvation, his wife is carrying out her responsibility as helpmate to the tsar in spiritual matters. This role is heightened in *The Tree of the Russian Realm,* which shows Mariia, who labors for the success of her husband's petition to Christ for help and salvation, as an intercessor before the Virgin Mary. In spite of the compositional and stylistic innovations in both these icons, their religious interpretation of the tsaritsa's role reflects the continued validity of the concept of the tsaritsy as helpmates to the tsars and spiritual intercessors for their realm in the seventeenth century.

3 The Tsaritsa as Ruler and Dynastic Link

THE MUSCOVITE TSARITSA'S ability to intercede with the divine for the welfare of the Russian realm and her role as a vessel that conveyed God's blessing to her son, the future tsar, added a larger dimension to her position insofar as they attributed to her the power to act on behalf of the realm and to assure the continued prosperity of the ruling dynasty. The tsaritsa's perceived capability to take on functions of government and to preserve dynastic continuity particularly came to the fore in the late sixteenth and early seventeenth centuries when the demise of Tsarevich Ivan Ivanovich and the frailty and childlessness of his surviving brother, Tsar Fedor Ivanovich, confronted Muscovite Russia with the specter of political and dynastic turmoil. Although experts in the history of medieval Russian women generally consider the late sixteenth century and the ensuing Time of Troubles as times of obstacles to women's participation in political life, the absence of a male heir to the throne and the need to create a new ruling dynasty heightened the already established political and dynastic significance of the tsaritsa.[1] The example of Fedor Ivanovich's wife, Irina Godunova, shows that, rather than being incapacitated by her inability to bear a son, she became the focus of an image-building campaign that proclaimed her capacity to act as an independent ruler in her own right and to serve as a dynastic bridge to the new line of her brother, Boris Godunov. Moreover, the activities of two royal wives and mothers—Boris Godunov's wife, Mariia Grigor'evna Skuratova-Bel'skaia, who ruled for her son, Fedor, after her husband's death, and Mariia Fedorovna Nagaia, the seventh wife of Ivan IV and mother of his last child, Dmitrii—suggest that in spite of the stresses of the late sixteenth and early seventeenth centuries, royal women continued to affirm their influence in defining the Russian tsardom. Irina Godunova's proclaimed ability to succeed Fedor Ivanovich as a ruler paved the way for her sister-in-law's prominence in the Godunov regime after her husband's death. The Muscovite notion that a tsaritsa could preserve dynastic stability gave Mariia Grigor'evna the visibility of a regent and ruler and also increased the political and social influence of Mariia Nagaia. Although the latter did not rule in her own right, she played a crucial role in Russia's search for a legitimate ruler.

Irina Godunova

As the study of the myth of the "pious tsaritsa Anastasiia" has shown, the balance between the perceived "feminine" (supportive and private) and "masculine" (independent and public) aspects of the role of the tsaritsa often shifted in the Muscovite period. The perception of the Muscovite tsaritsa was affected by political factors, notably dynastic considerations, ecclesiastical support for the role of the tsaritsa, circumstances that determined her social position, and the tsaritsa's own initiative in shaping her role. If the marital bond between the tsar and his wife was stable, the "feminine" element was more likely to determine the role of the tsaritsa. If, however, the royal familial unit collapsed or appeared to be threatened, the tsaritsa's perceived "masculine" qualities came visibly to the fore. This phenomenon can be most readily observed in the development of Irina Godunova's role in the face of a looming dynastic crisis that threatened to leave Russia without an heir to the throne.

During Fedor Ivanovich's reign (1584–1598) his wife, Irina, participated actively in the affairs of government. S. F. Platonov points out that she took part in deliberations of matters concerning both the state and the church. Irina is the first tsaritsa ever to be mentioned in official correspondence. S. M. Kashtanov relates the appearance of Irina's name in government documents to Boris Godunov's pretensions to the throne after Dmitrii Ivanovich's death in 1591.[2] A. A. Zimin, however, points out that Irina's name was used in an official context already in 1587. Contemporary sources tell us that Irina attended receptions for foreign high-ranking ecclesiastical dignitaries, such as the patriarch of Constantinople, Jeremiah (July 21, 1588), and the metropolitan of Trnovo, Dionisii (June 20, 1591). According to Giles Fletcher, Irina, "being a woman of great clemency and withal delighting to deal in public affairs of the realm," compensated for her husband's inefficiencies as a ruler and took over functions such as the granting of pardons, "in her own name by open proclamation, without any mention at all of the Emperor."[3] Irina's independent decision-making is also evident from a petition by Fedor Likharev to Patriarch Filaret in 1627, which states that in 1598 Irina had sent a charter and a military roster to Riazan' to organize the manpower on Russia's southern frontier. Moreover, Irina's name featured prominently in the correspondence of leaders of the

Orthodox church abroad with the Russian government.[4]

The transfer of power to Irina after Fedor Ivanovich's death posed a familiar problem to the Muscovite scheme of succession through the male line. As Elena Glinskaia's regency for her son Ivan IV proves, a theoretical framework had already been created in the early sixteenth century to include women in the scheme of succession when the continuity of the ruling dynasty was at stake.[5] The idea of a woman on the Muscovite throne reappeared in 1553 during the sudden illness of Tsar Ivan IV. On March 12 of that year Prince Vladimir Andreevich Staritskii, the tsar's relative and friend, swore an oath to serve the infant Tsarevich Dmitrii and his mother, Anastasiia, in case of Ivan's death. The text of a similar oath by Vladimir Andreevich (drawn up in the following year after little Dmitrii's death and the birth of Ivan Ivanovich) notes that the tsar, concerned with the survival of his own bloodline, had nominated Anastasiia in his testament as his successor in the event of his second son's death. The tsar's insistence that Vladimir was not to listen to his mother, Evfrosiniia Staritskaia, who might conspire against Ivan Ivanovich and Anastasiia, suggests that he intended to keep the Muscovite throne in his immediate family, even if it meant that a woman would rule.[6] While Ivan's plans for Anastasiia eventually came to nothing

7. The Golden Palace of the Tsaritsy, described by Arsenios Elassonis, who attended a reception by Irina Godunova in the chamber in 1589. The original Golden Palace of the Tsaritsy experienced architectural modifications (arches, tie-bars) and restoration efforts, which complicate the evaluation of the entire fresco program of the room. Still, the preponderance of female images on the walls and the ceiling is evident.

(because of the tsar's recovery or because of the boyars' dissent, who may well have frowned at the possible disruption in the power balance at court), the notion of a reigning tsaritsa was not forgotten.[7] In the late sixteenth century, the ability to act outright as a public figure was attributed to Irina Godunova in the frescoes of the Golden Palace of the Tsaritsy (see Figure 7).[8]

No complete scholarly description and evaluation of the frescoes of the Golden Palace of the Tsaritsy exist. Zabelin mentions the official function of the Golden Palace as a reception room but pays little attention to the fresco motifs, which he vaguely calls "biblical or historical."[9] Arsenios Elassonis—who accompanied Jeremiah, the patriarch of Constantinople, on his visit to Moscow in 1589 and saw the Golden Palace of the Tsaritsy during a reception given by Irina—noted that the room was filled with images featuring the Virgin Mary with the Christ child on her lap, angels, saints, and martyrs. According to Arsenios, the domed ceiling was covered with vegetation and animal motifs, sculpted in gold, and featured forests, the grapes of Rhodos, and birds. Although Arsenios's description may not be accurate, at the very least his account attests to the presence of images on the walls and to Irina Godunova's use of the Golden Palace as a reception chamber.[10] Very likely Arsenios confused some of the frescoes with icons—the east wall features the Virgin with the Christ child, and the north wall contains the image of the martyr Fedor Tiron. During the Time of Troubles the room apparently fell into disrepair so that it needed to be remodeled under Mikhail Fedorovich. Conceivably the frescoes were repainted during the reign of Mikhail Romanov, who had the chamber repaired.[11] This work would have been completed before the construction of the Church of the Savior in 1636, which caused structural damage to the Golden Palace below, requiring it to be reinforced with two stone arches. The arches covered a number of existing frescoes, which disrupted the sequence of images in several cycles.[12] If the earliest layer of the uncovered frescoes dates from the early seventeenth century, there is good reason to believe that they followed the original murals closely, since Muscovite artists usually followed old patterns when they repainted murals.[13]

Since the Golden Palace of the Tsaritsy served as an official reception chamber for Irina Godunova, we can assume that the images on its walls were meant to illuminate her position as a tsaritsa. A study of the five major fresco cycles, which all feature saintly royal women, reveals a common theme, reinforcing the notion of the Russian court that Irina could act as a legitimate ruler in her own right. The various cycles express this message in their depictions of royal women who earned the privilege of independent action through their commitment to the Orthodox faith.

The connection of royal women and the theme of victory in, of, and through the true faith is evident in two compositions on the ceiling of the Golden Palace, *The Dream of Constantine* and *The Discovery of the True Cross of Christ by Empress Helena*.[14] The composition *The Dream of Constantine* (which shows Constantine sleeping and then riding into battle with his right hand pointing up to the sky) depicts the supernatural experience of the still pagan Constantine the night before the battle with his rival Maxentius at the Milvian Bridge in 312 A.D.[15] Constantine saw the sign of a cross in the sky, and a voice told him: "Conquer by this." Taking heed, Constantine had the sign of the Christian cross painted on his soldiers' helmets and indeed emerged victorious the next day.[16] The image celebrates the official recognition of the Christian community by the Roman Emperor. The fresco adjacent to it reminds the viewer that Constantine's act was later reinforced by his mother, Helena, who, by discovering the True Cross of Christ in Jerusalem and taking it to Constantinople, laid the final foundation for the Christian rule on earth.[17]

The composition *The Discovery of the True Cross* in the Golden Palace of the Tsaritsy consists of three scenes (see Figure 8). On the left Empress Helena—wearing a blue gown with golden trim, a red cape, purple shoes, and a crown over a white head cloth—bows to a bishop to receive his blessing. Both Helena and the ecclesiastic (whom early versions of the Helena legend identify as Macarius, Bishop of Jerusalem) wear nimbs. Further to the right Helena, seated on a throne and surrounded by a group of men and women, converses with a well-dressed man wearing a long beard. An array of fragmentary inscriptions identifies the scene as the moment when Helena ordered the discovery of the True Cross. The scene depicts the so-called Judas Cyriacus legend, according to which the empress called a large assembly of Christians and Jews after her arrival in Jerusalem. Convinced that the Jews were responsible for hiding Christ's cross, she ordered the Jewish leaders to search for men in their midst who knew where it lay buried.[18] The formality of the assembly explains why Helena is depicted seated on a throne. The third scene also relates to the Judas Cyriacus legend. The fresco shows a Jew sitting in a dark hole in a deserted place and raising his hands toward the empress in a petitionary pose. The same Jew, kneeling and raising his hands up to the sky, appears again on the right, this time in the company of a nimbed Bishop Macarius, who stands in prayer. The image represents the passage in the Cyriacus legend where Helena, angered by Judas's refusal to divulge the cross's whereabouts, had him thrown into a well for seven days without food. Eventually Judas petitioned her and complied with her wishes. He dug at the place where his father had told him the cross was hidden, but instead of one cross he found three. In order to find out which was the True Cross of Christ, Judas carried the crosses to the city center and waited for a sign. When the True Cross eventually resurrected a dead man whom mourners were taking to the funeral, Judas himself became a Christian believer.[19]

The unusual selection of images of the Helena legend in the murals of the Golden Palace of the Tsaritsy resulted in the creation of the image of a pious empress who was able to do battle with the unbelievers and to defend Christian institutions. In contrast to known pictorial representations of the legend, the Golden Palace frescoes do not depict the central subject of the composi-

8. The Golden Palace of the Tsaritsy: The Discovery of the True Cross. From left to right the fresco shows the arrival of Empress Helena in Jerusalem and her being blessed by Macarius, Bishop of Jerusalem; Helena's inquiries about the location of the cross of Christ; and her punishment of Judas Cyriacus.

tion, the True and Life-Giving Cross of Christ, suggesting that the designers were not interested in highlighting the miraculous power of the cross.[20] By focusing on Judas suffering his punishment in a well, the murals of the Golden Palace emphasized the adversary relations between Helena and the Jews (characteristic of the Judas Cyriacus legend) and the empress's power to force Judas into compliance. The inclusion of Macarius in the composition (who does not appear at all in the Cyriacus legend) served to highlight the empress's piety and her close cooperation with the church.[21] The praying Judas at the end of the cycle expresses Helena's final victory in her dealings with Judas, who has converted to the Christian faith. On the whole, the ceiling frescoes of the Golden Palace demonstrate how the establishment of a Christian empire, foreshadowed by the dream of Constantine, ultimately was achieved through the commitment of a woman ruler to the Christian faith.

Contemporaries of Irina Godunova would have easily made the connection between the image of the pious Helena and the tsaritsa. Like the Byzantine and early medieval Western societies, Muscovites applied the Saint Helena typology to their royal women. The Kievan princess Ol'ga and the Muscovite tsaritsy Elena Glinskaia and Anastasiia Romanovna all were considered avid imitators of the Byzantine empress.[22] In 1585 the patriarch of Alexandria, Silvester, encouraged Irina in a letter that she should be a "worthy disciple of Saint Helena, the empress and mother of the emperor and apostle Constantine." The decisive, independently acting, pious Helena could be used as a model for the Russian tsaritsa in connection with her support for the establishment of a Russian patriarchate at a time when Moscow felt itself surrounded by opponents to the Christian faith. In a letter to Patriarch Jeremiah dated March 9, 1592, Tsar Fedor Ivanovich stated that, after long deliberations, he and his wife both had felt the need for the establishment of a Russian patriarchate. Such a move would uphold Orthodoxy in Muscovy since Rome had succumbed to the heretical teachings of Pope Formosus.[23]

The themes of conversion and victory through the faith associated with a female ruling figure are also apparent in the sequence of images illustrating the baptism of Saint Ol'ga in Constantinople in the upper register of the east wall of the Golden Palace. In the center of the cycle we see a female figure in a medallion wearing a red tunic with gold trim, a blue cape, red shoes, and a crown over a white veil. An inscription identifies the figure as Saint Ol'ga. Four individual scenes, arranged from left to right, highlight her visit to Constantinople.[24] The first image in the northeastern corner of the room shows Ol'ga's trip to Constantinople in a covered carriage drawn by two horses.[25] The next scene represents Ol'ga's meeting with the Byzantine emperor (see

9. The Golden Palace of the Tsaritsy: The meeting of the Kievan Grand Princess Ol'ga with the Byzantine emperor John Tzimisces. On the left, the Byzantine empress Theophano watches the meeting.

10. The Golden Palace of the Tsaritsy: Ol'ga's conversation with the Byzantine emperor. Ol'ga and Tzimisces are seated on separate thrones and wear crowns. Ol'ga wears purple shoes while the emperor wears sandals. Since Ol'ga is still pagan, her crown is not nimbed.

11. The Golden Palace of the Tsaritsy: Ol'ga's baptism. Ol'ga rises from the baptismal font clothed in royal garb and adorned with crown and halo. John Tzimisces, who acts as her godfather, and the Byzantine patriarch welcome the newly converted Russian princess.

Figure 9). Ol'ga stands before the emperor, who sits on a golden throne. On the left an empress, surrounded by four male advisers and a group of women, watches the event.[26] To the left of the medallion featuring Saint Ol'ga, we see the Kievan princess's conversation with the Byzantine emperor John Tzimisces, which is mentioned in the saint's *vita* (see Figure 10).[27] Ol'ga is seated on a chair covered with purple cloth. Surrounded by a group of female servants, she talks to Tzimisces on the right, who is seated on a large round throne. Again Ol'ga appears with a crown and purple shoes while the emperor wears a nimbed crown. The outcome of her conversation with Tzimisces, her actual conversion and christening, is depicted in the southeastern corner of the Golden Palace (see Figure 11). Against the background of a whitewashed cathedral with five cupolas, surrounded by church servants and a crowd of noblemen, the princess rises from a baptismal font. Fully clad in a blue robe with gold trim, a head cloth, and a crown, Ol'ga is now depicted with a halo, a sign of her conversion to the Christian faith. She reaches out to the emperor, her godfather, who is helping her step out of the font.

The intention behind the images of the Ol'ga cycle in the Golden Palace is evident both in the choice of the story and in how the main characters are depicted. The fresco designers deliberately opted against the depiction of the original account of Ol'ga's trip in the *Russian Primary Chronicle*, which focuses primarily on Ol'ga's request for baptism, her instruction in the faith by the patriarch, and her clever thwarting of the emperor's plan to marry her. Instead they chose to illustrate the sixteenth-century *vita* of Saint Ol'ga, which served as an apology for the Muscovite autocracy.[28] The calculated use of the *vita* is evident in the depiction of the Byzantine empress Theophano, who, according to Ol'ga's *life*, had previously been married to emperors Romanus II and Nikephoros Phocas, and who had collaborated with Tzimisces in the murder of Nikephoros.[29] In the reception scene Ol'ga and the empress wear purple shoes (an indication of imperial status in Byzantium) while the emperor is clad in sandals. The emperor is the only person wearing a nimbus. Only the emperor and Ol'ga wear crowns, identifying them as independent heads of state.

The symbolism of these features speaks to the issue of the transfer of royal power, which occupied Russia during the time the frescoes were painted. The purple shoes of the two women signify that the bloodline of the royal dynasty was maintained by the wives of the rulers. Just as Ol'ga did not need to marry a man of Byzantine imperial blood to establish her legitimacy as a ruler, Irina Godunova could carry on the dynastic continuity of the Rurikides through the female line. The *vita* of Saint Ol'ga insists that during his first meeting with Ol'ga, John Tzimisces asked her to marry him.[30] Ol'ga, who knew of the emperor's scandalous relations with Theophano, outwitted him by requesting to be baptized. While the absence of a halo on Ol'ga's head marks her yet pagan status, Theophano's illegal union with the emperor may explain the conspicuous absence of a halo and crown on her head. In contrast, Ol'ga's crown shows she enjoyed the same status

12. *Radzivil Chronicle,* fol. 31r: Ol'ga's conversation with the Byzantine emperor (on the left) and her baptism. Neither Ol'ga nor the emperor wears a halo. In the baptismal scene the Kievan princess is shown naked.

as the Byzantine emperor in her capacity as ruler of Kiev. The message is that, like Ol'ga, Irina could execute the functions of government without restrictions imposed by her gender. The vehicle by which the power to rule could be conferred on a woman was the Christian faith. By championing the cause of Orthodoxy, Irina could attain the same legitimacy as Ol'ga had achieved through her baptism.

To gain an appreciation for the message of the Ol'ga cycle in the Golden Palace of the Tsaritsy, it is useful to compare the arrangement and execution of the individual scenes with those of known iconographic models. The only extant copy of the fifteenth-century *Radzivil Chronicle*, which essentially repeats the Ol'ga tale of the *Russian Primary Chronicle*, contains two colored miniatures that highlight the major events of the story. Eliding the depiction of Ol'ga on the road and her reception in Constantinople, the first miniature shows Ol'ga's conversation with the emperor and her baptism following their meeting (see Figure 12). In the next illumination Constantine and Ol'ga share a throne. Ol'ga rebuffs Constantine's wedding proposal and announces her plans to return to Russia. From the right three servants approach, carrying precious vessels as farewell gifts.[31]

While the miniatures in the *Radzivil Chronicle* depict the events of the Ol'ga tale in chronological order, the Golden Palace frescoes represent

Ol'ga's baptism as the climax of her visit to Constantinople. The illustration of Ol'ga's trip sets the scene of the story. The following reception scene (not mentioned in the chronicle account) presents Ol'ga standing in all the royal regalia and pomp necessary to make her appear a ruler in her own right. The large throngs of people around her underscore her status. This scene replaces the farewell reception in the *Radzivil Chronicle*, which is much more modest and, in addition, compromises Ol'ga's position vis-à-vis the emperor with whom she shares a seat.

The different focus of the miniatures in the *Radzivil Chronicle* and the Ol'ga cycle in the Golden Palace is also evident in the details of the compositions. In the chronicle neither the emperor nor Ol'ga are nimbed. Ol'ga wears neither a crown nor the imperial purple and appears without servitors. Perhaps the most noticeable difference in the two Ol'ga cycles is found in the baptismal scene. In the miniature in the *Radzivil Chronicle* a completely naked Ol'ga, with her long blond hair falling over her shoulders, is seated in the baptismal font. Only the emperor and the patriarch, who is nimbed, witness her conversion. The contrast between the pagan bare-breasted Ol'ga in the miniature and the pious, royally clad, and acclaimed female ruler in the mural is striking.[32] Moreover, the designers of the Golden Palace murals did not completely follow Byzantine convention in that they depicted the christening of their heroine in front of a large number of witnesses.

The implications of the fresco cycle depicting Ol'ga's baptism are twofold. On one hand the event celebrated Ol'ga's personal rejection of paganism and the introduction of Christianity in Russia. The *vita* of Saint Ol'ga praised the saint for being the first to destroy the pagan ways of her country and to lay the foundation of the true faith in Russia. Through Ol'ga's conversion and activity as a teacher of the faith, Russia had become a friend of God. On the other hand, by emphasizing Ol'ga's choice of chastity, the fresco cycle focused on her female strength. The significance of Ol'ga's refusal to remarry can be gleaned from the saint's *vita*, which links Ol'ga's chastity to the saint's capability to intercede with God for the salvation of the Russian realm.[33]

The connection of Ol'ga's gender with her intercessory function is particularly evident in the *vita*'s interpretation of the Fall. The *vita* skillfully invokes the Christian tenet that woman was the cause not only of the Fall but also of eternal salvation, by equating Ol'ga's achievement with that of the myrrh-bearing women from whom "Christ received resurrection from the dead."[34] Ol'ga's ability to work for the salvation of man ultimately rested on the peculiarity of her sex, which made her more sensitive to the divine than her male counterpart.[35] This sensitivity may render the female more vulnerable to the snares of evil, as in the case of Eve, but it was also the source of great spiritual strength. Ol'ga is portrayed as a "younger, new disciple of Christ" who eradicated paganism in her realm and "broke the weapons of the oldest enemy, the mighty devil, who seduced Eve, and chased him out of Russia."[36]

The themes of the Ol'ga cycle provided an effective justification for the choice of Irina Godunova as successor of her husband, Fedor, to the Muscovite throne. The presentation of Ol'ga's chastity as a laudable virtue underscored the idea fostered by the tsar and his brother-in-law that Irina could function as a head of state in her own right, without the guidance of a husband. Ol'ga's example showed that a woman ruler could muster the necessary strength to protect the welfare of the realm. Ultimately, the basis of Irina's political power was constructed in religious terms. The significance of the royal woman lay in her saint-like status, which gave her the ability to intercede with God for the well-being of the realm.

This tendency to strengthen the political position of the tsaritsa by building up her religious prestige is also evident in the cycle of Saint Theodora, a Byzantine ruler who restored the worship of icons in her realm at the church council of 843. Two scenes on the south wall of the Golden Palace show Theodora, marked by a crown and a halo, standing at the bedside of her dying husband, Theophilus, with an icon of the Virgin in her hands (see Figure 13). In the first scene Theophilus, wearing a crown but no nimbus, reclines on his bed while a man in boyar dress stands behind him and looks on. In the following scene to the right, the dying man embraces an icon of the Savior. His crown hovers above his head, a sign that his end is near. Behind Theodora stands a group of men in secular dress. The boyar figure now has moved away from the head of the bed and joined them. The

13. The Golden Palace of the Tsaritsy: The Byzantine emperor Theophilus on his deathbed. The fresco is divided into two scenes. On the left the dying iconoclast (wearing a crown, but no nimbus) is tended by his wife, Theodora, who offers to him an icon of the Virgin. On the right Theophilus embraces an icon of Christ, signifying Theodora's success in converting him from heresy.

two images illustrate the claim, which (according to the *Chronicle of Theophanes Continuatus*) Theodora made to Patriarch Methodius—that in his last hours Theophilus, an iconoclast, had repented his heretical actions and had asked for images. Before giving up his spirit, he had fervently kissed the icons the empress had extended to him.[37]

The choice and execution of the images portraying Theophilus's death in the Theodora cycle of the Golden Palace of the Tsaritsy clearly shows the commissioners' intention to portray only pious, independently acting female rulers. The designers consciously selected the illustration of the "Tale of the Absolution of Emperor Theophilus" rather than the respective episode in Theodora's *vita*, which ascribes to her a lesser role in the conversion of her husband. Whereas the "Tale" portrays Theodora as a concerned wife who is urging her dying husband to accept the veneration of icons, the *vita* states that Theodora fell asleep during her lamentations at her husband's bedside and saw a vision of the Virgin with the Christ child. A number of angels in the Virgin's company reproached Theophilus for his iconoclasm and beat him. As the empress awoke, her husband was experiencing convulsions and moaned repeatedly that he was being beaten on account of his rejection of the icons. The empress continued to keep vigil and in her prayers interceded with God for her husband. Eventually Theophilus experienced relief from his pain and anguish when the *logothetes*, the eunuch Theoktistos, put an amulet around the emperor's neck and Theophilus kissed the religious image on it.[38] The *vita* portrays Theodora merely as a concerned pious wife while it ascribes the actual conversion to Theoktistos, who wielded influence at the court. In the Byzantine *Manasses Chronicle*, which follows this interpretation, Theodora is depicted standing behind her husband and holding his head in her hands. A group of six men approach the bed from the right. One of the figures, who presumably represents Theoktistos, offers to Theophilus a small icon with an image of the Virgin.[39] The switched role of Theodora and Theoktistos (the man in boyar dress) and the eunuch's role as mere onlooker in the Golden Palace murals underscore the central position of the empress in the Russian image cycle. The depiction of Theodora offering icons to her dying husband clearly credits her with the ultimate conversion of her husband from heresy to the true faith.

The close association of Empress Theodora with the salvation of her husband may also be observed in the two monumental scenes on the lower register of the west wall of the Golden Palace, left of the entrance, representing Theodora's and Methodius's visions of Theophilus's eventual salvation, as contained in the "Tale of the Absolution of Emperor Theophilus" (see Figure 14). The tale states that—in Theodora's vision—the people of Constantinople dragged the naked Theophilus, with his hands bound behind him, through the streets to the Bronze Gate of the city. There the judge, sitting in front of an icon of Christ, set Theophilus free because of his wife's faith and tears, ordering him to be untied and given over to his wife. Theodora joyfully led him away. Methodius's vision occurred during a service for the heretical Theophilus. When the patriarch reached for the book in which the names of the heretics were listed, an angel of God appeared to him and told him that God had pardoned Theophilus. When Methodius awoke from his dreamlike experience and checked the book, he found that Theophilus's name had been erased.[40] The murals on the west wall of the Golden Palace show Theodora sleeping to indicate her vision. In the lower left part of the image, a group of nimbed men leads Theophilus, who wears only his crown and a white loincloth, toward Christ, who sits in the center of the composition with his hands raised in judgment. Theophilus is the only figure in the composition who does not wear a halo, a sign of his sinful nature. In the left corner Theodora watches the event. She is again depicted in the center of the image, kneeling at Christ's feet and raising her hands in a petitionary gesture, while her husband stands behind her with his hands still tied behind him. The nature of her petition and Christ's granting of it are revealed in the scene immediately to the right, where Theodora is leading her husband away while Theophilus is looking back over his shoulder at the place of divine judgment.[41] The empress's

14. The Golden Palace of the Tsaritsy: The salvation of Theophilus according to the visions of his wife, Theodora, and Patriarch Methodius. In the first scene (on the left), Theophilus, wearing only a crown and a loincloth, is led before Christ the judge. Theodora kneels before the enthroned Christ to petition for her husband. The empress then leads the pardoned Theophilus away from the scene of judgment. The second scene (on the right) shows Methodius retrieving a blank scroll from an opening in the altar.

successful intercession for her husband is also the subject of the scene immediately to the right, which depicts Methodius's dream. Theodora joins the patriarch and a number of clergy in the celebration of the liturgy before an altar. With his right hand raised, an angel looks at a book that lies in front of him on the altar. In the lower half of the image, the patriarch is kneeling before an opening in the altar out of which he pulls a blank scroll.

The story of the death of Emperor Theophilus, who left behind a young son and a realm racked by religious crisis, could easily be associated with the impending turmoil following Tsar Fedor Ivanovich's death in Muscovite Russia. The supporters of Irina's succession to the throne had much to gain by proclaiming her similarity to the Byzantine empress, who not only maintained dynastic continuity by acting as regent for her son Michael after Theophilus's death but also reintroduced peace and stability in the realm.[42] Theodora's endeavors to save her husband's soul signified an act of personal piety with wider, public implications and thus echoed the Muscovite concept of the tsaritsa as a helpmate of the tsar and intercessor for the realm.

The comparison of Irina Godunova with Saint Theodora strengthened Irina's dynastic legitimacy. Already Iosif Volotskii in his *Prosvetitel'* had held up Theodora (in her role as defender of the faith) as a model for the Russian ruler.[43] The frescoes on the pillars in the Cathedral of the Annunciation in the Kremlin show that, in the mid–sixteenth century, the empress Theodora was considered a member of the family of ruler saints, which Metropolitan Makarii referred to in his address to the young royal couple in 1547.[44] Theodora and her son Michael are depicted together with Constantine and his mother, Helena; Vladimir and Ol'ga; and Aleksandr Nevskii and Ivan Kalita on the southwestern and northwestern pillars of the cathedral.[45] On the basis of her piety, Theodora, along with the rest of the named saints, was considered a distant relative of the Russian tsar. By invoking her name in connection with Fedor Ivanovich's wife, the courtly elite that supported Irina's succession to the throne attained a persuasive justification for promoting her candidacy.

The religious foundation of Theodora's (and by deduction, Irina Godunova's) right to rule is expressed in yet another monumental composition located immediately to the right of the entrance on the west wall of the Golden Palace of the Tsaritsy. The image commemorates the reestablishment of icon worship during Theodora's reign at the Council of Constantinople in 843, commonly referred to as the Triumph of Orthodoxy. (see Figure 7)[46] Theodora, her son Michael, and Patriarch Methodius are seen participating in a procession of icons. In the center of the composition a group of men of all ages carry an Orthodox cross, an icon of Christ, and a banner with an embroidered image of *Christ Not Made By Hands (Acheiropoietos)*. To the right of them four veiled women, some of them kneeling, hail the passersby. The empress, her son, and the patriarch—all of them nimbed—watch the procession with their arms raised in prayer.[47]

Theodora's commitment to image worship earned her a reputation as an exemplary believer, a fact that was expressed in the late sixteenth-century Muscovite polemical literature directed against the Protestants.[48] Clearly at a time when the Russian realm faced possible encroachment from its neighbors in the West (the Catholic Polish-Lithuanian Commonwealth and Protestant Sweden), the association of Theodora with the Muscovite tsaritsa was meant to calm concerns about Russia's role as a bastion of the true faith. Like Theodora, Irina Godunova, who was a proponent of the establishment of a Russian patriarchate, could be relied on to champion the cause of Orthodoxy in Russia.[49]

Irina's commitment to the Orthodox faith is reflected also in two compositions grouped around a medallion with the image of Saint Irina (Irene) in the upper register of the south wall of the Golden Palace. The presence of a crown and royal dress suggests that we are dealing with the empress Irene who had been responsible for the restoration of icons in the Byzantine empire at the Council of Nicaea in 787. To the left of the medallion a royal woman, accompanied by a servant, receives a book. The figure extending the book cannot be discerned because it is now covered by the arch that was installed for structural reasons. Very likely the scene denotes Patriarch Tarasius tendering the Council of Nicaea's decision to Irene.[50] To the right of the medallion a royal woman kneels before a figure in patriarchal garb while a group of people looks on. The patriarch blesses the woman, who then walks away with her train. Although the composition is not identified by a description, it is possible to surmise that it depicts Tarasius's blessing of Irene.[51]

Although Irina Godunova's name saint was the martyr Irene, who was celebrated on May 5, it is likely that the frescoes of the Golden Palace of the Tsaritsy conjured up a connection between Godunova and the Byzantine empress whose feast falls on August 9.[52] The empress was known in late-sixteenth-century Russia through hagiographic and monastic tracts. The *Prosvetitel'* referred to her condemnation of heretics. In his letter to Tsaritsa Irina from April 29, 1593, the patriarch of Alexandria, Meletius, proclaimed Irina Godunova's similarity to the blessed Empress Irene.[53] Placing illustrations of Irene's deeds on the walls of the Golden Palace of the Tsaritsy where the tsaritsy would receive high-ranking church dignitaries, the designers could be sure that the message of their iconographic program would be understood.

The association of the tsaritsa with the support of the Orthodox faith is expressed also in several compositions on the north wall of the Golden Palace. The figure in the medallion on this wall is identified as Saint Sofiia. The image to the left shows a royal woman with a train of servants approaching a patriarch before an altar.[54] Given the fact that the female figure depicted in the medallion and in the adjacent scene is wearing a crown, it is safe to assume we are dealing with another Byzantine empress. A likely candidate is Sophia, the wife of Justin II (565–578), who exercised political power during the time of her husband's madness. Under the influence of the orthodox patriarch John Scholasticus, Sophia engaged in the persecution of the heretical Monophysites. Sophia distinguished herself through her patronage of the cult of the Virgin Mary and numerous translations of icons and relics.[55]

All the pictorial cycles in the Golden Palace of the Tsaritsy discussed so far expressed the Russian tsaritsa's legitimacy and competence to rule by upholding her similarity to previous saintly ruler women, who were remembered in the hagiographic literature of Muscovite Russia. The choice of the compositional themes provided a planned response to the issue of dynastic continuity through the female line that preoccupied Russia in the late sixteenth century. The contemporary implications of the frescoes of the Golden Palace of the Tsaritsy are most readily discerned in the fresco cycle located in the lower register of the north wall. This cycle depicts the campaign of the Georgian princess Dinara against the Persian ruler and her victory over him in four individual scenes from left to right.[56]

The literary model for this fresco cycle, the *"Povest' o tsaritse Dinare"* ("Tale about Tsaritsa Dinara"), in all likelihood was composed in Metropolitan Makarii's circle in the middle of the sixteenth century.[57] The story, which is based on two historical figures—the Georgian princess Tamara (1184–1212), who inherited the throne of George III and distinguished herself in victories over the Turks, and Dinara, another Georgian princess who in the tenth century defended the Orthodox faith in western Georgia—espoused the themes of the continued struggle against the infidel, a system of government in which royal power is derived directly from God, and the sharing of ecclesiastical institutions in secular wealth. Dinara's struggle with the Persian ruler, who demanded tribute, bears overtones of Moscow's struggle with Kazan' in the first half of the sixteenth century. Her victory with the help of the Virgin Mary, in spite of the hesitation of her boyars, recalls the efforts made in contemporary Muscovite literary works (both secular and ecclesiastical) to free the position of the tsar from boyar influence and stress its legitimacy by divine grace.[58] In the late sixteenth century, the tale enjoyed popularity in the diplomatic circles of the Muscovite court.[59]

A careful juxtaposition of the individual images of the Dinara cycle in the Golden Palace of the Tsaritsy and their underlying literary model shows that in their illustrations the artists consciously chose only scenes with a gender-specific content. As a result of this selection process, the older interpretation of the tale was adjusted to a new context, which sought to justify the notion of dynastic succession through the female line with the claim that, through the Christian faith, gender-specific roles could be transcended.

The gender-specific aspects of the Georgian princess are clearly expressed in the first scene of the Dinara cycle, located immediately to the right of the door in the western sector of the north wall (see Figure 15). Dinara, wearing a crown and a nimbus over her loose hair (a sign of her virginity), is seated on a throne. Several bearded men in boyar dress address the princess while a group of women in white veils watches the scene from behind the throne.[60]

The composition depicts the moment when according to the *"Povest' o tsaritse Dinare,"* Dinara incited the hesitating boyars to make war on the infidel:

> Take courage [literally: manliness] and shake female weakness off from yourselves . . . let us chase off female weakness from ourselves and take care of our treasures. For when a woman conceives in her womb, she will also start to be ready; so should you who have received wealth and honor, and who are filled with pride . . . .[61]

The passage reflects a scenario in which the kind of warrior spirit that is commonly associated with men was nowhere to be found. The seriousness of the political situation led to a redefinition of the concept of courage, which was construed no longer in masculine, but in feminine terms. The skillful wordplay on male courage *(muzhestvo)* and the condition of the female womb (*zhenochrev"stvo*, that is, female weakness) not only gives a derogatory impression of the boyars but also proclaims the necessity to reverse the traditional gender roles. The boyars' model was supposed to be the pregnant woman who during gestation lives in a state of constant readiness. Dinara also used the imagery of a woman giving birth in her

15. The Golden Palace of the Tsaritsy: the Georgian princess Dinara enthroned; her pilgrimage to the Sharbenskii Monastery; the beginning of her campaign against the Persian tsar. The frescoes portray the maiden as a crowned ruler, who through her pious patronage of the Virgin's shrine gains the strength to take on her realm's infidel enemies in battle.

prediction of the Persians' defeat: "As a woman in pain suffers from the great torment of her body when the moment of birth approaches, so the Persians [will experience] great exhaustion."[62] While her male counterparts were clearly incapacitated by the predisposition of their gender, Dinara could shed her traditional female role and perform the tasks of a man: "Let us move quickly against the barbarians, and I, a girl, will also go. I will take up manly strength and gird my loins with arms, put on armor, place a helmet on my female head, and take a spear into my girl's palm."[63]

The blatant reversal of traditional gender roles in the Dinara story had to be based on powerful arguments in order to gain acceptance. As in the case of the other woman figures depicted in the Golden Palace of the Tsaritsy, religion provided the necessary ideological backing for the concept in question. According to the *"Povest' o tsaritse Dinare,"* the Georgian princess learned about military valor from the Scriptures.[64] God, Christ, and the Virgin justified her struggle to defend her country against the infidel.

In order to assure supernatural support for her pugnacious endeavor, Dinara set out on a pilgrimage to the Sharbenskii Monastery near Tabriz to pray at the Virgin's shrine. This event is depicted in the second composition of the Dinara cycle, which bears the inscription: "Tsaritsa Dinara walked barefoot over the sharp stones" (see Figure 15).[65] On the left Dinara, followed by a few female servants and several boyars, walks barefoot toward the entrance of a monastery. On the right the tsaritsa raises her hands in prayer before an icon of the Virgin. In the foreground she appears again, kneeling before the icon to implore the Virgin for support.[66]

Dinara's visit to the Sharbenskii Monastery ultimately had two goals. First, it meant to secure divine support for her military venture. Second, the princess sought from the Virgin the legitimization of her assumption of a male role. Dinara's prayer reminds the Virgin that it was she who had entrusted her with the rule over her father's realm. Dinara ends her plea that the Mother of God help her fend off the attack of the "proud and savage Persian" with the words "and give your weak child strength."[67]

The remaining frescoes of the Dinara cycle illustrate the final confrontation between Dinara and the Persian ruler. The third composition shows Dinara, dressed in warrior garb, speeding into battle on a white steed while her troops follow suit (see Figure 15).[68] The scene illustrates the passage found in the second redaction of the *"Povest' o tsaritse Dinare,"* which describes Dinara's setting out against the Persians:

> And she left the church, mounted her horse, and said to her commanders: "Friends and brothers! I want to lay down my head before you for the property of the Mother of God, for our honor, and for all the Orthodox people in our realm. If you do the same, may God help us and his immaculate mother extend her support to us. If you do not do so, may God destroy you, and may the Virgin deliver you into slavery and plunder, as happened to the Jewish priests." And she went out from her realm to meet the Persian.[69]

The last fresco, immediately to the right of the arch, depicts Dinara's victorious entrance into Tabriz (see figure 16). Dinara, in military garb, rides toward the city gate on her white horse, followed by her troops. In her right hand she holds a spear on which the head of the Persian ruler is displayed. The text accompanying the fresco composition reads: "She captured the Persian tsar, cut off his head, put it up on her spear, and carried it into the Persian town of Tabriz."[70] In the upper left corner of the image, Dinara is again depicted, this time without crown, in the company of one of her female servants. She is conversing with a group of monks on the left.

Both battle scenes of the Dinara cycle emphasize the accord between Dinara and the Virgin, on which the liberation of her homeland ultimately rested. In the speech underlying the third composition, Dinara pledged her life to the Virgin. The last scene shows the successful result of the princess's pact with the divine. Dinara's public display of the Persian ruler's head denotes her complete defeat of the enemy. More significantly, it also testifies to the fact that with the help of God and the Virgin, natural female weakness could be overcome. This thought is clearly expressed in Dinara's previous response to the Persian ruler's demands for tribute: "If I receive victory over you from Christ, my God, and help from his mother, I will step on your royal body with my woman's leg, and I will cut off your head. Then what honor will I receive, having defeated the Persian tsar

16. The Golden Palace of the Tsaritsy: Dinara's victorious entrance into Tabriz. Dressed in military garb and riding on a white horse, Dinara approaches the city gate of Tabriz. Her triumphant display of the defeated Persian tsar's head on a spear expresses the message that pious royal women could function as effective defenders of the Christian faith.

with a woman's prowess."[71] The emphasis on the Virgin's role in Dinara's assumption of male functions is also evident in the eulogy of the Virgin following the victory:

> Such help did the most Immaculate One give to a weak child, and she displayed such prowess in the female sex, and from such a girl's voice so many Persian warriors were frightened, and with such piercing of her spear the maiden confused them, and from such speed of a girl and from her voice all the Persians died from fear, and she gave such courage to a girl in a foreign land and placed such a state in the hands of a weak girl, and such wit did the Virgin give her![72]

The Virgin's continued support for the princess after the decisive battle with the Persians is recalled in the scene of Dinara conversing with the monks. The image refers to Dinara's delivering all the spoils of war to the monastery of the Virgin, as she had pledged during her previous visit to the shrine. In her bargain with the divine she in return received continued supernatural protection for her realm.[73]

With regard to the issue of Irina Godunova's succession to the throne, the frescoes of the Dinara cycle in the Golden Palace of the Tsaritsy made two strong statements in Irina's favor. First, by presenting the heroine as an energetic and successful figure, the cycle promoted the idea that gender was not a hindrance in the succession of the royal dynasty. Formally the battle scenes of the Dinara cycle connect with the theme of Constantine's victory over Maxentius, which is depicted on the vaulted ceiling. The visitor of the Golden Palace would easily have seen the correlation of the maiden ruler with the mighty Roman emperor. Second, just as the Virgin's support assured Dinara's success, the religious sanction of Irina Godunova's role ultimately was thought to benefit the realm as a whole.

Like all the other frescoes in the Golden Palace of the Tsaritsy, the Dinara cycle was carefully crafted to highlight the political potential the Georgian princess possessed as a result of the spiritual disposition of her gender. Conceivably an antecedent of a seventeenth-century manuscript of the *Kazan' Chronicle*, which included segments of the Dinara tale, might also have served as a model for the Golden Palace frescoes. Although the illustrations for the text were never executed, the captions accompanying them identify three scenes that all appear in the Golden Palace.[74] The five miniatures in the only extant illustrated copy of the *"Povest' o tsaritse Dinare"* (located in a seventeenth-century miscellany) suggest that—as in the fresco cycles of Saints Helena, Ol'ga, and Theodora—a careful selection of images also took place in the Dinara cycle.[75] The miniatures are not finished (they represent only black-and-white drawings) and do not constitute a complete cycle.[76] Of the five illustrations only the first is found in the Golden Palace. The Uvarov copy shows Dinara, wearing a crown over her long, loose hair, surrounded by female servants. Seated on a high throne, she receives several noblemen.[77] In the second miniature we see Dinara with a book in her hand next to a table on which lie several more books. Several nobles, one holding a scroll and another a book, stand under an arch to the right. The following image shows the Persian tsar receiving a Georgian ambassador. To the right three Persian messengers, marked by their tall turbans, speed off on galloping horses.[78] In the fourth miniature Dinara, seated on a throne, receives the three Persian diplomats who are bringing precious vessels as gifts.[79] The last image shows Georgian troops riding back to the Persian ruler's palace where they deliver presents to the shah.[80] The five miniatures closely follow the major themes of the *"Povest' o tsaritse Dinare,"* Dinara's enthronement, her familiarity with the Scriptures that caused her father to select her as his successor, and her negotiations with the Persians.[81] If the designers of the Golden Palace murals were familiar with the artistic and literary models of the *Povest'*, the absence of most of these images in the Golden Palace must be explained by the different focus of the illustrated tale in the Uvarov copy. The painter of the miniatures traced the details of the ambassadorial exchange without being held hostage by the anti-Persian polemic of the tale. Rather than taking a hostile attitude toward her enemy, Dinara follows the common decorum of diplomatic gift exchange. Such a depiction of Dinara would have seriously undercut the concept of the pious tsaritsa the commissioners of the Golden Palace were so eager to propound. Unlike the Dinara of the Uvarov miniatures, the Georgian princess in the Golden Palace frescoes is nimbed. In order to eliminate any notion that Dinara might have been interested in a compromise with her infidel foe, the designers of the murals eliminated all images containing references to negotiations. In order to avoid any doubt about Dinara's legitimacy as a ruler, they also dropped the second image, which explains Dinara's qualifications for assuming the throne. As a result the entire cycle in the Golden Palace becomes focused on Dinara's confrontation with the Persian infidel. The designers of the Golden Palace murals only chose those scenes that underscored Dinara's piety, independent action, and strength.

In view of the close connection between text and image in the Dinara cycle of the Golden Palace, the contemporary viewer who was familiar with the story possibly saw in the frescoes yet another connection between Dinara and Irina Godunova. While all other women depicted in the Golden Palace at one point had been wives and were mothers, Dinara had preserved her virginity, evident in her unveiled hair. According to the *"Povest' o tsaritse Dinare,"* this factor influenced her father to hand over the reign of Georgia to her.[82] The tale presents her abstinence from physical relations as both a virtue and a benefit for the realm. Given the saintly reputation Tsar Fedor Ivanovich enjoyed already during his lifetime, similar sentiments could have been easily applied to Irina Godunova. For Boris Godunov and his supporters, the concluding statement in the *"Povest' o tsaritse Dinare*" that, after ruling thirty-eight years, the chaste Dinara "passed the power on to her relatives" provided a convenient justification for their claim that Irina safeguarded the smooth transition from one dynasty to another.[83]

Given the paucity of sources, we may never know what sort of arrangements the Godunovs and their supporters had in mind with regard to Fedor's succession. The frescoes in the Golden Palace of the Tsaritsy, however, affirm the scholarly view, expressed notably by A. A. Zimin, that the transfer of power to Irina after the death of the last Rurikide in 1598 was not nominal, but real. Several sources reporting the event note that the Russian subjects swore an oath to recognize Irina as the next ruler shortly after Fedor Ivanovich passed away.[84] Zimin points out that Irina consciously rejected the responsibility to rule and thus refutes the idea that she was merely a puppet figure of her brother.[85] The frescoes further explain the elaborate ritual involved in the transfer of the reign from Irina to Boris. The seventeenth-century *Piskarev Chronicle* mentions that on February 21, 1598, Patriarch Iov with his holy synod, the boyars, gentry, and common people walked with crosses to the Novodevichii Monastery to petition Irina, who had become a nun there, to transfer the reign to Boris. Irina allegedly initially refused.[86] Even if by that time Boris's succession was hardly in doubt, the public nature of the procession proves that Irina's right to the throne and her privilege to nominate her successor were generally recognized. This is supported in the correspondence of Patriarch Iov following Boris's accession to the throne and in written oaths to Boris.[87] Moreover, the frescoes also provide an answer to the question why Irina was the first Muscovite tsaritsa to be recorded in the official prayer lists, and why these lists name Irina before Boris and his family.[88]

The pictorial themes in Irina's reception hall testify that by the late sixteenth century an elaborate ideology had developed that proclaimed the acceptability of a female ruler in Muscovite Russia. To achieve their aim, the framers of this ideology (who have to be sought in the close circle of Godunov supporters at the Muscovite court and who acted upon the instigation of Boris, and possibly even Irina) exploited traditional stories of pious princesses, proclaiming the capacity of these women to act as capable rulers on the basis of their high spiritual status. The fresco program of the Golden Palace of the Tsaritsy showed royal women introducing Christianity into their realm and combatting heresy within and the infidel outside their territory. Any depictions of women who were socially dependent on their husbands or other family members are conspicuously absent. All the figures depicted are virgins, widows, or independently acting mothers. Saint Helena does not appear together with her illustrious son in one image. Theodora's salvation of her husband occurred when she was already recognized as a ruler. The absence of married women in the murals suggests that the designers of the frescoes consciously transcended the image of the tsaritsa as helpmate of the tsar, which had largely determined Anastasiia

Romanovna's role. At the same time they also deemphasized the aspect of private spirituality in their heroines. The female figures depicted in the Golden Palace murals all excelled in religious acts that affected the spiritual well-being of their realm; none of the frescoes celebrates them for ascetic deeds in a privatized context.

The image of the tsaritsa, developed under the pressure of solving Muscovite Russia's problem of dynastic continuity, was considerably more masculine than in periods when succession seemed assured. The positive interpretation of Dinara displaying the head of the Persian ruler on a spear on the walls of the tsaritsa's reception room implies that Irina's role as a tsaritsa was thought to be determined less by her gender than by the exigencies of the contemporary situation. In this respect the developments in Muscovy in the 1580s and 1590s confirm the observation by a number of feminist scholars that, in periods of social dysfunction, women's status tends to improve, that is, women are able to assume roles normally reserved for men.[89] Whereas these scholars generally focus on political and socioeconomic factors influencing women's lives, in the case of the Muscovite tsaritsy the justification of the expansion of their role into the man's sphere came from religious tradition and was endorsed by the ecclesiastical hierarchy. That one of the most fervent supporters of the new dynastic arrangement in Fedor Ivanovich's reign was Patriarch Iov suggests that, in spite of its concern with maintaining the natural dominant role of the male over the female (expressed so vividly in the didactic literature of the Church Fathers), the Orthodox church did not oppose strong women at any cost.[90] The participation of the church in the definition of the role of the Muscovite royal wife in the second half of the sixteenth century augmented the Muscovite tsaritsa's religious prestige, which in turn led to an increased acceptance of her involvement in the salvation politics of the Muscovite state.

Mariia Grigor'evna Skuratova-Bel'skaia

Tsaritsa Mariia Grigor'evna Skuratova-Bel'skaia was a complex figure whose image diverged widely from her actual role. She was the daughter of a feared *oprichnik* and the wife of the first non-Rurikide tsar, who lived out his life under the suspicion of having his only possible rival for the throne—Ivan IV's son from his uncanonical union with his last wife, Mariia Nagaia—murdered. These circumstances made Mariia Grigor'evna one of the least liked tsaritsy in Muscovite history.[91] Contemporary foreign travelers in Russia left highly unflattering descriptions of her. According to William Parry, Mariia was an ugly, overweight woman, who was not in the best of health.[92] Isaac Massa called her an evil Jezebel who gave treacherous advice to her husband. He further noted that she was "a true Semiramis at heart" who constantly nursed ambitious plans to exploit her sister-in-law Irina's childlessness to become a tsaritsa herself.[93] If we disregard the bias of this invective, which associates Godunov's wife with illegitimate power, we find that the historical Mariia Grigor'evna commanded the same dynastic and political position as her sister-in-law Irina Godunova had enjoyed. In order to guarantee that the throne would smoothly pass to his son, Fedor, Boris Godunov endowed the matriarch of his line with sufficient prestige. Mariia featured prominently in donation charters of the Godunov family to foreign ecclesiastical dignitaries and native monastic institutions with her own presents, both before and after Boris's ascendance to power.[94] Mariia's significance with regard to the Godunov dynastic scheme is also evident in the portrayal of her name saint, Mary Magdalene, among the personal protector saints of the Godunov family in icons and embroideries commissioned by her husband.[95]

Mariia Grigor'evna's participation in her husband's efforts to consolidate his dynastic position served as a good preparation for her role after Boris Fedorovich's death on April 13, 1605. Political observers with varying sympathies for the Godunov regime ascribe the initiative in the subsequent transfer of power to his widow and Fedor Borisovich's mother. According to Isaac Massa, Tsaritsa Mariia Grigor'evna exploited the opportunity of the moment to enlarge her own power as tsaritsa, even though she knew that her increased visibility could put her in harm's way.[96] The account of the Time of Troubles attributed to Ivan Mikhailovich Katyrev-Rostovskii states that Mariia summoned Patriarch Iov and his synod and the great boyars to an assembly in the Kremlin and petitioned them to declare their loyalty to her son.[97] The details of the loyalty oath the assembled agreed to swear make clear that Mariia Grigor'evna was aware of her pivotal role in the transfer of the throne. The formula of the oath demanded that all social ranks of the realm declared their loyalty first to "Tsaritsa and Grand Princess Mariia," and then to her children, Tsar Fedor and Tsarevna Kseniia. A letter by Patriarch Iov to the Siberian town Pelymsk confirms the same order.[98] The fact that during the ceremony the assembly kissed the cross first to Godunov's widow suggests that it acknowledged her position as ruler in the same way it had accepted Irina Godunova, her sister-in-law, as the immediate successor of Fedor Ivanovich. If the Muscovites had seen Mariia Grigor'evna simply as a regent for her still youthful son, it would have sufficed to mention her second in the oath formula.

The formula of the oath sworn to the Godunov family in 1605 clearly states the challenges that Mariia Grigor'evna and her children faced from both outside and inside the Muscovite government. The long list of stipulations attached to the loyalty oath (which included the usual references to the subjects' obligation to show their goodwill to the ruler and to refrain from intrigue, desertion, and treason) expressed an inordinate fear of personal harm that Mariia and her children might suffer through the actions of witchcraft and sorcery.[99] The subjects were required not to contemplate other rulers, such as Semen Bekbulatovich, who had received the title Grand Prince from Ivan IV for a short while. They were to avoid any contact with the newly risen pretender, who claimed to be Dmitrii of Uglich (Ivan IV's and Mariia Nagaia's son) and were to report Dmitrii's activities to Moscow.[100] In addition to a possible dynastic challenge, Mariia and her family ostensibly feared a loss of control over their government and the decline of orderly procedure. This is evident in a special oath that members of the secretarial staff *(pod'iachie)* had to swear. The oath stipulated that they had to act truthfully in all matters concerning their mistress and lord and that they had to refrain from divulging state secrets, stealing money from the treasury, taking bribes, and falsifying documents.[101]

In all these eventualities Mariia Grigor'evna's recourse was without doubt limited. In the absence of political muscle, the tsaritsa and her family invoked God, the Virgin, the royal protector saints Peter, Aleksii, and Iona and the Muscovite clergy to punish those who would disregard the oath.[102] In the days and weeks following her and her son's accession to the throne, Mariia Grigor'evna, undaunted by the difficulties before her, did everything in her power to preserve the position of her family. With Patriarch Iov's help she spread the news about the transfer of power after Boris Fedorovich's death. In her capacity as tsaritsa, she herself sent a circular letter to all the towns in the Russian Empire in which she insisted that their inhabitants kiss the cross to her son. In order to undercut the influence of the False Dmitrii, she launched an investigation into the activities of his supporters. Judging from a letter to the tsaritsa and her son from the *voevoda* of Uglich dating from May 25, 1605, the tsaritsa had expressed her concerns about a black priest named Antonii, who had spread rumors about the pretender. The resulting inquest, however, did not have the desired result: in spite of the apparent application of torture, the priest denied any knowledge about the False Dmitrii's intention to incite the citizens of Uglich to rise up against the Muscovite government.[103]

The challenge presented by the False Dmitrii to the Godunov dynasty explains Mariia Grigor'evna's anxiety about the fate of her rival, Mariia Nagaia (the mother of the true Dmitrii of Uglich). According to Massa, a rumor already circulated in Moscow during Boris Godunov's lifetime that, after the appearance of the False Dmitrii, Mariia Grigor'evna summoned the last spouse of Ivan IV (then known as the nun Marfa) to Moscow and interrogated her personally about her son's death in Boris's bedchamber. Even though Mariia Grigor'evna nearly blinded her in a fit of rage with a lit torch, Marfa insisted that her son was still alive and had been taken out of the country (although she knew he was dead and buried). The Godunov matriarch had reason to fear Nagaia in spite of her monastic status. Nagaia's confirmation of the rumored survival of Tsarevich Dmitrii could have devastating consequences for the new dynasty. Mariia Grigor'evna, recognizing the potential political impact of her rival, a tsaritsa in her own right, took pains to increase Nagaia's social isolation.[104]

In addition to dealing with issues of loyalty and treason, Tsaritsa Mariia Grigor'evna devoted her attention to a variety of legal and administrative matters. The Godunov matriarch issued charters in her own name and in that of her son. The tsaritsa was also the focus of numerous petitions by subjects who had been displaced or ruined by the recent Lithuanian incursions on Russian territory. In all of the petitions Mariia Grigor'evna was addressed as the undisputed mistress of the Russian realm. Significantly, her name was placed before that of her son.[105]

Ironically the public aspects of Tsaritsa Mariia Grigor'evna's power that are evident in her dynastic politics and administrative activities may well have been an important reason for her eventual demise. The murder of Mariia Grigor'evna and her son Fedor on June 10, 1605, by members of the Muscovite aristocracy who went over to the pretender's camp undoubtedly is related to the crisis of dynastic legitimacy Russia faced during the Time of Troubles. Still, the question remains: Why did the murderers—Vasilii Mosalskoi, Mikhalka Molchanov, and Andrei Sheleoedinov—not follow the traditional practice of removing unwanted tsaritsy to a monastery?[106] Platonov's explanation that the Godunovs were destroyed because they were too weak to rule leaves one wondering about the bloodthirsty behavior of the boyars toward a regime they did not have to fear.[107] The disgraceful treatment of the members of the Godunov dynasty is much more plausible if one assumes that both the ruling tsaritsa and her son represented an insurmountable obstacle to the boyars' plans. While any attempt to replace the ruling dynasty necessitated the effective removal of the last male heir, Mariia's forceful death may well be explained by the rising importance of the tsaritsa in political, ecclesiastical, and other affairs of the realm since the late sixteenth century. Massa's view that Mariia Grigor'evna usurped part of the public power of the tsar hardly holds considering Irina Godunova's sanctioned participation in matters of state. By issuing documents and settling disputes, Boris's wife merely followed in the footsteps of her generally esteemed sister-in-law. The very visibility Mariia had gained by Boris's image-building campaign, which was designed to strengthen the legitimacy of his line, made it impossible for the princely aristocracy to shove her aside peacefully. Undoubtedly Mariia suffered from the rumor of the Godunovs' involvement in the murder of Dmitrii of Uglich, and she had little time after her and her son's accession to the throne to build loyalties among the boyar factions. Nevertheless, the fact that the murderers, in order to avoid a popular reaction, felt it necessary to insist she and her son had drunk poison suggests that the populace at large extended to Mariia the respect due a tsaritsa and might have taken unkindly to her violent exit from the political scene.[108]

The role of Mariia Grigor'evna during her husband's reign and after his death shows how the idea that a tsaritsa could preserve dynastic continuity gained currency in Muscovite Russia in the late sixteenth and early seventeenth centuries. The image-building campaign surrounding Irina Godunova paved the way for her sister-in-law to be recognized as a dynastic bridge between her late husband and her adolescent son. Although technically Mariia Grigor'evna should have held the status of regent, the dynastic challenge presented by the False Dmitrii caused her elevation to the position of an independent ruler. Loyalty oaths and letters from the time following Boris Godunov's death attest to Mariia's prominence in the Godunov regime. Her violent end leads one to conclude that, in early seventeenth-century Muscovy, royal women were seen as transmitters of dynastic continuity and as preservers of legitimate government.

Mariia Fedorovna Nagaia

As the seventh and last wife of Tsar Ivan IV, Mariia Fedorovna Nagaia's chances to play an important role in the dynastic scheme of the Muscovite autocracy were highly doubtful. In 1580, when the tsar concluded his last marital union, he already had two grown sons. Mariia Fedorovna therefore seemingly would never play the role of mother of the future ruler of Muscovy. Her position at the royal court was further weakened because the Orthodox church considered the tsar's seventh marriage uncanonical.[109] For these reasons it is hard to believe, even given the worst of circumstances—the murder of Tsarevich Ivan and the forced tonsure of his wife Elena Sheremeteva on November 9, 1581—that Mariia Nagaia might have profited from these events. Nevertheless, while the Russian realm focused on Ivan IV's second son, Fedor, as the new successor to the Russian throne, Mariia Fedorovna and the Nagoi clan still seem to have nourished hopes to become late players in the game of succession. Mariia and her natal kin may well have been encouraged by the limited physical and mental capacities of Fedor Ivanovich and by the birth of Mariia's son, Dmitrii Ivanovich, on October 19, 1582.[110] Mariia Fedorovna's own actions from the time of her wedding onward, and particularly after the birth of her son, make clear that she was fully aware of the potential inherent in her position as tsaritsa and that she intended to exploit the opportunity presented to her by her elevation to the status of royal mother. Although none of the later wives of Ivan IV were enshrined in myth as had been the first tsaritsa, Anastasiia Romanovna, Mariia Fedorovna could count on the fact that the myths concerning the tsaritsa's role and her ritual functions were not yet forgotten.[111] Mariia therefore ignored the uncanonical aspect of her marriage and comported herself as a true mother of the realm, even after the death of her son Dmitrii in Uglich on May 15, 1591.

The first evidence that Mariia Fedorovna sought to exploit her dynastic potential as tsaritsa comes from a pall she commissioned on February 23, 1581, in honor of Saint Sergius of Radonezh. The inscription on the large shroud, which features the full-size figure of the saint and an image of the Old Testament Trinity with Abraham and Sarah, states that the pall was made for the blessed great miracle-worker Sergius "during the reign of the pious tsar and grand prince Ivan, at the order of his tsaritsa and grand princess Mariia, in the presence of their children, the pious tsarevich Prince

Ivan and his tsaritsa, Princess Elena, the pious tsarevich Prince Fedor and his tsaritsa, Princess Irina."[112] The liturgical gift names Mariia Fedorovna as the exclusive donor among all her new royal relatives, which shows that the tsaritsa used the pall as a platform to advertise her own position in her new family. Her donation to Saint Sergius, the traditional protector saint of the royal family, expresses her intention to assume the responsibility for the well-being of her adopted children. The absence of any reference to Ivan IV as co-donor suggests that Mariia did not view herself merely as a helpmate to her husband in carrying out his religious duties. Instead, by invoking Saint Sergius's benevolence and thus setting herself up as the intercessor for the royal family, she claimed her own space at the Muscovite court.

Mariia Fedorovna's eagerness to build up her own prestige as tsar mother can be observed in a little-studied tapestry that carries the inscription "In the reign of the great lord, Tsar and Grand [Prince] of all Russia, Ivan Vasil'evich, Tsaritsa and Grand Princess Mariia Fedorovna [donated this image] of the Most Pure Mother of God [to] the Church of the Transfiguration on July 30, 1583."[113] The central panel of the pall features an image of the Virgin with the Christ child. The image is flanked by the full-size nimbed figures of John the Baptist on the left and Saint Demetrius of Thessalonike on the right. The pall also features the images of the Old Testament Trinity and Saint Sergius of Radonezh.[114] Both the images and the accompanying text on the tapestry express the donor's desire to give the birth of Tsarevich Dmitrii the aura of religious sanction. As N. A. Maiasova points out, the central panel depicts the Virgin of Jerusalem whose feast day coincided with Dmitrii Ivanovich's birthday.[115]

That Saint Sergius, who was credited with inspiring the womb of royal wives and with protecting the royal offspring, appears on the tapestry supports the conclusion that Marfa Fedorovna sought to proclaim her son's legitimate royal rank. From this perspective, the depiction of little Dmitrii's name saint, Demetrius of Thessalonike, alongside the patron saint of his father, John the Baptist, may be construed as an attempt by the tapestry's donor to insist on her son's right to be counted as a legitimate successor to Ivan IV. The date of the embroidery, which was executed before Dmitrii was even a full year old, betrays a certain urgency. It is known that Ivan during his last two years was not in good health and could be expected to pass away within the near future.[116] Moreover, if Mariia dedicated her liturgical gift to the Cathedral of the Transfiguration in Uglich, the donation may have expressed the tsaritsa's concern that, after her husband's death, she and her son would be permanently confined in Uglich, which Ivan IV had assigned to Dmitrii Ivanovich as an appanage.[117]

The events following Ivan IV's death in 1584 bear out the assumptions both that Mariia Fedorovna had staked the claim to her son's legitimacy and that she had feared her and her kin's removal from the court. Although (if one is to believe the *Inoe skazanie*) Ivan IV had tried to forestall the neglect of his wife and youngest son by Fedor Ivanovich's brother-in-law and adviser, Boris Godunov (by placing them into the care of the princes Ivan Petrovich Shuiskii, Ivan Fedorovich Mstislavskii, and Nikita Romanovich Iur'ev-Zakharin), the tsaritsa and her child were dispatched to Uglich soon after Fedor Ivanovich's accession to the throne on May 1, 1584.[118] Other members of the Nagoi clan were dispersed and imprisoned in remote towns.[119] The Godunovs' exiling the royal mother and son to Uglich so quickly after Ivan's death suggests they were seen as a threat to Tsar Fedor Ivanovich and his in-laws, who nourished their own designs to succeed the frail tsar to the throne. Boris Godunov and his adherents probably took seriously Mariia Fedorovna's statements concerning her son's legitimacy. Upon his return to Russia in 1586, Horsey observed that Fedor Ivanovich was concerned about the dynastic claims staked by Mariia and her kin.[120]

Historians have often maintained that, because of her uncanonical union with Ivan IV, Mariia Nagaia would not have been able to provide the realm with legitimate offspring, even if the Rurikide dynasty died out with Fedor Ivanovich.[121] The speedy removal of the Nagie from the Muscovite court after Ivan's death, however, and Mariia Fedorovna's undaunted insistence on the recognition of her status as royal mother before and after her departure to Uglich suggest that the conventional scholarly wisdom relies too heavily on the notion that the religious sanction of a royal marriage in Muscovite Russia completely eclipsed other considerations, such as blood relations, in the construction of royal legitimacy. Scholars have generally neglected both the Nagie's position regarding this issue and popular attitudes toward Tsaritsa Mariia Fedorovna and instead have raised the question of her and her son's legitimacy only in the context of Tsarevich Dmitrii's demise in Uglich on May 15, 1591.[122] Much has been made of the fact that, in the aftermath of the incident, Mariia Nagaia openly accused Boris Godunov of murdering her son to eliminate any competition for the royal inheritance.[123] Although many scholars have used the tsaritsa's statement to support the claim that the Godunovs were responsible for the tsarevich's death, more recent studies of the findings of the Commission of Inquiry, which investigated the matter shortly after Dmitrii's death, have made clear that neither Mariia nor any of the other accusers were present during Dmitrii's death. The majority of eyewitnesses confirmed that the tsarevich had inflicted fatal wounds on himself during an epileptic fit. Under the circumstances, Vernadsky's view that Mariia's statement was the result of long-standing fears that her son might fall prey to an assassination attempt seems to be most plausible.[124] The tsaritsa's hasty conclusion makes sense in light of her struggle with the Godunovs concerning her own recognition and her son's role in the succession scheme. Mariia Nagaia's involvement in the murder of the men accused of killing her son and in inciting the population of Uglich against Muscovite officials before the arrival of the Commission of Inquiry shows that the tsaritsa was a force the Godunovs had to reckon with, and that she enjoyed a certain amount of popular support.[125] The tsaritsa's special treatment in the inquest, that is, her private interview with Metropolitan Gelasius in place of her appearance before the commission, also proves that she continued to command the public respect due a tsaritsa.[126]

Whatever the circumstances of Tsarevich Dmitrii's death, there are reasons to believe that, in the mind of many Muscovites, Mariia Nagaia's role as tsaritsa was not diminished by her uncanonical union with Ivan IV. In his *Vremennik, d'iak* Ivan Timofeev (Mariia's contemporary) called her a strong advocate of dynastic continuity and legitimate government. Timofeev notes that being a royal mother, her sorrow over the death of Tsarevich Dmitrii was incomparable to normal expressions of grief since it affected the realm at large.[127] The respect the tsaritsa enjoyed and her insistence that her son had been murdered (a view that, contrary to the Commission's findings, became the dominant interpretation of the Uglich event) must have alarmed the Godunov faction, which was engaged in a propaganda campaign to raise the prestige of its own tsaritsa, Irina Godunova. Desperate in their desire to silence any further claims by a rival clan, the Godunovs had Mariia Fedorovna tonsured and sent to a distant monastery near Cherepovets on the Vyksa River.[128] In the end this measure showed little success. Just as Solomoniia Saburova, who had been forced to take the veil, continued to enjoy respect behind her monastic walls, Tsaritsa Mariia, who took the monastic name Marfa, retained her visibility. Moved from her original monastery to the Goritskii Monastery on the Sheksna River, she dedicated a chapel in the Cathedral of the Resurrection there in honor of her son.[129] The monastic confinement seems to have increased rather than silenced concern about the tsaritsa's fate. Describing the bleak existence of the tsaritsa in a desolate place, without sufficient food and clothing, and calling her exile a second murder after that of her son, Timofeev expressed deep sympathy and admiration for the royal nun's perseverance.[130]

Marfa Nagaia's efforts to maintain her public image paid off during the crisis that ensued after Boris Godunov's death in 1605. Pitted against her rival Mariia Grigor'evna, who suffered from the rumor of her complicity in Tsarevich Dmitrii's murder, the monastic royal mother was handed a golden opportunity when Grishka Otrepiev made his bid for the Russian throne, claiming that he was Dmitrii Ivanovich, who had survived the Uglich incident. In general, most Russian sources tend to exonerate Marfa Nagaia of any wrongdoing in her relations with the False Dmitrii because of their understandable bias against the pretender. Influenced by the attitude of the subsequent Shuiskii regime toward the tsaritsa, Russian sources claim that the pretender, who visited her in her monastery on the Vyksa, deceived her and forced her into acknowledging him as her son.[131] Although Grishka Otrepiev initially may well have exerted pressure on Marfa Nagaia to support his pretense, her history of insisting on her own agenda makes it difficult to believe she played the role of the revived tsarevich's mother out of sheer desperation. This is supported by the rumor reported by Isaac Massa that Marfa persisted in her claim that her son was still alive even when Tsaritsa Mariia Grigor'evna threatened her physically during an interrogation.[132] Even though the incident is not corroborated by other sources, Massa's contention that Marfa provided fuel for the dissemination of the rumors surrounding the pretender is difficult to reject. Cooperation with the pretender offered the exiled nun the opportunity to return with her kin to Moscow.[133] Finally she could play the role of tsar mother, which had been denied her for so long. Since many members of the political elite, such as Timofeev, sympathized with Nagaia, she ran little risk of being found out and punished. While Russia branded Mariia Grigor'evna as the evil tsaritsa, Marfa could exalt her own status by using her royal prestige to help legitimate Otrepiev's power as tsar.

A close examination of the nature of Marfa's cooperation with Otrepiev suggests that the pretender was cognizant of the goodwill and respect the Muscovite people bore the mother of the unfortunate tsarevich and was prepared to make concessions to her in return for her tacit acknowledgment of his claims. His decision to return Marfa from her monastic exile to Moscow and to settle her in the Monastery of the Ascension in the Kremlin (where most women of the Muscovite ruling house lay buried) suggests Otrepiev exploited old Muscovite notions that attributed to the tsaritsy the ability to guarantee dynastic continuity and the well-being of the realm in times of crisis.[134] According to Massa, upon her return to Moscow the Russian people at large treated Mariia as a legitimate tsaritsa and expected her judgment concerning Otrepiev's identity to end the dynastic turmoil. The pretender and his alleged mother reunited in front of a crowd of people two miles outside Moscow where both of them performed a "scene of sobbing and tears" that stirred the hearts and minds of the onlookers.[135]

Her close cooperation with Otrepiev undoubtedly bolstered Nagaia's desire for public recognition and led to her involvement in affairs of the realm.[136] The *Novyi letopisets* maintains that the False Dmitrii lovingly treated her like his natal mother.[137] Massa points out that Mariia's lie concerning her son led to her recognition as a royal mother and to her excellent treatment. She was assigned quarters in the Monastery of the Ascension in the Kremlin where she lived "as a sovereign."[138] From Massa's and Bussow's remarks that the tsar visited with his mother daily after her arrival in Moscow one may conclude that Marfa was kept informed of matters of state in spite of her monastic retirement. The old tsaritsa seems to have participated in the wedding negotiations concerning the tsar's Polish bride, Marina Mniszech. When Marina arrived in Moscow, Marfa was the first to receive her. According to Arsenios Elassonis, the royal nun participated in the wedding preparations of her future daughter-in-law, who stayed with her for eight days in the monastery.[139] Possibly the pretender hoped that his Orthodox mother would be able to make his Latin bride more acceptable to his Russian Orthodox subjects.

Marfa Nagaia's role as guarantor of dynastic continuity that justified her social and political prominence also comes to the fore in the formula of the loyalty oath demanded by the pretender from all ranks of Muscovite society in June 1605.[140] The frequent appearance of Marfa's name in the oath suggests that the pretender counted on the goodwill toward his reign that his mother would evoke among his subjects. In the face of the doubts about his background and his competition with the Godunovs, Mariia Nagaia represented a kind of touchstone for the Russian people, which the False Dmitrii cleverly exploited.[141] The oath demands that Dmitrii's subjects avoid any contact with Fedor Borisovich and his mother and refrain from acts of treason and sorcery against the new tsar and his mother. Just as the loyalty oath in the Godunov regime had to be sworn first to Boris's widow and then to his son, Grishka Otrepiev stipulated that the Russians kiss the cross to "our mistress, Tsaritsa and Grand Princess, the nun Marfa Fedorovna of all Russia, and to our lord born to her, Tsar and Grand Prince Dmitrii Ivanovich of all Russia."[142] The position of her name and the phrase "our lord born to her" unequivocally demonstrate that the pretender relied on Marfa Nagaia's ability as tsar mother to function as a bridge between her late husband, Tsar Ivan, and her alleged son. The tsaritsa thus was credited with the ability to guarantee dynastic continuity when the regular mechanism of succession had been disrupted.

The pretender's claim that his mother—regardless of her uncanonical marital status or her monastic vocation—could assure legitimate succession in Muscovy found a strong supporter in the Orthodox church. In a circular letter sent by Patriarch Ignatii to several Siberian settlements on June 3, 1605, to inform them about Dmitrii Ivanovich's coronation, he stipulated that Marfa Fedorovna be included in their prayers for their new leader. To avoid possible confusion about the exact places in the liturgy where the names of the new tsar and his mother had to be mentioned, the patriarch provided a detailed outline for all possible services. The most striking aspect of his instructions is that Marfa Nagaia's name consistently preceded the names of Tsar Dmitrii and Patriarch Ignatii in the litanies during the hours, the liturgy, and in the prayers for their health and long life in the church service. In all cases Marfa Nagaia was to be addressed as "Mistress Tsaritsa and Grand Princess, the nun Marfa Fedorovna of all Russia."[143]

The real or perceived close association of Marfa Nagaia with the pretender makes it perhaps surprising that the tsaritsa was not swept up by the Muscovites' murderous wrath that eventually cost Grishka Otrepiev and many of his followers their lives on May 17, 1606. Nevertheless, events following the pretender's assassination show Marfa Nagaia adjusting very quickly to the radical political changes that put Prince Vasilii Ivanovich Shuiskii on the Russian throne. In a circular letter she sent to the *voevoda* Ivan Nikitich Godunov only four days after the bloody revolt in Moscow, she turned on her alleged son, claiming that he had deceived her and threatened her and members of her kin with death.[144] Clearly seeking to exonerate herself from any guilt the Muscovites might attribute to her because of her acquiescence in the False Dmitrii's conduct, she claimed that during her stay in Moscow he had placed her in complete isolation. Nevertheless, she had tried to inform the boyars in secret that Boris Godunov had her son killed in Uglich. In her defense Marfa Nagaia skillfully portrayed herself as a weak, unprotected, long-suffering royal widow and orphaned mother. She manipulated the Muscovites' tendency to associate their tsaritsa with the defense of the Orthodox faith so that she herself would appear to take the side of the righteous Russians against the Latin impostor. Ignoring her previous part in the wedding arrangements of the False Dmitrii, she complained of his violations of Orthodox practices. Feigning outrage that Otrepiev had not baptized his bride and that he had crowned her queen according to Western coronation practices, she fed the anti-Latin sentiment of the masses. Her public statement culminated in the outrageous claim that she, Tsaritsa Marfa, along with the high-ranking ecclesiastics of the realm and the leading boyars and gentry members, had selected the new tsar, Prince Vasilii Ivanovich Shuiskii.[145]

Marfa's letter from May 21, 1606, gives us a rare insight into her understanding of her political position. Faced with possible retribution or even death, Marfa skillfully played the card of female weakness to facilitate the change of her loyalty to the new ruler. Although she undoubtedly knew she was completely at Shuiskii's mercy, she pretended to carry out her traditional royal duty as guarantor of dynastic continuity by endorsing him as the next tsar. While Marfa saved her own face with this action, she ran little risk of exposure since Vasilii Shuiskii experienced the same need to bolster his legitimacy that had brought Marfa and the pretender together.[146]

Tsar Vasilii Shuiskii's subsequent treatment of Marfa Nagaia strongly suggests that he followed his predecessor's strategy of using the tsaritsa to solidify his own dynastic position. The mutually beneficial arrangement between the boyar tsar and the last consort of Ivan IV is particularly evident in the ceremonial translation that took place when Shuiskii ordered the true Dmitrii Ivanovich's remains brought from Uglich to Moscow to undermine any further claims of the pretender's supporters. While the inquiry into the condition of Dmitrii Ivanovich's body and its transfer and solemn reburial in the Cathedral of the Archangel on June 3, 1606, are well attested in seventeenth-century Russian chronicles and tales of the Time of Troubles, the role his mother played in this process has so far received little attention.[147] All of the contemporary sources describing the event attribute to Marfa Fedorovna a central role in identifying Dmitrii Ivanovich's remains and attesting to their sanctity.[148] When the casket with the boy's relics (which had been found in an undisturbed state and were therefore considered holy) arrived at the outskirts of Moscow, the tsar, Marfa Nagaia, members of the ecclesiastical hierarchy, the boyar and gentry elites, and the people of Moscow greeted it by the city gate with crosses. According to Tsar Vasilii Shuiskii's circular letter and Marfa Fedorovna's letter to Elets, the tsar and Marfa together examined Dmitrii's remains in the presence of the holy synod and the people and then ordered the relics to be displayed to all participants in the procession.[149] The prominent role of Marfa Fedorovna in this religious ceremony, which had far-reaching political implications, can only be understood in the context of Tsar Vasilii Shuiskii's need for the general recognition of his rightful place on the Russian throne and in light of the Muscovite belief that the tsaritsa represented a receptacle of royal prestige. The *Novyi letopisets* states outright that Vasilii Shuiskii ordered the translation of Dmitrii's relics to counter treasonous and disloyal sentiments toward him in the Muscovite populace. Considering the pretender's previous claims, however, it became absolutely essential that, upon their arrival in Moscow, the relics were authenticated beyond any shadow of a doubt before they would be placed forever in the final resting place of his illustrious ancestors, the Cathedral of the Archangel Michael.[150] Under these circumstances the identification of the tsarevich's body by his natal mother underscored the legitimacy of Shuiskii's position.

The ritual of the verification of the relics, however, not only aimed at establishing Dmitrii's authenticity but also was concerned with determining his sanctity, which was crucial to the boyar tsar, who himself lacked the aura of religious sanction. The dual intent behind Marfa Nagaia's participation in the ceremony did not escape Isaac Massa, who ascribes to the tsaritsa the leading role in convincing the inhabitants of Moscow that they had been visited by a saint:

> When they came out of the city, the body was there on a bier set upon a carriage. The tsar, the lords, and the bishops came and gazed at it. The tsarina did the same, and cried out: "Oh, I see him now, the true Dmitry, murdered at Uglich! And by the grace of God, his body is as fresh as if they had just put him in the coffin!" Hearing these words, all the people began to praise and thank God, and they covered the bier. I would have liked to look at it too if they had let me, and many monks and priests were as anxious to see it as I was, but no doubt they were afraid that we would be too curious and profane this sacred corpse. It was borne into the city like a saint and holy man [sanct en heiligen].[151]

Marfa Nagaia's prominent role in the authentication and canonization of Dmitrii of Uglich's remains clearly served the boyar tsar's need for dynastic legitimacy and religious sanction. Moreover, it gave the tsar mother an opportunity to silence the concerns about her past association with the pretender, to ally herself publicly with the new ruler, and to invoke the people's sympathy for her own person. It is striking that Marfa Nagaia did not content herself with identifying her son but also testified to the undisturbed state of his remains, which denoted their holiness, although the present members of the church hierarchy might easily have performed this task.[152] The ritual of authenticating relics, which was traditionally reserved to leading ecclesiastics, provided her with the means to appeal to the Muscovites as a mouthpiece of the divine. By declaring the arrival of Dmitrii the saint, she conjured up images of the pitiful murder of the innocent child. At the same time, she reminded the Muscovite subjects of God's mercy. Following the public examination, the participants all thanked God and asked forgiveness from Dmitrii, who began to work miracles on the way to the Kremlin.[153] The entire incident shows that Shuiskii's efforts to bolster his legitimacy were intricately tied up with Marfa Fedorovna's successful manipulation of an established religious ritual, a manipulation aimed at proclaiming her association with the divine will and the good fortune of the Russian land. This enhanced Marfa's own prestige and ensured her a continued safe future.

The argument that Marfa Fedorovna's participation in the translation of Dmitrii Ivanovich's relics not only benefited Tsar Vasilii Shuiskii, but also served to advance the tsar mother's visibility and to assure her the continued support of the Muscovite people is further supported by Marfa Nagaia's public appearance in the Cathedral of the Archangel Michael following the solemn translation of her son's remains to his permanent resting place. According to Shuiskii's circular letter and Marfa's letter to Elets, the tsaritsa in a dramatic performance appealed to the tsar and all those attending the ceremony for forgiveness for her past behavior. She confessed that she was guilty of acquiescing in the pretender's claims and of not exposing him sooner. Knowing that he was not her son, she had become responsible for much bloodshed. In her defense she asked her audience to consider that she had acted against her own will, that she had been imprisoned and deprived of contact with her kin, and that the pretender had threatened to kill her if she gave him away.[154] The image of the repentant, unprotected tsar mother who had lost her son and suffered oppression by several of the previous rulers could not help but stir the hearts of those present. For those who may have had reason to resent her silence, her confession in the presence of her saintly son, the new miracle-worker of Muscovy, made a refusal of her requested pardon impossible. Moreover, by pardoning Dmitrii's mother, the Muscovites purged themselves of any guilt they themselves bore for the havoc created by the pretender. Shuiskii, who was indebted to Marfa for her support of his royal position, predictably forgave her "so that she would not remain in sin and be condemned by the whole world."[155] In his own words, his decision was motivated by his sense of mercy and his respect for the royal nun's ex-husband, Tsar Ivan, and his pious son, Tsarevich Dmitrii. In order to give his pronouncement additional weight, he asked the holy synod and the Orthodox community at large to pray for the absolution of Marfa Nagaia's sins.[156]

The close cooperation between the boyar tsar and the politically seasoned tsaritsa continued after the translation of Tsarevich Dmitrii's relics. The letter that Marfa Nagaia sent to the inhabitants of the town of Elets makes it clear that Shuiskii continued to rely on her ability to act as conciliator between him and his political opponents. It states that the tsar had previously written to Elets about the translation of the true Dmitrii's remains to Moscow to assure the population of the town that the pretender's claims had been false. Hearing about the continued disloyalty of Elets to

Tsar Shuiskii, Marfa Fedorovna appealed to the inhabitants of the town to acknowledge Vasilii Shuiskii—whose reign had been blessed by her saintly son himself—as the tsar of Muscovy. As proof for the recent events, she sent them an icon of Saint Dmitrii of Uglich.[157]

Marfa Nagaia's letter to Elets represents a good example of the Muscovite notion that the wives of the previous Muscovite tsars continued to be valued for their ability to contribute to a smoother and calmer transition of power in periods of political confusion. It also makes clear that Nagaia was conscious of the political influence she wielded as a result of her function as tsar mother. By promoting the cult of her son, she not only rehabilitated her own position at the Muscovite court but seized an opportunity to work for the peace and stability of the realm. Her final blessing of the inhabitants of Elets and her wishes for peace reflect the traditional duty of the tsaritsa as the mother of the realm.

Marfa Nagaia's reputation as a distinguished tsar mother survived into the Romanov period. After her death she was buried in the prestigious Monastery of the Ascension in the Kremlin.[158] Marfa Ivanovna—Tsar Mikhail Fedorovich's mother, who had suffered much from the phenomenon of pretense—took great care to honor the memory of her previous rival. On October 24, 1616, she gave one hundred rubles to the Trinity-Sergius Monastery for the commemoration of "the mistress tsaritsa and grand princess, the nun Marfa Fedorovna."[159] Marfa Ivanovna also made sure that the Rurikide tsaritsa would be remembered locally in Uglich, the site of her exile and her son's untimely death. In two charters issued by Marfa Ivanovna to the female Monastery of the Epiphany in Uglich on February 28, 1629, and November 30, 1630, she stipulated that the sisters enter Marfa Fedorovna's name into the memorial registers of their monastery.[160] By appearing as the sponsor of her previous rival's commemoration, Marfa Ivanovna made sure that the notion of the tsaritsa as mother of the realm persisted into her own time, when it could be attributed to her own person.

. . .

An examination of the construction of dynastic continuity in medieval Russia after Ivan IV's death shows that the royal mothers played a significant role in contributing to the survival and the stability of the Muscovite autocracy. Royal motherhood gave these women unprecedented visibility in public life but also exposed them to repression and physical harm. Survival often depended on their ability to defend the claim of their sons and to associate themselves with the proclaimed legitimate heir to the throne. In doing so, royal mothers actively promoted myths that expressed their ability to act as links between dynasties and as intercessors for the present ruler. The case of Marfa Fedorovna shows that a tsaritsa could manipulate traditional religious rituals to boost the legitimacy of the government she supported and to associate herself with the greater good of the country. In essence the phenomenon of pretense empowered Nagaia by giving her the authority to identify the true successor to the throne. In the same vein, her involvement in the canonization of Tsarevich Dmitrii not only gave political and religious sanction to Vasilii Shuiskii's reign but also enhanced her own prestige.

The threat of dynastic and political turmoil in the late sixteenth and early seventeenth centuries afforded the Muscovite tsaritsy the opportunity to fulfill their potential as rulers in their own right and as preservers of dynastic continuity. The need for a new ruling dynasty, which resulted from the childlessness of the last Rurikide ruler, drove the Muscovite court to emphasize the political acumen of his wife, Irina Godunova. If the Muscovite tsardom was to retain an air of legitimacy under the rule of Boris Godunov (Irina's brother and Fedor Ivanovich's adviser), Tsaritsa Irina's key role in linking two bloodlines must be underscored. The iconographic program of Irina's reception chamber, the Golden Palace of the Tsaritsy, skillfully advertised her status as an independent ruler by comparing her to famous royal women who had succeeded their male relatives to the throne because of their strong commitment to the Orthodox faith. Considering that Irina Godunova was credited with the ability to perpetuate legitimate autocratic rule in Russia, the wide range of activities undertaken by Mariia Grigor'evna Skuratova-Bel'skaia and Mariia Fedorovna Nagaia in their capacity as tsar mothers must not be viewed as a usurpation of power. These women made the most of their role as royal mothers, which gave them political, legal, and economic influence in addition to social prestige. In a period when royal succession was no longer controlled by one kin group, however, women did not stake the claims of their sons unpunished; Mariia Grigor'evna paid for her bid for power with her life, Marfa Nagaia spent years of her life in monastic isolation. Nevertheless, the example of the last wife of Ivan IV shows that, if a tsaritsa managed to survive, her traditional reputation as guarantor of dynastic legitimacy could help secure her continued social and political influence at the Muscovite court. The trust that members of the Russian political elite (and if we are to believe Isaac Massa, even the populace at large) placed in an uncanonical wife of one of their previous tsars would be difficult to explain if Mariia Nagaia did not stand within a time-honored tradition that saw the wives and mothers of their rulers as guardians of the realm's physical and spiritual well-being. Although Mariia Nagaia did not rule in her own right, ultimately the Muscovite concept that a tsaritsa could preserve dynastic continuity because of her role as intercessor for the realm empowered her to play a significant part in Russia's struggle for a legitimate government.

4 The Royal *Terem* in the Early Romanov Period

THE INVESTIGATION of the social realities and ideological concepts that shaped the lives of Muscovite royal women and these women's efforts to improve their status has so far primarily focused on the mothers and wives of the Russian tsars. The observant reader who wonders about the role of royal daughters and sisters in the Muscovite autocratic system should keep in mind that, before the late 1620s, female royal offspring played only a small role at the Muscovite court. In the fifteenth century, the grand princes' daughters were strategically married to important Russian or foreign rulers, as the cases of Grand Princess Anna Vasil'evna of Riazan' and Ivan III's daughter Elena demonstrate.[1] Although these women often stayed in touch with their parents and occasionally played a limited role in the Russian ruler's political maneuverings, they did not leave a lasting impression on the social life and ideological aspirations of the court. In the sixteenth century the question of the role of the royal daughters in Muscovy was a moot one: neither Solomoniia Saburova nor Elena Glinskaia produced girls, and Anastasiia Romanovna's female children died in infancy. Ivan IV's later marriages also were without female offspring, and Irina Godunova's only child, Feodosiia, passed away prematurely. Under these circumstances the tsar's private life naturally focused on his wife, the tsaritsa. This situation, however, changed in the reigns of Boris Godunov, Mikhail Fedorovich, and Aleksei Mikhailovich when the tsars' daughters became an integral part of the royal *terem*, the living quarters of the female members of a Russian ruler's family. The historian cannot help wondering how the role of both tsaritsy and tsarevny was perceived in seventeenth-century Muscovy. Two questions in particular beg for further investigation.

First, to what degree was the tsaritsa's proclaimed role as spiritual helpmate to and intercessor for the tsar realized within the confines of the *terem?* Second, to what extent did the royal daughters share in their mothers' role? To answer these questions requires a reevaluation of the common scholarly theory of the seclusion of royal women in Muscovite Russia.

Modern Russian and Western evaluations of the family life of the medieval Russian tsars have tended to follow the Russian historian I. E. Zabelin who, nearly a century and a half ago, stated that the living space of the Muscovite royal family was sharply divided into two spheres. While the tsar occupied the public space at court, his wife, sisters, and under-age children were relegated to a secondary private sphere, the royal *terem*.[2] This assumption, which equated the public sphere with the male-dominated realm of politics and its private equivalent with female domesticity, corresponded to commonly held nineteenth-century notions about men's and women's places in society. The separation theory, however, does not necessarily nor adequately describe medieval Russian notions of public and private life and of the division of roles between the genders. With regard to the Muscovite royal *terem* in particular, several questions arise: to what extent does the distinction between public and private roles apply to male and female members of the tsar's family in the seventeenth century? How was the seclusion of the wives, sisters, and daughters of the tsars constructed? A study of the royal *terem* under Mikhail Fedorovich and Aleksei Mikhailovich suggests that neither Zabelin's view of a separation of the public and private spheres nor his assumption that Muscovite royal women lived a secluded life accurately represent the historical truth. Rather, as at many Western medieval courts, the personal and private sphere was inextricably intertwined with the public affairs of state, which provided royal women with an opportunity to cross any socially sanctioned boundaries between the worlds of men and women.[3]

Whereas many scholars of the nineteenth and twentieth centuries have concerned themselves with the institution of the *terem*, few have concentrated on the development of this social phenomenon within the Kremlin walls. (One important exception is Zabelin.) In general the social historians of Russia have focused their attention on the hazy origins of the *terem*, which have been attributed to such varied factors as the Byzantine monastic influence, the Mongol oppression, and the deleterious effect of the Muscovite autocracy and the medieval Russian church on the traditional Russian family.[4] More recently Nancy Shields Kollmann has shed light on the *terem*'s function within the Muscovite social elite. Although she argues convincingly that noble families exploited the control over their women to assure the smooth functioning of their political system, she never addresses the extent to which the women living in the *terem* led secluded lives. Instead, Kollmann (although with caution) repeats Zabelin's claim that female seclusion intensified in the seventeenth century.[5]

Although the royal *terem* in the Kremlin may not be entirely representative of this social institution at large, a study of the activities of the female members of the tsar's family at the very least can help combat traditional preconceptions about the *terem*. It is not surprising that scholars who generally consider the institution of the *terem* a negative phenomenon in the history of Russian women also view its royal variant in a dim light. Philip Longworth calls the royal *terem* a place "where life was mainly given over to gossip and good works."[6] Susanne McNally, who in her dissertation wrote extensively on the *terem*, charges that the adoption of this institution by the Russian rulers led to the loss of political and economic power of their wives and daughters, privatization, and therefore trivialization of their role, and even to a decline in moral conduct and authority.[7] These sweeping generalizations, however, are not easily verifiable in specific circumstances. Although the living quarters of the female members of the tsar's family in the seventeenth century were kept separate from his own private quarters and were located far from the halls of public power, the women of the early Romanov dynasty were neither reduced to meaningless routine activities nor insulated against the harsh political reality of their time.[8]

With the successful second marriage of Mikhail Fedorovich the Romanov regime, which had emerged victoriously from the Time of Troubles, set out to structure anew the family life of the Russian ruler. Several of the Russian tsaritsy—such as Mariia Fedorovna Nagaia and Marina Mniszech—and Mikhail Fedorovich's own mother, Marfa Ivanovna, had led rather peripatetic lives during their country's experience of dynastic and social turmoil, so it is understandable that the wives and daughters of the new tsar received their own secure place at the court. Although seventeenth-century descriptions of Muscovy note the close confinement of Russian royal women, the impressions of their authors very likely result from their lack of personal familiarity with the life in the royal *terem*.[9] In the case of foreign travelers to Muscovy, their assumption that the tsar's female relatives led a quiet and boring life may well have to be attributed to a cultural misunderstanding. In reality the Romanov *terem* was structured so that its senior female members, in particular the tsaritsy, exercised administrative, social, and even spiritual functions that empowered them in their private sphere and reached into the public arena as well.

The *terem* was important in the life of the royal court; it did not represent merely an informal family arrangement but had an administrative structure over which the tsar's wife herself presided. The tsaritsa supervised an array of noble attendants and simple servants consisting of wet nurses, textile workers, a wardrobe mistress, and a female judge in charge of settling disputes among members of the *terem* staff. Loyalty oaths sworn to Mikhail Fedorovich and Aleksei Mikhailovich included declarations of faithful service to their wives and mothers by the various groups in the *terem*.[10] Although the appearance of the tsaritsa's name in oaths of this type represented a regular occurrence in Muscovite Russia, separate statements by members of her entourage arose first in the Romanov period. This development, which parallels the inclusion of lower government servants in loyalty oaths to the tsar, suggests that the *terem* participated in the gradual bureaucratization of the Muscovite government in the seventeenth century.[11] The wives of the Romanov tsars devoted themselves to the arrangements of weddings for the servants in their household and the distribution of dowries, which often included large land grants. Since many of the noble women serving in the *terem* were close relatives of the royal couple, the tsaritsa played a significant part in the autocracy's efforts to assure and reward loyalty and to undercut political rivalry.[12] Although the royal *terem* had its own structure and rules, its respect for personal relations corresponded to the political life at the Romanov court at large.

The argument proposed here—that the women in the *terem* of the first two Romanov tsars were not secluded objects of the autocracy without a function but, rather, exercised a meaningful and respected role at court—is further supported by the tsaritsy's preoccupation with administrative matters. Already Mikhail Fedorovich's mother had managed her own properties and exercised judicial authority over her subjects.[13] Marfa Ivanovna had carried on her own correspondence and used her own seal.[14] The wives of Mikhail Fedorovich and Aleksei Mikhailovich regularly received written petitions from their subjects. In a letter dated November 30, 1641, a Katka Sokolova petitioned Evdokiia Luk'ianovna for her yearly payment for a cell the tsaritsa had acquired on one of her pilgrimages to the Alekseevskii Monastery. The petition was promptly granted, and one of the tsaritsa's relatives, Fedor Stepanovich Streshnev, issued the money.[15] The document proves that the tsaritsa carried on economic transactions and counted as an independent legal persona to whom subjects had direct recourse; it also testifies to the *terem*'s close interaction with the male world of the court.

The *terem*'s administrative structure also made it possible for the wives of the Romanov tsars to function as arbiters in legal disputes. In 1653 the nun Evfrosiniia appealed directly to Mariia Il'inichna when a certain Ivan Devulia and a widow named Avdot'ia abducted one of her wards, the girl Makrinka, under the pretext that the tsaritsa wanted to marry the girl to one of her servants and had ordered the bride to be brought to the Kremlin for inspection. The nun's complaint led to an immediate investigation of the matter. (Unfortunately the outcome is not known.) Russian subjects often petitioned the tsaritsa to intervene in legal matters concerning their relatives. Kotoshikhin points out that these pleas for help usually met with success.[16]

The tsaritsa's acknowledged ability to arbitrate in matters concerning her subjects earned her respect. John Struys, who witnessed the funeral of Mariia Il'inichna in 1669, mentions the lamentations of the common subjects who "oftentimes in distress were accustomed to address themselves to her, as a Mediatrix."[17] During the uprising in Moscow on June 1, 1648, the crowd that complained to the tsar about the heavy hand of Moscow's city officials sought to enlist the help of Mariia Il'inichna. When the rioters stormed the house of Aleksei Mikhailovich's governor, Boris Ivanovich Morozov, out of respect for the tsaritsa they spared Morozov's wife, Anna (who was Mariia Il'inichna's sister), from their murderous wrath. Morozov himself eventually was saved because Aleksei Mikhailovich invoked his close kinship ties to his wife.[18]

The ability of the wives of the Romanov tsars to transcend the private sphere of the *terem* and to become engaged in matters usually associated with the public organs of government is particularly visible in the correspondence between representatives of the Romanov government and Mariia Il'inichna from 1654–1655 when the plague struck Moscow. Even a casual examination of the correspondence reveals the tsaritsa's familiarity with many of the Muscovite officials. In her letters Mariia Il'inichna frequently inquired about the condition of high-ranking servitors.[19] At a time when the tsar was on his Smolensk campaign, the Muscovite authorities in charge of day-to-day governmental affairs addressed the tsaritsa (who had left Moscow with the entire royal family to escape contagion) for advice on how to deal with the chaos caused by the epidemic. When Prince Mikhail Petrovich Pronskoi received orders from the tsar to send money and supplies, he left the final decision—whether to carry out the tsar's command and risk the spreading of the plague among the tsar's troops—to the tsaritsa. After Pronskoi's death Ivan Andreevich Khilkov requested instructions from Mariia Il'inichna on how to counter the breakdown of order in the capital.[20] The tsaritsa took resolute action to prevent the spreading of the plague, especially to the tsar and his troops, and to the royal family. As a safety precaution she had the main roads from Moscow to Smolensk, Pereslavl', Suzdal', and Iur'ev Pol'skoi blocked by soldiers. In a letter from September 9, 1654, she instructed the *syn' boiarskii* Fedor Golianishev to check on the origins of provisions merchants from Uglich had purchased for the tsar and the royal family in order to ascertain whether the goods had not been contaminated. She also decided that the supplies the tsar had requested from Moscow were not to be sent to Smolensk.[21] Mariia Il'inichna also sought to minimize the exposure of the populace to the fatal disease. In several letters to the Muscovite officials in the Kremlin, she insisted they should make sure that both natives and foreigners avoided the capital. The Kremlin gates were to be closed and people in infected houses to be quarantined. Mariia Il'inichna forbade the minting of new money during the year of the plague to prevent contagion through its circulation. She made provisions for the burial of the dead in prison to stop the disease from spreading there. On a more personal level, the tsaritsa took care of the families of servitors fleeing from the plague. A petition by the *pod'iachii* Dementii Bashmakov that the tsaritsa protect the life and property of his wife met with success.[22]

The public aspects of the tsaritsa's authority can also be seen in Mariia Il'inichna's interest in the maintenance of peace in the capital. In a letter she wrote from the Koliazinskii Monastery to the *okol'nichii* Ivan Andreevich Khilkov, she ordered the musketeers *(strel'tsy)* to patrol the Kremlin and the White Town to guard against robbery and vandalism. In order to assure the cooperation of the troops, she arranged for the pay of the *strel'tsy* who had survived and remained in Moscow from *prikaz* money. As the plague abated, the tsaritsa requested details about the identity of the robbers.[23]

In dealing with the health and safety crisis in the capital, Mariia Il'inichna involved herself in nearly every aspect of government, with the exception of foreign affairs.[24] A letter issued in the name of Tsarevich Aleksei Alekseevich on September 16, 1654, asked the *voevoda* of Uglich to prepare a collection of legal fines and to send them to the tsaritsa in the Koliazinskii Monastery. The tsaritsa herself prohibited the collection of the head tax in Moscow out of fear that the process might aid in the spread of the disease. Mariia Il'inichna also displayed concern about the impact of the plague on the economic life in the capital, notably people's ability to buy foodstuffs at the markets when merchants succumbed to the illness. When a fire broke out in the Frolov Tower in the Kremlin, she received a report on the inquest concerning this incident. Moreover, the tsaritsa gave instructions that the prisons be guarded and that those in charge of governing barricade themselves in the Kremlin, refrain from receiving people, inform the tsar in Smolensk of further matters, and keep appropriate records.[25]

While the correspondence between the Muscovite government officials and the tsaritsa from 1654–1655 clearly points to the involvement of the wife of the Romanov tsar in matters of government, the tsaritsa's authority was not necessarily deemed identical with that of the Russian ruler. The qualitative, rather than quantitative, difference in the authority of the male and female members of the medieval Russian ruling family is evident in the different tone one encounters in Mariia Il'inichna's letters and in documents issued in the name of the infant tsarevich Aleksei Alekseevich. While both parties expressed concern about their own safety, the tsaritsa alone inquired about the condition of her subjects. The association of the tsaritsa with a kinder and gentler form of authority and the attempt to give the tsarevich a tough image is particularly evident in a letter from Aleksei Alekseevich dated October 10, 1654. In the correspondence the tsar's successor threatened people from infected areas who were trying to approach him on the road with the death penalty.[26]

The internal administrative structure of the *terem* and the tsaritsa's ability to intervene on behalf of her subjects suggest that the Romanov women's confinement in specific chambers of the Kremlin did not necessarily exclude them from public life. Although the wives of the Romanov tsars did not enjoy the same visibility as their predecessors during the Time of Troubles—who carried on the business of government and issued decrees in their own names and in those of their sons—they nonetheless occupied an important place in the Romanov regime.[27] Their removal from the daily contact with the population of Moscow created a mystique that associated them with a space untainted by the unsavory aspects of political life. As occupants of the royal *terem*, the tsaritsy were close to the Russian rulers, but untouched by the tough reality of the male world of government. The charisma enjoyed by the royal women as a result of their personal influence and unassailable neutrality enabled them to appear as facilitators of social justice and peace in the realm. Their success depended on the separation of the male and female spheres at the court. In a period when the Russian government became increasingly bureaucratized, access to the tsar through his family represented another option to the Muscovite population. At the same time, the administrative structure of the royal *terem* in the seventeenth century assured close communication between the *terem* and the main organs of government. Through their ritual confinement in their private quarters in the Kremlin and their resulting social prestige, the wives of the Romanov rulers bridged the realms of the public and the private. The overlapping of the public and the private spheres within the Muscovite royal family especially comes to the fore in the correspondence of the tsaritsa with government officials in Moscow during the crisis years of 1654 and 1655. From her self-imposed exile, Mariia Il'inichna directed pressing matters concerning health and security in her realm in the absence of the tsar.

The fallacy of the seclusion argument is also evident in the public aspects of the position of the seventeenth-century tsaritsy that arose out of their religious role. The written correspondence received in the *terem* quarters suggests that these women maintained a high profile in the Orthodox world abroad. As during the reign of Boris Godunov, the hierarchs of the Eastern Orthodox church, who regularly approached the Russian government for funds, sent separate petitions to the tsaritsy. Theophanes, the patriarch of Jerusalem, inundated Mikhail Romanov's second wife, Evdokiia Luk'ianovna Streshneva, with specific requests for liturgical objects and vestments, for example. In a letter from 1629, he expressed his gratitude to the tsaritsa for her contributions to the renovation of the Church of the Resurrection, likening her to "the holy tsaritsa Helena, who built many churches and erected the holy sites."[28] Two decades later his successor, Patriarch Paisius, employed the same vocabulary in his correspondence with Mariia Il'inichna.[29] Paisius befriended Aleksei Mikhailovich's first wife in hopes of receiving her charity for his beleaguered community of Jerusalem. Judging from a letter the patriarch sent to her in December 1652, the two had become good friends during his visit to Moscow. The patriarch profusely thanked her for her hospitality and her generous gifts for the Holy Sepulcher and reminisced that the tsaritsa had wanted him to stay longer. He insisted he would have complied with her wishes had it not been for the necessity to put his patriarchate in order. The letter concludes with the hierarch's complaint about Arsenii Sukhanov, whom the tsar had attached to Paisius's retinue, evidently to keep an eye on the patriarch's activities.[30]

Although the correspondence between heads of the Eastern Orthodox church and the Muscovite tsaritsy does not necessarily reflect native Russian perceptions of the role of the Romanov wives, it proves that the tsaritsa's sphere of activity was not confined to mundane tasks associated with the private quarters of the royal women in the Kremlin. As the wife of Russia's Orthodox ruler, the tsaritsa was considered to share her husband's interest in the well-being of the true faith abroad. For this reason the leaders of the Eastern Orthodox churches abroad sent separate letters to the tsars' wives rather than appending notes conveying their respect and best wishes to their correspondence with the tsars. The tsaritsa also represented a source of charity that was well worth tapping; although generally the tsar's gifts exceeded in value those of his spouse, her consistent donations were considerable.[31] Paisius's remarks about his treatment by Mariia Il'inichna in Moscow and his concern about Sukhanov's report to the tsar suggest that he ascribed to her a certain amount of influence.

The tsaritsy's contributions to the Russian Orthodox church provided them with another opportunity for greater public visibility. Their ability to transcend the private aspects of the *terem* quarters is particularly evident in their participation in royal donations of liturgical objects. Inscriptions on the donated objects or records of the gifts contain direct references to the charitable activities of the royal wives. In 1653 and 1654 Mariia Il'inichna and her husband donated two altar crosses to the Cathedral of the Annunciation in the Kremlin. Evdokiia Luk'ianovna's name appears on the Royal Gate completed in 1643 for the Church of the Holy Trinity in the Trinity-Sergius Monastery. In 1650 Mariia Il'inichna and Aleksei Mikhailovich donated a tapestry with the composition *The Appearance of the Virgin to Saint Sergius* to the same institution.[32] In several cases the tsaritsy bestowed liturgical objects on monasteries in their own name. On January 30, 1652, Mariia Il'inichna donated a printed book featuring the *Spiritual Ladder of Saint John Climacus* to the Nikolo-Shartomskii Monastery in the Vladimir region. As late as 1694, Peter the Great's mother, Natal'ia Kirillovna Naryshkina, commissioned a silver cross for the female Monastery of the Dormition in the town of Aleksandrov in return for prayers for her own health and that of her son and grandson.[33]

Supporters of the seclusion theory generally point out that the women of the Romanov household seldom appeared in public, and that when they did they were generally shielded from the gaze of their subjects. In the same vein, these scholars emphasize that the royal women usually attended the liturgy in a separate ceremony (often held at night), surrounded only by close court attendants and friends.[34] Although the royal women did not participate in the public state rituals carried out by the tsar and the secular and ecclesiastical elite on Palm Sunday, Good Friday, Epiphany, or the Festival of the Blessing of the Waters on August 1, they were not categorically barred from religious ritual of any kind. Paul of Aleppo's observation that the women in the *terem* were sent food or vessels of holy water blessed during the religious ceremony on the named feast days points to their integration into the Orthodox community. The royal women were generally included in the customary acts of gift giving by religious institutions. On Easter the patriarch himself blessed the tsaritsa's Easter eggs. The screening off of the tsaritsa during her attendance of liturgical services as well did not mean that Muscovite society did not value her presence in church. Paul of Aleppo observes that Mariia Il'inichna received the blessing of the ecclesiastic celebrating mass at the end of the service. Patriarch Nikon even seems to have encouraged the tsaritsa to attend the liturgy during daytime in the presence of her subjects. The archdeacon notes that he had a special chair made for her for this purpose. When services were held for the protection of the tsar and his realm, the tsaritsa was usually present.[35]

Living in the royal *terem* did not prevent the women of the Romanov family from maintaining close contact with important ecclesiastical figures. Paul of Aleppo points out that Patriarch Nikon and Patriarch Macarius both visited the tsaritsa in her quarters during the Easter celebrations held in the tsar's absence. On that occasion Mariia Il'inichna received the metropolitans and archimandrites of the realm as well. The tsaritsa seems to have been able to make friends with the visiting foreign patriarchs. In addition to the patriarch of Jerusalem, Paisius, she also extended her hospitality to the patriarch of Antioch.[36]

The capability of the tsaritsy during the Romanov period to transcend their isolation in the *terem* by means of their religious activities may also be gleaned from the frequency of their visits to holy shrines in the realm. After Mikhail Fedorovich's accession to the throne, his mother, who had accompanied him since childhood on his peregrinations across Russia, concentrated her efforts on assuring her son's divine support by praying frequently at the shrines of Russian saints. The extant correspondence between the tsar mother and her son and her previous husband, Patriarch Filaret, shows that Marfa Ivanovna participated in the tsar's annual visits to the Trinity-Sergius Monastery. She also accompanied him on trips to the monastery of Makarii Unzhenskii and the Ugreshskii Nikolaevskii Monastery.[37] After the tsar's marriage to Evdokiia Luk'ianovna, the young wife joined her mother-in-law on the traditional outings to the Trinity-Sergius Monastery and eventually took over this responsibility entirely.[38] This custom continued under Aleksei Mikhailovich. Only one week after her wedding, Mariia Il'inichna accompanied her husband on a pilgrimage to the Trinity-Sergius Monastery.[39] Two years later the royal couple set out on an extensive journey to pay its respects at the Trinity-Sergius Monastery, the Makarii Koliazinskii Monastery, and the shrines of Dmitrii of Uglich and Anna of Kashin.[40]

The frequent participation of the wives and mothers of the Romanov tsars in royal pilgrimages makes it hard to agree with scholars who maintain that the *terem* system intensified in the seventeenth century, implying that the confinement of its inhabitants became more severe and resulted in a privatization of their role.[41] The tsaritsy clearly still enjoyed the right to leave the Kremlin, although their mobility was regulated. The tsar himself expected his sisters, wife, and children to visit him during his military campaigns. In 1654 he met with his family in Viaz'ma. The ritualization of their personae, expressed in customs such as the veiling of their faces and bodies in public, did not necessarily lessen their impact on their subjects.

Pilgrimages provided important points of contact between the populace at large and the tsar's wife, who displayed her pious commitment to the subjects of the realm through generous almsgiving.[42]

The tsaritsy's expense accounts, which diligently recorded individual charitable donations during their traditional visits to the Trinity-Sergius Monastery, enable us to reconstruct the interaction between the tsaritsa and the commoners during outings with a religious purpose. As soon as the tsaritsa left the Kremlin, her entourage was mobbed by crowds petitioning her for alms. Many people approached her with specific requests for food and clothes. In every village she passed, the tsaritsa had to stop to show her kindness to the local monks and nuns, priests and their wives, and widows and children. In many instances she left generous money contributions to poorhouses. All along the road to and from the pilgrimage site, the tsaritsa distributed money to needy individuals, and those who brought her delicate foods were handsomely rewarded for their hospitality.[43] The tsaritsa's expense accounts corroborate Kotoshikhin's statements that the tsaritsa accompanied her husband on pilgrimages to monasteries in Moscow in order to feed monks and distribute alms and that she often visited poorhouses and displayed her generosity to the poor.[44]

The exposure of the wives and mothers of the Romanov tsars to the concerns and needs of the common people during these pilgrimages, which occurred frequently, suggests that in the seventeenth century, through their religious activities, the tsaritsy not only attained popular respect but also played a social welfare role. The Romanovs, like their Rurikide predecessors, expected their wives to support them in their governmental tasks by concentrating their efforts on the social welfare of their state. On Thursday after Pentecost, the tsaritsa joined her husband and the patriarch in a display of almsgiving and in the attendance of a liturgical service for people who had drowned or had been murdered and for all deceased foreigners.[45] Together with the tsar, Mariia Il'inichna doled out daily allowances to the poor and the prisoners. Referring to her participation in the ritual of visiting the prisons in Moscow on Good Friday, the English traveler Samuel Collins testifies to the tsaritsa's supportive function vis-à-vis the tsar, who "buys out some that are in debt, and releases others that are criminal, as he thinks fit: He pays great sums for such as he is inform'd are really necessitated. His Czaritsa buys out women."[46] Paul of Aleppo as well comments on the tsaritsa's involvement in matters of public welfare. According to the archdeacon, the first wife of Aleksei Mikhailovich built the convent of Saint Savva in Moscow for the purpose of settling some seventy Cossack nuns there whom the tsar had brought to Moscow from Smolensk and Mogilev.[47] Following in the footsteps of their illustrious dynastic ancestor, Anastasiia Romanovna, the wives of the Romanov tsars pursued charitable causes to assure God's blessing for their realm. This responsibility necessarily directed their interests and actions beyond the walls of the *terem* and thus increased their visibility in Muscovite society.

Beyond providing her with the possibility to escape the private life within the Kremlin walls and to contribute to the maintenance of her people's well-being, the religious role of the tsaritsa involved her directly in church matters of a public nature. The Romanov women engaged the help of the supernatural for the protection of their dynasty and promoted the cults of icons and saints that were expected to protect the fortunes of their realm. A striking example of a tsaritsa engaging the protector saints of the royal family on a personal level is found in a pall Evdokiia Luk'ianovna dedicated to Saint Aleksandr Svirskii in 1645. The pall contains medallions featuring the name saints of the royal couple, Saint Michael Maleinos and Saint Eudokia, and those of their children, Saints Alexius, Anna, Irene, and Tatiana.[48] The wife of the first Romanov tsar displayed a vivid interest in miracle-working icons and saints. When the icon of the Virgin of Kazan' appeared to Sofiia, a nun in the Monastery of the Virgin in Kazan', Evdokiia wanted to see the nun personally. After Abbess Anfisa refused to let the sister go to Moscow, the tsaritsa dispatched letters to both Anfisa and Sofiia to press her demand.[49] On February 26, 1634, Evdokiia contacted her previous spiritual guide, the *protopop* Maksim, in Novgorod to enlist his help in procuring information about all miracle-workers in the Novgorod region. The *protopop* complied with her wishes and offered to have all those local *vitae* and miracle-stories that were not known in Moscow copied, should the tsaritsa order it.[50] The tsaritsa had a keen interest in the holy shrines of Novgorod, their patron saints, and their miraculous activities. Already in the previous year, Evdokiia Luk'ianovna and her family had commissioned a shroud for the tomb of the Novgorodian saint Antonii Rimlianin, which was located in the Antoniev Monastery.[51] Clearly Evdokiia Luk'ianovna considered it her business to disseminate the reputation of local holy men in the center of the Muscovite realm and to manage the divine goodwill vis-à-vis the ruler and his realm.

The mediating role in spiritual matters ascribed to the Romanov wives is particularly evident in their veneration of saints who were regarded as special protectors of the Muscovite rulers. When in January 1630 Patriarch Filaret had to leave Moscow, Tsaritsa Evdokiia Luk'ianovna promised to pray for the success of his trip to the Muscovite saints Peter, Aleksii, and Iona. Paul of Aleppo notes Mar'ia Il'inichna's presence at a vigil in honor of Saint Peter, the first metropolitan of Moscow, who was seen as a powerful spiritual intercessor for the tsar. Paul marveled at the steadfastness of the attendants, who stood bareheaded and motionless despite freezing temperatures. The archdeacon, poorly adjusted to the northern climate, claims that his attempt to abandon the liturgy because of the intolerable frost was thwarted by the tsaritsa, who stood in his way.[52]

Their pious behavior earned the wives of the Romanov tsars a certain amount of religious authority. When in 1654 the plague struck Moscow during the tsar's absence and Patriarch Nikon removed himself and the royal family from the capital to escape contagion, the populace expected Mariia Il'inichna to take on the task of providing the spiritual care to those left behind, a responsibility that normally fell to the church leaders. In August 1654 Prince Mikhail Petrovich Pronskoi contacted Mariia Il'inichna in the Koliazinskii Monastery about a religiously motivated popular uprising that had occurred in Moscow. According to Pronskoi, the populace objected to the recent destruction of new-style icons by Patriarch Nikon and brought damaged icons to the Kremlin, insisting that they should be repainted.[53] According to Paul of Aleppo, many Muscovites blamed the plague on their patriarch's unholy act. At a loss about how to proceed in the case, Pronskoi turned to the tsaritsa for a decision. Mariia Il'inichna promptly claimed the authority to uphold the patriarch's position with regard to the icons.[54] Mariia further expressed her concern about the impact of the plague at home in a letter she sent from the Trinity-Sergius Monastery to Pronskoi on August 27, 1654. In an effort to silence the wrath of God, she sent a copy of the icon of the Virgin of Kazan' and an image of a miracle-worker to Moscow. She ordered the local secular and ecclesiastical hierarchies to gather the commoners and greet these images with liturgical chants and candles, and then take them to the Cathedral of the Dormition in the Kremlin. There they were to sing the liturgy and pray to God to deliver them from the scourge that had befallen them.[55]

It is clear from the tsaritsa's correspondence with Pronskoi that, in matters concerning her subjects' interaction with the divine, she enjoyed large discretionary powers. Mariia Il'inichna's letter was composed in her own name and that of Aleksei Alekseevich, her infant son, and only cursorily acknowledged Patriarch Nikon's blessing in the matter. In view of Nikon's shameful abandonment of the flock that God had entrusted to his care, the tsaritsa's initiative in the matter is quite striking, insofar as she ordered the performance of traditional religious rituals normally controlled by the male church hierarchy.[56] Since Mariia Il'inichna gave her instructions with the patriarch's approval, her role in caring for the spiritual well-being of her subjects must have been sanctioned by tradition.

Mariia Il'inichna's initiative to ensure the spiritual salvation of the inhabitants of Moscow at a time when the capital was without its secular and religious leaders makes clear that her religious authority enabled her—at the very least during times of crisis—to reach out to the public and issue orders to its benefit. In some instances her decisions impinged on the prerogatives of the secular and ecclesiastical authorities. In a letter from October 3, 1654, the tsaritsa ordered the closure of the Kremlin gates to protect the Cathedral of the Dormition and the holy relics and liturgical objects of the Kremlin churches. In a letter to Prince Mikhail Petrovich Pronskoi, which Mariia issued from her camp on the River Nerl' on September 7, 1654, she responded to his inquiry concerning the visions of the woman Stefanidka Kolizhenka and her brother Tereshka. As the plague took more victims in Moscow, claims to supernatural experiences arose. Stefanidka and her brother insisted they had seen a holy female figure, but upon investigation they could not agree on her identity and started to accuse each other of lying. When the inquiry did not make progress, Pronskoi sent the testimony to the tsaritsa and asked her for instructions. Mariia Il'inichna promptly decided that both brother and sister were untrustworthy. In another letter from September 7, 1654, Mariia insisted that the few surviving priests in the Cathedral of the Dormition in the Kremlin continue to celebrate the liturgy.[57] On September 22, 1654, the tsaritsa asked Pronskoi for detailed information about the effect of the plague on the city's monasteries and inquired about the names of the monastic and clerical personnel that had survived the calamity.[58]

The content of Mariia Il'inichna's letters to Pronskoi reveals a side of this seventeenth-century tsaritsa that scholars have not yet sufficiently appreciated.[59] Pronskoi's appeal to Mariia in the matter of Stefanidka Koluzhenka and her brother illustrates Mariia's unquestioned authority in matters of the faith. The authentication of visions and other miraculous experiences generally fell to the patriarch and the tsar in seventeenth-century Russia.[60] Clearly the perception existed that, in the absence of both these authorities, the tsaritsa could be trusted to make the correct decision. Mariia Il'inichna was fully aware of the impact of her decision not only on the two persons who allegedly experienced the visions but on the state of affairs in Moscow at large. By categorically denying the truthfulness of Stefanidka and Tereshka's supernatural experience, she undercut possible religiously motivated upheaval in the capital. In the same vein she encouraged the regular performance of the liturgy to give the suffering population access to traditional spiritual care. All in all the tsaritsa's instructions reflected her deep concern for the continued functioning of social and political institutions and the health of her friends and advisers in the Kremlin. Far from her private living quarters in the Moscow citadel, she made decisions in her capacity as spiritual intercessor that affected the lives of a large number of her subjects.

It is not surprising, considering the tsaritsa's religious prestige and her reputed ability to intercede with the tsar, that Mariia Il'inichna became involved in the struggle between religious reformers and the proponents of Old Belief. The tsaritsa was acquainted with Archpriest Avvakum, who together with the metropolitan of Kazan', Kornilii, in June 1552 petitioned her and the tsar to support Stefan Vonifat'ev's candidacy for patriarch of the Russian church.[61] In the struggle over the necessity of religious reform in Russia, Mariia Il'inichna seems to have favored Avvakum's stance. The archpriest was good friends with her kinswoman Anna Petrovna Miloslavskaia, who received him during his stay in Moscow.[62] Avvakum notes in his autobiography that the tsaritsa disagreed with his forced tonsure in 1666 and saved him from capital punishment. When in 1667 Avvakum refused to recant his position, the tsar made a last effort to persuade him to change his mind by asking the archpriest to consider the feelings of his royal wife and children.[63]

The tsaritsa's visibility in the controversy over religious reform in the second half of the seventeenth century reached beyond the person of Avvakum. The circle opposing Nikon's reforms after his accession to the patriarchal seat recognized the value of Mariia Il'inichna's religious prestige and tried to capitalize on it by appealing to her capacity as a mediator in spiritual matters. The tsaritsa was present during the defrocking of Login, archpriest of Murom, by Patriarch Nikon and may have tried to intercede for him. When Ivan Neronov, a priest with wide appeal, objected to Nikon's reforms and was arrested, Avvakum and Daniil of Kostroma appealed to Aleksei Mikhailovich and his wife for his release, a clear sign that they considered the tsaritsa to have influence in affairs of the church. The arrest of Avvakum and Daniil did not stop Neronov from sending his own petition to Mariia on May 2, 1654, to plead for his friends in return.[64] The letter, which is addressed to "the servant of the great God and our Savior Jesus Christ . . . Mistress Tsaritsa and Grand Princess Mariia Il'inichna," reflects Neronov's belief that it was the tsaritsa's business to stop religious persecution in the Russian realm and to impress upon the tsar the wrongful suffering of Avvakum and Daniil. The priest urged her to appear with her recently born son Aleksei Alekseevich before her husband and to plead with him to settle the religious discord in the country before setting out on his Polish campaign. Calling the patriarch an enemy of the church, Neronov predicted the failure of Aleksei Mikhailovich's military venture if Nikon's reforms were not stopped. The direct, polemical tone of the letter suggests that Neronov was comfortable stating his position before the tsaritsa at a time when, according to Neronov's own admission, Aleksei Mikhailovich had ordered him to refrain from sending the tsar any further messages. This impression is reinforced by his expressed desire to see his mistress and to converse with her in person.[65]

In spite of the eventual failure of the Old Believers to garner the support of the royal couple, the relations between Mariia Il'inichna and Nikon's opponents show that the Romanov women were considered champions of the Orthodox faith in Russia, not only in narrow court circles but also among clerics of the church. Like Irina Godunova who had been involved in the establishment of the first Russian patriarchate, Mariia Il'inichna had the right to help choose a successor to the patriarchal seat. The dissenters to Patriarch Nikon's policies addressed her as a patroness of their cause and counted on her active support. In none of their appeals did they treat the tsaritsa merely as a pious figure who was well disposed to their beliefs, but who lacked significance. Ivan Neronov's letter proves that the Old Believers counted on Mariia Il'inichna's action in their battle for the survival of the true faith in Russia.

The integral role the wife of the Romanov tsar played in both the secular and religious affairs of the Muscovite realm is reflected in a series of twelve laments Simeon Polotskii composed on the occasion of Mariia Il'inichna's death in 1669. The *Freny, ili plachi vsekh sanov i chinov pravoslavnago Rossiiskago tsarstva o smerti blagovernyia i khristoliubivyia gosudaryni tsaritsy i velikiia kniagini Marii Il'inichny (Threnodies or Dirges of all Ranks and Orders of the Orthodox Russian Realm about the Death of the Pious and Christ-loving Mistress Tsaritsa and Grand Princess Mariia Il'inichna)* project a composite image of the tsaritsa's major functions from the perspective of the Muscovite realm's political, social, and economic institutions.[66] The tsar's lament composed by Polotskii praised Mariia Il'inichna as a helpmate to her husband in all matters, whether personal, governmental, or spiritual. The threnody of the holy church council expressed the same sentiment, calling the tsaritsa a precious jewel and a golden crown that God had bestowed upon the tsar, a rock of the realm, and the confirmation of the entire government. The laments of the clergy, the monasteries, and the poor, orphans, and widows highlight the tsaritsa's charitable activities and call her a communal mother to all.[67] The tsaritsa's ability to intercede for her subjects comes to the fore in the lament of the Russian towns.[68] The Orthodox army appreciated her inclination to reward distinguished servitors and to promote them in rank. For the Russian troops, the tsaritsa represented an intercessor before God who prayed for their safety and victory. Like the prayers of Moses on the mountain, Mariia's supplications in her chambers were considered holy. Without them the army did not dare move against the enemy.[69] Finally, the church militant appreciated Mariia Il'inichna's cooperation with the tsar in removing religious dissenters from Moscow the second Jerusalem.[70]

The major themes of the laments composed by Polotskii surprisingly parallel those found in the documentary sources. Polotskii merely elaborated on commonly held notions of the tsaritsa's role in Muscovite society. The threnodies point to Mariia Il'inichna's placement at the nexus between the public and private. Through her personal religious disposition, the wife of the Romanov tsar transcended the boundaries between the female living quarters of the *terem* and the male sphere of government.

. . .

Thus, the Romanov wives' association with a structured life in the *terem* was not synonymous with physical and social isolation and an inability to influence public events. The discussion must now turn to an examination of the impact of the *terem* on the remaining female members of the royal family, that is, the tsar's sisters and daughters. The social position of the Romanov tsars' female children differed from that of the tsaritsa insofar as they remained unmarried.[71] Boris Godunov had still tried to find a suitor for his daughter, Kseniia, and Mikhail Fedorovich expended considerable effort to arrange a wedding for his daughter Irina. Both matches failed because of the unwillingness of the foreign grooms to convert to Orthodoxy.[72] The religious barrier foiled future plans to marry the Muscovite tsars' female children to foreign princes. At the same time, the Romanovs were unwilling to accept one of their own noble subjects into their family. Although Kotoshikhin insists that the lower social status of a Russian suitor represented an insurmountable obstacle to marrying a tsarevna, the tsars' objection to a Russian son-in-law or brother-in-law stemmed more likely from the memory of the circumstances of the demise of the Rurikide line (that is, Boris Godunov's influence over his frail brother-in-law) and from the desire of the new regime to distance itself from other noble kin groups in the realm.[73] From this perspective, McNally's argument that the tsarevny of the seventeenth century were deprived of the option of influencing public life by functioning as links between families undoubtedly holds true. Nevertheless, one cannot simply assume that the tsarevny's passive social role in marriage politics meant that they led trivial lives within the confines of the *terem*.[74] A close examination of the role of the sisters and daughters of Aleksei Mikhailovich suggests that the tsarevny of the Romanov period shared in the respect and function of the tsaritsa. Like their mothers, the tsarevny were intimately familiar with the political events affecting the court and represented sources of spiritual support for the tsar when he was exposed to political or personal dangers.

The daughters of Mikhail Fedorovich and Aleksei Mikhailovich retained a certain amount of visibility by sharing in the charitable activities of their respective mothers. Requests by hierarchs of the Eastern Orthodox church for alms often included specific petitions to the Russian tsarevny. In 1649 the patriarch of Jerusalem, Paisius, provided Mikhail Fedorovich's daughters Irina, Anna, and Tat'iana with lists of liturgical vestments, vessels, and icons that were needed by his religious establishments. The practice continued into Peter the Great's reign.[75]

The daughters of the Romanov tsars received regular public attention at the court in Moscow. Mikhail Fedorovich made it a habit to observe the name days of his daughters along with that of his wife.[76] While these feasts were regularly celebrated with banquets in both the tsar's and the tsaritsa's chambers, the tsar often used these occasions to demonstrate his goodwill toward his subjects. The tsar elevated several men to the rank of boyar on May 5 and July 25, 1635, in honor of Irina Mikhailovna's and Anna Mikhailovna's name saints.[77] The tsar also was known to pardon subjects during the feast days of his daughters' personal saints.[78] Aleksei Mikhailovich fastidiously continued his father's practice and celebrated the name days of his wife, sisters, and children even during his absence from Moscow on military campaigns.[79] The personal attention the Romanov tsars paid to their sisters and daughters and their display of royal largesse and mercy on the tsarevny's name days suggest that the tsarevny, like their mothers, were intricately woven into the fabric of court life, which consisted of both public and private strands.

Aleksei Mikhailovich, who based his public performance on well-functioning domestic relations, relied heavily on his sisters to assure that all his family members were well cared for and lived together in harmony. According to Kotoshikhin, the tsar's sisters had the arduous task of guarding his bride from injurious acts by boyar families before his wedding. The *Mazurinskii Chronicle* states that in 1681 Tsar Fedor Alekseevich even sought the advice of his sisters concerning a second marriage.[80] In his letters to his family from the Smolensk campaign, Aleksei Mikhailovich repeatedly implored his sisters not to abandon his wife and children, who were his most precious possessions, but to take care of them and live in concord with them.[81] The tsar may have been concerned about the condition of his pregnant wife and enlisted his sisters' help to make certain of her safe delivery. The sisters seem to have accepted this responsibility. Shortly before Aleksei Alekseevich's birth in 1654, Irina Mikhailovna gave thirty rubles to a female monastery in Aleksandrov with the stipulation that the nuns pray for the pregnant tsaritsa. Aleksei Mikhailovich placed great trust in Irina's ability to care for his male offspring. After the birth of his first son, Tsarevich Dmitrii, in 1648, he appointed his elder sister as the child's godmother.[82] Aleksei himself seems to have projected his feelings for his mother onto Irina after Tsaritsa Evdokiia Luk'ianovna had passed away. During the tsarevna's lifetime he directed most of his correspondence with his family to her and regularly addressed her in his letters as "my mistress and mother, the pious tsarevna and grand princess Irina Mikhailovna."[83] Paul of Aleppo notes that the tsar regularly sought the advice of his elder sister, who had served as his governess in his youth.[84] The endowment of Irina Mikhailovna with the status of symbolic motherhood suggests that the tsarevny of the early Romanov period essentially shared in the tsaritsy's duties to act as helpmates to the tsar and to look after the success of his dynasty and his realm.

Since the tsar himself provided the link between the *terem* members and the outside world, it appears fruitful to investigate the direct communication between the Russian ruler and his women for its implications for their perceived and actual roles. The extant correspondence between Aleksei Mikhailovich and his family (seventy letters written between 1654 and 1675) provides an excellent opportunity to define the construction of royal female seclusion in the Romanov period. The letters, which have been studied so far only for their political information (such as details of the tsar's Smolensk campaign), also contain a wealth of information about the *terem* members' knowledge of current issues. The tsar expected his family to stay closely in touch with him during his absences from Moscow. In order to express his bond with the members of his family from afar, he penned personal notes in his own hand at the end of the dictated letters. He apologized profusely when circumstances prevented him from doing so. For example, in a letter from June 3, 1654, he regretted that a headache had interfered with his writing a separate note.[85] The tsar obviously expected that his female family members would handle his mail personally although they, too, used the help of scribes to answer it.[86] Unfortunately none of the women's letters seem to have survived, but Aleksei Mikhailovich referred frequently to his family's messages to him in the field.[87] On the whole, the tsar kept in close touch with his domestic circle, even in times of intense military activity. During his 1554 and 1555 campaigns he wrote home an average of once a week.

Judging from the content of Aleksei Mikhailovich's letters, the *terem* structure did not insulate royal women from the difficulties generally associated with the male sphere of action. Aleksei Mikhailovich's letters to his sisters, wife, and children distinguish themselves by the pragmatic details with which he expected his family to be familiar. Beyond the exchange of terms of endearment and inquiries concerning the health of the royal family, the tsar imparted to the members of his *terem* vital information concerning his military campaign. The tsar usually did not send home polished accounts of successful parts of his campaign, but he shared with his family his immediate experience on the road. Once the tsar wrote home about his frustration with a particularly slow troop muster.[88] Each of his letters from the Smolensk campaign gives details of his exact whereabouts. Often the tsar identified his planned date of departure and his next intended stop along his campaign route.[89] The tsarevny and the tsaritsa also received reports about tactical problems posed by rough roads, the reconnaissance of enemy territory, the coordination of troop contingents, the fortification of enemy towns, and the maintenance of supplies in the field.[90] The tsar shared with them his knowledge of his enemy's troop movements and strength.[91] After an armed confrontation he sent home a detailed description of the battle and its outcome regardless of whether he had been victorious or not. The tsar often included a comparison of the enemy's losses and his own casualties.[92] He particularly rejoiced to his family about the capture of spies and important enemy figures and itemized the booty his troops amassed.[93]

The tsar's detailed accounts of his military ventures to his family reveal that—in contrast to Kotoshikhin's assertion—he expected his female family members to keep current about matters of war and peace. The tsarevny and the tsaritsa shared in the Russian ruler's plans, challenges, anxieties, and failures in the field in spite of their physical removal from this traditionally male sphere of action. Although it is impossible to establish with any degree of certainty the royal women's competence in military matters, the very fact that they were regularly inundated with information of this type suggests that the *terem* was not the site only of leisurely activities such as embroidery and pleasurable games, as Zabelin suggests.[94] The tsar's own desire to communicate his experience on the battlefield provided the opportunity to his wife, sisters, and children to acquire practical knowledge of Russia's enemies and of the art of warfare, which they could foster if they so chose.

In addition to providing information about his confrontation with his enemies, the tsar shared with his womenfolk at home his observations on the performance of the Muscovite political elite in the field.[95] The women were not spared gruesome reports of the fate of traitors, such as that of the *syn' boiarskii* Vaska Mikhailov *syn'* Neelov from Smolensk, who was captured, forced to confess, and eventually quartered. The tsar, however, also took pains to pass on the names of individuals in his regiments who had distinguished themselves in his service. When on June 29, 1654, the boyar Vasilii Petrovich Sheremetev achieved the capitulation of Polotsk after a successful battle, the *terem* members found out about it.[96]

Aleksei Mikhailovich's correspondence with his family members concerning his commanders in the field reached beyond an enumeration of their achievements or failures. In 1655 the tsar informed his female relatives of the death of his *stol'nik* Semen Ivanov *syn'* Shein after six days of suffering. When during the 1656 campaign Aleksei Mikhailovich's close adviser, Prince Nikita Ivanovich Odoevskii, informed the tsar that his son Fedor had died in his lord's service, the Russian ruler attached Odoevskii's note to him to one of his own letters to his family. Since the prince had asked for royal kindness for his son's surviving wife and children, it is likely that the tsar in his absence placed the task of looking after Fedor Nikitich's family on his female relatives in the *terem*. A letter by Mariia Il'inichna and her son Aleksei dating from October 3, 1554, testifies to the tsaritsa's initiative in making the final arrangements for the burial of Prince Maikhail Petrovich Pronskoi. The tsaritsa also took care of Pronskoi's surviving daughter.[97] At the very least, the fact that the tsar passed Odoevskii's note on to his tsaritsa and tsarevny suggests that they closely followed the fate of leading kin groups at the court.

Tsar Aleksei Mikhailovich's regular correspondence with his wife, sisters, and children contributed to a widening of the intellectual confines of the royal *terem* and acquainted the female sphere with the hard political and military reality. It demonstrates that the tsarevny, just as their mother, were expected to play a direct role in the events involving the tsar by acting as perpetual intercessors for him before God. Scholars of the royal *terem* in favor of the seclusion theory base much of their argument on Kotoshikhin's assertion that the tsar's sisters and daughters lived a hermitic life marked by prayer, fasting, and the shedding of tears. These scholars, however, do not analyze the meaning of this image. Kotoshikhin's description of the life of the tsarevny does not necessarily represent evidence for their cruel treatment by an autocratic system that found no use for them. Kotoshikhin, who himself was a Russian subject and thus familiar with the institution of the *terem*, may simply have referred to a known sociocultural construct.[98] His allusion to the tsarevny's devotion to prayers, fasting, and weeping in seclusion conjures up the images of nuns, who through their commitment to pious deeds not only strive to achieve their own salvation but incur God's favor for the community at large. The gift of tears, *umilenie,* was one of the most highly prized spiritual qualities in Muscovite Russia. Fasting and praying generally were seen in medieval Russia as God-pleasing actions. Paul of Aleppo marveled at the strict fasting and prayer schedule of both the tsar and the tsaritsa during Lent.[99]

The remark by Kotoshikhin, a previous clerk in the Foreign Office *(Posol'skii prikaz),* may not have been so much a scathing criticism of the Russian autocrat's neglect of his female relatives as a shrugging off of the royal women's spiritual role, which was widely accepted in Russia. This argument finds support in the correspondence of Aleksei Mikhailovich with his sisters, wife, and children. In his letter from May 26, 1654, he encouraged his female kin to place their trust in God so that He would strengthen them in their fasting and praying. The tsar expected his womenfolk to pray regularly for his health and his success in the campaign and often attributed his military successes to their intercessory prayers.[100] In his correspondence Aleksei Mikhailovich liked to equate the spiritual task of the tsarevny to that of the patriarch of Russia, who traditionally prayed for the tsar's success in times of crisis.[101]

The religious connotation of the position of all female members of the royal *terem* surfaces as well in Aleksei Mikhailovich's accounts of his devotional activities and spiritual experiences during the campaign. Thus he told his family when the cross of Constantine the Great arrived in his camp from Mount Athos. The cross that once had helped Constantine to victory over his foe Maxentius strengthened Aleksei in his conviction that his campaign found God's favor. The tsar informed his family whenever he received communion. In each instance he ascribed the fact that God considered him worthy of receiving the body of Christ to the cleansing intercessory prayers of his nearest female kin. Aleksei Mikhailovich also felt duty bound to relate his most private spiritual experiences to the members of the royal *terem* in the expectation that they would rejoice with him. Thus in August 1656 he wrote them about a vision in which Saints Boris and Gleb ordered him to consecrate a church to the Russian royal martyr saint Dmitrii in the captured town of Kokkenhausen.[102] The letters relating to the tsar's pious experiences during his campaign in many ways parallel his customary correspondence from the pilgrimage path.[103] Both types of communication served to instruct the royal women about the spiritual status of the autocracy, which they were to monitor and protect. From this perspective, it is not surprising that some of the tsarevny, like the tsaritsa, became involved in the struggle over Old Belief. According to Avvakum's autobiography, Tsarevna Irina Mikhailovna took mercy on his suffering in exile and sent him clothes during his stay in Tobolsk.[104]

. . .

Past evaluations of the structure of the royal *terem* in seventeenth-century Muscovy have generally assumed a sharp dividing line between the public and the private spheres at the court of the first two Romanov tsars. The assignment of the Russian ruler's wife, sisters, and daughters to a secluded area in the Kremlin has led scholars to the conclusion that the autocracy deliberately secluded its women from public life. As a result women's ability to exert influence on affairs of state or to play any meaningful social or cultural role was seriously curtailed. Although the Romanovs undoubtedly practiced ritual seclusion of their women, a clear understanding of the structure and function of the royal *terem* can be gained only by an evaluation of the exact relationship between the perceived public and private aspects of family life in the Kremlin. The details emerging from this study suggest that the royal *terem* was a complex institution that contained both public and private elements, resulting in an overlapping of the traditional male and female spheres of action. The relegation of the Romanov women to gender-specific living quarters in the Kremlin did not simply follow an earlier, sixteenth-century tradition because the period of dynastic confusion had thoroughly disrupted royal family life and released the tsaritsy into an insecure political arena. The fear of further erosion of the tsar's position posed by intense court rivalries drove the Romanovs to regulate the conduct and influence of their women. The resulting ritualization of the roles of the tsaritsy and tsarevny—although disturbing from a modern feminist perspective—did not inevitably lead to a trivialization of their lives. Within their women's sphere, the tsaritsy and tsarevny retained a great deal of legal, economic, and administrative autonomy. The ritual seclusion of the Romanov women did not entail complete spatial confinement and isolation from the issues of the day. Under more or less controlled circumstances, these women often left the Kremlin and even the capital and interacted with their subjects during pilgrimages. While his female relatives were residing in the *terem*, the tsar himself kept them informed about current events, significant political and military figures, and the tedious details of governing. As a result, the tsaritsa, her children, and royal sisters-in-law residing with her in the women's quarters had the opportunity, if they so chose, to acquire a certain amount of practical and technical knowledge of statecraft.

A critique of the popular seclusion theory must not only address the Romanov women's opportunity to transcend the physical boundaries of the *terem* but also consider the extent of the social impact and cultural significance of these women. The involvement of both the tsaritsy and the tsarevny in the issuing of royal pardons and the practice of charity shows that, in spite of their ritual seclusion (or possibly on account of it), the Romanov women served as facilitators of social justice and peace. The correspondence of Aleksei Mikhailovich with female members of his family suggests that he considered them active supporters in his struggle to protect and maintain the well-being of his realm. Perhaps the significance of the wives, sisters, and daughters of the Romanov tsars for the functioning of the autocracy is most evident in their religious role. Their perceived ability to act as personal spiritual intercessors for the tsar and as guardians of the Orthodox faith in their country gave them a great deal of prestige. It placed them at the nexus between the spheres of earthly government and the divine will, the control of which was deemed crucial to the success of the Muscovite government. Within the autocratic regime of seventeenth-century Russia, the Romanov women did not represent mere pawns but, rather, actively promoted the goals of the tsardom. Therefore, rather than regarding the confines of the royal *terem* as a wall that prevented women from having contact with the world at large and from exerting any public influence, we might be better served to view the *terem* as a kind of osmotic membrane that allowed women to enjoy social prestige and to participate in matters of state from a safe distance.

5 Sofiia Alekseevna, the Tsarevna as Ruler

IN CONTRAST TO ALL OTHER Muscovite royal women, Sofiia Alekseevna, the sixth child of Tsar Aleksei Mikhailovich, has been the subject of numerous studies. Struck by the tsarevna's political visibility during her regency for her brothers Ivan and Peter from 1682 to 1689, historians in Russia and abroad have been quick to compare her to her famous half brother, who forcefully hurled Russia into the modern period. This approach predictably placed Sofiia Alekseevna's accomplishments in an unfavorable light. The many scholars who stood in awe of Peter the Great as a ruler and innovator were bound to find fault with his sister, who contested his sole rule. Apologists for Peter criticized Sofiia Alekseevna's governing skills and her reluctance or inability to bring about lasting cultural change in Russia and accused her of being infatuated with power and intrigue—the former a trait traditionally reserved to men, the latter all too readily ascribed to women. At best scholars saw her as a transitional figure who prepared the way for Peter's reforms. At the opposite end of the scale, critics of Sofiia's regency indulged in lurid descriptions of her private life and unflattering utterances about her physical appearance and femininity.[1]

Under these circumstances the recent studies by Lindsey Hughes, A. P. Bogdanov, and Elizabeth Zelensky, which focus on Sofiia Alekseevna's regency for its own sake, represent a refreshing change.[2] All three authors emphasize the cultural and political creativity of the regent's court and its receptiveness to Western ideas in its conceptualization of the Russian autocracy. Hughes in particular sheds light on Sofiia Alekseevna's accession to power in 1682, which she sees as a lucky coincidence of accidents of birth and death in the royal family, the result of court rivalries, social and economic tensions resulting in the uprising of the musketeers *(stre'ltsy),* and the regent's personal ambition.[3] This assessment treats Sofiia's regency as a unique phase in Russian history, during which Muscovite traditions gradually gave way to the conventions of the modern Russian state. The themes of modernization and westernization also underlie the studies of Bogdanov and Zelensky, who seek to discover the roots of Russia's new concept of sovereignty in the Imperial period in the artistic productions of the court culture of the 1680s.

The sustained scholarly interest in Sofiia Alekseevna's regency undoubtedly has helped to separate myth from fact regarding her accomplishments as a person and ruler and to illuminate the political and cultural creativity in the decade before Peter's accession to power. Nevertheless, the question as to how a royal daughter could assume and retain the position of a female ruler in a highly structured patriarchal environment in spite of the presence of two brothers has not yet found a satisfactory answer.[4] Hughes and Zelensky, who both are sensitive to the challenges Sofiia Alekseevna faced as a female sovereign, essentially treat her role as woman ruler as a new phenomenon in Russian history. In Hughes's view, the fourth daughter of Aleksei Mikhailovich managed to assert herself in this role by balancing traditional social restrictions and religious requirements imposed on royal women with her own formulation of royal rituals, titles, and literary and artistic portrayals of her person. Zelensky as well proceeds from the assumption that Sofiia Alekseevna's success as a sovereign ultimately depended on her skill to overcome the marginalization of women by their patriarchal environment through the creation of new legitimacy-granting paradigms, such as "Sofiia the Wisdom of God."[5] None of these interpretations, however, provides a ready answer to the puzzle as to why there was little outcry against the appearance of a female ruler in 1682. They do not explain how it was possible for a royal daughter without any apparent political experience and right to rule to rise out of the obscurity of the *terem* chambers and take over the reins of government. Furthermore, if indeed medieval Russian social, cultural, and political traditions were so hostile to the idea of a woman ruler, why did Sofiia Alekseevna and her court resort so much to the gender-specific symbolism of Muscovite royal myths and rituals to strengthen the regent's position?

A complete reinterpretation of Sofiia Alekseevna's achievements would go far beyond the scope of this study. Nevertheless, the focus of this book on the construction of the ideal and the actual roles of the Muscovite royal women invites an inquiry into possible connections between the social, religious, and political conditions that shaped Sofiia's position as a regent and that of her female ancestors. Even if we allow for the progressive westernization of the Russian court culture from the 1670s onward, the simultaneous interest of the court ideologues in traditional Orthodox rituals and myths, evident in their construction of Sofiia's image as a ruler, justifies such an endeavor.[6] Rather than adopting the stance that Sofiia Alekseevna was essentially a modern ruler who struggled to free herself from the constraints of a medieval environment, this study chooses to investigate how this royal daughter manipulated the patriarchal structures that shaped her childhood and adolescence in order to boost her political visibility.[7] The evidence suggests that both Sofiia's ascendance to power in 1682 and her role as regent for her two brothers were sanctioned by socioreligious conventions surrounding royal wives and daughters, which were flexible enough to accommodate new, even secular, notions of sovereignty in Russia. Although Sofiia Alekseevna was the first tsarevna to take the reins of government, the similar function of tsaritsy and tsarevny in the royal *terem* of the late seventeenth century provided her with an opportunity to claim for herself the throne-worthiness of a tsar's wife—so evident in the cases of Irina Godunova and Mariia Grigor'evna. The blurred distinction between the role of royal wives and daughters is also observed in the mythopoeic endeavors of the court designed to justify Sofiia's position in the ruling trinity alongside her two brothers. The court rhetoric and its visual expression in royal portraiture constructed the regent's power in feminine terms, often employing identical or similar metaphors that had been applied previously to the tsaritsy. This feminine interpretation of Sofiia's position as autocrat existed throughout her seven-year regency and persisted alongside more masculine conceptions, which surfaced after 1686 in the wake of plans to make her a crowned ruler.

The roles of the tsarevny and tsaritsy in the royal *terem* in the late seventeenth century were bound to inform decisively the political future of Sofiia Alekseevna. Unfortunately the dim view most scholars take of the institution of the *terem* prevents them from appreciating its positive impact on the royal daughter. Experts on Sofiia Alekseevna's life and career tend to stress her physical seclusion from public life in her youth and to repeat Kotoshikhin's and Meyerberg's assertions that the royal *terem* oppressed its members with rote, meaningless, and unintellectual tasks, reducing their lives to an existence of unending drudgery and boredom.[8] If the royal *terem* had any redeeming value at all, it was to be found in the "aura of exclusivity" that aided Sofiia Alekseevna in establishing her authenticity as a ruler. In general, however, scholars emphasize Sofiia's pathbreaking endeavor to rid herself from the *terem*'s constraints, a feat facilitated by Tsaritsa Natal'ia Kirillovna Naryshkina's innovations in the royal family life.[9] The findings in this current study regarding the role of the tsaritsy and tsarevny in the early Romanov period, however, suggest that the conventions surrounding these women are not necessarily proof of their low political and social status and inability to rule. A closer look at the perception of the members of Sofiia Alekseevna's family and their behavior suggests that to a large extent Sofiia Alekseevna owed her emergence on the political scene in 1682 to the conditions of the royal *terem*, which functioned as a receptacle of royal blood and legitimacy.

When, in the seventeenth century, the tsars produced numerous daughters who grew to adulthood, the prospect of the proliferation of royal blood in the female line affected the status of the tsarevny profoundly. Scholars are right to point out that the autocracy's fear of rivals for the throne resulting in the stipulation that royal daughters were not allowed to marry affected the tsarevny's social position adversely insofar as they could not function as links between kin groups.[10] Their effective removal from the marriage market, however, and their confinement in the *terem* (along with their mothers and future sisters-in-law) did not erase the fact that they shared in the special blood status of the tsars' line, a kind of throne-worthiness that extended to all the immediate members of the royal family. While this particular quality did not constitute a right to rule per se, it could be used in a dynastic emergency—when mature male blood was not available—to justify a claim by any female member of the royal *terem*.[11] The perceived participation of royal daughters in the throne-worthiness determined by blood is evident already in the inclusion of Tsarevna Kseniia Borisovna Godunova in the loyalty oath required by Tsaritsa Mariia Grigor'evna and Tsar Fedor Borisovich from their subjects in 1605, and in the rape and forced tonsure of the unfortunate tsarevna by the False Dmitrii.[12] During the reigns of the first two Romanov tsars, it had been common practice to make subjects swear the oath of allegiance not only to the tsar, but to the entire royal family.[13] In 1682 when Tsar Fedor Alekseevich's death left the realm without a viable male successor, resulting in a conflict between the Miloslavskii branch of the royal family (which backed Fedor's handicapped brother, Ivan) and the Naryshkin faction (which rallied behind Peter, the son of Aleksei Mikhailovich and his second wife, Natal'ia), the idea of the throne-worthiness of the royal *terem* members presented itself as an opportunity to the royal women in either camp to grasp the reins of government.

The notion of the tsarevny's throne-worthiness seems to have been widely accepted in the 1680s. Records in the Chancellery of Military Affairs *(Razriadnyi prikaz)* from the early period of Sofiia Alekseevna's regency show that, after Fedor Alekseevich's death, loyalty oaths continued to be sworn to the entire royal family.[14] Sil'vestr Medvedev's account of the events of 1682 (composed approximately two years later) states that the secular and ecclesiastical authorities, together with the women of the royal *terem*, had jointly decided to establish Sofiia Alekseevna as regent for the two tsarevichi. Regardless of their veracity, the rumors circulating in the fall of 1682—that Ivan Khovanskii had plotted to kill Natal'ia Kirillovna and Sofiia Alekseevna—imply that both the tsar mother and her step-daughter represented legitimate royal authorities, who had to be reckoned with. In the same vein, the accusation that Ivan Khovanskii's son Andrei intended to marry a tsarevna and to force the remaining royal daughters to live as nuns in distant monasteries demonstrates that the female royal children were credited with the ability to convey the right to rule because of their blood ties to the previous ruler.[15]

The tsarevny themselves seem to have entertained the notion of their throne-worthiness. Accustomed to the rhetoric of court poetry, which eulogized them as "sovereign ladies" *(gosudaryni)*, a title usually reserved to the tsars' wives, they came to claim this title for themselves. According to the inscription of a tapestry donated by Mariia Alekseevna in 1687, the tsarevna referred to herself by the same title—expressing sovereignty—that she ascribed to her siblings Ivan, Peter, and Sofiia.[16] Her sister Marfa Alekseevna seems to have sympathized with the notion of a royal daughter on the throne as well. During the *strel'tsy* uprising of 1698, which aimed to restore Sofiia Alekseevna to power, Marfa informed her sister (then confined in the Novodevichii Monastery) of the revolt. Peter the Great, who had interrogated both Marfa and Sofiia, feared the interference and possible competition of the two sisters so much so that he resorted to the time-honored practice of forced tonsure to remove them from the public eye.[17] In his attempt to break up the network of royal women, Peter also moved against his aunt Tat'iana Mikhailovna, who supplied the confined Tsarevna Sofiia with news. In October 1698 he restricted the visiting privileges of his sisters and Tat'iana Mikhailovna at the Novodevichii Monastery to Easter, the monastery's main feast day, and extreme emergencies.[18]

In addition to relying on the throne-worthiness of all royal women in the *terem*, Sofiia Alekseevna also could draw on the women's traditional role as advisers and supporters to the tsar to advance her claim to the regency for Ivan Alekseevich and his younger brother, Peter. The phenomenon of a tsarevna counseling a brother in affairs of state can already be observed in the case of Sofiia's father, who during his youth sought the advice of his elder sister Irina Mikhailovna. According to Paul of Aleppo, Aleksei Mikhailovich respected her for her educated and sensible decisions. In his adult years the tsar continued to share information concerning political matters with Irina Mikhailovna and other female members of his family, as the letters by the tsar from his Polish campaign in 1654–1656 prove. Sofiia Alekseevna had ample opportunity to familiarize herself with the tsar's responsibilities as ruler while she was growing up in the *terem*. Since infancy her name was included in her father's letters to his wife, sisters, and children in which he described his daily activities.[19]

During Sofiia Alekseevna's regency, the tradition that the tsarevny functioned as the confidants of the Russian ruler was cleverly exploited by her court poets, who sought to elevate her status through elaborate odes. In his first eulogy for Sofiia after her official recognition as regent, Sil'vestr Medvedev, who metaphorically described the Russian autocracy as a double-headed eagle whose heads represented the two tsars, referred to the royal daughters and wives as the bird's wings that made its soaring flight possible, that is, as guarantors of the autocracy's success. In the later part of Sofiia's regency, the eagle-wing metaphor was married to the "Sophia the Wisdom of God" paradigm associated with the regent. In his interpretation of the Novgorodian variant of the image "Sophia the Wisdom of God" from August 1689, Ignatii Rimskii-Korsakov eulogized the regent's surviving aunts, Anna and Tat'iana, as the wings of Divine Wisdom. Sofiia Alekseevna is presented as a guide and counselor to her brothers.[20] The same theme emerges in a dedication ascribed to Karion Istomin, which dates from the first year of Sofiia's regency. The author compared the tsarevna to Pulcheria, the sister of the Byzantine emperor Theodosius II, who imposed on herself and her sisters a vow of chastity to protect her child brother's right to the throne. The poem stresses the royal stock of the pious Pulcheria, who governed during her brother's minority, and points out how she imparted her wisdom to the young Theodosius and instructed him in affairs of state.[21] The court poetry exemplifies the Muscovite elite's awareness of the notion that tsarevny, just as the tsars' wives, could function as helpmates to the tsars. It also shows how Sofiia Alekseevna's regency was based to a large degree on traditional notions concerning the transfer of power to a female of royal descent in times of dynastic crisis. If a tsarevna was allowed to function as mentor and adviser for her tsar brothers, the inclusion of her name in royal rescripts and her participation in matters of the court was but a logical further step.

Just as the legitimacy of ruling royal wives was based on their perceived affinity to the divine, Sofiia Alekseevna's right as a tsarevna to govern for her brothers ultimately depended on her reputation for piety, which could induce God to bestow his favor on the Russian realm. Aleksei Mikhailovich had regularly asked his sisters and daughters to pray for his success. In the 1680s the connection between the tsarevny's austere life-style, their angelic chastity, and devotional activities can be observed repeatedly in the court literature. In his funeral oration for Fedor Alekseevich from 1682, Sil'vestr Medvedev called the mourning tsarevny "members of the angelic order." Karion Istomin praised the tsarevny's continuous prayers, their abstinence, charity, and mercy in his *"Panegiris,"* the preface of a book he dedicated to Sofiia Alekseevna on September 17, 1687. Ignatii Rimskii-Korsakov expressed similar sentiments in his exegesis of the Novgorod Sophia icon. In his dedication from 1682–1683, Karion Istomin celebrated Sofiia for her patience in prayer, her assiduous commitment to fasting, and her undaunted faith in Christ. In another oration composed in connection with the dedication of the book *Bogovidnaia liubov' (God-like Love)* in March 1687, the same author praised her for her piety and eagerness to resort to prayers whenever she encountered adversity in her position as a ruler.[22]

The perceived connection between the tsarevny's religious lifestyle and the fortunes of the autocracy (and, by implication, the Russian realm at large) makes it difficult to agree with Zabelin and Hughes, who interpret Sofiia Alekseevna's monastic and ascetic tendencies as a private phenomenon and a throwback to old-fashioned traditions that impeded the full expression of her abilities as a ruler.[23] Although scholars generally focus on Sofiia's claim to function as a sovereign co-ruler, a claim that came to fruition after 1686, they have ignored that, whereas her brothers were referred to as "great sovereign tsars," she alone consistently was given the title "great sovereign lady and pious tsarevna."[24] The gender-specific formulae in addressing the royal siblings make it clear that the conventions of the royal *terem* carried with them their own legitimizing force, which Sofiia could take advantage of. In the 1680s the notion of the "pious tsarevna" represented a viable alternative to the concept of the pious Orthodox tsar in defining the position of a female ruler.

Sofiia Alekseevna's awareness of the royal *terem*'s potential role in sanctioning a female ruler is also evident in her desire to tap the prestige inherent in the position of the tsaritsa to strengthen her own claim to rule. Sofiia's joint actions with various tsaritsy in 1682 were designed to show off the tsarevna's equal status to that of a tsaritsa. In order to appear as a mediator in the conflict between the court factions and as a proponent of the rightful heir to the throne, Sofiia associated herself with the widow of the late tsar, Tsaritsa Marfa Matveevna Apraksina. When rumors circulated that Ivan Alekseevich might have fallen victim to a Naryshkin plot, the two women made a public appearance on May 15, 1682, to present the unharmed tsarevich to the crowd.[25] According to Heinrich Butenant's account, Sofiia Alekseevna and Marfa Matveevna both openly engaged in negotiations with Ivan Andreevich Khovanskii and other nobles on the Kremlin grounds the following day. The same source states that the two women jointly defended the honor of the royal throne by standing up against Ivan Naryshkin, who allegedly tried on the royal regalia. They again appeared, on May 17, this time with Tsaritsa Natal'ia Kirillovna, to plead with the *strel'tsy* for Naryshkin's life.[26] In all cases the tsarevna demonstrated her capacity to fulfill the traditional roles of a legitimate tsaritsa as peacemaker, caretaker of the royal throne, and pious intercessor. Sofiia Alekseevna's appearance next to the late tsar Fedor Alekseevich's wife, the accepted vehicle of a dynastic transfer of power, further underscored the legitimacy of her position. Sofiia's readiness to share the limelight with her rival, her stepmother Natal'ia Kirillovna, illustrates her ability to manipulate to her own advantage the legitimizing potential inherent in the tsaritsa's position. Sofiia's joint appearance with the tsaritsa expressed the message that she claimed the same position vis-à-vis Ivan Alekseevich that her stepmother held with regard to her son Peter. At the same time, her intercession for a member of the Naryshkin clan showed her capacity of displaying compassion and mercy, which was usually associated with the role of the tsaritsa. The following day, May 18, Sofiia exercised her right to plead alone; by asking the crowd to show mercy to Natal'ia's father, she effectively stepped into her stepmother's role.[27]

The conscious appropriation of aspects of the tsaritsa's image by Sofiia Alekseevna is particularly evident in the tsarevna's involvement in religious ritual. To assume (as Hughes does) that Sofiia engaged in a "feminized version of that 'nightmare religiosity' created at the court of her father," because it lent her an aura of exclusivity, represents a misunderstanding of both Sofiia's model of piety and the image it conveyed. Throughout her regency Sofiia emulated the charitable activities usually—though not exclusively—associated with the tsaritsa. She commissioned religious architecture in the new baroque style, along with icons and other liturgical objects, and attended the consecration of chapels and churches. In a panegyric to Sofiia Alekseevna from September 17, 1687, Karion Istomin praised her for her generous gifts to monasteries and poorhouses and her rich endowments of churches in Russia. Moreover, Sofiia Alekseevna also imitated the tsaritsa's involvement in pilgrimages to monasteries and other holy sites, and in the processions of icons.[28] During a service in the Cathedral of the Dormition on February 22, 1687, for the troops departing for the first Crimean campaign, Sofiia witnessed the consecration of banners, crosses, and icons that were to accompany and protect the troops. She was seated on the throne that was customarily reserved for the tsar's wife.[29]

Sofiia also sought to appropriate the tsaritsa's role as spiritual intercessor. Throughout her regency her name appeared together with those of her brothers on banners that were sent to various commanders in the field.[30] In one of the banners Sofiia Alekseevna's name saint, the martyr Sophia, is portrayed with those of her brothers Peter and Ivan in the act of worshiping the image of *Christ Not Made By Hands*. Saint Sofiia's petition for the success of the regiment to which the banner was assigned is implied by the analogous composition on the reverse side, which shows the metropolitan saints Aleksii, Peter, and Iona and Saint Sergius of Radonezh praying before the Virgin of the Sign.[31] During the second Crimean campaign in 1689, Sofiia Alekseevna undertook numerous pilgrimages separately from her brother Peter.[32] Sofiia Alekseevna's extant letters to Prince Golitsyn (composed in cypher and sent to him in the field) express the assumption that she could function as a petitioner before God for the success of the Russian realm against the infidel enemy. Just as Ivan IV had expected his wife to undertake arduous pilgrimages and pray for him in 1552, Golitsyn evidently instructed Sofiia to visit monasteries and engage in prayer. Following the custom of the pious tsar wives, the tsarevna humbly undertook the required trips, on foot, to the shrines of the protector saints of the Russian realm, including the site of Saint Sergius of Radonezh's relics.[33]

The religious role associated with the tsaritsa represented a safe source, which Sofiia Alekseevna could exploit to increase her legitimacy as a ruler without overstepping the boundaries of the patriarchal norms surrounding the tsardom. Throughout her reign the regent never laid claim to the traditional male royal regalia, the crown and cross of Monomakh, nor did she make any effort to insert herself into state rituals focusing on the Christ-like person of the tsar, such as the Palm Sunday and Epiphany ceremonies.[34] In the same vein, her public appearances did not prevent her from observing the rules of the *terem*. When she set out to attend the blessing of banners in the Cathedral of the Dormition in 1687, she entered the main church through a separate walkway from the Church of the Deposition of the Robe, as was customary for the royal women.[35] Although Sofiia Alekseevna clearly manipulated time-honored practices associated with the tsaritsy to elevate her own prestige, the accusations in later accounts of her regency by members of Peter the Great's camp that she shamelessly ignored custom by participating in religious processions are polemical and specious in nature.[36] It is significant that, although Tsar Peter may personally have disapproved of the visibility his sister displayed on these occasions, his letter to his brother Ivan from September 8–12, 1689, in which he points out Sofiia's transgressions regarding the royal dignity, does not refer to any violations of religious ritual on her part.[37]

Sofiia Alekseevna's efforts to appropriate the myth of the pious tsaritsa in order to further her prestige and legitimacy are evident in her conscious pursuit of the epithet "defender of the true faith." Hughes holds that the regent modeled her image of a champion of Orthodoxy after that of her father. Contemporary court poetry, letters, and accounts of Sofiia's regency suggest, instead, that the roots of this symbolism are to be found in the feminine sphere of the royal *terem*.[38] Sofiia Alekseevna's court ideologues, when presenting her handling of religious issues in the 1680s, consistently applied to the regent the theme—already evident in the frescoes of the Golden Palace of the Tsaritsy—of royal women who through their advocacy of the true faith became strong, masculine rulers in their own right.

The confrontation between Sofiia Alekseevna and a number of rebellious Old Believers on July 5, 1682, provided an opportunity to drive home the point that, regardless of her sex, her ascendance to power was pleasing to God and thus divinely sanctioned. Medvedev's account of the affair carefully links her ability to rule with her courage to stand up against God's enemies, the schismatic Old Believers. When, in a disputation in the Palace of Facets, Prince Ivan Khovanskii (who sided with the Old Believers) forcefully challenged the patriarch to hear their grievances, Sofiia fearlessly took up the cause of the established church. The decision of Tsaritsa Natal'ia Kirillovna and a number of tsarevny to accompany her underscores the fact that the regent's stance was not unprecedented but was hallowed by a century-old tradition of royal women acting as champions of the faith because of their superior spiritual position.[39] Medvedev, who emphasizes the danger Sofiia exposed herself to by accepting Khovanskii's proposition, presents her as a "true protectress of the holy Orthodox church," who was willing to give her life for the faith.[40] While members of the traditional male church hierarchy, including the patriarch, are portrayed as fearful and in need of an intercessor, Sofiia can rely on her God-given "masculine, strong ardor" to foil Khovanskii's evil plans and to protect the church from the onslaught of the heretics. Her refusal to be intimidated by the brawling schismatics led her to silence the vocal Old Believer Nikita Pustosviat, to threaten the crowd with the departure of the royal *terem* from the Kremlin, and to order the troops to persecute the religious dissenters after the conclusion of the meeting. In the aftermath of Sofiia Alekseevna's confrontation with the Old Believers, the regent and her followers carefully exploited the occasion to press their point of Sofiia's divinely sanctioned position. In his dedication from July 28, 1683, the court poet Karion Istomin repeatedly eulogized Sofiia's pugnacious disposition, which intimidated the schismatics, and credited her with bringing peace to the church.[41] Contemporary domestic and foreign sources concur that the regent took a personal interest in bringing the perceived rebels against God to justice. Three years after Sofiia's ascendance to power, July 5, the day of Sofiia's debate with the Old Believers, was declared an official holiday in honor of the tsarevna's victory over the schismatics.[42]

The efforts of the royal court in the 1680s to sanction Sofiia Alekseevna's role as a ruler by declaring her a champion of the Orthodox faith were further aided by the regent's identification with the interests of the Russian Orthodox hierarchy in her dealings with Russia's non-Christian foes. The official characterization of the enemy Tatars (whom Sofiia's government campaigned against in 1686) as evil infidels who destroyed churches, defiled icons and other sacred objects, and sold Orthodox Christians into slavery made Sofiia appear as a determined protector of the Orthodox church and its flock. The treaty of 1686 openly expressed Sofiia's commitment to liberate all Christians from the Muslim yoke. The regent herself displayed her commitment to the Christian faith in religious processions in honor of the soldiers fighting in the Crimean campaigns.[43] Even when the second Crimean campaign had a dismal outcome, Sofiia Alekseevna attended a thanksgiving service at the Novodevichii Monastery to heighten her image as a defender of the church against the infidels. Her promotion of the establishment of a metropolitanate of Kiev under the aegis of the patriarch of Moscow and her attainment of Poland's nominal agreement to tolerate its Orthodox subjects in 1685 and 1686 served to strengthen the impression that her unwavering adherence to the true faith worked to the benefit of all Russian Orthodox Christians and thus legitimated her position as a ruler.[44] Panegyric works such as Ivan Bogdanovskii's dedication of the book *Dary sviatogo dukha (Gifts of the Holy Spirit),* produced in Chernigov in 1688, skillfully connected the regent's anti-Uniate stance with her divinely sanctioned position in the Russian government.[45]

The endeavors of ideologues at Sofiia Alekseevna's court to exploit the accepted notion that through a strong commitment to the faith, a royal woman could transcend the traditional social and political limitations placed on her sex and appear as a ruler in her own right are also evident in repeated comparisons of the regent with illustrious women figures from the Old Testament and its apocrypha. As Lois Huneycutt points out, already in the ninth century, Hrabanus Maurus had dedicated commentaries on the books of Esther and Judith to Queen Judith, the second wife of the Carolingian king Louis the Pious, in which he asked her to imitate the lives of these biblical women. Pope John VIII petitioned the wife of Charles the Bald to act as a champion of the imperial church, taking Queen Esther as her model. The Esther *topos* also appears in conjunction with a number of queens of the Later Middle Ages, such as Margaret, Queen of Scotland, her daughter Mathilda, and Jeanne of Champagne-Navarre, the wife of Philip the Fair. In all cases it denoted the royal women's ability to reject their own comfortable lifestyle to bring about peace for the church and their subjects.[46] In the late seventeenth century, many of Sofiia Alekseevna's learned supporters became interested in the strong women of the Old Testament as well. Sil'vestr Medvedev is known to have read interpretations of the books of Judith, Ruth, and the Song of Songs. The story of Esther was among the first theater plays in Russia to be performed at the court of Aleksei Mikhailovich.[47] The images of outstanding women one encounters in the Old Testament and the apocryphal texts found their way into the panegyrical literature devoted to the regent. Conscious comparisons of Sofiia Alekseevna with such women can be found in Medvedev's account of the events of 1682, Karion Istomin's dedication from July 28, 1683, Osip Titov's introduction to the book *Zvezda presvetlaia (The Most Bright Star)* from 1686, and Ignatii Rimskii-Korsakov's panegyrical composition in honor of the troops departing on the first Crimean campaign, which dates from March 14, 1687. Orthodox foreigners applied female Old Testament images to the regent. Thus the Likhudes brothers eulogized Sofiia Alekseevna as a "valiant Judith," "holy Suzanna," and "chaste Deborah" in their 1687 Easter oration, and the patriarch of Constantinople, Dionysius IV Mouselimes, likened her to Deborah, Judith, and Esther in a letter from 1688.[48]

Among the few scholars who have studied in detail the panegyrics to Sofiia Alekseevna, only Zelensky has noted the significance of the regent's comparison with female protagonists of the ancient Israelites. Although Zelensky rightly points out these women's gift of reason and wisdom, a close look at the relevant passages in the Old Testament and the apocrypha reveals the preponderant theme of strong female figures who protected the Hebrew faith and their people from hostile forces in times of severe distress and who subsequently became respected leaders of their community.[49] The Jewish woman Esther risked her life to gain justice from her husband, the Persian king, for her oppressed people and to elevate the status of her kinsman Mordecai's house. Through her influence the Israelites received the right to assemble and protect themselves. In turn the Hebrews recognized Esther's spiritual authority and allowed her to set the time of the Purim holidays (Esther 2:2–10:3). Deborah, a prophetess and judge in Israel, led the Israelites into battle against their Canaanite oppressors. A married woman, she abandoned her feminine role to give moral support and advice to the Israelite commander Barak in the field. With the voice of God speaking through her, Deborah was instrumental in her people's victory over the troops of the Canaanite Sisera (Judg. 4:4–5:15). Judith, the wealthy and beautiful widow of Manasseh, impressed her countrymen so much with her severe asceticism that they put their fate into her hands when Holofernes, general of Nebuchadnezzar, tried to subjugate them by cutting off their water supply. Through a ruse she gained access to Holofernes's tent and cut off his head, while still preserving the purity of her body and faith. Like Deborah, Judith advised the Israelites on how to defeat the enemy troops. The high priest Joakim blessed her before she led the men and women of the Israelites in a victory celebration.[50]

The handlers of Sofiia Alekseevna's image incorporated the theme of the strong Old Testament women who fought for their religion and the welfare of their people into their portrayals of the regent to give her political status the aura of divine sanction. In his account of the events of 1682, Medvedev compared Sofiia to Deborah, Judith, and Esther to prove that she was an instrument of God, who stood by his chosen people in times of severe distress. In his dedication to Sofiia from July 28, 1683, Karion Istomin as well likened the regent's commitment to the protection of the Orthodox church, her victory over the Old Believers, and her liberation of Christians from the yoke of the infidel to Deborah's defeat of the proud Sisar.[51]

In the wake of the efforts of the Muscovite court after 1686 to ascribe to Sofiia Alekseevna the position of an independent ruler in her own right, the tsarevna's association with the Old Testament heroines served as a convenient tool to overcome the lacking tradition of an officially crowned female ruler in Russia. In his panegyrical introduction to the book *The Most Bright Star* from January 1686, the undersecretary *(pod'iachii)* from the Novodevichii Monastery, Osip Titov, deliberately emphasized the gendered aspects of the theme of Deborah, defender of the Hebrew people and its religion, to make a case for Sofiia's sovereign status. According to Bogdanov, who examined the copy dedicated to the regent, in the introductory miniature (folio 2v), four angels crown the Virgin, who herself places one crown on the heads of the tsars Ivan and Peter, and a second one on that of Patriarch Ioakim.[52] The miniature illustrates the divine origin of the secular and spiritual authorities in Muscovite Russia. In the subsequent text these authorities are compared to the leaders of ancient Israel, echoing the common notion of Russia's identity with the second Jerusalem. The crowns the Virgin hands down are to remind the leaders receiving them of their common spiritual obligations. Sofiia Alekseevna's inclusion in the group of Russia's divinely sanctioned leaders is stressed immediately after the introduction of the New Jerusalem theme (folios 6v and 6r). In his wishes that God bless and strengthen the Russian tsars as he previously blessed Moses and David, Titov included Sofiia's role model: "And with them her who judged the people who had been previously chosen and loved by God, Deborah, clever like a man and most wise."[53]

Titov's reference to Deborah's capacity to think like a man not only served to remind his audience of Sofiia Alekseevna's political acumen but represented a device to overcome any disadvantage of status associated with her sex by appealing to her divine approval. In the Old Testament spiritual hierarchy, Deborah ranked lower than Moses and David. The image of the New Jerusalem, however, prepared the ground for the notion that the tsarevna could assume the position of a male ruler by setting the discourse on royal power into the framework of salvation history, in which gender differences are outweighed by spiritual status. Just as the frescoes of the Golden Palace of the Tsaritsy proclaimed Irina Godunova's capacity to rule by portraying her Byzantine and Georgian models in their masculine role of defenders of the faith, Titov's panegyric manipulates the gendered language of the Deborah story to uphold Sofiia's divinely approved status as an autocrat in her own right. His address ends in a praise of the ruling trinity consisting of Ivan, Peter, and Sofiia.[54]

Throughout the remaining years of Sofiia Alekseevna's regency, the court resorted to the practice of comparing the regent with biblical women who through the power of the spirit overcame the weakness of their sex. Karion Istomin credited her with the gift of Judith (that is, strength) in his *"Panegiris"* of 1687. In a letter of Patriarch Dionysius IV Mouselimes to Sofiia Alekseevna dating from 1688, the patriarch implored her to take up weapons and to save her own people from the onslaught of the Muslims, just as God once rescued the Hebrews with the help of Deborah, Judith, and Esther. The language of warfare in the patriarch's address to the tsarevna freed her from any social and political restrictions associated with her sex. At the same time, the reference to the Old Testament heroines' victory over their enemies, which was assured because of their alignment with God, made Sofiia Alekseevna appear as a divinely chosen ruler. The same notion is also obvious in the oration composed by the Likhudes brothers Ioannikii and Sofronii for the Muscovite ruling trinity on March 27, 1687, for the celebration of Easter. The authors address Sofiia Alekseevna as "a second Judith, a most holy Susanna, and a most chaste Deborah," who should rejoice "because a crown has been prepared for you in heaven, not from very precious, transitory, and temporal jewels, but from God's grace and the spirit around the divine throne. A crown and scepter has been made for you because you have confirmed the scepters of your ancestors with your wisdom and manly courage."[55] The passage clearly derives the regent's right to be endowed with royal regalia and to stake a claim to the heritage of the previous Russian tsars from her imitation of the biblical heroines. Like Irina Godunova before her, Sofiia Alekseevna could adopt the position of a male sovereign because of her ability to acquire masculine traits by vigorously pursuing her commitment to the Orthodox faith.

The court poets' choice of Old Testament heroines in their eulogies of Sofiia Alekseevna reflects their sensitivity to the tsarevna's unusual position in government. In contrast to the tsaritsy, who gained the potential to act as rulers through marriage and (when possible) subsequent motherhood, Sofiia's role as royal daughter did not inherently carry a similar claim and therefore needed to be enhanced. It is not surprising, then, that comparisons of the tsaritsy with Old Testament women focused on the themes of marriage and motherhood that described the royal wives' attained status. The frescoes of the Golden Palace of the Tsaritsy elaborate on Irina Godunova's potential as a tsaritsa by comparing her with other pious female rulers. In contrast, the Old Testament women associated with Sofiia Alekseevna do not enjoy royal status and attain their visible public role only through extraordinary acts. Even Esther in the end is not remembered for exercising her power as a queen, but for challenging the authority of her royal husband for a spiritual cause. By invoking Old Testament heroines such as Esther, Judith, and Deborah, the court poets thus both reflected and overcame Tsarevna Sofiia's uncommon position as a political leader.

The indebtedness of Sofiia Alekseevna and her supporters to the mythopoeic traditions surrounding the image of the Muscovite ruler's wife also appears in the central myth of the tsarevna's regency, which equated Sofiia with "Sophia the Wisdom of God." Scholars such as Bogdanov, Hughes, and Zelensky have recently emphasized the innovative aspects of the Sophia imagery, which in their view prepared the ideological ground for a female ruler in a waning Muscovy ruled by patriarchal norms. On account of its androgynous nature, the imagery is supposed to have initiated the depersonalization of government characteristic of the Imperial period. Even a cursory look at the bulk of panegyric works produced during Sofiia Alekseevna's regency, however, reveals that the various authors employed sophic terminology quite freely and used it in different contexts.[56] Quite often several conceptualizations of Sofiia's Sophic image coexist side by side in a single work written by one author. It is not surprising, considering this poetic flexibility and the already observed fondness of the panegyrists for the traditional notions of the pious female ruler, to find in their works a conflation of these notions with the concept of the Divine Sophia.

The experimentation of court ideologues with the customary feminine religious symbolism surrounding the person of the tsaritsa and their creative fusion of this symbolism with a new theological concept of a female ruler are particularly evident in the development of the myth of Sofiia Alekseevna's divinely inspired, translucent, virginal womb. The Muscovite myth of the blessed womb of the tsaritsa, which treated the tsar's wife as a conduit of divine grace imbuing the future heir to the throne, was married to the Sophic imagery. In the process the blessed womb of the tsaritsa became transformed to denote the tsar daughter's immaculate light-filled body, which functioned as a vessel of divine providence. Whereas previously the myth of the divinely inspired womb legitimized the position of the tsaritsy even if they were not mothers (that is, in the case of Solomoniia Saburova), in the 1680s it justified the rule of an unmarried tsar daughter by ascribing to her the ability to be pregnant with Divine Wisdom, which symbolized both good government and God's sanction of it.

Although Sofiia Alekseevna was named after the martyr saint Sophia, celebrated on September 17, it became common practice even during her childhood to ascribe to her the qualities of another Sophia, who was held to be the personification of the Divine Wisdom.[57] In the dedication of his book *Venets very (The Crown of the Faith),* Simeon Polotskii called the twelve-year-old tsarevna a seeker of the heavenly wisdom, who lived her life in her name.[58] Polotskii's equation of this wisdom with book knowledge, which he wished the tsarevna to pursue, was later developed in the panegyrics of the regent's court poets, Karion Istomin's eulogy of Sofiia Alekseevna in conjunction with his petition for the establishment of an academy in Moscow in 1682–1683, and Medvedev's dedication to the regent designed to commemorate the charter for the Graeco-Latin-Slavonic Academy in 1685. In both cases the authors expressed the conviction that, through the study of Divine Wisdom, Sofiia could acquire the virtues of justice, "male courage," and the favor of God without which no sovereign could rule.[59]

Bogdanov, Zelensky, and Hughes are undoubtedly right in their view that the introduction of the concept of the Divine Sophia enabled Sofiia Alekseevna's supporters to attribute to the regent the qualities of a male ruler. Nevertheless, it would be wrong to assume that the creators of this legitimating device treated the tsarevna as a liminal figure whose gender-based legal and dynastic weakness needed to be compensated with masculine values.[60] It is striking that, in his request to Sofiia to institute the pursuit of science in Russia, Karion Istomin proposed to the regent that she model herself not only after the example of her late brother Fedor, who promoted learning in Russia, but after her mother, Mariia Il'inichna, who displayed great interest in the education of her son Aleksei. In the same way Sofiia was to treat her people like a good mother, who gave her children spiritual nourishment.[61] In his appeal to Sofiia Alekseevna to found an academy in 1685, Medvedev held up to the regent a feminine model of wisdom as well. The court poet maintained that, just as the Kievan princess Ol'ga had revealed "the light of faith" to Russia, Sofiia was to kindle the light of science in Russia.[62] In both cases the connection of royal women with knowledge—whether religious or scientific—proved beneficial to their realms and thus could function as a condition for a capable female sovereign in Muscovite Russia.

Since the concept of wisdom could be attributed to both men and women in Muscovite Russia, it is not surprising that Sofiia Alekseevna's panegyrists seized on it to develop a powerful mythical construct that proclaimed the tsarevna's undisputed status as a ruler. Familiar with the notion expressed in the myth of the blessed womb of the tsaritsy that royal women could function as divinely inspired vessels, the court poets cast the tsarevna as a vessel or house filled with the light of heavenly wisdom. The resulting new image of "Sofiia the house of God" or of "Sofiia the virginal translucent womb" reconfigured elements of the theological concept of the Divine Sophia to present the tsarevna as a medium through which God communicated his divine blessing to the Russian Orthodox realm.[63]

The symbolic connection between Sofiia Alekseevna the ruler and the concept of the Divine Sophia did not hinge on a simple identification of the tsarevna with the fourth hypostasis in the divine trinity, as one might expect, but instead centered on the notion of Sofiia functioning as a vessel of her divine counterpart. In *Venets very* Polotskii praised the tsarevna for seeking out the divine wisdom contained in the knowledge of God and in the pursuit of sacred law "as gold in a vessel." In 1682 Sil'vestr Medvedev applied the "Sophia the house of God" metaphor to Sofiia Alekseevna in his first eulogy to the tsarevna, found in the preface to the lament on the occasion of Tsar Fedor Alekseevich's death.[64] Medvedev called Sofiia the house of the sun, which in antiquity had been considered the residence of the gods. According to the Christian tradition, the house of the sun was erected by Divine Wisdom, who built herself a temple made of seven pillars.[65] Sofiia Alekseevna, the vessel in which God chose to reside, would derive great spiritual stature and strength from her close association with the divine if she always heeded God's advice just as the biblical Judith had done—she had preserved her chastity throughout her dealings with Holofernes.[66]

Since God bestowed on his cherished vessel the gifts of his divine wisdom (strong faith, deep love for God and one's neighbor, unshakable hope, kindness, humility, good government, and foresight), Sofiia could acquire the qualities of a model ruler through her symbiosis with the divine. Medvedev's intention to use the metaphor of the house of God for a politico-dynastic purpose is clearly expressed in his statement at the end of the eulogy composed in 1682 that the eyes of the Russian eagle (whose two heads and two wings denoted, respectively, the two tsars Ivan and Peter and the tsaritsy and tsarevny) always looked up to "Sofiia the house of God," and that the eagle's heart was filled with Sofiia's God-given wisdom.[67] In his eulogy to the regent from January 21, 1685, the poet pointed out the beneficial aspects of the symbiosis between the divinity and the earthly tsarevna. By settling in her soul, the Holy Spirit rendered Sofiia's mind wise and focused all her energy to the good. As a result the tsarevna became a medium that communicated the will of God to the Russian people. Since she held God's identity within herself, she, too, became sacred like a cathedral. By submitting to God's wish to make her soul his residence, Sofiia Alekseevna herself became a participant in divine grace. Thus the "vessel of God" metaphor does not treat the regent as a passive host, as Zelensky holds, but empowers her with the right and the capacity to act in the political arena. Medvedev insists that as a result of her role as vessel of God, Sofiia could work for the well-being of her subjects. Blessed with the divine gifts of faith, hope, love, kindness, truth, justice, wisdom, male courage, and restraint, she was bound to be the perfect ruler.[68]

As a successful ruler Sofiia Alekseevna had to capture the Wisdom of God and impart it to her people. In order to demonstrate this interaction between God, Sofiia, and the Russian people, Medvedev inserted a light motif into the metaphor "Sofiia the vessel of God." Already in his first eulogy to Sofiia Alekseevna, he described the house of God as a bright dwelling with numerous windows made out of glass and crystal. Aware of the fragility of these two materials, Medvedev was careful to avoid the suggestion that the regent displayed any signs of weakness but instead declared that crystal stemmed from ice and snow, which in time hardened on the mountaintops into a glistening substance, while ashes heated by fire eventually yielded clear glass. In the same way the love of God with which Sofiia Alekseevna was imbued fortified the structure of his house and rendered it beautiful.[69] At the same time, the transparency of glass and crystal, a quality that undoubtedly impressed seventeenth-century man, allowed the content of the house of the sun, that is, the Wisdom of God, to radiate out on the Russian eagle in undiminished splendor. Therefore, rather than juxtaposing feminine fragility with masculine strength and clarity (as modern scholars are apt to do), Medvedev focused on the qualities of strength and translucency, which complemented each other in the person of Sofiia Alekseevna.[70] Just as the fire had transformed powdery, dull grey ashes into compact, shining glass, God's wisdom had endowed the tsarevna with all the necessary attributes of an ideal strong ruler, regardless of her gender. The light motif created a bridge between the notion of Sofiia Alekseevna as the divinely chosen vessel and the claim that the tsarevna could function as an effective ruler.

Medvedev's particular use of the light motif to empower the tsarevna is not surprising, considering the imagery that developed around the women of the royal *terem* in the Romanov period. While the association of a light motif with rulers may have had a long tradition in medieval Russia, as Zelensky points out, scholars have not yet paid attention to the common attribution of this theme to royal women in the syllabic court poetry of the second part of the seventeenth century.[71] Simeon Polotskii liked to apply a light motif to Aleksei Mikhailovich and his family. In a set of verses he composed for the tsar's return from Riga in October 1656, he likened the tsar to the sun; his wife to Diana, the goddess of the moon; his son Aleksei to daylight; and the tsarevny to the stars.[72] Polotskii's disciple, Sil'vestr Medvedev, skillfully transformed the light motif into a tool to endorse Sofiia Alekseevna's rightful position as a ruler in his first eulogy to Sofiia in 1682:

> Your most bright highness, because you were honorably created as a vessel not only from bright [glass], but from the most bright glass of the house of the royal, most bright highness, you will be honored as a royal daughter not only by man, but by God himself: for the daughters of kings are honored by you, says the royal prophet to God.[73]

Karion Istomin also employed the light motif in connection with the "Sofiia the house of God" metaphor in his dedication of the book *God-like Love* in 1687. Calling Sofiia a "cathedral built to Jesus Christ," he maintained that "the son of God praises his name in you. Your kindness flows joyously so that through you wisdom begins to shine in the realm."[74]

The employment of the light motif by Sofiia Alekseevna's panegyrists to justify the extraordinary visibility of a royal daughter in the Russian government is understandable if one considers that, in the court poetry of the second half of the seventeenth century, the motif was used to describe the superior spiritual disposition of the tsarevny. Simeon Polotskii repeatedly praised the bodily asceticism and charitable spirit of Aleksei Mikhailovich's sisters and daughters. In his "Sermon on the Day of Gregory of Neokaisareia," which was part of an early draft of his *Vecheria dushevnaia (Spiritual Supper),* Polotskii compared the tsarevny to the wise virgins of the New Testament, who "decorated the lamps of their souls, filled them with the oil of mercy and generosity, and lit the fire of the love of God for the coming of the heavenly bridegroom."[75]

Polotskii's intention to use the biblical parable of the wise virgins to emphasize the close affinity of the tsarevny to the divine is particularly evident in his skillful exploitation of the story's nuptial imagery. In one of his eulogies to the tsarevny, he draws a parallel between the desire of Christ the groom to enter the hearts of the royal virgins and the visitation of the Virgin Mary by the divine spirit:

> Having preserved his mother as the immaculate Virgin, as it was befitting for the son of God, who is a warm lover of purity and a most generous preserver of those who preserve it, He now rests in a mean manger, guarded by the Virgin; and the most pure God, who is a king himself, wants to enter into your pure hearts, [the hearts] of royal daughters. He wants to light up your precious souls with the light of his grace and live in you. With him you will dwell, and he will add his light to your brightness.[76]

The passage clearly demonstrates the intricate connection between the light motif and the metaphor of a royal daughter serving as a vessel or house of God. Just as God entered into the pure body of the Virgin Mary, he now chose the tsarevny as his favorite dwelling place on account of their spiritual lifestyle. The act of the divine in-dwelling itself is marked by a light motif. Icons of the Annunciation usually show a ray of light above the heads of the Virgin and the Archangel Gabriel.[77]

The new application of the theme of a miraculous visitation or conception to royal daughters in the seventeenth century demanded certain adjustments. While the myth of the blessed womb of the tsaritsy served to maintain their reputation as mothers of the realm in times of dynastic crisis, the image of motherhood as a device to express royal women's spiritual role in the tsardom was less suitable for the unmarried sisters and daughters of Aleksei Mikhailovich. As paragons of chastity and kindness, they were more easily portrayed as the brides of Christ. In the works of Polotskii and other panegyrists of the later seventeenth century, the theme of the divine visitation of royal women focused less on the act of a conception or birth than on the intense intimacy experienced by the bridal couple, which ultimately overcame the lesser "brightness" of the bride. As a result the royal daughters themselves shared in the qualities of Christ.

Sensitive to the fact that the nuptial imagery of the metaphor of the wise virgins could be used to underscore the divine approval of Sofiia Alekseevna's regency, her supporters associated the metaphor exclusively with the ruling tsarevna. In his eulogy from July 28, 1683, Karion Istomin praised Sofiia's virginal chastity, which caused God to choose her as a dwelling place. In his words she betrothed herself willingly to Christ, who was a most loving fiancé to her. In his letter to Sofiia Alekseevna from 1686, the patriarch of Constantinople, Dionysius IV Mouselimes, ascribed to the regent the chastity of the five wise virgins, who set out to meet their heavenly fiancé.[78]

Like the myth of the blessed womb of the tsaritsa, the notion of "Sofiia the virginal and translucent vessel of God" demanded a fertility theme to underscore the regent's beneficial impact on her subjects and her resulting legitimate status as a ruler. Although Sofiia was celebrated as a virgin, her union with Christ the groom made her a fruitful bride. When Medvedev developed his "Sofiia the house of God" metaphor in 1682, he stressed that the royal receptacle of the divine was filled with the light of Divine Wisdom and the gifts of the Holy Spirit, which could flow from the translucent human vessel to be shared by her worthy subjects. In his panegyrical address to Sofiia Alekseevna from September 17, 1687, Karion Istomin also used the fertility theme to underscore his contention that the tsarevna could function as a sovereign regardless of her sex because God had chosen her as a receptacle for his divine gifts:

> In the female sex as well we will see clearly
> how the gifts shine beautifully in them;
> So we see blessedness in Sarah,
> strength in Judith.
>
> Your most bright highness,
> the spirit of God adorns [you] with all [gifts]
> like a vessel God made
> and chose for himself.
>
> Like a great and uncounted treasure
> in the royal chambers, which is filled with all good,
> so Sofiia is filled entirely
> with the gift of God.

As Medvedev before him, Karion Istomin treated "Sofiia the house of God" as an organic entity that became pregnant with the spirit flowing from its creator. The divine blessing, however, did not remain locked up in the virgin's womb but irradiated the entire realm. In Istomin's words, everybody benefited from "Sofiia the treasure of God."[79]

The message underlying the "Sofiia the house of God" metaphor—that is, that the regent ruled with divine favor and consequently was bound to keep her government strong and her subjects safe—also represents the topic of Ivan Shchirskii's engraving from 1683, which served as the frontispiece of Lazar Baranovich's *Blagodat' i istina (Grace and Truth).* This well-studied engraving states the significance of Sofiia Alekseevna's contribution to the Russian government and its subjects in allegorical form (see Figure 17).[80] Careful analysis of Orthodox iconographic conventions and a comparison of the visual imagery with its literary counterparts reveal that Medvedev's metaphor of "Sofiia the house of God" became instrumental in defining the

17. Ivan Shchirskii. Frontispiece to *Blagodat' i istina* from 1683 (Russian National Library, St. Petersburg). In the upper register God Father crowns Sofiia Alekseevna's adopted name saint, Sophia the Divine Wisdom, who carries images of Russian tsars on her wings. Below Wisdom the house with seven pillars protects the Russian eagle from the onslaught of enemies. The pavilion of the Divine Wisdom supports two tsar brothers, who are blessed by Christ. The image expresses the prominent role of Sofiia Alekseevna in the ruling trinity made up of Sofiia and her brothers Ivan and Peter.

regent's ruler image in the early years after her brother Fedor's death.[81]

Shchirskii's frontispiece to *Grace and Truth* is organized in three compositional layers. The upper register of the composition is dominated by the figure of a winged maiden with long loose hair, a sign of her virginity. She is separated from the rest of the image by a triangular band of clouds, marking the celestial sphere. Amid dense rays of light, God Father places a crown upon the maiden's nimbed head. Her wings feature six medallions with the portraits of unnamed Muscovite tsars, three on each side. All of the rulers hold a scepter and an orb, and four of them wear a crown of Monomakh as a symbol of their royal legitimacy. The two bareheaded figures placed on the tips of the virgin's wings are in the process of receiving divine investiture. On the left Christ reaches down another crown of Monomakh. On the right the Holy Spirit in the shape of a dove hovers above the recipient, with the royal regalia in its claws.

The coronation theme in the upper register is repeated in an inverted fashion in the center of the composition. Christ extends both his hands in a gesture of blessing to two young tsars, who stand one on either side of him. Both wear royal garb and are equipped with the traditional ruling regalia, scepter and orb, the chest cross, and the crown of Monomakh of the type worn by seventeenth-century Russian rulers.[82]

The middle and lower layers of the image are organically connected in that Christ and the two tsars stand on three pedestals attached to the dome of a large pavilion, which occupies the center of the lower register. The structure consists of seven ornately decorated Corinthian columns, placed on an elevated platform. Between the pillars the fortifications, secular buildings, and churches of a distant town can be seen.[83] Outside the walls, on either side of the pavilion, we see the figures of an Orthodox hierarch, a tsar, and a tsaritsa in praying posture. The theme of royalty appears again within the columned structure where the two-headed Russian eagle, depicted with two hearts and three crowns, is readying itself for battle. Raising a shield with its left claw and a bundle of flashing lightening bolts with its right, the eagle stares at the battle raging around the pavilion. From the clouds above, angels in classical armor hurl spears, arrows, and lightening bolts at the troops below, who flee in panic, leaving the dead behind. Mounted warriors clad in Roman armor and with their swords raised pursue their enemies, who wear turbans and follow banners featuring the Muslim half moon.[84]

The theme of battle pervading all three layers of the composition expresses an overall feeling of heightened danger. Although the recent death of Tsar Fedor may well have contributed to a sense of military instability in the Russian realm (as A. P. Bogdanov claims), the decisive participation of the forces of heaven in the armed conflict suggests a larger, eschatological framework for the image. The apocalyptic mood is indicated by the two bands of inscriptions flanking the wings of the virgin, which cite Rev. 12:14: "And to the woman were given two wings of a great eagle."[85] The battle pits the forces of good (that is, the angels, whose classical armor may well have been designed to trigger associations with the idea of Moscow the Third Rome) against the forces of evil (embodied by the Muslim infidels).[86] The involvement of the celestial forces in the battle against God's enemies is expressed in the inscriptions accompanying the two armed archangels to the left and to the right of the winged maiden: "The angel of the Lord encampeth round about them that fear him, and delivered them" (Ps. 34:7) and "Let their way be dark and slippery: and let the angel of the Lord persecute them" (Ps. 35:6).[87]

The eschatological theme that occupies a large part of the composition on either side of the engraving serves as a stark contrast to the theme of crowned rulers, which runs vertically through the central part of the image. Zelensky took notice of the triangular design pattern of crowned royalty in the image, which is formed by the winged virgin and the clouds surrounding her, the configuration of the tsars and the blessing Christ below, and the outline of the eagle's body in the pavilion. Struck by the tension between the triangular design and the theme of dual monarchy (expressed by the coronation of the two tsars and the two hearts of the double-headed eagle), Zelensky concluded that the winged virgin—the iconographic representation of "Sophia the Wisdom of God"—did not denote the regent Sofiia Alekseevna ruling with her brothers in a triumvirate. Instead Zelenskii argued that the figure represented a symbol of complete sovereignty and harmony.[88]

The iconographic conventions of seventeenth-century Russian religious painting regarding the cloud pattern suggest a different interpretation. As in Ushakov's icon *The Tree of the Russian Realm,* the clouds mark the boundary between the eternal heavenly sphere above and the events on earth below. The separation between the spheres of God and man allowed the composer of the image to express the view of Sofiia Alekseevna's divinely approved status as a regent without violating existing conventions concerning the absolute power of her male siblings.[89] In the frontispiece God's approval of the Russian tsardom is depicted in the medallions on the wings of the Russian eagle, which feature Russian rulers with regalia.[90] The investiture of two young tsars by Christ and the Holy Spirit confirms that God intended the tsardom to continue in Peter and Ivan. At the same time, the participation of God Father in the act of royal investiture in the center makes clear that the maiden crowned by God was not merely a symbol of good government in Muscovy, but denoted Tsarevna Sofiia. As in the contemporary panegyrical literature, Sofiia's ruler potential is based on her intimate relationship with the divine. Sofiia, who is depicted without scepter and orb, receives her crown directly from the Godhead and bathes in the light of Divine Wisdom emanating from the triangular haloes worn both by God and the tsarevna. The beneficial effect of Sofiia's celestial coronation is evident in the assured manner she spreads the wings of the eagle that sustain the Muscovite sovereigns.

The divinely sanctioned triumvirate in Muscovite government hinging on the pivotal role of Sofiia Alekseevna is also reflected in the composition immediately below the celestial sphere. The blessing the two royal figures receive from Christ denotes the legitimacy of the two tsars Ivan and Peter on the Russian throne. Christ's mandate to each of the brothers is contained in two inscriptions. The one between Christ and the tsar on the left (presumably Ivan Alekseevich)—"Prosper and rule!"—is an adaptation of Jer. 23:5: "Behold, the days come, saith the Lord, that . . . a King shall reign and prosper, and shall execute judgment and justice in the earth." While this reference to King David implies the conferment of the established legal authority to rule on Ivan, the shortened passage of John 21:15—"Peter, do you love me? Feed my lambs"—on the right (presumably directed to Ivan's brother Peter) conveys a more spiritual mandate to care for the Christian flock. The legal and spiritual aspects of power (consistent with the two different investitures of the tsars on the eagle's wings in the upper register—one by Christ and the other by the Holy Spirit) were meant to be complementary. This message is reinforced by the citation of Matt. 18:20 and of Ps. 133:1 in the inscriptions above Christ and on both sides of the two tsars: "For where two are gathered together in my name, there am I in the midst of them" and "Behold, how good and how pleasant it is for brethren to dwell together in unity!" The divine approval of Ivan's and Peter's joint rule, however, did not guarantee the peace and stability of their realm. For the Muscovite autocracy to survive the cosmic struggle between good and evil, it needed strong support. This notion is expressed in the pavilion structure, which represents a parallel theme to the wise virgin above. The inscription on the dome referring to Prov. 9:1 makes the theme of Divine Wisdom explicit: "Wisdom hath builded her house, she hath hewn out her seven pillars."

The image of the pavilion, the house of heavenly Wisdom, represents an iconographic counterpart to the metaphor of the vessel of the divine ascribed to Sofiia Alekseevna in the panegyrical literature of the 1680s. The primary purpose of the structure made out of seven columns was the maintenance and the protection of the Russian autocracy. The careful observer notices that the pillars support not only the arched roof but also the royal brothers, who stand on pedestals mounted on the entablature of the columns.[91] The inscription on two medallions fastened to the two outer pillars "I bear up the pillars of it" (Ps. 73:3) reinforces the notion that the house of Wisdom was designed to buttress the Russian autocracy. The close association between Sofiia, the sacred dwelling of Divine Wisdom, and the Muscovite government is further supported by the presence of the Russian eagle in the house of Wisdom, by the union of the eagle's two hearts in one vessel, and by the three crowns upon its two heads. "Sofiia the house of Divine Wisdom" represented a bulwark that protected the Russian eagle from the onslaught of the forces of evil. Sofiia's close association with the divine assured the success of the Russian autocracy.

The frontispiece of Baranovich's *Grace and Truth* demonstrates the continued influence of traditional gender-specific notions in the construction of Sofiia Alekseevna's royal sovereignty. An analysis of the iconography of the engraving and the accompanying inscriptions disproves the conventional view that the frontispiece does not attribute to the tsarevna the status of a sovereign ruler.[92] The sophic theme pervading the composition does not extol Sofiia Alekseevna's identity with the fourth hypostasis of God to attribute to her a male royal status that is equal to that of her brothers. Instead, by drawing on the customary myth of royal women functioning as vessels of the divine, it conceives the tsarevna as an intercessor for the autocracy before the Godhead, who in his love for her complies with her wishes. As a result Sofiia, the chosen vessel of Divine Wisdom, also becomes the Russian eagle's favorite residence, which protects him from adversity. At the same time the vessel's ability to defend the eagle and its realm from the infidel reminds the viewer of the Muscovite myth of the tsars' wives acting as defenders of the Orthodox faith. In this sense the iconography of Shchirskii's engraving corresponds to the repeated association of the "Sofiia the Divine Wisdom" theme with heroines of the Old Testament in the panegyrical literature. Finally, the intimacy between the maiden in the upper register and the Godhead, a result of her virginal purity, becomes an ultimate justification for Sofiia's royal sovereignty. Although the image does not feature a royal portrait of the historical Sofiia, her legitimate right to rule with her brothers is indicated by the coronation of the wise maiden in the celestial sphere and the third crown on the eagle's heads directly below this scene in the earthly realm.

Sofiia Alekseevna's ideological spin doctors skillfully adapted mythopoeic devices traditionally used to bolster the position of the tsars' wives. In doing so they showed their deep appreciation for the gender-specific aspects of an autocratic system constructed in religious terms. Aware of the unprecedented position Sofiia Alekseevna claimed in the Russian government as the daughter of a tsar, her supporters often sought to avoid arguments about her legitimacy by placing the regent into the respected group of pious royal women rulers. As accepted defender of the realm or a blessed vessel of the divine, Sofiia could claim that her mandate to rule came directly from God without having to encroach on her two brothers' right to the throne. Neither of these concepts limited Sofiia's ruler potential in any way. Although they made the tsarevna appear as a mere mediator who conveyed God's grace to the Russian realm, her assumed affinity to God provided an independent explanation of her legitimacy.

To a large extent Sofiia Alekseevna's adherence to traditional notions of female royal power was responsible for the success of her seven-year regency. By appearing as a helpmate to her two royal brothers, an intercessor for her realm, and a defender of the Orthodox faith, the tsarevna avoided a direct confrontation with the tsarevichi's legitimate claim to power. Rather than claiming her brothers' sovereign rights, Sofiia manipulated the ritual practices usually associated with the wives and mothers of the tsars. The appearance of her name in royal rescripts can be related to precedents involving Muscovite tsaritsy since the time of Irina Godunova.[93] Similarly, Sofiia's habit of receiving foreign diplomats personally in a special ceremony has its roots in the royal wives' customary reception of high ecclesiastics visiting the royal family from abroad. The elaborate ceremonial witnessed by the Swedish ambassador Kerstin Gullenstierna in the Golden Palace on May 28, 1684, recalls the meetings of Irina Godunova and Mariia Il'inichna with the patriarchs Jeremiah and Macarius. Sofiia, seated on a throne and attended by female servants and high political figures, exchanged greetings and wishes for health with her guest.[94] Since audiences of this type by the regent usually followed a similar ceremonial involving the two tsars, one finds it difficult to agree with Hughes that Sofiia usurped the traditional male diplomatic protocol.[95]

While Sofiia Alekseevna's adherence to medieval notions of female rule is evident in her deportment throughout her regency, it would be wrong to assume that once adopted by the tsarevna, these notions remained static and unchallenged. As both Bogdanov and Hughes have convincingly argued, after the Permanent Peace with Poland in 1686, the tsarevna moved to advertise her equal position in the ruling trinity more openly by adopting the title Autocrat traditionally reserved for the male rulers of Russia.[96] The title Sofiia, Autocrat of all the Russias appeared not only in government documents but on military banners and gold coins that were minted in the aftermath of the first Crimean campaign.[97] The latter also contained a ruler portrait of Sofiia with a crown and a scepter. Although the tsarevna was not depicted with the crown of Monomakh (traditionally reserved for male rulers), her very appearance on the coins as a single royal woman with a crown and a scepter was unprecedented.[98]

The innovations in the area of royal etiquette had profound implications for the perception of Sofiia's power as a female sovereign. As intercessor for the realm, defender of the faith, or the house of Divine Wisdom, she essentially derived her mandate to rule not only from God's grace, as the tsars did, but from her contribution to the religiously constructed body politic of the tsardom. Sofiia's title Autocrat and her ruler portrait on the coins, however, counteracted the notions that as a regent she had to justify her role in government in any way. Rather than insisting on the traditional gendered notion of the tsardom, they placed the regent on an equal footing with her brothers.

It is tempting to attribute this shift in the notion of female sovereign rule in Muscovy to the personal ambition of Sofiia Alekseevna or to the influx of new Western political ideas, but the regent's cautious approach to and the timing of the adoption of her new title and ruler portraits suggest a more compelling explanation.[99] In 1686 the fourteen-year-old Tsar Peter was rapidly approaching maturity. Although the tsarevna could be assured of her continued control over her disabled brother Ivan, her victory over the maternal kin of her half brother in 1682 made Peter's acceptance of her co-rule less likely once he had come of age. Since the medieval model of female sovereignty with its assumption of the harmonious cooperation of all ruling members in the tsardom was ill suited to deal with the acrimony between Sofiia and Peter, the tsarevna began to explore new ways to enhance

18. Eagle portrait of Sofiia Alekseevna (Russian Museum, St. Petersburg). The portrait shows Sofiia Alekseevna with a scepter, orb, and crown. The two-headed eagle in which the portrait is inscribed features personifications of the traditional imperial Western values. The sword and plume in its claws express strength and a commitment to learning. The image is devoid of religious themes and eclipses the role of Sofiia's brothers in government.

her power. Both the regent's much discussed interest in the possibility of her coronation and the ruler portraits featuring her with the symbols of Russian government (the two-headed eagle, a crown, scepter, and orb) and the personifications of the traditional imperial values (see Figure 18) reflect her perceived need to strengthen her position with a new ruler ideology that radically redefined her position within the ruling trinity.[100]

Sofiia Alekseevna's new ruler image—which gradually emerged from 1686 onward, alongside traditional expressions of her power—broke with the customary gendered notion of the tsardom. While the medieval concept of the Russian autocracy encompassed the active participation of the tsar's immediate female kin in government by means of their religiously constructed role, Sofiia could only succeed against her fully grown half brother if she disavowed her part in the mutually inclusive role of both sexes in the Muscovite government. The result of such a decision, however, placed Sofiia in a dilemma, since she implicitly had to deny the entire Russian Orthodox tradition of the pious tsaritsy and tsarevny that sanctioned her position in the first place. In August 1687 the regent received a taste of the consequences of her unorthodox approach to her own ruler ideology when her supporter Fedor Shaklovityi failed to garner the *strel'tsy*'s support for her coronation as tsar.[101] According to the archimandrite of Mount Athos, Isaiah, who functioned as an ambassador of the patriarch of Constantinople to Russia, the Russian patriarch Ioakim fervently opposed Sofiia's coronation in the presence of two living tsars, because it violated the rules of the Apostles and the Church Fathers.[102] Patriarch Ioakim's reaction to the proposed coronation of Sofiia Alekseevna is striking insofar as he was not concerned with the impact of Western ideas on the construction of the tsardom, but with the undermining of its Orthodox theological basis.

Several of the artistic and literary works that were produced during the last two years of Sofiia's regency to increase her political authority prove that the patriarch's trepidation was justified. Although the court ideologues continued to exploit the image of Divine Wisdom in their portrayals of Sofiia Alekseevna, they deemphasized the notion of Sofiia as a translucent vessel collecting the divine grace and channeling it to her brothers and her realm at large. Instead, they used the image of the Wisdom of God to emphasize the tsarevna's supreme status in the ruling trinity.

According to Ivan Perekrest's testimony in the treason trials following Sofiia's fall from power, one of Sofiia's lost ruler portraits featured the three sovereigns Ivan, Peter, and Sofiia below the images of God Father, the Son, and the Holy Spirit.[103] At Fedor Shaklovityi's instigation, Perekrest's family commissioned the portrait after the first Crimean campaign as a frontispiece to a book of eulogies in honor of the regent. While the composition by and large seems to have followed the principles of Shchirskii's frontispiece to *Grace and Truth* in 1683, it deviated from the latter in one crucial detail. Whereas the 1683 engraving focused on the benefits of Sofiia's close relationship with the divine for the Russian tsardom, the image commissioned by Perekrest showed the seven gifts of the Holy Spirit emptying out on Sofiia alone. The implied superior position of the tsarevna in government vis-à-vis her brothers was clear to Sil'vestr Medvedev, who received his own copy from Shaklovityi. According to his later testimony, Medvedev was struck by the boldness of the print's symbolism but hesitated to inform Shaklovityi of his reservations.[104]

The ambivalence on the part of one of Sofiia Alekseevna's most ardent supporters toward the portrait of Sofiia with the divine gifts reflects the shift in the tsarevna's ruler ideology in the later years of her regency and the dangers it posed. Medvedev's concept of "Sofiia the translucent vessel of Divine Wisdom" based the regent's claim to sovereignty on the medieval notion of the religiously sanctioned symbiosis of the male and female members of the royal family. By associating the divine gifts exclusively with the tsarevna, the very premise of his concept of female sovereignty was undermined. While the degendering of tsardom evident in the lost portrait made it possible for Sofiia to appear as a visibly absolute ruler in her own right, it also undermined the religious roots of the Muscovite autocracy. Clearly realizing the implications of Sofiia's proposed coronation as tsar, Medvedev once openly told Shaklovityi that the patriarch would never agree to it.[105]

From a theological perspective, the transcendence of the medieval construction of Sofiia Alekseevna's position as a female ruler ultimately demanded a reinterpretation of the entire "Sophia the Wisdom of God" paradigm in connection with the regent. If the tsarevna was to appear as the only divinely chosen ruler of Russia, it was more effective to compare her directly with the fourth hypostasis in the divine entity than to label her the house of Divine Wisdom. An early example of this trend can be found in Lazar Baranovich's letter to Sofiia from September 20, 1686, in which he bases her claim to rule on the fact that her scepter was wise.[106] The final step in the evolution of Sofiia's ruler ideology is evident in Ignatii Rimskii-Korsakov's oration *"Svitetel'stvo ko obrazu sviatyia neizrechennye Sofii-Premudrosti slova bozhiia. O rossiiskom blagoslovennom tsarstvii"* ("Witness to the Image of the Holy Inexpressible Sophia, the Wisdom of the Word of God. About the blessed Russian Realm"), composed for official recitation on August 15, 1689, but never delivered because of Peter's takeover two weeks later. In the eulogy Rimskii-Korsakov allegorically interprets the Russian government in terms of the traditional iconography of the Novgorod Sophia icon, which shows the crowned and winged figure of Sophia, the fourth hypostasis of God, seated on a throne with seven legs, and with her feet placed on a stone (see Figure 19). She is flanked by the Virgin of the Sign on the left and John the Baptist holding a scroll on the right. Immediately above Sophia, who wears a regal tunic, Christ is seen blessing her with both hands. In the star-dotted heavens above six angels surround a throne featuring Christ's martyr instruments. Rimskii-Korsakov systematically assigned each component of the image a contemporary connotation. The Divine Wisdom seated on the throne denoted Sofiia the regent, while the Christ figure above her symbolized the true

Wisdom of God. The wings of the seated Wisdom stood for the regent's aunts, Anna and Tat'iana, who supported her. The seven legs of the throne signified the seven church councils, which represented the Orthodox foundation of the Russian government. Sofiia Alekseevna's close association with the Orthodox tradition was further expressed by the scroll in her hands, which in Rimskii-Korsakov's view referred to her function as intercessor for and defender of the faith. The stars in the firmament symbolized the members of the secular and ecclesiastical elites of Muscovy, while the six angels before the altar stood for the tsarevna's sisters, who devoted themselves to prayers on behalf of the realm. They were joined in their task by the Virgin of the Sign below. Her companion on the right, John the Baptist, represented the name saint of the regent's natal brother, Tsar Ivan, while the rock under Wisdom's feet referred to the Apostle Peter, the name saint of Peter Alekseevich.[107]

Rimskii-Korsakov's interpretation of the main forces in the Russian government in his allegorical treatment of the Novgorod Sophia icon clearly demonstrates the shift in Sofiia Alekseevna's ruler image in the later years of her regency. Placed on a throne and adorned with a royal garb and a crown, Sofiia's name saint is the only figure portrayed with ruler insignia.

19. Novgorod Sophia icon from the fifteenth century (Kremlin Museums, inventory no. Zh-1413; 97 Bl. s.; 480 sob.). Sophia the Wisdom of God, clad in royal garb and wearing a crown, is seated on a throne while the Virgin (on the left) and John the Baptist adore her. Immediately above, Christ blesses the figure of Wisdom. In the upper register, six angels worship the instruments of the Passion. The icon inspired court ideologue Ignatii Rimskii-Korsakov to ascribe to Sofiia Alekseevna supreme power over her brothers Ivan and Peter (identified by John the Baptist and the rock under Wisdom's feet).

Tsar Ivan simply acts as a facilitator of Sofiia's rule. Rimskii-Korsakov's identification of Sofiia's stepbrother with the rock under Wisdom's feet (Saint Peter's name denotes "rock," and the Apostle functioned as the rock of the church) drives the point home that, within the Russian ruling trinity, Aleksei Mikhailovich's daughter played the most eminent and prestigious role. Commanding the royal regalia and Christ's blessing, she alone could claim full sovereignty. In Rimskii-Korsakov's 1689 paradigm of royal power, Sofiia Alekseevna no longer represents a regent who rules for her brothers but one who rules over them. The concept of "Sofiia the vessel of God" that radiates divine wisdom onto the Russian realm is transcended in the notion of Sofiia the absolute ruler.

The ruler image of Sofiia Alekseevna underlying the lost portrait sponsored by Perekrest and Rimskii-Korsakov's allegorical approach to the Novgorod Sophia icon might have corresponded by and large to the traditional canons of Muscovite painting and literature, but it did not adhere to the Russian Orthodox notion of a gendered tsardom. Rimskii-Korsakov's panegyric of 1689 contained the same thoughts as the inscription on the Bloteling portrait, which compared Sofiia with strong female rulers, Semiramis of Mesopotamia, Elizabeth of Britain, and Pulcheria of Byzantium.[108] Characteristically the verses on the portrait do not refer to the gender-specific task of the three women but instead commemorate their respective eternal fame, royal stature, and mental acumen, values often associated with Western absolute rulers.[109] The subversion of the traditional notion of the Orthodox tsar in Sofiia's eagle portraits (which portray the tsarevna with a scepter, orb, and crown), the lost image of Sofiia Alekseevna, and Rimskii-Korsakov's last eulogy to the regent explains the vigorous campaign against these images and the banning of the performance of the oration during Peter the Great's reign. In spite of the lip service these artistic expressions of royal power rendered to the notion of the divinely approved position of the tsarevna, their silence about Sofiia Alekseevna's duty toward her brothers ultimately presented a direct challenge to their royal authority. It is not surprising that in his first letter to his brother Ivan after his overthrow of Sofiia Alekseevna, Tsar Peter reclaimed his and his brother's exclusive prerogative to God's favor and all royal titles and regalia.[110] By 1689 the tsarevna no longer appeared primarily as a divinely sanctioned female helpmate to her siblings but as a ruler who sought legitimacy outside the traditions of the royal family. Perhaps it is ironic that in her efforts to give her regency a more permanent character, Sofiia Alekseevna undermined the medieval concept of a gendered autocracy, which had enabled her to rise to power. In the end it may have made little difference since the success of any governmental system in late seventeenth-century Russia depended on the voluntary or forced consensus of all members of the ruling trinity. In the final struggle with Peter and the Naryshkin clan, Sofiia Alekseevna was not so much a victim of a Russian misogynist tradition as a loser in a struggle for political power.

An overall evaluation of Sofiia Alekseevna's regency must take into account her skillful manipulation of the symbolism associated with the Muscovite notion of a gendered tsardom, which entailed a division of duties among the immediate members of the ruling family. As a royal daughter, Sofiia from childhood participated in the rituals and myths surrounding Aleksei Mikhailovich's *terem*, which celebrated the tsarevny as spiritual intercessors for the tsar. Even more important, the regent and her followers were aware of the ideological force hidden behind the image of the pious tsaritsa and consistently sought to harness this force to the tsarevna's person throughout her years in power. In designing Sofiia Alekseevna's ruler image, her ideological handlers attributed to her the roles of a charitable caretaker of her subjects, spiritual intercessor for her realm, and defender of the true faith. The appropriation of these roles enabled the tsarevna to gain public visibility without violating the sensibilities of the Muscovite patriarchy. Considering the tsaritsa's accepted status as helpmate to the tsar, Sofiia Alekseevna's regency on behalf of her younger brothers could be interpreted as a morally high-minded and pious act that upheld and strengthened the autocracy in a time of dynastic crisis. In essence, rather than curtailing the tsarevna's opportunities to rise to political power (as most scholars assume), the ritual and mythical traditions surrounding the female members of the tsar's *terem* paved the way to her legitimate accession to the regency.

The adherence of Sofiia Alekseevna's regime to the traditional, medieval concept of tsardom is particularly evident in the religious overtones of her ruler image as it presented itself in royal ritual, panegyrical works dedicated to the regent, and a number of her ruler portraits. Whether she appeared as a devout tsarevna on a pilgrimage to assure the well-being of her realm or as a second Judith or Deborah upholding the faith of her people in the face of an attack on its religion, the religious connotation of her image provided assurance that Sofiia's role within the ruling trinity proclaimed in 1682 was consistent with the religious foundation of the tsardom in general. The regent's acceptance of a religiously constructed ruler image allowed her to overcome any obstacles posed by her gender. By embracing the Muscovite notion that royal women functioned as vessels of the divine, Sofiia Alekseevna claimed the illustrious position as a mediator of divine grace vis-à-vis her brothers and the realm. The resulting myth, "Sofiia the translucent house of Divine Wisdom," sanctioned her position as a protector of the autocracy and a benefactor to her realm.

Sofiia Alekseevna's reliance on the rituals and myths connected with the royal *terem* in the creation of her own ruler image suggests that her power as a regent was constructed primarily in feminine terms. As defender of the faith, mediator of Divine Wisdom, or virginal intercessor for the autocracy, she essentially fulfilled the helpmate role ascribed to the female component in the androgynous head of the tsardom. Sofiia's continued political influence ultimately depended on the acknowledgment of her position, which in view of the kinship rivalries within the royal family was less likely to occur when Sofiia's half brother Peter approached the end of his minority. To counter his bid for power, from 1686 onward Sofiia's ideological handlers increasingly attributed to the regent masculine symbols of power, which gave her the aura of a sovereign ruler in her own right. Tragically, by promoting her coronation and her exclusive monopoly of the divine gifts of a ruler, Sofiia's supporters destroyed the basis of power that had enabled her to attain a prominent position in the Russian autocracy by realizing her apportioned gender role. This change in the conceptualization of Sofiia's power, which alienated the traditionalists in the Muscovite state, in the end only played into the hands of the ambitious Peter, who was poised to wrest the reins of government from her.

Conclusion

HISTORIANS OF THE FAMILY LIFE of heads of state, whether they are of royal or of non-noble blood, generally ascribe to their wives an obligatory, but secondary role. In a world where the leadership of a country—both real and ceremonial—is still largely seen as a male affair, the wives of rulers and presidents often appear as alien figures that take their place in the public sphere merely by the force of circumstance. Tradition or state protocol generally seek to create "meaningful" roles for these women, which express their commitment to the work of their spouses. Such roles generally include the reception of political guests, beautification of the male environment of government (one thinks of Jacqueline Kennedy's campaign to refurbish the White House), the practice of charity, and the dissemination of culture. From a modern perspective, these duties are clearly gender-biased since they largely pertain to the domestic, private sphere. In essence these activities make the wives of political leaders appear as glorified hosts, housekeepers, and mothers, defined and circumscribed by the vehicle of public ritual.

If the wives of world leaders do not share directly in the political authority of their husbands, this does not mean, however, that they exercise no influence at all in the body politic, nor is it true that their position is entirely derived from that of their spouses. The personal influence of a First Lady on her husband more than once has affected political decisions in the White House. Eleanor Roosevelt and Diana, Princess of Wales, both developed a relationship with their respective people that broke through the barriers established by protocol and earned them independent prestige and fame. Political observers, historians, and sociologists, and even the media in recent times have increasingly directed their attention to the hidden power of the wives of presidents and princes, a power not derived from office, but familial status.

The wives of the medieval Russian tsars to a large extent would have been able to identify with the roles of their modern counterparts. From the time of Sofiia Paleolog to the regency of Sofiia Alekseevna, the royal women of Muscovy entertained high-ranking visitors to the Russian state. The women of the first two generations of the Romanov dynasty commissioned artistic projects designed to decorate the Kremlin. The medieval Russian chronicles, court and church records, and donation charters repeatedly testify to the grand princesses' and tsaritsy's commitment to alms-giving and other charitable acts. Through their interaction and correspondence with members of the Eastern Orthodox church abroad, the wives of the Muscovite tsars appeared as ambassadors of Russian culture. Medieval Russian royal women also would have understood the power of familial status that gives the spouses (and, in Muscovy, the mothers) of heads of state wide-ranging influence in political matters. The mothers of the grand princes of Moscow acted as advisers and political mediators to their oldest sons. Irina Godunova exercised governmental authority in the place of her frail husband, foreshadowing Sofiia Alekseevna's visible display of political decision-making a century later. The eminent position of the tsaritsy as mothers of the realm, sometimes coupled with their charitable roles, gave Mariia Nagaia, Solomoniia Saburova, and Anastasiia Romanovna a degree of independent prestige not unlike that enjoyed by Eleanor Roosevelt or Princess Diana.

Still, the position of the royal women of Muscovite Russia, the challenges they faced, and the means they employed to meet them are in many ways fundamentally different from those associated with wives of modern world leaders. When evaluating the roles of medieval Russian grand princesses and tsaritsy, we must keep in mind that this role was shaped by social norms alien to the modern experience. Although a Muscovite royal woman would have agreed that one of the bases of her authority and prestige was the family, the very concept of family was endowed with infinitely more significance and meaning in a period that did not yet separate clearly the personal and private from the public sphere. In contrast to most modern examples, the role of Muscovite royal women was to a large degree defined by religious norms. For better or worse, in every generation the grand princesses and tsaritsy had to respond to the expectations of the Russian Orthodox church, both ideological and practical. The church essentially provided the language for the conceptualization of the tsaritsa's role in the same way it coined the concept of the blessed and pious tsar. Russian Orthodoxy also took it for granted that the tsars' wives would affirm the spiritual quality of their position in acting out the religious ritual prescribed for them, such as that associated with pilgrimages, care for the needy, and alms-giving to monastic and ecclesiastical institutions. In essence Muscovite royal women constantly performed a balancing act juggling the requirements of their families, the autocracy, and the church. In the process they put their own stamp on their relationship with these institutions. The vehicle they employed for this purpose was the language of religious myth.

Our understanding of the status of medieval Russian royal women ultimately hinges upon the realization that the lives of the tsars' wives were informed by historical constructs specific to their time and place. Nineteenth- and twentieth-century scholars have generally failed in their efforts to uncover the achievements of these women precisely because they let themselves be influenced by contemporary notions of the role of women in society and the state. Ivan Zabelin's tremendous effort a century and a half ago to uncover the details of the Muscovite tsaritsy's daily lives in the end leaves us with a two-dimensional view of these women because of his inability to imagine them as actors and contributors on the political stage. Modern scholars have been unduly influenced by a distaste for autocratic systems and a (Western) feminist disillusionment with established religion. They generally see Muscovite women, royal and nonroyal, primarily as victims. None of these explanatory models satisfy, however, since they all assume that medieval Russian royal women were singularly and unilaterally dependent on one institution. In reality the lives of Muscovite royal women were infinitely more complex and dynamic than modern experts have dared to admit.

Throughout the Muscovite period, the position of royal women was governed by the family principle. The complicated pattern of the interaction of Muscovite royal women and male members of their immediate kin created both hardships and opportunities for the grand princesses and tsaritsy. Muscovite royal women associated with the Rurikide house and the Godunov family were persecuted because of their key role in dynastic politics. On the other hand, they served as advisers and helpmates to their husbands and oldest sons and acted as social and spiritual intercessors for the Russian rulers. They maintained these roles in spite of the gradual formalization of Muscovite governmental structures evident in the separation of male and female space in the Kremlin and the evolution of gender-specific state ritual. This division, however, was not synonymous with the removal of royal women from public life to an artificially created private sphere. In Russia before the eighteenth century, the public and private were intricately intertwined. As in early medieval Western Europe, political matters were conceived in personal and familial terms. The wives and daughters of the first two Romanov tsars enjoyed the confidence of the Russian rulers. During Aleksei Mikhailovich's Smolensk campaign, Mariia Il'inichna issued instructions regarding the maintenance of public health and order in the capital. In times of military or dynastic crisis, Muscovite royal women came to the fore to defend the interests of the realm. In a sense the creation of the royal *terem* and exclusively female royal rituals shone the spotlight on the special significance held by the Muscovite royal women in the political system of the tsardom.

The importance of the Muscovite rulers' wives in the autocratic system of government emerging in the sixteenth and seventeenth centuries can be gleaned from the proliferation of myths surrounding the personae of Russian royal women. Chronicles, hagiographic works, and liturgical inscriptions of the period all aimed at adding a spiritual dimension to the tsaritsa's role. In their efforts to create a religious aura for the Russian ruler, which would underscore the superiority of his new position, the framers of the ideology of tsardom displayed a tremendous interest in the pious tsaritsa. In the hands of the ideological spin doctors, the image of Solomoniia Saburova became transformed from that of an infertile tsar's wife to that of a saintly defender of the Orthodox realm and a protector of her people. At the end of the sixteenth century, traditional stories surrounding the Kievan Grand Princess Ol'ga and the pious Byzantine empresses Helena, Theodora, and Irene became tools in the hands of Godunov sympathizers to proclaim Boris Godunov's legitimate right to the throne—because of his sister's position as the last tsaritsa of the Rurikide dynasty. Using religious myth to elevate Irina Godunova to the level of her saintly models (who all acted without male guidance to defend the true faith in their countries), they attributed to the last Rurikide tsaritsa the ability to function as an independent ruler in times of crisis.

These schemes of spiritualizing the position of the tsaritsa were clearly aimed at strengthening the institution of the tsardom as a whole. The reinterpretation of Solomoniia Saburova's figure underscored the notion that the Muscovite autocracy was divinely sanctioned. When faced with the problem of maintaining dynastic continuity in their realm, the proponents of the Muscovite autocracy did not hesitate to manipulate the image of their tsaritsy to serve their needs. The politics of images observed in the frescoes of the Golden Palace of the Tsaritsy were the product of narrow court interests pursuing at any cost the success of the Godunov clan. Nearly simultaneously, supporters of the Romanov family carefully fostered the myth of the "pious tsaritsa Anastasiia," to derive the legitimacy of the Romanov line from the first wife of Ivan IV.

If the autocracy's interest in positive images of Muscovite royal women was self-serving, the mythopoeic efforts of advocates of a strong centralized government nevertheless benefited the tsaritsy by reinforcing their importance for the tsars and for the realm at large. If grand princesses had acted as mediators in their families, after the official establishment of the tsardom they became spiritual intercessors for the Russian rulers and their subjects. This function heightened the visibility of the royal wives. As intercessors for their husbands, they engaged in publicly recognized liturgical activities that were aimed at securing the support of the divine for the tsardom. As caretakers of their subjects, throughout the sixteenth and seventeenth centuries they practiced charity and enforced social justice. The myth-making schemes associated with the rise of the tsardom worked to the advantage of royal women, endowing their role as wives and mothers with a dynastic significance hitherto unknown in Russia. The equation of Irina Godunova with Princess Dinara and Saints Irene, Theodora, Helena, and Ol'ga resulted in Irina's elevation to an independently acting ruler. In similar fashion the court poetry and court-sponsored art of the late seventeenth century used biblical analogies to create an ideological foundation for the regency of Sofiia Alekseevna. The constant association of the Muscovite royal women with the maintenance of the true faith in Russia gave the tsaritsy and tsarevny unprecedented spiritual authority. The involvement of Irina Godunova in the establishment of the Russian patriarchate or Mariia Il'inichna's intervention in the religious turmoil in Moscow in 1654–1655 would have been unthinkable had their actions not been sanctioned by long accepted religious myths. In a similar way the involvement of Irina Mikhailovna, Mariia Il'inichna, and Sofiia Alekseevna in the Old Believer controversy can be understood only if we keep in mind that Muscovites were used to seeing their royal women as champions of the true faith.

The mythopoeic activities surrounding the persona of the Muscovite tsaritsa, however, were not geared solely to strengthening the Muscovite autocracy. The religious symbolism attached to the tsars' wives also gives insight into the dynamic interaction between these women and existing social norms and political exigencies, as well as into their engagement in transforming their sociocultural roles. Muscovite royal women did not respond passively to the definition of their position by promoters of the autocracy. They actively used the power of religious myth and ritual to create for themselves a meaningful role within a largely male-centered political system. The example of Sofiia Paleolog shows that a Muscovite royal mother—faced with the dynastic claims of the offspring of her husband's former wife—won the upper hand by linking her own body with the notion of tsardom by divine grace. Her successors Solomoniia Saburova, Anastasiia Romanovna, Mariia Temriukovna, and Irina Godunova all used the myth of the tsaritsa's blessed womb to strengthen their position in their battle with infertility (which could end in their physical removal from the court). From the middle of the sixteenth century on, the wives of the Russian tsars patronized the cults of several saints whom they credited with the ability to protect the health of royal children. Confronted with the specter of infant mortality, these women reinforced the notion that the future of the autocracy was dependent on their pious works. In their hands myth and ritual became powerful instruments that not only helped define the ideology of tsardom but also wrote royal women into that definition, thus giving their arduous lives meaning and significance.

The fact that the myths and rituals Muscovites associated with their royal women were almost exclusively religious in nature raises the issue of the role played by the Orthodox church in defining the image of the grand princesses and tsaritsy. In view of the widespread dissemination in medieval Russia of the traditional Christian didactic literature, presenting women as weak and corrupting elements in God's creation, the virtual absence of this concept in Muscovite religious writings composed about or directed to Muscovite royal women is surprising. Rather than comparing the tsaritsy with Eve, literary and visual sources stress their similarity to the Virgin Mary. The myth of the tsaritsa's blessed womb in essence assumes a likeness between these women and the Mother of God, whose conception of Christ was considered divinely inspired. Mariological imagery was employed also to underscore the tsaritsy's perceived intercessory function between the divine and the tsars and their realm. The use of religious language for the enhancement of the position of royal women is also evident in the frequent association of the tsaritsy with acclaimed Orthodox female saints. Although most of these mythopoeic activities arose on Russian soil, their models lay in the Byzantine tradition. This circumstance strongly refutes the commonly held view inspired by Zabelin that the Byzantine religious heritage influenced the position of medieval Russian women negatively.

The full impact of traditional religious symbolism on the position of the wives of the medieval Russian rulers can be grasped only if we appreciate the flexibility of the mythical language and the sophistication in its application to the tsars' wives. The mythical language that defined the role of the Muscovite royal women, in both its written and its visual forms, was multi-semic in character. This allowed the framers of the ideology of tsardom to adjust individual myths to the circumstances that figured prominently in the life of a tsaritsa in each generation. For example, in his wedding sermon of 1547, Metropolitan Makarii applied to Anastasiia Romanovna the myth of the tsaritsa's spiritual affinity to Saint Helena, in order to underscore the notion that Moscow could become a second Jerusalem. In the frescoes of the Golden Palace of the Tsaritsy, the myth expressed Irina Godunova's ability to act as a ruler in her own right on account of her role as a pious advocate of the true faith. For Evdokiia Luk'ianovna, the Helena myth simply represented an incentive for generous almsgiving. The icon *The Veneration of the Cross* underscored the notion that, in her likeness to Saint Helena, Mariia Il'inichna could act as a spiritual intercessor for her royal husband. Throughout the Muscovite period, those in charge of developing the concept of the tsaritsa took advantage of the flexibility in the interpretation of the religious myths and applied them selectively to any given situation.

If the Eastern Orthodox arsenal of religious imagery ultimately proved to be a source for Muscovite royal women from which they drew prestige and power, this outcome was sanctioned by members of the ecclesiastical and monastic ranks in medieval Russia and the Orthodox communities abroad. Numerous examples testify to the close cooperation, in the construction of the royal wife's image, of the tsaritsy with members of the Orthodox church hierarchy. If Solomoniia Saburova and Anastasiia Romanovna played a vital role in the invention of the myth of the tsaritsa's blessed womb, the longevity of the myth ultimately must be ascribed to figures such as Metropolitans Makarii and Afanasii, who encouraged the royal wives in their endeavors and promoted the dissemination of the myth in contemporary chronicle literature and hagiography. Similarly, the elevation of the religious status of the Muscovite tsaritsa to that of the Byzantine saint and imperial mother, Saint Helena, was supported by an array of Orthodox hierarchs in

Russia and abroad from the second half of the sixteenth century onward. The interaction of the royal wives with Orthodox clerics and monks often took on an intimate character. Patriarch Iov served as a close spiritual adviser to Irina Godunova, whom he treated as an heir to the throne left vacant by the last Rurikide tsar. Irina and her Romanov successors entertained cordial relations with a number of Eastern Orthodox patriarchs who appreciated the patronage of the royal women. The professed friendship between these ecclesiastical authorities and the tsaritsy belies the assumption of many experts both East and West that the institutional church by its very nature is hostile to the concept of strong, independently acting women.

The image and role of Muscovite royal women in many ways parallels the representations and functions of queens in medieval Europe. The comparison of royal wives and mothers with biblical counterparts or saints of the early Christian era goes back as far as the Merovingian and Carolingian periods. Western European queens often were valued as patrons of religious institutions, helpmates to their husbands, intercessors for their subjects, and caretakers of the poor. In times of political turmoil and stress, Merovingian and Ottonian royal women exercised economic and legal control in their territories, made political decisions, and acted as effective regents for their sons. Carolingian queens functioned as confidantes and advisers to their husbands, while their Capetian and Norman counterparts cemented their respective royal governments with their dynastic connections.

Still, in many respects, the Muscovite tsaritsy enjoyed a unique position. Medieval Russia never separated the person of its ruler from that of his wife. Queenship as a category distinct from kingship was not acceptable to Muscovites, as is shown by their moral outrage about Marina Mniszech's coronation in 1605. The Muscovite refusal to consider the tsaritsa a persona apart from the tsar may be explained by the circumstance that medieval Russia never participated in the trend to desacralize the image of rulers and to define their position in government in legal terms, a trend that Western Europe had experienced since the eleventh century. The absence of a legal definition in the sixteenth century led Metropolitan Makarii to define the autocracy as a family enterprise in which the royal husband and wife carried out separate but mutually supportive tasks. Unable to draw upon Western legal concepts of the power of a sovereign, Makarii developed the older Muscovite notion that matters of state concerned the immediate members of the grand-princely family, both male and female. The efforts of the metropolitan and other supporters of an autocratic government to endow the tsardom with a religious dimension also led to the spiritualization of the tsaritsa's position. The tsardom, embodied in the ruling couple, represented the sum of the religious deeds of its members. While the tsar was accountable to God for the physical and spiritual well-being of his realm, his wife was to support him in his task by carrying out pious acts of social justice and kindness. Her spiritual potential placed her in an intermediary position between God and the tsar and therefore made her an intercessor for her husband before the divine. The tsaritsa's function was an integral part of the tsardom that assured its continued success. This explains why royal women who were forced to take the veil by their husbands continued to command respect from subsequent rulers, who cherished their support.

The findings of this study that the royal wives of Muscovy were tightly woven into the structure of the tsardom, the success of which they helped guarantee, raise questions about the often expressed scholarly opinion that the medieval Russian autocrat wielded unfettered, absolute power.[1] This view, which rests upon the assumption that the tsar's sovereign authority was uncurbed by laws or representative institutions, has recently been challenged by scholars such as Nancy Kollmann, Valerie Kivelson, and Donald Ostrowski.[2] The interpretation of the tsar's power advanced by these scholars stresses the cooperation between the tsar and the ruling elite, the negotiated interaction of the provincial gentry with the Muscovite ruler in the seventeenth century, and the ability of the church and the boyar council to affect the tsar's decisions. While these scholars examine political and social aspects of the tsardom to show that the Mucovite ruler was far from embodying an Oriental despot, this study implies that the tsar also was not an absolute ruler in a cultural sense. The religious construction of the tsardom not only bound the tsar to Christian ethics, as Michael Flier and Daniel Rowland have pointed out, but it made the person of the Russian ruler dependent on his wife, who shared in his duties of government before God. Even though Muscovite ideologues could not conceive of an unharmonious relationship between the tsar and the tsaritsa, which would have lessened the tsar's authority, their assumption that, in affairs concerning the well-being of the realm, the Muscovite autocrat relied on the pious intercession of his spouse ultimately makes the nature of his authority appear less absolute.

The Muscovite notion that the tsardom was not embodied by the male ruler alone but included his spouse, whose persona was inseparable from that of the tsar, in essence meant that the medieval Russian tsardom was an engendered concept. Undoubtedly the day-to-day affairs of the Russian government—diplomatic negotiations, the administration of law, and the collection of taxes—were usually conducted by the tsar or his staff. But the complex interaction between tsar, tsaritsa, and God could confront scenarios (notably in times of crisis) in which the tasks of the members of the ruling couple were redistributed. Fedor Ivanovich and Aleksei Mikhailovich engaged in religious activities to such an extent that they occasionally eclipsed their wives in the performance of their customary duty. Vice versa it was possible for Irina Godunova and Mariia Grigor'evna to take on traditionally male functions of government.

The flexible combination of masculine and feminine potencies in the Muscovite ruler couple may give us a new understanding of the tradition of female rule in Imperial Russia. Scholars investigating the origin of this tradition generally focus on the regency of Sofiia Alekseevna for her brothers Ivan and Peter, which Sofiia manipulated to attain the status of a sovereign ruler in her own right. While much attention has been paid recently to Sofiia's image-building campaign, the search for the ideological basis of Sofiia's status as a ruler appears to have been unduly biased toward the last years of her reign, in which her supporters at court experimented with attributions of Western, secular symbols of power to the tsarevna. The evidence from official government documents argues for Sofiia's gradual emergence as a sovereign ruler. It is therefore not surprising that Sofiia's ruler image did not represent a sharp break from medieval Russian notions of tsardom. The cultivation of the image of the pious tsarevna Sofiia, her portrayal as a champion of the Orthodox faith, and her proclaimed likeness to biblical figures all find precedents in the Muscovite past. As in the case of the Muscovite tsaritsy, religious symbolism provided a means to demonstrate the legitimacy of an independent female ruler. The identification of Sofiia Alekseevna with Sophia the vessel of Divine Wisdom, which was the root metaphor for the tsarevna's political authority, represents a clever variant of the Muscovite myth of the blessed womb of the tsaritsa. The court ideologues of the later seventeenth century displayed creativity in making the necessary adjustments that the shift from the concept of a ruling tsaritsa to that of a ruling tsarevna required. In view of the established Muscovite notion that the tsardom was a gendered, familial concept, the replacement of the husband-wife relationship with a triune concept of government that comprised Sofiia and her two brothers was not such a radical step as is commonly assumed. As in the case of the royal wives and mothers, Sofiia's leading role in the triune rule was justified by her presumed superior spiritual virtues.

If in the end Sofiia could not hang on to the reins of power, her failure was not synonymous with a Russian rejection of female rule. Peter the Great may have presented his sister's regency as a feminine abuse of power for his own selfish reasons, but in the end he facilitated the succession of his wife Catherine to the throne. Perhaps the celebrated westernizer and social and cultural innovator was more indebted to Muscovite traditions than we have until now been willing to believe.

Glossary

d'iak	secretary in Muscovite chancellery system; often in charge of administrative matters; ranks higher than *pod'iachii*
gosudarynia	sovereign lady; title used by the wives and daughters of the Romanov tsars
gubnaia zapis'	provision concerning provincial government
hegumen	abbot of an Orthodox monastery
katapetasma	liturgical curtain separating the sanctuary from the part of the church in which the believers gather
kliuchar'	sacrist; church official in large church or cathedral who is responsible for the safe storage of liturgical objects; holds the keys to the church
kondakion	sermon in verse celebrating saints or feasts; a hymn
logothetes	high official at Byzantine court in charge of departments; administrative title
mamka	nanny; a woman usually from a boyar family serving in the royal *terem*
minei	from Greek *menaia;* liturgical books containing hymns and prayers for the annual celebration of saints organized by month; in medieval Russia, the *minei* often contained *vitae* and homilies to the saints, similar to the *menologia.*

namestnik	provincial governor; vicegerent (fell out of use in sixteenth century)
okol'nichii	second-highest noble rank after boyar
oprichnina	governmental experiment by Ivan IV known for its terror, 1564–1570
pod'iachii	undersecretary; clerk in Muscovite chancellery system
poluustav	semi-uncial
Posol'skii prikaz	Foreign Office; Department of Foreign Affairs
prikaz	chancellery
protopop	archpriest
Razriadnyi prikaz	Chancellery of Military Affairs
sakkos	richly ornamented liturgical vestment worn by patriarchs, metropolitans, and bishops
skoropis'	cursive
stol'nik	Muscovite court rank denoting a courtier with less than *duma* rank
strelets/strel'tsy	musketeer/musketeers
syn' boiarskii	junior boyar, member of gentry, who serves in provincial cavalry
terem	living space of female members of Muscovite noble or royal household
troparion	basic strophic unit of a hymn
umilenie	spiritual disposition associated with humility and gift of tears
vita	a saint's *life;* hagiographical genre
voevoda	provincial governor or military commander
zhertvennik	sacrificial altar

Appendix

Genealogical Charts

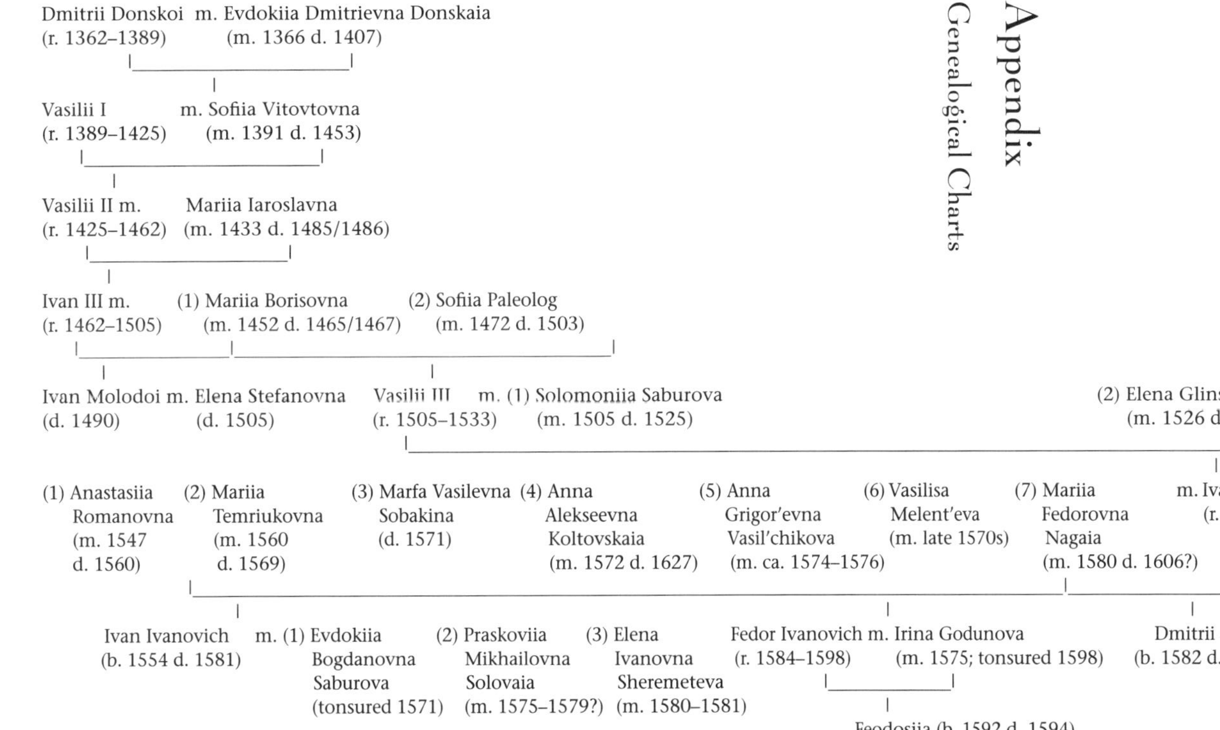

The Godunov Dynasty

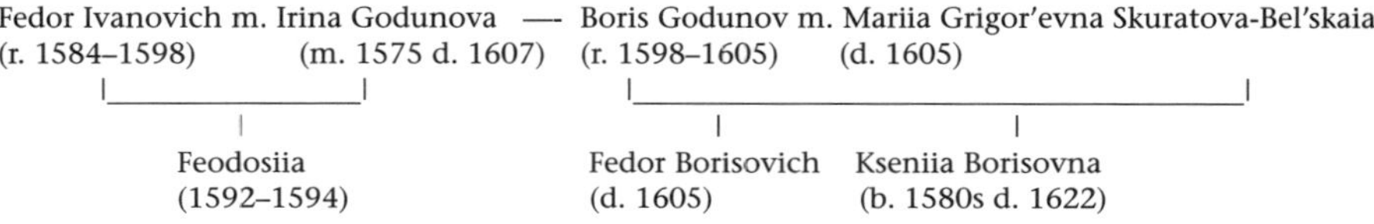

The Pretender and his Fictitious Dynastic Claim

Ivan IV m. (7) Mariia Fedorovna Nagaia
(r. 1547–1584) (m. 1580 d. 1606?)

First False Dmitrii m. Marina Mniszech
(r. 1605–1606) (crowned 1606 d. 1614)

The Romanov Dynasty (Simplified Chart)

Nikita Romanovich (d. 1586) — Anastasiia Romanovna (m. 1547 d. 1560) m. Ivan IV (r. 1547–1585)

Fedor Nikitich (d. 1633) m. Mariia (Marfa) Ivanovna Shestova (d. 1631)

Mikhail Fedorovich (r. 1613–1645) m. (1) Mariia Vladimirovna Dolgorukaia (d. 1624); (2) Evdokiia Luk'ianovna Streshneva (m. 1626 d. 1645)

(2) Natal'ia Kirillovna Naryshkina (m. 1670 d. 1694)	(1) Mariia Il'inichna Miloslavskaia (m. 1648 d. 1669)	m. Aleksei Mikhailovich (r. 1645–1676)	Irina (b. 1627 d. 1679)	Pelagiia (b. 1628 d. 1629)	Anna (b. 1630 d. 1692)	Marfa (b. 1631 d. 1632)	Sofiia (b. 1634 d. 1636)	Tat'iana (b. 1636 d. 1706)	Evdokiia (b. d. 1637)

Aleksei Mikhailovich m. (1) Mariia Il'inichna Miloslavskaia; (2) Natal'ia Kirillovna Miloslavskaia

Aleksei (b. 1654 d. 1670)	Fedor (r. 1676 -1682)	Ivan (r. 1682 -1696)	Evdokiia (b. 1650 d. 1712)	Marfa (b. 1652 d. 1707)	Anna (b. 1655 d. 1659)	Sofiia (b. 1657 r. 1682–1689 d. 1704)	Ekaterina (b. 1658 d. 1718)	Mariia (b. 1660 d. 1723)	Feodosiia (b. 1662 d. 1713)	Evdokiia (b. d. 1669)	Peter the Great (r. 1682 –1725)	Natal'ia (b. 1673 d. 1716)	Feodora (b. 1674 d. 1678)

The Marriages of Aleksei Mikhailovich's Sons:

Fedor Alekseevich (r. 1676–1682) m. (1) Agaf'ia Semenovna Grushetskaia (m. 1680 d. 1681)
(2) Marfa Matveevna Apraksina (m. 1682 d. 1715)

Ivan Alekseevich (r. 1682–1696) m. Praskov'ia Fedorovna Saltykova (m. 1684 d. 1723)

Peter the Great (r. 1682–1725) m. (1) Evdokiia Fedorovna Lopukhina (m. 1689 d. 1731)
(2) Ekaterina I Alekseevna (m. 1712 d. 1727)

Abbreviations

AAE *Akty sobrannye v bibliotekakh i arkhivakh Rossiiskoi imperii Arkheograficheskoi ekspeditsiei Akademii nauk.* 4 vols. St. Petersburg, 1836.

AI *Akty istoricheskie, sobrannye i izdannye Arkheograficheskoi kommissiei.* 5 vols. St. Petersburg, 1841–1842.

Bakhrushin, "Politicheskie tolki" Bakhrushin, S. V. "Politicheskie tolki v tsarstvovanie Mikhaila Fedorovicha." In *Trudy po istochnikovedeniiu, istoriografii i istorii Rossii epokhi feodalizma (nauchnoe nasledie).* Ed. B. V. Levshin. Moscow, 1987. 87–118.

BAN Biblioteka Akademii nauk (Library of Academy of Sciences, St. Petersburg).

Blagoveshchenskii Sobor *Blagoveshchenskii sobor Moskovskogo Kremlia. K 500-letiiu unikal'nogo pamiatnika russkoi kul'tury.* Ed. I. Ia. Kachalova, N. A. Maiasova, and L. A. Shchennikova. Moscow, 1990.

Bushkovitch, *Religion* Bushkovitch, Paul A. *Religion and Society in Russia. The Sixteenth and Seventeenth Centuries.* New York, 1992.

ChOIDR *Chteniia v Imperatorskom obshchestve istorii i drevnostei rossiiskikh pri Moskovskom universitete.* Moscow, 1845–1919.

Chubinskaia, "Ikona" Chubinskaia, V. G. "Ikona Simona Ushakova 'Bogomater' Vladimirskaia,' 'Drevo Moskovskogo gosudarstva,' 'Pokhvala Bogomateri Vladimirskoi' (opyt istoriko-kul'turnoi interpretatsii)." *TODRL* 38 (1985): 290–308.

Claus, *Stellung* Claus, Claire. *Die Stellung der russischen Frau von der Einführung des Christentums bei den Russen bis zu den Reformen Peter des Großen.* Munich, 1959.

Collins, *Present State* Samuel Collins. *The Present State of Russia, in a Letter to a Friend at London*. London, 1671.

DAI *Dopolneniia k Aktam istoricheskim, sobrannym i izdannym Arkheograficheskoi kommissiei*. 12 vols. St. Petersburg, 1846–1872.

DDG Cherepnin, L. V. *Dukhovnye i dogovornye gramoty velikikh i udel'nykh kniazei XIV–XVI vv*. Moscow, 1950.

Dimitrijević, "Dokumenti" Dimitrijević, M., ed. "Dokumenti koji se tiču odnosa između srpske crkve i Rusije u XVI veku." *Spomenik*. Ed. Srpska Kraljevska Akademija, vol. 39, drugi razred, br. 35 (1903): 16–42.

DR *Dvortsovye razriady po vysochaishemu poveleniiu izdannye II otdeleniem sobstvennoi ego Imperatorskago velichestva kantseliarii*. 4 vols. St. Petersburg, 1850–1855.

DRG Komitet dlia izdaniia Drevnostei Rossiiskago gosudarstva. *Drevnosti Rossiiskago gosudarstva*. 6 vols. Moscow, 1849–1853.

Drijvers, *Helena Augusta* Drijvers, Jan Willem. *Helena Augusta: The Mother of Constantine the Great and the Legend of the Finding of the True Cross*. Leiden, 1992.

DRV *Drevniaia rossiiskaia vivliofika*. Ed. N. I. Novikov. 2d ed. 20 vols. Slavistic Printings and Reprintings 250. 1788–1791. The Hague, 1970.

Flier, "Breaking the Code" Flier, Michael S. "Breaking the Code: The Image of the Tsar in the Muscovite Palm Sunday Ritual." In *Medieval Russian Culture*. Vol. 2. Ed. Michael S. Flier and Daniel Rowland. California Slavic Studies 19. Berkeley, 1994. 213–42.

Flier, "Iconography" Flier, Michael S. "The Iconography of Royal Procession: Ivan the Terrible and the Muscovite Palm Sunday Ritual." In *European Monarchy: Its Evolution and Practice from Roman Antiquity to Modern Times*. Ed. Heinz Duchhardt, Richard A. Jackson, and David Sturdy. Stuttgart, 1992. 109–25.

Flier, "Iconology" Flier, Michael S. "The Iconology of Royal Ritual in Sixteenth-Century Muscovy." In *Byzantine Studies: Essays on the Slavic World and the Eleventh Century*. Ed. Speros Vryonis, Jr. New Rochelle, 1992. 53–76.

GIM Gosudarstvennyi istoricheskii muzei (State Historical Museum, Moscow).

Goehrke, "Witwe" Goehrke, Carsten. Die Witwe im alten Rußland." *Forschungen zur osteuropäischen Geschichte* 38 (1986): 64–96.

GTG Gosudarstvennaia Tret'iakovskaia Gallereia (Tret'iakov Gallery, Moscow).

GTG. Katalog Antonova, V. I., and N. E. Mneva. *Gosudarstvennaia Tret'iakovskaia Gallereia. Katalog drevnerusskoi zhivopisi XI–nachala XVIII vv*. 2 vols. Moscow, 1963.

Herberstein, *Notes* Herberstein, Sigismund von. *Notes upon Russia: Being a Translation of the Earliest Account of that Country entitled Rerum Moscoviticarum Commentarii*. Ed. and trans. R. H. Majors. 2 vols. 1851–1852; New York, 1963.

Howes, *Testaments* *The Testaments of the Grand Princes of Moscow*. Ed. and trans. Robert Craig Howes. Ithaca, N.Y., 1967.

Hughes, *Sophia* Hughes, Lindsey. *Sophia, Regent of Russia 1657–1704.* New Haven, 1990.

HUS *Harvard Ukrainian Studies.*

Kämpfer, *Herrscherbild* Kämpfer, Frank. *Das russische Herrscherbild von den Anfängen bis zu Peter dem Großen.* Recklinghausen, 1978.

Kamen' Kraeug"l'n" *Kamen' kraeug"l'n": Rhetoric of the Medieval Slavic World. Essays presented to Edward L. Keenan on his Sixtieth Birthday by his Colleagues and Students.* Ed. Nancy Shields Kollmann, Donald Ostrowski, Andrei Pliguzov, and Daniel Rowland. HUS 19. Cambridge, Mass., 1995.

Kapterev, *Kharakter* *Kapterev, N. F. Kharakter otnoshenii Rossii k pravoslavnomu vostoku v XVI i XVII stoletiiakh.* 2d ed. Slavistic Printings and Reprintings 107. 1914. Reprint, The Hague, 1968.

Kliuchevskii, *Drevnerusskiia zhitiia* Kliuchevskii, V. O. *Drevnerusskiia zhitiia sviatykh kak istoricheskii istochnik.* 1871. Reprint, The Hague, 1968.

Kollmann, *Kinship* Kollmann, Nancy Shields. *Kinship and Politics. The Making of the Muscovite Political System, 1345–1547.* Stanford, 1987.

Kotoshikhin, *O Rossii* Kotoshikhin, Grigorii. *O Rossii v carstvovanie Alekseija Mixailoviča.* Ed. A. E. Pennington. Oxford, 1980.

Levin, *Sex and Society* Levin, Eve Rebecca. *Sex and Society in the World of the Orthodox Slavs, 900–1700.* Ithaca, N.Y., 1989.

McNally, "From Public Person" McNally, Susanne. "From Public Person to Private Prisoner: The Changing Place of Women in Medieval Russia." Ph.D. diss., State University of New York at Binghamton, 1976.

Nikolaeva, *Sobranie* Nikolaeva, T. V. *Sobranie drevnerusskogo iskusstva v Zagorskom Muzee.* Leningrad, 1968.

Novombergskii, *Slovo i delo* *Slovo i delo gosudarevy. Protsessy do izdaniia Ulozheniia Alekseia Mikhailovicha 1649 goda.* Ed. N. Novombergskii. Vol. 1. Moscow, 1911.

OSP *Oxford Slavonic Papers.*

Paul of Aleppo, *Travels* Paul of Aleppo. *The Travels of Macarius, Patriarch of Antioch, written by his Attendant Archdeacon, Paul of Aleppo, in Arabic.* Trans. F. C. Belfour. 2 vols. London, 1836.

PL *Pskovskie letopisi.* Ed. A. N. Nasonov. Moscow, 1941–1955.

Posol'skaia kniga *Posol'skaia kniga po sviaziam Rossii s Gretsiei (pravoslavnymi ierarkhami i monastyriami) 1588–1594 gg.* Ed. V. I. Buganov and M. P. Lukichev. Moscow, 1988.

***PRG*, vol. 1** *Pis'ma russkikh gosudarei i drugikh osob tsarskago semeistva.* Ed. Arkheograficheskaia kommissiia. Vol. 1. Moscow, 1848.

***PRG*, vol. 5** *Pis'ma russkikh gosudarei i drugikh osob tsarskago semeistva.* Ed. Arkheograficheskaia kommissiia. Vol. 5. Moscow, 1896.

PSRL *Polnoe sobranie russkikh letopisei.* 41 vols. to date. St. Petersburg and Moscow, 1846–1989.

PSZ *Polnoe sobranie zakonov Rossiiskoi imperii.* Sobranie pervoe. 45 vols. St. Petersburg, 1830.

RGADA Rossiiskii gosudarstvennyi arkhiv drevnikh aktov (Russian State Archive of Ancient Acts, Moscow).

RGB Russkaia gosudarstvennaia biblioteka (Russian State Library, Moscow).

RH *Russian History/Histoire russe.*

RIB *Russkaia istoricheskaia biblioteka, izdavaemaia Arkheograficheskoiu kommissieiu.* St. Petersburg and Leningrad, 1872–1927.

RNB Russkaia natsional'naia biblioteka (Russian National Library, St. Petersburg).

Rowland, "Biblical Military Imagery" Rowland, Daniel. "Biblical Military Imagery in the Political Culture of Early Modern Russia: The Blessed Host of the Heavenly Tsar." In *Medieval Russian Culture.* Vol. 2. Ed. Michael S. Flier and Daniel Rowland. California Slavic Studies 19. Berkeley, 1994. 182–212.

RR *Russian Review.*

Russia's Women *Russia's Women: Accommodation, Resistance, Transformation.* Ed. Barbara Evans Clements, Barbara Alpern Engel, and Christine D. Worobec. Berkeley, 1991.

SEER *Slavonic and East European Review.*

SGGD *Sobranie gosudarstvennykh gramot i dogovorov khraniashchikhsia v Gosudarstvennoi kollegii inostrannykh del.* 5 vols. Moscow, 1813–1894.

Slovar' knizhnikov *Slovar' knizhnikov i knizhnosti drevnei Rusi.* Ed. D. S. Likhachev. 3 vols. in 5 parts to date. Leningrad, 1987–1993.

SR *Slavic Review.*

TODRL *Trudy Otdela drevnerusskoi literatury Instituta russkoi literatury (Pushkinskogo doma) AN SSSR.* 50 vols. to date. Moscow and St. Petersburg, 1934–1997.

Zabelin, *Tsarei* Zabelin, I. E. *Domashnii byt russkikh tsarei v XVI i XVII st.* 2d ed. Moscow, 1872.

Zabelin, *Tsarits* Zabelin, I. E. *Domashni byt russkikh tsarits v XVI i XVII st.* 2d ed. Moscow, 1872.

Zimin, *V kanun* Zimin, A. A. *V kanun groznykh potriasenii, predposylki pervoi krest'ianskoi voiny v Rossii.* Moscow, 1986.

Notes

Introduction

1. Kremlin Museums, inventory no. TK-4. Excellent color reproductions of the *sakkos* and a detailed description of its imagery and inscriptions can be found in N. A. Maiasova, ed., *Srednevekovoe litsevoe shit'e. Vizantiia, Balkany, Rus'. Katalog vystavki. XVIII mezhdunarodnyi kongress vizantinistov. Moskva, 8–15 avgusta, 1991 g.* (Moscow, 1991), no. 10, pp. 44–51. For a discussion of the *sakkos,* see Elisabeth Piltz, *Trois sakkoi byzantins: Analyse iconographique* (Stockholm, 1976), 31–33, 48–49; Pauline Johnstone, *The Byzantine Tradition in Church Embroidery* (Chicago, 1967), 95; Tano Papas, *Studien zur Geschichte der Messgewänder im byzantinischen Ritus* (Munich, 1965), 119–20. For the origin of the *sakkos* as a liturgical vestment, see Papas, *Studien zur Geschichte,* 125–30; Piltz, *Trois sakkoi,* 13–26; A. P. Kazhdan, ed., *The Oxford Dictionary of Byzantium* (New York, 1991), 3:1830.

On Fotii's ecclesiastical appointment and travel to Russia, see *PSRL,* vol. 27, p. 97 *(Nikanorov Chronicle).* Obolensky argues that the *sakkos* was a personal gift from the Byzantine emperor to Fotii, who is depicted in the *sakkos* to the left of John VIII; Dmitrii Obolensky, "Some Notes concerning a Byzantine Portrait of John VIII Palaeologus," *Eastern Churches Review* 4, no. 2 (1972): 141–42. However, it is equally possible that the work served a larger function by representing a showpiece of contemporary Russo-Byzantine relations. For Fotii's activities in Russia, see A. E. Presniakov, *The Formation of the Great Russian State: A Study of Russian History in the Thirteenth to Fifteenth Centuries,* trans. A. E. Moorhouse (Chicago, 1970), 311; J. L. I. Fennell, *A History of the Russian Church to 1448* (London, 1995), 162–69.

2. All figures are identified by either Greek or Slavic inscriptions. On the martyrs see Piltz, *Trois sakkoi,* 50; John Meyendorff, *Byzantium and the Rise of Russia* (Crestwood, N.Y., 1989), 187–88. Vasilii I sent his daughter to Constantinople in 1409; see *PSRL,* vol. 27, p. 97 *(Nikanorov Chronicle).* Russian sources date the marriage

to 1411, Byzantine sources to 1414; see A. A. Zimin, *Vitiaz' na rasput'e. Feodal'naia voina v Rossii XV v.* (Moscow, 1991), 86; Obolensky, "Some Notes," 141; A. A. Vasiliev, *History of the Byzantine Empire, 324–1453* (Madison, 1964), 2:588.

The presentation of John VIII in the great *sakkos* of Fotii has puzzled some scholars, who point out that John was not crowned co-emperor with his father, Manuel, until 1421. Some Byzantine sources, however, mention that John was already given the imperial title Basileus before 1408; Obolensky, "Some Notes," 143–44; Nicolas Oikonomides, "John VII Palaeologus and the Ivory Pyxis at Dumbarton Oaks," *Dumbarton Oaks Papers,* no. 31 (1977): 332–33.

3. For depictions of the family of the Kievan grand prince Iaroslav the Wise in the frescoes of Saint Sophia in Kiev and of Grand Prince Mikhail Iaroslavich of Tver' and his mother, Oksiniia, in a Russian copy of the *Chronicle of Hamartolus* from ca. 1400, see Kämpfer, *Herrscherbild,* figs. 60–61 (p. 110); fig. 72 (p. 143); also see pp. 111–16 and 148–49 for a discussion of the images.

4. The term *Byzantine Commonwealth* was coined by Dmitrii Obolensky in *The Byzantine Commonwealth: Eastern Europe, 500–1453* (Crestwood, N.Y., 1982), 13–16.

5. See Presniakov, *Formation,* 310; Fennell, *History,* 163–66.

6. On the negative impact of the Russian autocracy on women in Muscovite society and culture, see McNally, "From Public Person," 81–101; Claus, *Stellung,* 114–23; Zabelin, *Tsarits,* 294–95. For the most recent studies of medieval Russian women, see *Russia's Women,* 1–94; Levin, *Sex and Society;* Nada Boškovska, *Die russische Frau im 17. Jahrhundert* (Cologne, 1998).

7. On the impact of the events of 1453 on Muscovite notions of the power of their ruler, see Iaroslav Pelenski, "The Origins of the Official Muscovite Claims to the 'Kievan Inheritance'," *HUS* 1 (March 1977): 51.

8. John Carmi Parsons, ed., *Medieval Queenship* (New York, 1993); Louise Olga Fradenburg, ed., *Women and Sovereignty,* Cosmos: The Yearbook of the Traditional Cosmology Society, vol. 7 (Edinburgh, 1992); also see Lois L. Huneycutt, "Intercession and the High-Medieval Queen: The Esther Topos," in *Power of the Weak: Studies on Medieval Women,* ed. Jennifer Carpenter and Sally-Beth MacLean (Urbana, Ill., 1995); John Carmi Parsons, "The Queen's Intercession in Thirteenth-Century England," in *Power of the Weak,* 147–77; Elizabeth McCartney, "Ceremonies and Privileges of Office: Queenship in Late Medieval France," in *Power of the Weak,* 178–219; Pauline Stafford, *Queens, Concubines, and Dowagers: The King's Wife in the Early Middle Ages* (Athens, Ga., 1983), 99–114. Jane Tibbetts Schulenburg's treatment of the subject suffers from an anachronistic assumption that the medieval queens' sphere of action was defined in either public or private terms; see Jane Tibbetts Schulenburg, "Female Sanctity: Public and Private Roles, ca. 500–1100," in *Women and Power in the Middle Ages,* ed. Mary Erler and Maryanne Kowaleski (Athens, Ga., 1988), 117–19.

9. For a recent assertion of the public/private dichotomy, see Jürgen Habermas, *The Structural Transformation of the Public Sphere: An Inquiry into a Category of Bourgeois Society,* trans. Thomas Burger (Cambridge, Mass., 1989).

10. See for example John Carmi Parsons, "Ritual and Symbol in the English Medieval Queenship to 1500," in *Women and Sovereignty,* 60–61; Parsons, "Queen's Intercession," 147–49; Fradenburg, "Introduction," in *Women and Sovereignty,* 7–9.

11. Daniel Rowland, "Ivan the Terrible as a Carolingian Renaissance Prince," in *Kamen' kraeug"l'n",* 594–606.

12. For Carolingian Europe, see Rosamond McKitterick, *The Frankish King-*

doms under the Carolingians, 751–987 (London, 1983), 77–105. For Muscovy, see Nancy Shields Kollmann, *By Honor Bound: State and Society in Early Modern Russia* (Ithaca, 1999); Kollmann, *Kinship*. Valerie Kivelson notes the tension between the personal and religious nature of Muscovite political ideology and the bureaucratization of the tsarist government from the mid–seventeenth century on; see Valerie Kivelson, *Autocracy in the Provinces: The Russian Gentry and Political Culture in the Seventeenth Century* (Stanford, 1996).

13. Huneycutt, "High-Medieval Queen," 129.

14. K. J. Leyser, *Rule and Conflict in an Early Medieval Society: Ottonian Saxony* (Oxford, 1989), 48–73.

15. Elaine Pagels, *Adam, Eve and the Serpent* (New York, 1988), xxvii–xxviii.

16. Stanislaw Roman, "Le statut de la femme dans l'Europe Orientale (Pologne et Russie) au moyen âge et aux temps modernes," *Recueils de la Société Jean Bodin pour l'histoire comparative des institutions* 12 (1962): 392; McNally, "From Public Person," 142–43, 148–58; Nancy Shields Kollmann, "The Seclusion of Elite Muscovite Women," *RH* 10, pt. 2 (1983): 170–87. Nada Boškovska provides a much more cautious evaluation of Russian women in the seventeenth century; see Boškovska, *Die russische Frau,* 209–22. Russianists (including medieval Russianists) have already begun to reevaluate the definition and role of the private in Russian history. On October 4–6, 1996, the University of Michigan sponsored a conference on the topic "Private Life in Russia: Medieval Times to Present." For new insights about the private in medieval Russia, also see Nancy Shields Kollmann, "The Meaning of the Private in Seventeenth-Century Russia," and Valerie Kivelson, "Private Property à la Russe: Maps and the Outlines of Ownership in the Seventeenth Century" (papers delivered at Privacies Seminar, University of Michigan, Ann Arbor, October 3, 1998).

17. Hughes, *Sophia,* 266–74.

18. Zimin, *Vitiaz',* 31.

19. McNally, "From Public Person," 102–24.

20. A. V. Dobriakov, *Russkaia zhenshchina v do-mongol'skii period* (St. Petersburg, 1864), 100.

21. For general treatments of these issues, see Presniakov, *Formation;* J. L. I. Fennell, *The Emergence of Moscow, 1304–1359* (Berkeley, 1968).

22. William G. Doty, *Mythography: The Study of Myths and Rituals* (University, Ala., 1986), 127.

23. Flier, "Breaking the Code," 213–42; Flier, "Iconography," 109–25; Flier, "Iconology," 53–76; Rowland, "Biblical Military Imagery," 182–212; Daniel Rowland, "Did Muscovite Literary Ideology Place Limits on the Power of the Tsar (1540s–1660s)?" *RR* 49, no. 2 (April 1990): 112–56; Daniel Rowland, "Moscow—the Third Rome or the New Israel?" *RR* 55, no. 4 (October 1996): 591–614.

Chapter 1: The Myth of the Tsaritsa's Blessed Womb

1. See for example McNally, "From Public Person," 2–3, 34, 53, 73; Alexandre Eck, "La situation juridique de la femme russe au moyen âge," *Recueils de la Société Jean Bodin pour l'histoire comparative des institutions* 12 (1962): 407–8; Goehrke, "Witwe," 68–69.

2. McNally, "From Public Person," 13–14, 20, 100; Goehrke, "Witwe," 68.

3. McNally, "From Public Person," 8, 34; Eck, "La situation juridique,"

409–41; Goehrke, "Witwe," 75–76. On the granting of immunities, also see N. L. Pushkareva, *Zhenshchiny drevnei Rusi* (Moscow, 1989), 52.

4. See for example Eck, "La situation juridique," 408; Zimin, *Vitiaz'*, 31; McNally, "From Public Person," 14, 34, 70, 91, 93.

5. This is supported by Nancy Shields Kollmann's findings that the Muscovite political system with its focus on family relations and loyalty bonds did not significantly change under Ivan III; see Kollmann, *Kinship and Politics*. For an in-depth discussion of the role of Muscovite royal wives and mothers in the formation of the Muscovite state, see Isolde Thyrêt, "The Grand Princesses of Moscow and the Rise of the Medieval Russian State" (paper presented at the Thirty-Seventh Annual Meeting of the Midwest Medieval History Conference, University of Notre Dame, October 26–27, 1998); and Isolde Thyrêt, "The Grand Princesses of Moscow and the Ideology of Dynastic Continuity" (paper presented at the Early Russian History Workshop, Illinois Summer Research Laboratory on Russia and Eastern Europe, University of Illinois, Urbana, June 15–19, 1998).

6. For the issues surrounding the rise of Moscow, see Presniakov, *Formation*.

7. *DDG*, no. 12, pp. 33–34. Also see Howes, *Testaments*, pp. 126–27 for the original Russian text; pp. 208, 212 for an English translation. Subsequent references indicate the English translation first; references to the Russian original published in Howes follow in hard brackets.

8. The fact that Vasilii stayed at the court of his father's enemy, Vitovt, at the time the will was composed might have aroused Donskoi's suspicions about the intentions of the Lithuanian ruler, who was offering his daughter Sofiia in marriage to Vasilii. On this point, also see McNally, "From Public Person," 83; L. V. Cherepnin, *Russkie feodal'nye arkhivy XIV–XV vekov* (Moscow, 1948–1951), 1:62; *DDG*, no. 12, pp. 35, 36; Howes, *Testaments*, 215, 217 [128, 130]. Also see *PSRL*, vol. 11, p. 90 *(Nikon Chronicle)*. The *Tver' Chronicle* and the *Moscow Chronicle Compilation of the End of the Fifteenth Century* obliquely refer to Vasilii's stay in Lithuania; see *PSRL*, vol. 15, col. 44; vol. 25, p. 214.

9. *DDG*, no. 21, pp. 59, 57; no. 22, pp. 62, 60. Howes, *Testaments*, 233, 227 [134, 132–33]; 240, 236 [137, 135]. Cherepnin, *Russkie feodal'nye arkhivy* 1:90; McNally, "From Public Person," 75. For the date of Vasilii's wills, see Howes, *Testaments*, 21. On Lithuania's political influence on Moscow at the time, see Presniakov, *Formation*, 291.

10. *DDG*, no. 61a, pp. 194, 197–98; Howes, *Testaments*, 243, 260 [137, 141].

11. Goehrke, "Witwe," 71.

12. *DDG*, no. 1a, p. 8; no. 1b, p. 10; Howes, *Testaments*, 184 [116, 118] (testament of Ivan Kalita); *DDG*, no. 4a, p. 16; no. 4b, p. 18; Howes, *Testaments*, 198–99 [121, 123–24] (testament of Ivan II).

13. *DDG*, no. 12, p. 35; Howes, *Testaments*, 214–15 [128].

14. *DDG*, no. 12, pp. 33, 35, 36; Howes, *Testaments*, 208, 214, 215, 217 [126, 128, 129–30].

15. *DDG*, no. 12, p. 36; Howes, *Testaments*, 217 [130]. On this point, also see McNally, "From Public Person," 75.

16. Redistribution of patrimonial lands: *DDG*, no. 61a, p. 197; Howes, *Testaments*, 259 [141]; obedience: *DDG*, no. 61a, pp. 194, 197; Howes, *Testaments*, 243, 259, 260 [137, 141].

17. *DDG*, no. 61a, pp. 194, 195; Howes, *Testaments*, 247, 250, 252 [138, 139]; for Sofiia Vitovtovna's bequests, see *DDG*, no. 57, pp. 175–78.

18. *PSRL,* vol. 6, p. 172 *(Sophia II Chronicle);* vol. 18, p. 195 *(Simeonov Chronicle);* vol. 25, p. 263 *(Moscow Chronicle Compilation of the End of the Fifteenth Century).* The *Sophia II Chronicle* dates from the early sixteenth century; see *Slovar' knizhnikov,* vol. 2, pt. 2, p. 60.

19. *PSRL,* vol. 25, p. 286; vol. 27, p. 131 *(Nikanorov Chronicle).*

20. Robert Michell and Nevill Forbes, eds. and trans., *The Chronicle of Novgorod, 1016–1471,* Camden Third Series, vol. 25 (London, 1914), 207; also see Pushkareva, *Zhenshchiny drevnei Rusi,* 51.

21. *PSRL,* vol. 18, p. 167 *(Simeonov Chronicle);* vol. 25, p. 246; also see Fennell, *History,* 234–36; Zimin, *Vitiaz',* 31, 34.

22. Marriage: *PSRL,* vol. 18, p. 237 *(Simeonov Chronicle);* vol. 25, p. 299. The *Sophia II Chronicle* mentions only Ivan's mother; *PSRL,* vol. 6, p. 197. Military response: *PSRL,* vol. 4, p. 153 *(Novgorod IV Chronicle);* vol. 6, p. 20 *(Sophia I Chronicle);* vol. 6, p. 224 *(Sophia II Chronicle);* vol. 25, p. 327. Also see Ia. S. Lur'e, *Dve istorii Rusi 15 veka* (St. Petersburg, 1994), 175. The *Tipografskaia Chronicle* refers to Mariia's involvement only indirectly; *PSRL,* vol. 24, p. 199.

23. *DDG,* no. 18, p. 51; Cherepnin, *Russkie feodal'nye arkhivy* 1:75–76; McNally, "From Public Person," 82.

24. Zimin, *Vitiaz',* 54–56; also see Cherepnin, *Russkie feodal'nye arkhivy* 2:353–58. The text of the *gubnaia zapis'* is found in *AAE,* vol. 1, no. 115, pp. 87–88; B. D. Grekov, ed., *Akty sotsial'no-ekonomicheskoi istorii severo-vostochnoi Rusi kontsa XIV–nachala XVI v.* (Moscow, 1952), vol. 3, no. 12, pp. 27–29.

25. McNally, "From Public Person," 82–83, 88.

26. *SGGD,* vol. 1, no. 95, pp. 228–30. On the circumstances surrounding the draft, see Cherepnin, *Russkie feodal'nye arkhivy* 1:194–96. For Mariia's illness, see *PSRL,* vol. 18, p. 243 *(Simeonov Chronicle);* vol. 24, p. 193 *(Tipografskaia Chronicle);* vol. 25, p. 298.

27. *PSRL,* vol. 4, p. 151 *(Novgorod IV Chronicle);* vol. 6, pp. 31–32 *(Sophia I Chronicle);* vol. 6, p. 195 *(Sophia II Chronicle);* vol. 18, pp. 242–43 *(Simeonov Chronicle);* vol. 24, p. 192 *(Tipografskaia Chronicle);* vol. 25, p. 297; Cherepnin, *Russkie feodal'nye arkhivy* 1:196.

28. *PSRL,* vol. 24, p. 194; vol. 8, p. 180; Presniakov, *Formation,* 355.

29. *DDG,* no. 61a, p. 197; Howes, *Testaments,* 259 [141].

30. *DDG,* no. 12, p. 35; Howes, *Testaments,* 214 [128].

31. Herberstein, *Notes,* 1:50–51; also see *PL* 1:103.

32. Novombergskii, *Slovo i delo,* vol. 1, no. 57, pp. 73–75. See also Bakhrushin, "Politicheskie tolki," 105–6.

33. Collins, *Present State,* ch. 2, p. 11. Johann Korb, who wrote during the time of Peter the Great, also mentioned infertility as a reason for the divorce and forced tonsure of royal women; see Johann Georg Korb, *Diary of an Austrian Secretary of Legation at the Court of Czar Peter the Great,* ed. and trans. Count Mac Donnell (London, 1863), 2:132. For a discussion of the major obstacles in the lives of the tsaritsy, see Zabelin, *Tsarits,* 293.

34. Levin, *Sex and Society,* 177–78; N. Gal'kovskii, *Bor'ba khristianstva s ostatkami iazychestva v drevnei Rusi* (Kharkov, 1913–1916), 2:94; and V. J. Mansikka, *Die Religion der Ostslaven* (Helsinki, 1922), 272–73.

35. Kotoshikhin, *O Rossii,* 30; Claus, *Stellung,* 48; Levin, *Sex and Society,* 171. For the ecclesiastical debate about the purification of women in the early fifteenth century, see A. S. Pavlov, ed., *Pamiatniki drevne-russkago kanonicheskago prava, vol.*

1: Pamiatniki XI–XV v. in *RIB,* vol. 6, no. 48, col. 416.

36. For a contrary view, see Anne Bassein, who considers Christianity "weak in supporting humans in their most intense and productive area of life." See Beth Ann Bassein, *Women and Death: Linkages in Western Thought and Literature* (Westport, 1984), 30.

37. For Sofiia's life before her arrival in Russia, see Joseph L. Wieczynski, ed., *The Modern Encyclopedia of Russian and Soviet History,* s.v. "Sophia (Zoe) Paleologos."

38. *PSRL,* vol. 6, p. 279. For the most recent interpretations of the events of 1497–1499, see Gustave Alef, "Aristocratic Politics and Royal Policy in Muscovy in the Late Fifteenth and Early Sixteenth Centuries," *Forschungen zur osteuropäischen Geschichte* 27 (1980): 79–81; Nancy Shields Kollmann, "Consensus Politics: The Dynastic Crisis of the 1490s Reconsidered," *RR* 45, no. 3 (July 1986): 236–67.

39. *PSRL,* vol. 12, pp. 246, 249, 255 *(Nikon Chronicle).* For the manuscript tradition of this sixteenth-century chronicle and its relation to other contemporary Muscovite chronicles, see B. M. Kloss, *Nikonovskii svod i russkie letopisi XVI–XVII vekov* (Moscow, 1980).

40. The shroud is reproduced in N. A. Maiasova, *Drevnerusskoe shit'e* (Moscow, 1971), no. 38. On the development of the cult of Saint Sergius, protector of the Rurikide dynasty, see Thyrêt, "'Blessed Is the Tsaritsa's Womb': The Myth of Miraculous Birth and Royal Motherhood in Muscovite Russia," *RR* 53, no 4 (October 1994): 481; David Miller, "The Cult of Saint Sergius of Radonezh and Its Political Uses," *SR* 52, no. 4 (winter 1993): 680–99.

41. For the inscription, see N. N. Voronin and V. V. Kostochkin, eds., *Troitse-Sergieva Lavra. Khudozhestvennye pamiatniki* (Moscow, 1968), 122. For the history and preservation of the tapestry, see T. Manushina, ed., *Khudozhestvennoe shit'e drevnei Rusi v sobranii Zagorskogo muzeia* (Moscow, 1983), 60–61; V. V. Filatov, "Ikona s izobrazheniem siuzhetov iz istorii Russkogo gosudarstva, *TODRL* 22 (1966): 280; M. V. Shchepkina, *Izobrazhenie russkikh istoricheskikh lits v shit'e XV veka* (Moscow, 1950), 8–11. The tapestry, located in the Historical Museum of the Trinity-Sergius Monastery (inventory no. 413), is reproduced in M. A. Il'in, *Zagorsk. Trinity-Sergius Monastery,* trans. Natasha Johnstone (Moscow, 1967), 71. For a detailed discussion of the imagery of the tapestry, see Thyrêt, "Blessed Womb," 480–84.

42. *PSRL,* vol. 25, p. 323; vol. 27, p. 281 *(Abbreviated Chronicle Compilation of 1493);* vol. 12, p. 40 *(Nikon Chronicle).*

43. Louis Réau, *Iconographie de l'art chrétien* (Paris, 1955–1959), 2:594–95.

44. On David, see ibid., 595. In Byzantium the emperor was often called a second David; see Otto Treitinger, *Die oströmische Kaiser- und Reichsidee nach ihrer Gestaltung im höfischen Zeremoniell* (Bad Homburg, 1969), 130–36. For Vasilii's name saints, see *PSRL,* vol. 25, p. 323; vol. 27, p. 281 *(Abbreviated Chronicle Compilation of 1493);* vol. 12, p. 190 left column; vol. 21, pt. 2, p. 555 *(Stepennaia kniga).* The *Stepennaia kniga* was composed in the 1560s at the order of the metropolitan of Moscow, Makarii. For a discussion of the possible authorship and intention and arrangement of the work and its sources, see *Slovar' knizhnikov,* vol. 2, pt. 1, pp. 73–79. On Basil of Parion's identity, see Thyrêt, "Blessed Womb," 483n.19.

45. A. A. Zimin, "O politicheskoi doktrine Iosifa Volotskogo," *TODRL* 9 (1953): 160–74. In this sense Sofiia Paleolog perpetuated a common Byzantine notion of rulership in Russia without introducing large-scale structural changes at the Muscovite court. On Sofiia's role in the dissemination of Byzantine imperial

values in Russia, see Lur'e, *Dve istorii,* 196; V. I. Savva, *Moskovskie tsari i vizantiiskie vasilevsy. K voprosu o vlianii Vizantii na obrazovanie idei tsarskoi vlasti moskovskikh gosudarei* (Kharkov, 1901), 1–57. On Sofiia's political standing, notably her contacts with foreign diplomats, see Pushkareva, *Zhenshchiny drevnei Rusi,* 57.

46. *PSRL,* vol. 25, p.323; vol. 27, p. 281 *(Abbreviated Chronicle Compilation of 1493).*

47. Günther Stökl, "Staat und Kirche im Moskauer Rußland. Die vier Moskauer Wundertäter," *Jahrbücher für Geschichte Osteuropas,* n.s., 29, no. 4 (1981): 490.

48. See John V. A. Fine, Jr., "The Muscovite Dynastic Crisis of 1497–1502," *Canadian Slavonic Papers* 8 (1966): 214–15.

49. *PSRL,* vol. 28, p. 93. The story is not included in the *Chronicle Compilation of the End of the Fifteenth Century.*

50. Sofiia Paleolog fell into disgrace with her husband at the end of 1497; for a treatment of the events of 1497, see Lur'e, *Dve istorii,* 214.

51. *PSRL,* vol. 4, p. 295 *(Novgorod IV Chronicle).* Zimin argues that Vasilii considered divorce for the first time in his will in 1523; see A. A. Zimin, *Rossiia na poroge novogo vremeni (Ocherki politicheskoi istorii Rossii pervoi treti XVI v.)* (Moscow, 1972), 294–95.

52. *AI,* vol. 1, no. 130, p. 192; Zabelin, *Tsarits,* 279–80 (love magic); Zimin, *Rossiia na poroge,* 295 (pilgrimage).

53. The tapestry is located in the Historical Museum of the Trinity-Sergius Monastery (inventory no. 409). For a reproduction see Nikolaeva, *Sobranie,* 139, fig. 68; *Zagorsk State Museum–Preserve of History and Art: An Illustrated Guidebook* (Moscow, 1988), 74–75. For a detailed discussion of the embroidery and its preservation, see N. E. Mneva, "Shit'e XVI–nachala XVII veka," in I. E. Grabar', V. S. Kemenov, and V. N. Lazarev, eds., *Istoriia russkogo iskusstva* (Moscow, 1953–1969) 3:678; Manushina, *Khudozhestvennoe shit'e,* 64–65.

Possibly a pall with the image of Saint Sergius and the Old Testament Trinity with Abraham and Sarah served as a companion piece to the tapestry. According to its inscription, the piece was fashioned for the shrine of Saint Sergius in 1525 as well; see Nikolaeva, *Sobranie,* 140, fig. 69; T. V. Nikolaeva, "Proizvedeniia russkogo prikladnogo iskusstva s nadpisiami XV–pervoi chetverti XVI v.," *Arkheologiia SSSR. Svod arkheologicheskikh istochnikov* E 1–49 (1971): 75–76.

54. For the literary and iconographic expressions of the theme of miraculous birth in the Byzantine and Slavic world, which might have served as models for Solomoniia's tapestry, see Thyrêt, "Blessed Womb," 486–87. For a discussion of the transmission of the story of the Maccabees, see ibid., 485n.29. The Maccabee brothers and their mother, Solomoniia (Shamone), were often depicted in icons featuring the feast of the Origin of the True Cross, which was also celebrated on August 1. For examples, see Hetty J. Roozemond–Van Ginhoven, *Ikon: Inspired Art: Icons from "De Wijenburgh"* (Echteld, Netherlands, 1980), fig. 42; Walter Felicetti-Liebenfels, *Geschichte der russischen Ikonenmalerei* (Graz, 1972), fig. 340. Also see Thyrêt, "Blessed Womb," 486n.32, for a sixteenth-century icon featuring Solomoniia, Eleazar, and the Maccabee brothers, which belonged to the Church of the Procession of the Life-Giving Cross in the Suzdal' Pokrov Monastery.

55. According to the *Letopisets nachala tsarstva,* which dates from the early 1550s, Vasilii III prayed to Saints Peter and Aleksii for offspring; see *PSRL,* vol. 29, p. 16; *Slovar' knizhnikov,* vol. 2, pt. 2, pp. 20–21. In 1514 Vasilii III founded a church in Leontii's honor and donated a shroud with Leontii's image to the saint; see *PSRL,* vol. 6, p. 254 *(Sophia II Chronicle);* vol. 13, pt. 1, p. 18 *(Nikon Chronicle);*

Nikolaeva, "Proizvedeniia," 71–72. The *Muscovite Chronicle Compilation of the End of the Fifteenth Century* includes Leontii of Rostov in the group of the special protector saints of the Muscovite grand princes; *PSRL,* vol. 25, p. 269. On the role of the Muscovite ecclesiastical hierarchy in the promotion of Saint Leontii's cult, see Gail Lenhoff, "Canonization and Princely Power in Northeast Rus': The Cult of Leontij Rostovskij," *Die Welt der Slaven* 37, nos. 1–2 (1992): 359–80; Stökl, "Staat und Kirche," 489.

56. Both chronicles were composed in the late 1520s–1530s at Metropolitan Daniil's court; see A. N. Nasonov, *Istoriia russkogo letopisaniia XI–nachala XVIII veka. Ocherki i issledovaniia* (Moscow, 1969), 389–94; A. N. Nasonov, "Materialy i issledovaniia po istorii russkogo letopisaniia, *Problemy istochnikovedeniia* 6 (1958): 248–50; N. A. Kazakova, *Ocherki po istorii russkoi obshchestvennoi mysli. Pervaia tret' XVI veka* (Leningrad, 1970), 212; A. A. Zimin, *Russkie letopisi i khronografy kontsa XV–XVI vv.* (The Hague, 1969), 17; and M. N. Tikhomirov, *Russkoe letopisanie* (Moscow, 1979), 164–65. Daniil died in 1547; see *Slovar' knizhnikov,* vol. 2, pt. 1, p. 182.

57. *PSRL,* vol. 24, pp. 222–23; Nasonov, *Istoriia,* 391–92.

58. Iu. K. Begunov, "Povest' o vtorom brake Vasiliia III," *TODRL* 25 (1970): 116.

59. Kloss, *Nikonovskii svod,* 192. For the reader's convenience, Russian titles translated into English have been italicized. For the development of a Muscovite ruler ideology, see Wieczynski, *The Modern Encyclopedia of Russian and Soviet History,* s.v. "Moscow the Third Rome"; Zimin, *Rossiia na poroge,* 323–63; Daniel Rowland, "Moscow," 591–614. For the cultural significance of the *Stepennaia kniga,* see David Miller, "The Velikie Chetii and the Stepennaia Kniga of Metropolitan Makarii and the Origins of Russian National Consciousness," *Forschungen zur osteuropäischen Geschichte* 26 (1979): 263–382.

60. *PSRL,* vol. 21, pt. 2, p. 554; for Sofiia's female children, see vol. 25, pp. 301, 303, 308.

61. *PSRL,* vol. 21, pt. 2, p. 554. The story is also included in the Shumilov copy of the *Nikon Chronicle;* see *PSRL,* vol. 12, pp. 190–91 right column. Kloss dates the Shumilov copy between 1574 and 1581; see Kloss, *Nikonovskii svod,* 223. On the connection of the tale with the events of 1499 rather than with Vasilii III's birth, see Thyrêt, "Blessed Womb," 489.

62. See for example *PSRL,* vol. 25, p. 323; vol. 27, p. 281 *(Abbreviated Chronicle Compilation of 1493);* vol. 12, p. 190 left column, p. 191 right column (early copies of the *Nikon Chronicle*). According to the Orthodox calendar (old-style) the Annunciation, a fixed holiday, was celebrated on March 25; the following day, March 26, was the feast day of Archangel Gabriel; see E. I. Kamentseva, *Khronologiia* (Moscow, 1967), 98.

63. *PSRL,* vol. 21, pt. 2, p. 606; also vol. 6, p. 265 *(Sophia II Chronicle).* On Vasilii III's and Elena's marriage in 1525, see *PSRL,* vol. 13, pt. 1, p. 45 *(Nikon Chronicle).* On Elena's background and political role after Vasilii's death in 1533 see Hartmut Rüß, "Elena Vasil'evna Glinskaja," *Jahrbücher für Geschichte Osteuropas* 19, no. 4 (December 1971): 481–98.

64. *PSRL,* vol. 21, pt. 2, p. 605. See Gen. 17:15–19, 18:15, 21:1–2; I Sam. 1:3–20; Judg. 14:2–14; Luke 1:5–25, 1:26–38. For Ivan IV's patron saint, see *PSRL,* vol. 21, pt. 1, pp. 48, 49. For the eschatological ramifications of the connection of Ivan IV with John the Forerunner, see Flier, "Iconography," 123–24, and Flier, "Iconology," 69.

65. *PSRL,* vol. 21, pt. 2, p. 629. The reference to Titus proves that the

episode does not predate Ivan's birth since it implies knowledge of his birthday, August 25, 1530, which coincided with the feast day of the apostles Bartholomew and Titus. See *PSRL,* vol. 13, pt. 1, p. 48 left column; vol. 13, pt. 1, p. 49 right column *(Nikon Chronicle).*

66. To date, no studies of infant mortality in medieval Russia exist but the situation in Muscovite Russia most likely resembled that in other premodern societies. For details, see Shulamith Shahar, *Childhood in the Middle Ages,* trans. Chaya Galai (London, 1992), 149.

67. See Thyrêt, "Blessed Womb," 490–91. For a nongendered analysis of Muscovite royal pilgrimages, see Nancy Shields Kollmann, "Pilgrimage, Procession, and Symbolic Space in Sixteenth-Century Russian Politics," in *Medieval Russian Culture,* vol. 2, ed. Michael S. Flier and Daniel Rowland, California Slavic Studies 19 (Berkeley, 1994) 163–81.

68. *PSRL,* vol. 29, p. 57 *(Letopisets nachala tsarstva);* vol. 13, pt. 1, p. 158 *(Nikon Chronicle);* vol. 13, pt. 2, pp. 459–60 *(Addenda to Nikon Chronicle).*

69. Anna died on March 17, 1551; *PSRL,* vol. 13, pt. 1, p. 161 *(Nikon Chronicle).* Another daughter, Mariia, also died in infancy; *PSRL,* vol. 21, pt. 2, p. 651 *(Stepennaia kniga).* Dmitrii Ivanovich was born in October 1552. For the varying interpretations of Dmitrii's death in sixteenth- and seventeenth-century Russian sources, see Thyrêt, "Blessed Womb," 491n.65.

70. BAN, Sobranie Petra Pervogo, A 37, fols. 19r–19v. The second redaction of this episode, contained in Chapter 20 of the *vita,* also refers to the parents' grief (fol. 23v). Chapter 19 is ascribed to the possible author of the *Stepennaia kniga,* Metropolitan Afanasii, who himself was born in Pereslavl'. The chapter is included in this chronicle but whether Afanasii specifically composed it for this purpose is still unclear. The supposed author of the following chapters, the *hegumen* Vassian of the Nikitskii Monastery in Pereslavl', retold the events of Chapter 19 in Chapter 20 of the *vita,* which is not contained in the *Stepennaia kniga;* see *Slovar' knizhnikov,* vol. 2, pt. 1, pp. 73–79, 307–9.

71. BAN, Sobranie Petra Pervogo, A 37, fol. 23v. Since the 1470s the metropolitan saint Iona enjoyed the same reputation as the miracle-workers Peter and Aleksii; see Stökl, "Staat und Kirche," 490. Saint Nikita was accorded the rank of miracle-worker at the church council of 1547; see Kliuchevskii, *Drevnerusskiia zhitiia,* 462.

72. For Anastasiia, see BAN, Sobranie Petra Pervogo, A 37, fol. 19v (Ch. 19), fols. 24r–24v (Ch. 20). For Mariia, see *PSRL,* vol. 13, pt. 2, pp. 365–66 *(Addenda to Nikon Chronicle).*

73. BAN, Sobranie Petra Pervogo, A 37, fols. 37r–37v (Ch. 22 of the *vita* of Saint Nikita of Pereslavl'). For the historicity of the event, see Thyrêt, "Blessed Womb," 493. For a discussion of Ivan IV's patronage of the monastery of Saint Nikita and the politics of production of royal offspring, also see A. L. Batalov, "Molenie o chadorodii i obetnoe stroitel'stvo tsaria Fedora Ivanovicha," in *Zakazchik v istorii russkoi arkhitektury,* ed. G. I. Revzin and V. V. Sedov (Moscow, 1994), *Arkhiv arkhitektury,* vol. 5, no. 1, 119.

74. *PSRL,* vol. 13, pt. 2, p. 383 *(Addenda to Nikon Chronicle);* BAN, Sobranie Petra Pervogo, A 37, fol. 34v. On Afanasii's role as spiritual adviser to Ivan and his wife, see *PSRL,* vol. 13, pt. 1, p. 204 *(Nikon Chronicle);* vol. 13, pt. 2, p. 333 *(Addenda to Nikon Chronicle);* vol. 29, p. 96 *(Letopisets nachala tsarstva).*

75. *AI,* vol. 1, no. 216; also see Zabelin, *Tsarits,* 285. The 1859 inventory list

of the Pafnut'ev-Borovskii Monastery mentions the donation by Elena Glinskaia of a tapestry featuring Saint Pafnutii in 1530, the year of Ivan's birth; see L. D. Likhacheva, "Pokrov Pafnutiia Borovskogo iz Gosudarstvennogo Russkogo Muzeia," *Pamiatniki kul'tury. Novye otkrytiia. Ezhegodnik 1977* (Moscow, 1977), 269. Claus mistakenly attributes Pafnutii's intervention to the birth of Ivan, son of Ivan the Terrible (Claus, *Stellung,* 116).

76. For the date of the *vita,* see RGB, f. 304. I., Collection of the Trinity-Sergius Monastery, no. 562; on Kornilii, see *Slovar' knizhnikov,* vol. 2, pt. 2, p. 123; also Kliuchevskii, *Drevnerusskiia zhitiia,* 303.

77. RNB, Pogodin Collection, no. 647, fols. 36v–37r, 39, 41, 43.

78. Pilgrimage in 1585: *PSRL,* vol. 29, p. 218 *(Aleksandro-Nevskaia Chronicle);* quote: Giles Fletcher, *Of the Rus Commonwealth,* ed. Albert J. Schmidt (Ithaca, N. Y., 1966), 120–21. For the dating of the *Aleksandro-Nevskaia Chronicle,* see Kloss, *Nikonovskii svod,* 227–31.

79. See T. V. Nikolaeva, *Drevnerusskaia zhivopis' Zagorskogo muzeia* (Moscow, 1977), 137, fig. 236; 138–39, fig. 237. For a sketch of Golovkin's life, see T. V. Nikolaeva, "Troitskii zhivopisets XVI v. Evstafii Golovkin," in *Kul'tura drevnei Rusi,* ed. A. L. Mongait (Moscow, 1966), 177–83.

80. RGB, f. 37 (Bolshakov Collection), no. 422, fols. 420r–422v. The manuscript, a miscellany written in *poluustav,* seems to date from the seventeenth century. Although copies of the *vita* of Saint Antonii Siiskii are numerous, this seems to be the only one to contain the story. To date, this *vita* has been neither published in its entirety nor studied in detail; see "Zhitie Antoniia Siiskogo," in *Slovar' knizhnikov,* vol. 2, pt. 1, pp. 247–48.

81. RNB, O.IV.17, fols. 10r–29v. For a description of the source, see Thyrêt, "Blessed Womb," 495n.94. Feodosiia Fedorovna was born in 1592, three years after Irina's marriage to Fedor Ivanovich, and died in 1594; see S. F. Platonov, *Ocherki po istorii smuty v Moskovskom gosudarstve XVI–XVII vv.* (Moscow, 1937), 153; *PSRL,* vol. 14, pt. 1, p. 45 *(Novyi letopisets).*

82. RNB, O.IV.17, fols. 24r–25v. The story is found in the apocryphal gospel of James, 1–4:2.

83. RNB, O.IV.17, fol. 28. According to the *Aleksandro-Nevskaia Chronicle,* Irina indeed implored the Virgin to intercede for her fertility; *PSRL,* vol. 29, p. 219.

84. RNB, O.IV.17, fol. 29v (support of all-Russian saints), fols. 25v–26r (emulation of Hannah).

85. Dimitrijević, "Dokumenti," no. 28, pp. 36–37. Also see ibid., no. 34, p. 40, no. 35, p. 42, for the performance of prayers for Irina's fertility in other Serbian houses.

86. *Posol'skaia kniga,* 53; also see Batalov, "Molenie o chadorodii," 124. For further examples of requests for prayers for royal offspring directed to Eastern hierarchs, see *Posol'skaia kniga,* 111, 120–22, 125–26, 137, 140, 143, 145.

87. Arsenios Elassonis, *Document relatif au patriarchat moscovite 1589,* translated from Greek to French by Prince Augustin Galitzin (Paris, 1857), 72 (my translation), also 55–59, 62, 67.

88. Ibid., 67–68 (my translation).

89. For examples, see *AAE,* vol. 3, no. 156, p. 222; vol. 3, no. 169, p. 247; vol. 4, no. 23.II, p. 36; vol. 4, no. 23.I, p. 36; vol. 4, no. 181, p. 232. Novombergskii, *Slovo i delo,* no. 119, pp. 196–97.

90. "Skazanie Avraamiia Palitsyna ["Narration of Avramii Palitsyn"]," in *RIB,*

vol. 13, 2d ed., col. 1247; also see B. A. Uspenskii, *Semiotik der Geschichte* (Vienna, 1991), 76–77.

91. S. F. Platonov and V. V. Maikov, eds., "Fedora Griboedova Istoriia o tsariakh i velikikh kniaziakh zemli russkoi," in *Pamiatniki drevnei pis'mennosti i iskusstva* (St. Petersburg and Leningrad, 1879–1925), 121:65; for information on the author's life and the composition of the *History,* see ibid., I-XVI, 69. Platonov and Maikov fail to prove their assumption that Gribcedov's work was to serve primarily as a reader for the tsar's children. Most likely the work was commissioned by the court to showcase the Romanov dynasty (ibid., XI-XII).

92. *SGGD,* vol. 3, no. 72, p. 279. A draft of the patriarch's sermon in the wedding roster for the aborted marriage of Aleksei Mikhailovich and Evfimiia Vsevolozhskaia in 1646 contains the same comparisons; see RGADA, f. 135, otdel IV, rubrik 2, no. 2, fol. 14r.

93. *SGGD,* vol. 3, no. 72, p. 287. On the Muscovite royal wedding ritual, see Daniel Kaiser, "Symbol and Ritual in the Marriages of Ivan IV," *RH* 14, nos. 1–4 (1987): 247–62.

94. Zabelin, *Tsarits,* 315, 319; see also *PRG,* vol. 1, no. 255, p. 200.

95. *PSRL,* vol. 34, p. 194. The chronicle, which survives in only one copy, dates from the early seventeenth century; *PSRL,* vol. 34, p. 5.

96. *Sluzhba i zhitiia Sergiia i Nikona* (Moscow, 1646), ch. 54, 121r–122v. For the ensuing debate about the veracity of Azar'in's miracles, see S. Smirnov, "O predislovii k zhitiiu prepodobnago Sergiia pisannom kelarem Simonom Azar'inym," *Vremennik Imperatorskago Moskovskago obshchestva istorii i drevnostei rossiiskikh* (1851): sect. III.1, p. 2; Simon Azar'in, "Kniga o chudesakh pr. Sergiia," ed. S. O. Platonov, in *Pamiatniki drevnei pis'mennosti i iskusstva* 70: 5–6.

97. S. I. Maslenitsyn, *Iaroslavskaia ikonopis'* (Moscow, 1973), fig. 46. The icon depicts a standing Saint Sergius in the center panel. Twenty-four frames in the surrounding border depict traditional scenes from the saint's life. The background of the center panel features additional episodes of the saint's posthumous miracles described by Simon Azar'in. In the second half of the seventeenth century, another panel was added to the bottom of the icon, depicting the battle of Kulikovo Pole. For a detailed description of the icon, see ibid., 32–34. The icon is now located in the regional museum of Iaroslavl' (inventory no. I-394).

98. Filatov, "Ikona s izobrazheniem," 276, 281, 283.

99. RGB, f. 37, Bolshakov Collection, no. 26, fols. 130r–33r (portents, prophesies, stories), 133r–34r (blessing of Natal'ia's womb).

100. A. P. Sumarokov, *Polnoe sobranie vsekh sochinenii v stikhakh i proze,* ed. N. Novikov (Moscow, 1787), 2:9 (Peter), 241 (Paul); Uspenskii, *Semiotik,* 291 (my translation).

101. See Parsons, "Ritual and Symbol," 66.

102. Herberstein, *Notes* 1:50–51. Solomoniia took the monastic name Sofiia.

103. *PSRL,* vol. 26, p. 313 *(Vologodsko-Permskaia Chronicle); PL* 1:103 *(Pskov I Chronicle).*

104. See *AI,* vol. 1, no. 130, p. 192 (detailed description of two specific incidents with sorceresses); Herberstein, *Notes* 1:51.

105. Herberstein, *Notes* 1:51. Also see A. A. Zimin, *Formirovanie boiarskoi aristokratii v Rossii vo vtoroi polovine XV–pervoi treti XVI v.,* ed. V. I. Buganov (Moscow, 1988), 275; A. A. Zimin, *Gosudarstvennyi arkhiv Rossii XVI stoletiia. Opyt rekonstruktsii* (Moscow, 1978), 1:50. According to later popular lore, Solomoniia's alleged son

was buried in the Suzdal' Pokrov Monastery; see I. Tokmakov, *Istoricheskoe i arkheologicheskoe opisanie Pokrovskago devich'iago monastyria v gorode Suzdale* (Vladimir, 1913), 46.

106. *PSRL,* vol. 24, pp. 222–23; Nasonov, *Istoriia,* 391–92.

107. Begunov, "Povest' o vtorom brake," 116 (quote and reference to monastic virtues).

108. Ibid.

109. *PSRL,* vol. 8, p. 271 *(Voskresensk Chronicle);* see also vol. 13, pt. 1, p. 45 *(Nikon Chronicle);* vol. 21, pt. 2, p. 604 *(Stepennaie kniga).*

110. While S. O. Shmidt sees in the *"Povest'"* a polemical tract written in the 1540s against Vasilii's remarriage and association with the Glinskie, N. A. Kazakova argues it was composed in the 1570s. Zimin also favors a later dating of the text. See S. O. Shmidt, "O vremeni sostavlenii 'Vypisi' o vtorom brake Vasiliia III," in *Novoe o proshlom nashei strany. Pamiati akademika M. N. Tikhomirova,* ed. V. A. Aleksandrov (Moscow, 1967), 110–22; Kazakova, *Ocherki,* 117; A. A. Zimin, "O metodike izuchenii povestvovatel'nykh istochnikov XVI v.," in *Istochnikovedenie otechestvennoi istorii* 1 (Moscow, 1973), 197, 200; Zimin, *V kanun,* 138. For further interpretations of the *"Povest',"* see *Slovar' knizhnikov,* vol. 2, pt. 2, pp. 231–32.

111. *PSRL,* vol. 34, p. 15. The chronicle dates from the second half of the sixteenth century; see *Slovar' knizhnikov,* vol. 2, pt. 2, p. 300.

112. Andrei Kurbskii, "Istoriia o velikom kniaze Moskovskom," in *Pamiatniki literatury drevnei Rusi. Vtoraia polovina XVI veka,* ed. L. A. Dmitriev and D. S. Likhachev (Moscow, 1986), 218. For the controversy over the dating of the Kurbskii correspondence and the *History,* see Edward L. Keenan, *The Kurbskii-Groznyi Apocrypha: The Seventeenth-Century Genesis of the "Correspondence" Attributed to Prince A. M. Kurbskii and Tsar Ivan IV,* appendix by Daniel C. Waugh (Cambridge, Mass., 1971), 62–64; R. G. Skrynnikov, *Perepiska Groznogo i Kurbskogo. Paradoksi Edvarda Kinana* (Leningrad, 1973), 100–113; Edward L. Keenan, "Putting Kurbskii in His Place, or: Observations and Suggestions concerning the Place of the *History of the Grand Prince of Muscovy* in the History of Muscovite Literary Culture," *Forschungen zur osteuropäischen Geschichte* 24 (1978): 131–61; and Ia. S. Lur'e and Iu. D. Rykov, *Perepiska Ivana Groznogo s Andreem Kurbskim* (Leningrad, 1979).

113. V. Georgievskii, *Pamiatniki starinnogo russkogo iskusstva Suzdal'skogo Muzeia* (Moscow, 1927), Prilozhenie I, p. 47; the shroud is reproduced on pl. XII, fig. 2. According to Georgievskii, the shroud was donated in 1594 (Georgievskii, *Pamiatniki,* 21). See also Arkhiepiskop Filaret, *Russkie sviatye chtimye vseiu tserkoviu ili mestno. Opyt opisaniia zhizni ikh* (St. Petersburg, 1882), 569.

114. *AI,* vol. 2, p. 539; *RIB,* vol. 35, no. 53, cols. 86–89. The Shuiskie came from the Suzdal' region.

115. *RNB,* F.XVII.16, fol. 681r. The manuscript, a miscellany dating from the late seventeenth century, contains a short *vita* of Solomoniia, two miracles followed by a short *troparion* and a *kondakion,* and an additional seventeen miracles. In the description of Suzdal' by the sacrist *(kliuchar')* Ananiia dating from the seventeenth century, two additional miracles are mentioned; see Ananiia Fedorov, "Istoricheskoe sobranie o grade Suzhdale," *Vremennik Imperatorskago Moskovskago obshchestva istorii i drevnostei rossiiskikh* 22 (1855): Materialy, 185. Two more manuscripts dating from the eighteenth and nineteenth centuries (respectively) contain Solomoniia's miracles; see RGADA, f. 197, op. 51, no. 62, fol. 2r; RGB, f. 256, Sobranie Rumiantseva, no. 164, fols. 11r–12r. For a published version of

Solomoniia's *life* and miracles, which is based on unknown sources, see Tokmakov, *Istoricheskoe,* "Prilozheniia," 18–22.

116. RNB, F.XVII.16, fol. 681r; also see Tokmakov, *Istoricheskoe,* "Prilozheniia," 20 (miracle of 1602 and quote).

117. *Vladimirskie gubernskie vedomosti,* September 27, 1852 (no. 39), pp. 309–10; K. Tikhonravov, ed., *Vladimirskii sbornik. Materialy dlia statistiki, etnografii, istorii i arkheologii Vladimirskoi gubernii* (Moscow, 1857), 135. On the Shuiskii women in the Suzdal' Pokrov Monastery, see *Vladimirskie gubernskie vedomosti,* February 6, 1854 (no. 6), p. 96.

118. RNB, F.XVII.16, fol. 681v.

119. For a description of the misfortunes that befell Suzdal' in the seventeenth century, see S. I. Maslenitsyn, *Souzdal. Monuments d'architecture,* trans. Vladimir Maksimov (Leningrad, 1985), 10–11.

120. Fedorov, "Istoricheskoe," 56; Tokmakov, *Istoricheskoe,* "Prilozheniia," 16. Patriarch Iosif's call to sing the office for the dead for Solomoniia and to perform prayers to her confused the church historian Golubinskii, who contended that memorial services for and prayers to Solomoniia could not logically be combined; see E. Golubinskii, *Istoriia kanonizatsii sviatykh v russkoi tserkvi* (Moscow, 1903), 278n.2. Golubinskii proposed that the prayers were directed to Solomoniia's name saint. Kliuchevskii, however, points out that the confusion of memorial services and prayers was quite common in the medieval period (Kliuchevskii, *Drevnerusskiia zhitiia,* 388).

121. Count M. V. Tolstoi, ed., "Kniga glagolemaia opisanie o Rossiiskikh sviatykh," *ChOIDR* (1887): no. 4, sect. II, no. 388, p. 210; *Vladimirskie gubernskie vedomosti,* November 29, 1852 (no. 48), p. 317.

122. Tokmakov, *Istoricheskoe,* "Prilozheniia," 4 (blessed mother),11–12 (quotation).

123. Kotoshikhin, *O Rossii,* 19. For a discussion of witchcraft-related illness, see Claus, *Stellung,* 52.

124. See Claus, *Stellung,* 51. For the duties of these nannies and their rewards, see Kotoshikhin, *O Rossii,* 31; Edward Keenan, "Ivan the Terrible and His Women. Pt. 2: Dowagers, Nannies, and Brides" (typescript, Cambridge, Mass., 1981).

125. Augustin Baron de Meyerberg, *Relation d'un voyage en Moscovie,* trans. Prince Augustin Galitzin, Bibliothèque russe et polonaise (Paris, 1858), 2:118; also see McNally, "From Public Person," 156.

126. These letters are published in *PRG,* vol. 1, nos. 1–5, pp. 3–5; for the dating of the individual letters, see nos. 1–3, p. 309.

127. *PRG,* vol. 1, no. 2, pp. 3–4 (rebuke), no. 2, p. 4, (advice of servitors), no. 4, p. 4 (psychological disorder), no. 5, p. 5 (nutrition), no. 4, p. 5 (encouragement).

128. For grief counseling to noble women, see two letters directed by Maksim Grek to a Russian princess regarding the death of her son; D. M. Bulanin, ed., *Perevody i poslaniia Maksima Greka* (Leningrad, 1984), nos. 6–7, pp. 204–6; RGB, f. 256, Rumiantsev Collection, no. 264, fol. 164v–170v, fol. 298r–299r. For the attribution of the letters to Maksim, see Bulanin, *Perevody i poslaniia,* 204; and V. F. Rzhiga, "Neizdannye sochineniia Maksima Greka," *Byzantinoslavica* 6 (1936): 93. I am grateful to Hugh Olmsted for these references.

129. RNB, O.IV.17, fols. 10r, 14r, 18r, 16v–17r. Similar sentiments are expressed in the "Sermon of John Chrysostom about the excessive lamenting over babies"; Gal'kovskii, *Bor'ba khristianstva,* vol. 2, no. 18, pp. 176–78. Gal'kovskii's text is based on fifteenth- and sixteenth-century copies.

130. RNB, O.IV.17, fols. 16v, 17v, 18v. Also see the "Sermon of John Chrysostom about the excessive lamenting over babies"; Gal'kovskii, *Bor'ba khristianstva,* vol. 2, no. 28, p. 177.

131. RNB, O.IV.17, fols. 11r (normal life), 18r, 16v (childbirth).

132. The story is included in the first redaction of the *vita* and can be found in the March volume of Makarii's *Velikie chet'i minei;* see Arkhimandrit Iosif, *Podrobnoe oglavlenie Velikikh Chetiikh Minei vserossiiskogo mitropolita Makariia khraniashchikhsia v Moskovskoi Patriarshei (nyne Sinodal'noi) biblioteke* (Moscow, 1892), 2:60. I have consulted the text of the *vita* in RNB, Collection of the Novgorod Sophia Cathedral, no. 1491, fols. 194v–196r. The episode is also found in the second redaction, which was included in the *Stepennaia kniga; PSRL,* vol. 21, pt. 2, pp. 512–13. For a discussion of the dating of the *vita* and its redactions, see Kliuchevskii, *Drevnerusskiia zhitiia,* 240; *Slovar' knizhnikov,* vol. 2, pt. 1, pp. 270–73.

133. Shumilov copy of the *Nikon Chronicle* in *PSRL,* vol. 12, p. 191; also see *PSRL,* vol. 21, pt. 2, p. 555 *(Stepennaia kniga);* vol. 6, p. 272 *(Sophia II Chronicle).*

134. *PSRL,* vol. 21, pt. 2, p. 607 *(Stepennaia kniga).*

135. See for example *PSRL,* vol. 29, p. 9 *(Letopisets nachala tsarstva);* vol. 13, pt. 2, p. 409 (reference to pilgrimage of Vasilii III and Elena in 1534 in *Tsarstvennaia kniga*). For Ivan IV's and Anastasiia Romanovna's pilgrimages, see Kollmann, "Pilgrimage." The *Addenda to Nikon Chronicle* note the pilgrimages of Ivan and Mariia Temriukovna in September 1561, May 1563, June 1565, September 1565, December 1565, September 1566, and February 1567; *PSRL,* vol. 13, pt. 2, pp. 339, 367, 396–97, 399, 400, 404, 407.

136. *PSRL,* vol. 29, pp. 210–11 *(Aleksandro-Nevskaia Chronicle).*

137. Olearius, *The Travels of Olearius in Seventeenth-Century Russia,* ed. and trans. Samuel H. Baron (Stanford, 1967), 260–61; *PRG,* vol. 1, no. 8, p. 11; no. 10, p. 12; no. 71, p. 70; no. 76, p. 73; no. 123, p. 103; no. 146, p. 117; no. 175, p. 136; no. 182, p. 141; no. 213, p. 166; no. 255, p. 200; no. 365, p. 285. See also Zabelin, *Tsarits,* 315–30, and ibid., "Materialy," 7–14; I. E. Zabelin, *Troitskie pokhody russkikh tsarei* (Moscow, 1847); Paul of Aleppo, *Travels,* 2:136; also see *DR,* vol. 3, cols. 170, 173, 197, 199, 254, 258, 314, 316, 438; Korb, *Diary of an Austrian Secretary,* 121.

138. BAN, Sobranie Petra Pervogo, A 37, fols. 20r–20v; *PSRL,* vol. 21, pt. 2, pp. 651–52.

139. BAN, Sobranie Petra Pervogo, A 37, fols. 24v–26r, 26 (quote). Compare I Sam. 10:1, II Sam. 2:4. For the veneration of Saint Nikita's relics, see Kliuchevskii, *Drevnerusskiia zhitiia,* 44.

140. BAN, Sobranie Petra Pervogo, A 37, fols. 25v–264.

141. BAN, Sobranie Petra Pervogo, A 37, fols. 21r, 26r, 28r. According to the *Nikon Chronicle* and the *Lebedev Chronicle,* the royal family set out from Moscow on September 10, 1556; *PSRL,* vol. 13, pt. 1, p. 273; vol. 29, p. 250.

142. BAN, Sobranie Petra Pervogo, A 37, fol. 29r. The Museum of History and Art in Pereslavl' possesses two tapestries that resemble this description. One of them features Saint Nikita the Warrior and the Virgin Hodegetria on the reverse side. The other depicts Saints Nikita the Warrior and Nikita of Pereslavl' with the Old Testament Trinity, and on the reverse the Annunciation; see S. I. Maslenitsyn, *Pereslavl-Zalessky,* trans. N. Johnston (Leningrad, 1975), 123–25 (reproductions of shrouds), 120 (discussion). Since neither of the tapestries is dated with an inscription, one should treat with caution Maslenitsyn's assumption that they were donated by Anastasiia in 1556.

143. BAN, Sobranie Petra Pervogo, A 37, fols. 29r–29v.

144. *RIB,* vol. 13, 2d ed., cols. 283–84.

145. *PSRL,* vol. 13, pt. 2, pp. 328–29 *(Addenda to Nikon Chronicle).*

146. BAN, Sobranie Petra Pervogo, A 37, fol. 37r.

147. See for example *PRG,* vol. 1, nos. 8, 10, pp. 11, 12 (letters from August 25 and 26, 1619).

148. *PRG,* vol. 1, nos. 7, 74, pp. 11, 72 (letters from August 25, 1619, June 2, 1620).

149. *PRG,* vol. 1, no. 8, p. 11 (letter from August 25, 1619 requesting intercessory prayers); nos. 8–12, pp. 11–13 (pilgrimage in August 1619), no. 146, p. 117 (trip in May 1623).

150. Zabelin, *Tsarits,* 315–30. Saint Catherine was thought to be able to avert difficult births; ibid., 312. Pelagiia received communion on September 1, October 22, December 19, 1628, and again on January 6, 1629. The child died three weeks later; ibid., 318; *PSRL,* vol. 14, pt. 1, p. 153 *(Novyi letopisets).*

151. Zabelin, *Tsarits,* 312, 318, 320, 323, 327; *DR,* vol. 2, p. 156. According to Zabelin, the Romanov women regularly prayed to Saint Nikita of Pereslavl' at an altar dedicated in his name in one of their house chapels, the Church of the Birth of the Virgin in the Terem Palace (Zabelin, *Tsarits,* 312).

152. Kay F. Turner, "Contemporary Feminist Rituals," in *The Politics of Women's Spirituality,* ed. Charlene Spretnak (New York, 1982), 221.

Chapter 2: Helpmate to the Tsar and Intercessor for the Realm

1. Michael Cherniavsky, *Tsar and People: Studies in Russian Myths* (New York, 1969), 51; Paul A. Bushkovitch, "The Epiphany Ceremony of the Russian Court in the Sixteenth and Seventeenth Centuries," *RR* 49, no. 1 (January 1990): 1–17; Rowland, "Biblical Military Imagery," 17; A. A. Zimin, *I. S. Peresvetov i ego sovremenniki* (Moscow, 1958), 85.

2. Cherniavsky, *Tsar and People,* 71; Flier, "Breaking the Code," 213–42; Rowland, "Muscovite Literary Ideology," 112–56; also Robert Crummey, "Court Spectacles in Seventeenth-Century Russia: Illusion and Reality," in *Essays in Honor of A. A. Zimin,* ed. Daniel Clarke Waugh (Columbus, Ohio, 1985), 130–58. Paul Bushkovitch interprets the Palm Sunday ritual as a reflection of church-state relations in mid–sixteenth century Muscovy ("Epiphany Ceremony," 4).

3. RGB, f. 113, Volokolamsk Collection, no. 522, fols. 534v–540r (see esp. 534v, 537r). The text of the instructions is published in *DRV* 14:227–33 (see esp. 227, 229, 232, 233).

4. Zimin, *Peresvetov,* 78; Zimin, "O politicheskoi doktrine," 174.

5. RGB, f. 113, Volokolamsk Collection, no. 522, fol. 536v (also *DRV* 14:229).

6. Ibid., fols. 535r (also *DRV* 14:227), 539r (also *DRV* 14:231).

7. Since the early Middle Ages, Eastern and Western European ruler couples were compared with Constantine and Helena; see Drijvers, *Helena Augusta,* 183. Detailed descriptions of the *katapetasma* can be found in V. V. Stasov, "Zametki o drevnei russkoi katapetasme," *Izvestiia Imperatorskago arkheologicheskago obshchestva* 4 (1863): cols. 534–41, and in N. P. Kondakov, *Pamiatniki khristianskago iskusstva na Afone* (St. Petersburg, 1902), 246–48. For a study of the liturgical aspects of the curtain see Frank Kämpfer, "Ivan Groznyj und Hilandar," *Jahrbücher*

für Geschichte Osteuropas 19, no. 4 (December 1974): 499–519; also see pl. 1 for an excellent reproduction. For Ivan's ruler portrait in the *katapetasma,* see Isolde Thyrêt, "The Construction of the Tsar's Image at the Court of Ivan IV: The Case of the *Katapetasma* of 1555" (paper presented at the Twenty-Seventh Convention of the American Association for the Advancement of Slavic Studies, Washington, D.C., October 26–29, 1995).

8. RGB, f. 113, Volokolamsk Collection, no. 522, fol. 539v (also *DRV* 14:232).

9. Ibid., fols. 535v–536v, 537v, 539r (also *DRV* 14:227, 228–29, 231).

10. Ibid., fol. 537r (also *DRV* 14:229); quotation from fol. 538r (also *DRV* 14:230). Makarii's concept of marriage was adopted by the church council of the *Stoglav* in 1551, which developed it into a lay model for pious women; see N. Subbotin, ed., *Tsarskiia voprosy i sobornyia otvety v mnogo-razlichnykh tserkovnykh chinekh (Stoglav)* (Moscow, 1890), 116–17.

11. "But I would have you know, that the head of every man is Christ; and the head of the woman is the man; and the head of Christ is God" (I Cor. 11: 13); see Peter Brown, *The Body and Society: Men, Women and Sexual Renunciation in Early Christianity* (New York, 1988), 57; Jean Laporte, *The Role of Women in Early Christianity* (New York, 1982), 5. For a feminist reading of the passage, see Jo Ann McNamara and Suzanne F. Wemple, who unfavorably compare Eph. 5:22–33 with Gal. 3:28, which maintains the spiritual equality of the sexes; Jo Ann McNamara and Suzanne F. Wemple, "Sanctity and Power: The Dual Pursuit of Medieval Women," in *Becoming Visible: Women in European History,* ed. Renate Bridenthal and Claudia Koonz (Boston, 1977), 93.

12. *PSRL,* vol. 29, p. 79 *(Letopisets nachala tsarstva).*

13. On the eschatological aspects of the Muscovite tsardom, see Flier, "Iconology," 61, 68–69. The aspect of martyrdom is discussed in Rowland, "Biblical Military Imagery," 189–90.

14. For Metropolitan Makarii's intercession with God for the tsar's victory over Kazan', see *PSRL,* vol. 29, p. 86 *(Letopisets nachala tsarstva).*

15. For pilgrimages on June 21 and September 14, 1548, see *PSRL,* vol. 13, pt. 2, pp. 458, 459 *(Tsarstvennaia kniga).* For news of victory, see vol. 13, pt. 1, p. 221 *(Nikon Chronicle);* vol. 29, p. 115 *(Letopisets nachala tsarstva).* For the dedication of churches, see vol. 13, pt. 2, p. 320. Also see *PSRL,* vol. 29, p. 281, for a similar entry in the *Lebedev Chronicle.* The presence of the wives of Muscovite rulers at dedications of churches was not uncommon. On September 3, 1533, Elena Glinskaia attended the dedication of the stone church of the Ascension of the Lord in Kolomenskoe; *PSRL,* vol. 13, pt. 1, p. 65 *(Nikon Chronicle).*

16. See Mariia Makhan'ko, "Sobiranie v Moskve drevnikh ikon i relikvii v XVI veke, ego istoriko-kul'turnoe znachenie," *Iskusstvoznanie* 1 (1998): 112–41.

17. For a detailed description of the tapestry, see Shchepkina, *Izobrazhenie,* 13–15; also G. V. Popov, *Zhivopis' i miniatiura Moskvy serediny XV–nachala XVI veka* (Moscow, 1975), 45. For an attempt to identify the female figures in the tapestry, see Kämpfer, *Herrscherbild,* 158, 161. Since the tapestry does not identify figures by name, his view remains hypothetical.

18. *PSRL,* vol. 13, pt. 1, p. 273 *(Nikon Chronicle);* vol. 13, pt. 2, p. 305 *(Addenda to Nikon Chronicle);* vol. 29, p. 269 *(Lebedev Chronicle).*

19. See for example Claus, *Stellung,* 118–19.

20. See for example Herberstein's arrival in Moscow; Herberstein, *Notes* 2: 112–27.

21. *PSRL,* vol. 29, p. 287; also see *PSRL,* vol. 13, pt. 2, pp. 328–29 *(Addenda to Nikon Chronicle).*

22. E. N. Klitina, T. N. Manushina, and T. V. Nikolaeva, eds., *Vkladnaia kniga Troitse-Sergieva monastyria* (Moscow, 1987), 26–27. For Muscovite commemoration practices, see Ludwig Steindorff, *Memoria in Altrußland: Untersuchungen zu den Formen christlicher Totensorge,* Quellen und Studien zur Geschichte des östlichen Europa, vol. 38 (Stuttgart, 1994), 157–239.

23. N. F. Kapterev, "Snosheniia ierusalimskikh patriarkhov s russkim pravitel'stvom s poloviny XVI do kontsa XVIII stoletiia," *Pravoslavnyi palestinskii sbornik* 15, no. 1 (1895): 94.

24. The donor and the destination of the gift are identified by an inscription on the Gospel cover. For a good reproduction, see *Blagoveshchenskii sobor,* fig. 263; a cursory description is found on p. 93. The cover, which measures 13.4 by 8.4 inches, is now located in the Kremlin Museums (inventory no. KN-33; 316Bl.s.; 711 sob). The Gospel cover seems to have been inspired by a similar work commissioned by the boyar Fedor Koshka in 1393; see A. N. Svirin, *Iuvelirnoe iskusstvo Drevnei Rusi XI–XVII vekov* (Moscow, 1972), 84–85, fig. 36; T. V. Nikolaeva, *Prikladnoe iskusstvo Moskovskoi Rusi* (Moscow, 1976), 160–67.

25. For the significance of the image *The Queen Stands to Your Right* for Muscovite political culture, see Rowland, "Biblical Military Imagery," 190; Thyrêt, "Construction of the Tsar's Image."

26. *DRV* 14:232.

27. Thyrêt, "Construction of the Tsar's Image."

28. For the pall of 1389, see Maiasova, *Drevnerusskoe shit'e,* fig. 5. The Gospel cover of 1568 depicts Saint Nikita of Pereslavl' in monastic garb, with a long beard, holding an open scroll in the right hand. A similar depiction of the saint can be found in an embroidery Anastasiia may have donated to the Nikitskii Monastery in Pereslavl' in 1556; see Maslenitsyn, *Pereslavl-Zalessky,* 125, fig. 98. Saint Nikita appeared among the number of the official intercessors for the Russian realm as early as 1563; see *AI,* vol. 1, no. 168, p. 320.

29. *DDG,* no. 104, pp. 426–44; Howes, *Testaments,* 307–60 [155–73]. On the transmission of the text, see Howes, *Testaments,* 304–6; S. B. Veselovskii, "Dukhovnoe zaveshchanie Ivana Groznogo kak istoricheskii istochnik," *Izvestiia Akademii nauk SSSR. Seriia istorii i filosofii* 4, no. 6 (1947): 505–20.

30. *DDG,* no. 104, pp. 443–44; Howes, *Testaments,* 357–59 [172].

31. On arrangements of this type and the traditional widow's portion, see Ann M. Kleimola, "'In Accordance with the Canons of the Holy Apostles': Muscovite Dowries and Women's Property Rights," *RR* 51 (April 1992): 215–16.

32. *DRV* 11:239; P. Kh. Grebel'skii and A. B. Mirvis, "Rodoslovnoe drevo predkov Romanovykh" in *Dom Romanovykh. Biograficheskie svedeniia o chlenakh tsarstvovavshego doma, ikh predkakh i rodstvennikakh* (St. Petersburg, 1992).

33. *DDG,* no. 104, p. 444; Howes, *Testaments,* 360 [173] (oprichnina); *DDG,* no. 104, pp. 426–27; Howes, *Testaments,* 308, 309 [155] (quotations); *DDG,* no. 104, pp. 432–33; Howes, *Testaments,* 322–24 [161–62] (protector saints).

34. *DDG,* no. 104, p. 433; Howes, *Testaments,* 324 [162].

35. Dimitrijević, "Dokumenti," 36–37 (no. 28), 37–38 (no. 30), 38 (no. 31). For Arsenios Elassonis, see A. Dmitrievskii, *Arkhiepiskop Elassonskii Arsenii i*

memuary ego iz russkoi istorii po rukopisi trapezuntskago sumeliiskago monastyria (Kiev, 1899), 77. Fear of Ivan IV and awe for Fedor Ivanovich's simplicity were the other reasons mentioned.

36. Quotations found in RGB, f. 310 (Undol'skii Collection), no. 1153, fols. 38r–38v, and in *Sluzhba i akafist prepodobnomu ottsa nashemu Gennadiiu, Kostromskomu i Liubimogradskomu chudotvortsu: S prisovokupleniem skazaniia o zhitii ego i chudesakh* (Moscow, 1888), 17. The Undol'skii copy bears a watermark from the mid–eighteenth century. The earliest copies date from the seventeenth century; see Kliuchevskii, *Drevnerusskiia zhitiia,* 303; T. V. Bulanina, "Aleksei," in *Slovar' knizhnikov,* vol. 2, pt. 1, pp. 34–35. For a list of the manuscripts, see N. P. Barsukov, *Istochniki russkoi agiografii,* ed. Obshchestvo liubitelei drevnei pis'mennosti, 81 (St. Petersburg, 1882), cols. 114–15.

37. RGB, f. 310 (Undol'skii Collection), no. 1153, fol. 38v–39r; *Sluzhba i akafist,* 18.

38. Cited from A. N. Murav'ev, *Snosheniia Rossii s Vostokom po delam tserkovnym* (St. Petersburg, 1858–1860), 1: 159. The Englishman Jerome Horsey, who visited Muscovy in the late sixteenth century, also mentioned a connection between Anastasiia's personal religiosity and the well-being of the Russian realm: "The Empress became wise and of such holiness, virtue, and government, as she was honored, beloved, and feared of all her subjects"; see Lloyd E. Berry and Robert O. Crummey, comps., *Rude and Barbarous Kingdom: Russia in the Accounts of Sixteenth-Century English Voyagers* (Madison, 1968), 264.

39. P. G. Vasenko, *Boiare Romanovy i votsarenie Mikhaila Feodorovicha* (St. Petersburg, 1913), 31; A. A. Zimin, *Oprichnina Ivana Groznogo* (Moscow, 1964), 10, 12; McNally, "From Public Person," 98. Horsey also liked to juxtapose a "young and riotous" tsar with a wife who "ruled him with admirable affability and wisdom" (Berry and Crummey, *Rude and Barbarous Kingdom,* 264). This view provides a welcome contrast to the general notion that Anastasiia was a meek and pious creature; see for example N. M. Karamzin, *Istoriia gosudarstva Rossiiskago,* Slavistic Printings and Reprintings 189/1–12 (The Hague, 1969), vol. 8, ch. 3, p. 59; Claus, *Stellung,* 107; Vasenko, *Boiare Romanovy,* 26.

40. *SGGD,* vol. 3, no. 1, pp. 2–3. Kliuchevskii points out that, in spite of his election, Mikhail was considered a hereditary monarch because of his kinship ties with the Rurikides; see V. O. Kliuchevskii, *A Course in Russian History: The Seventeenth Century,* trans. Natalie Duddington (Armonk, N.Y., 1994), 65.

41. *SGGD,* vol. 1, no. 203, pp. 601, 617. Similar statements appear in the *1617 Khronograf,* the *Skazanie Avraamiia Palitsyna,* the *Inoe Skazanie,* the *Piskarev Chronicle,* and the *Pskov Chronicle;* see *RIB,* vol. 13, 2d ed., cols. 1319, 1235, 129; *PSRL,* vol. 34, p. 219, and vol. 5, p. 63.

42. *RIB,* vol. 13, 2d ed., cols. 279–80. For an excellent interpretation of this source, see Daniel Rowland, "Toward an Understanding of the Political Ideas in Ivan Timofeyev's *Vremennik,*" *SEER* 62, no. 3 (July 1984): 371–99.

43. Dmitrii of Uglich was canonized in 1606 when his relics were translated to Moscow; see S. F. Platonov, *Boris Godunov: Tsar of Russia,* trans. L. Rex Pyles, The Russian Series, vol. 10 (Gulf Breeze, 1973), 143–44.

44. *RIB,* vol. 13, 2d ed., cols. 1, 2; also see E. Kusheva, *Iz publitsistiki Smutnogo vremeni* (Saratov, 1926), 45–64.

45. I. E. Grabar' dates the image to the reign of Mikhail Fedorovich; I. E. Grabar', *Istoriia russkago iskusstva* (Moscow, 1909–1913), 6:386 (for a black-and-white

reproduction, 6:383). The icon is now located in the Tret'iakov Gallery (inventory no. 22209); for a short description, see *GTG. Katalog,* vol. 2, p. 485, no. 1015.

46. *SGGD,* vol. 1, no. 203, pp. 509, 624.

47. Platonov and Maikov, "Fedora Griboedova Istoriia," 26.

48. *SGGD,* vol. 3, no. 63, p. 261; *PSRL,* vol. 5, p. 65 *Addenda to Pskov Chronicles); PL* 1: 132; also see Zabelin, *Tsarits,* 232.

49. During their engagement, Evdokiia Luk'ianovna Streshneva and Mariia Vladimirovna Dolgorukaia were referred to only as "tsaritsa"; see *SGGD,* vol. 3, no. 72, p. 278; *DRV* 13:137–38.

50. *RIB,* vol. 13, 2d ed., cols. 1273–74.

51. Ibid., cols. 279–80 (Timofeev); Dmitrievskii, *Arkhiepiskop Elassonskii,* 172 (quotation).

52. Novombergskii, *Slovo i delo,* no. 4, pp. 4–6; Bakhrushin, "Politicheskie tolki," 93.

53. Platonov and Maikov, "Fedora Griboedova Istoriia," X, 24; on the sources for Griboedov's work, see XI-XIV. The eulogy clashes with the terse style of the genealogical segment. On Griboedov and Russian royal women, see for example ibid., 56, 57 (widowhood and death of Evdokiia Luk'ianovna), 58, 67 (wedding and death of Mariia Il'inichna).

54. For the only known copies, see RNB, Q.XVII. no. 142; GIM, Uvarov Collection, no. 441. Both copies date from the late seventeenth–early eighteenth century. The RNB text is published in A. N. Vlasov, "O pamiatnikakh Ustiuzhskoi literaturnoi traditsii XVI–XVII vv." in *Knizhnye tsentry drevnei Rusi XI–XVI vv.,* ed. D. S. Likhachev (St. Petersburg, 1991), 328–43. Vlasov dates the text to the second part of the seventeenth century. For the date and the organization of the text, see Vlasov, "O pamiatnikakh," 326. Saint Khristofor, who founded a hermitage sixteen miles from Solvychegodsk, left his fellow-monks in 1572 and died alone in the wilderness; see Barsukov, *Istochniki russkoi agiografii,* 579.

55. Vlasov, "O pamiatnikakh," 329. The author of the tale could not name the specific cause of Anastasiia's problem but probably knew about her general condition from the *vita* of Saint Nikita of Pereslavl', who is mentioned elsewhere in the text. Instead of providing details of Anastasiia's distress, the author invoked Gen. 3:16, which refers to women's inevitable pain associated with conception; see ibid., 327, 334, 329.

56. Ibid., 331–33.

57. B. N. Putilov and B. M. Dobrovol'skii, comps., *Istoricheskie pesni XIII–XVI vekov* (Moscow-Leningrad, 1960), nos. 263–66, pp. 456–63. For a discussion of the themes of the song, see Norman W. Ingham, "The Groza of Ivan Groznyi in Russian Folklore," *RH* 14, nos. 1–4 (1987): 228–29; also see 225–27 for the problems associated with the dating and reading of material of this type.

58. Ingham, "The Groza," 229n.9. Since the time of the composition of "The Death of the Tsaritsa" cannot be securely established, questions about the transfer of its ideas from the sphere of the court to the popular level must remain speculative; see ibid., 229. The evidence from the Lukh affair suggests, however, that already in the early seventeenth century the common Russian subjects showed interest in the commemoration of the "pious tsaritsa Anastasiia."

59. L. Uspenskii and V. Losskii, *Der Sinn der Ikonen* (Bern and Olten, 1952), 52; V. G. Chubinskaia, "Ikona Simona Ushakova 'Bogomater' Vladimirskaia,' 'Drevo Moskovskogo gosudarstva,' 'Pokhvala Bogomateri Vladimirskoi' (opyt

istoriko-kul'turnoi interpretatsii)," *TODRL* 38 (1985): 290.

60. Augustin Meyerberg, *Al'bom Meierberga. Vidy i bytovyia kartiny Rossii XVII veka,* ed. A. M. Loviagin (St. Petersburg, 1903), 27, fig. 64; Paul of Aleppo, *Travels* 2:211–13.

61. See, for example, E. S. Ovchinnikova, *Portret v russkom iskusstve XVII veka. Materialy i issledovaniia* (Moscow, 1955), 19–21. A more cautious view has recently been advanced by S. B. Mordvinova, "Istoriko-khudozhestvennye predposylki vozniknoveniia i razvitiia portreta v XVII v.," in *Ot Srednevekov'ia k Novomu vremeni. Materialy i issledovaniia po russkomu iskusstvu XVIII–pervoi poloviny XIX veka,* ed. T. V. Alekseeva (Moscow, 1984), 27. On the general features of Russian art in the seventeenth century, see Lindsey Hughes, "The 17th-Century 'Renaissance' in Russia: Western Influences in Art and Architecture," *History Today* (February 1980): 43.

62. The image *The Veneration of the Cross* exists only in a few copies. One copy is presently located in the Museum of Applied Art in the Kremlin. Painted by the icon painter Ivan Saltanov in February 1678 on a lavish black-and-gold background it was originally placed over the sacrificial altar *(zhertvennik)* in the Church of the Crucifixion in the Terem Palace; see "Izobrazhenie kresta gospodnia s predstoiashchimi emu tsariami i sviatitelem," in *DRG* 4:3. For a good reproduction see Gosudarstvennyi istoriko-kul'turnyi muzei-zapovednik "Moskovskii Kreml'," ed., *Moskovskii Kreml'. Patriarshie palaty* (n.p., 1994), 38. This church was erected in 1681 under Tsar Fedor Alekseevich; see G. Markova, comp., *The Great Palace of the Moscow Kremlin,* trans. M. Wilkinson (Leningrad, 1981), 32. On Saltanov, see Zabelin, *Tsarei,* 175; O. S. Evangulova, *Izobrazitel'noe iskusstvo v Rossii pervoi chetverti XVIII v.* (Moscow, 1987), 71. An apparent paper icon of *The Veneration of the Cross* dating from the seventeenth century is published in V. Trutovskii, "Romanovskaia tserkovno-arkheologicheskaia vystavka v Moskve," *Starye gody* 2 (1913): 36–43. An eighteenth-century copy of this composition is located in the Novgorod Museum. A copy dating from 1785 is found in the collection of the Novodevichii Monastery (inventory no. 1941); see N. F. Trutneva and M. M. Shvedova, *Russkie mastera zhivopisi i graviury XVI–XVIII vv. Katalog vystavki. Gosudarstvennyi ordena Lenina Istoricheskii Muzei* (n.p., 1989), pl. 44. The composition is further featured in an ivory once located in the Church of the Dormition on Sennaia Square in St. Petersburg, published on the last page of *Izvestiia Imperatorskago arkheologicheskago obshchestva* 10 (1884). For other examples, dating mostly from the eighteenth century, see T. M. Kol'tsova, "'Krestovyi obraz' Kiiskogo Krestnogo monastyria," in *Nauchno-issledovatel'skaia rabota v khudozhestvennom muzee: sbornik statei,* ed. E. I. Ruzhnikova (Arkhangelsk, 1998), 14–32.

63. He remains unidentified in the image from the Kremlin Museum and in the paper icon.

64. The Novodevichii copy adds "autocrat of all Great, Little, and White Russia" to Aleksei Mikhailovich's inscription. The ivory omits many of the more detailed inscriptions, perhaps because of limitations imposed by the material.

65. *DRG* 4:3; Kämpfer, *Herrscherbild,* 233. The St. Petersburg ivory gives an abbreviated summary of the inscription: "In the holy cross in the Monastery of the Cross on the island of Kii in the ocean there are gathered holy relic parts [which consist of] up to three hundred holy objects." The close connection of the image with Nikon's promotion of the cult of the True Cross is also evident in a variant composition of *The Veneration of the Cross* in the Golgotha Chapel of the

Cathedral of the Resurrection in the New Jerusalem Monastery, which was built in 1658 under the patriarch's supervision (Kämpfer, *Herrscherbild,* 233). The composition in the Golgotha Chapel was spread over three panels, which featured the Crucifixion in the center, Constantine, Aleksei Mikhailovich, and Nikon on the right, and Helena, Mariia Il'inichna, and Tsarevich Aleksei Alekseevich on the left; see Arkhimandrit Amfilokhii, ed., "Vypiska iz podrobnoi opisi imushchestvu Voskresenskago Novoierusalimskago monastyria, 1680 goda," *Izvestiia Imperatorskago arkheologicheskago obshchestva* 4 (1863): cols. 48–50; Kämpfer, *Herrscherbild,* 233. See M. Il'in, *Podmoskov'e* (Moscow, 1974), 195–202, for a description of the New Jerusalem Monastery. A number of Eastern and Western scholars have recently pointed out the significance of the symbolism of the New Jerusalem for Muscovite Russia; see Rowland, "Moscow"; Flier, "Iconology"; I. L. Buseva-Davydova, "Ob ideinom mysle 'Novogo Ierusalima' patriarkha Nikona," in *Ierusalim v russkoi kul'ture,* ed. A. L. Batalov and A. M. Lidov (Moscow, 1994), 174–81.

66. Kapterev, *Kharakter,* 63–71 (interest in relics); Zabelin, *Tsarei,* 175 (Saltanov image).

67. The connection of the icon with the New Jerusalem symbolism makes it unlikely that the image expressed Patriarch Nikon's claim—that his spiritual authority was to be valued higher than the secular authority of the tsar (M. G. Vernadsky's view). Nikon is not depicted with the imperial crown; see M. G. Vernadskii, "Note sur les vêtements sacerdotaux du patriarche Nikon," *L'art byzantin chez les Slaves. Les Balkans,* vol. 1, pt. 2, ed. Gabriel Millet, Orient et Byzance IV (Paris, 1930), 412–15. Moreover, Nikon is the only figure depicted in a kneeling position, which indicates his humble disposition.

68. Kämpfer, *Herrscherbild,* 234.

69. See for example Anthony Hippisley, *The Poetic Style of Simeon Polotsky,* Birmingham Slavonic Monographs, no. 16 (Birmingham, 1985), 26.

70. Kapterev, "Snosheniia," 58 (Theophanes), 150–51 (Paisius), 173–74 (Paisius quotation); *Materialy dlia istorii raskola za pervoe vremia ego sushchestvovaniia,* vol. 1 (Moscow, 1875), 79 (Neronov). On the Old Believers and other dissident movements in seventeenth-century Russia, see Georg Michels, *At War with the Church: Religious Dissent in Seventeenth-Century Russia* (Stanford, 1999).

71. B. A. Uspenskii, *The Semiotics of the Russian Icon,* ed. Stephen Rudy (Lisse, Belgium, 1976), 68.

72. The inscriptions on the icon are published in *DRG* 4:4. The inscription on the panel in the Church of the Resurrection adds a plea: "When I saw you, I was illuminated in the water during baptism; the evil Maxentius, who did not believe in you, drowned in the water. And now help those who honor and believe in you in all matters, and place those enemies opposing them at their feet. When at the Second Coming you will have Christ stand before us, grant us who honor you to stand without pretense at your right and to rejoice merrily in the heavens" (Arkhimandrit Amfilokhii, "Vypiska," col. 49).

73. The Golgotha panel, which flanks the crucifixion scene, emphasizes the notion of Christ's sacrifice for man. The phrase "you are the divine kingdom, protect those who beseech you" is substituted by the words "you are the divine sacrifice, protect those who sing to you" (ibid., col. 49).

74. The Golgotha composition, which focuses on the power of the cross, contains a more elaborate version: "O honorable cross of Christ, I recognized the heavenly light during the conception of my son Constantine, and I raised you

with my own hands from the womb of the earth at the advice of my son Constantine, and I erected in your honor a holy church to you. Defend us and the believers after us from all evil. And now we, who kneel before you and embrace you, have recognized you yourself and your holy power in the dead maiden, and through her who was resurrected by you I . . . spoke [the name of] Christ, who was crucified on you. As you have granted that girl resurrection, so grant all who honor you deliverance from all evil and eternal consolation, here and in the Last Judgment" (ibid., col. 50). For the Byzantine empress's role in the discovery of the Holy Cross and in the erection of the Holy Sepulchre in Jerusalem and for the miracles ascribed to the cross, see Drijvers, *Helena Augusta,* 101, 102, 106, 108.

75. Drijvers, *Helena Augusta,* 15–18.

76. Xantophulos's works were read in Russia by the court poet Sil'vestr Medvedev; see A. A. Prozorovskii, "Sil'vestr Medvedev (Ego zhizn' i deiatel'nost')," *ChOIDR* (1896): no. 2, sect. IV, p. 78.

77. For a detailed summary of the myth, see L. Rydén, *Bemerkungen zum Leben des heiligen Symeon von Leontius von Neapolis* (Uppsala, 1970), 35–38; also see Drijvers, *Helena Augusta,* 17n.43. The chapel of Ajios Jeórjios and Ajios Konstantínos in Pýrghos on Crete contains a rare fresco cycle that includes a depiction of the birth of Constantine; see Klaus Gallas, Klaus Wessel, and Manolis Borboudakis, *Byzantinisches Kreta* (Munich, 1983), 374–77, 376, fig. 339.

78. The inscription is found in the Novgorod and Novodevichii copies and the respective Golgotha panel.

79. See *DRG* 4:4.

80. *AI,* vol. 1, no. 173, p. 332 (intercessors); *DRG* 4:4 (quote). The corresponding Golgotha panel reads: "I fall to my knees and appeal to you, my most holy cross, enlighten my mind, ears, lips, tongue, breath, and eyes on the way to Christ's kingdom"; Arkhimandrit Amfilokhii, "Vypiska," col. 49. The reference to the Kingdom of Heaven expresses the eschatological theme underlying the Golgotha constellation.

81. GTG no. 28598 (*GTG Katalog,* vol. 2, pp. 411–12, no. 912). For reproductions of this icon, including close-up views of individual segments, see E. S. Smirnova, *Moskovskaia ikona XIV–XVII vekov* (Leningrad, 1988), pls. 199, 200; and E. S. Ovchinnikova, *Tserkov' Troitsy v Nikitnikakh. Pamiatnik zhivopisi i zodchestva XVII veka* (Moscow, 1970), 140–41, pls. 155, 156. The sizable icon (42 by 24.8 inches) was originally located in the Church of the Holy Trinity, which was built by the Muscovite merchant Grigorii Leont'evich Nikitnikov in Kitai Gorod in 1634 (Ovchinnikova, *Tserkov' Troitsy,* 5). The date and the author of the image are attested in two inscriptions on the bottom of the icon.

82. Both men are associated with the foundation of the cathedral in 1326; see *PSRL,* vol. 25, pp. 167–68 *(Moscow Chronicle Compilation of the End of the Fifteenth Century).*

83. G. Filimonov, "Simon Ushakov i sovremennaia emu epokha Russkoi ikonopisi," in *Sbornik na 1873 god,* ed. Obshchestvo drevne-russkago iskusstva pri Moskovskom publichnom Muzee (Moscow, 1873), sect. I., "Izsledovaniia," 36.

84. According to his *vita,* Prince Aleksandr Nevskii took monastic vows on his deathbed; see "Povest' o zhitii Aleksandra Nevskogo" in *Voinskie povesti drevnei Rusi,* ed. N. V. Ponyrko (Leningrad, 1985), 126. In sixteenth- and seventeenth-century Russian frescoes and icons, he is usually depicted as a monastic saint, wearing a dark hooded habit; see for example *Blagoveshchenskii sobor,* fig. 74, and *GTG. Kata-*

log, vol. 2, no. 397, p. 51; no. 1014, p. 484; no. 1020, p. 480. On the conceptualization of Aleksandr Nevskii as a monastic saint, see Werner Philipp, "Heiligkeit und Herrschaft in der Vita Aleksandr Nevskijs," *Forschungen zur osteuropäischen Geschichte* 18 (1973): 70–71.

85. For descriptions of the icon, see Kämpfer, *Herrscherbild,* 225–31; I. E. Danilova and N. E. Mneva, "Zhivopis' XVII veka," in Grabar', Kemenov, and Lazarev, *Istoriia russkogo iskusstva* 4:376–81; N. G. Bekeneva, *Simon Ushakov, 1626–1686* (Leningrad, 1984), 29–56.

86. Danilova and Mneva, "Zhivopis'," in Grabar', Kemenov, and Lazarev, *Istoriia russkogo iskusstva* 4:380; also see V. K. Bylinin and V. A. Grikhin, "Simeon Polotskii i Simon Ushakov. K probleme estetiki russkogo barokko," in *Barokko v slavianskikh kul'turakh,* ed. A. V. Lipatov (Moscow, 1982), 202; T. A. Anan'eva, *Simon Ushakov: Masters of World Painting* (Leningrad, 1971), 15–16.

87. A. I. Nekrasov, *Drevnerusskoe izobrazitel'noe iskusstvo* (The Hague, 1969), 353; Kämpfer, *Herrscherbild,* 230–31 (a similar view is expressed in Ovchinnikova, *Portret,* 21); Chubinskaia, "Ikona," 306, 290.

88. Ibid., 302. For the use of the Tree of Jesse motif in genealogical charts of medieval Slavic rulers, see a fourteenth-century fresco in the Church of the Dečani Monastery in Serbia, which depicts the Nemanjić dynasty. For a reproduction of the fresco, see Paul Johannes Müller, *Famous Frescoes,* trans. Una Tomašević (Belgrade, 1986), 99.

89. Chubinskaia determined that Ushakov's composition represented a composite of a number of iconographic themes that were developed in the Ukraine in the seventeenth century; Chubinskaia, "Ikona," 294–96. For a detailed discussion of the frontispiece of the *Spiritual Sword,* see Kämpfer, *Herrscherbild,* 231–32; Chubinskaia, "Ikona," 303–5. The image is reproduced in Kämpfer, *Herrscherbild,* 255, pl. 156, and in Chubinskaia, "Ikona," 305; the best reproduction is found in D. A. Rovinskii, *Podrobnyi slovar' russkikh graverov XVI–XIX vv.* (St. Petersburg, 1895), vol. 1, col. 30.

90. "Poslanie ko byvshemu patriarkhu Nikonu obsuzhdaiushchemu cherez pisanie knigu imenuemuiu 'Mech dukhovnyi'," in GIM, Synodal Collection, no. 130, fol. 213r; quoted from Chubinskaia, "Ikona," 304–5.

91. The genealogical aspect of the Tree of Jesse motif occurs again in the frontispiece of the *Truby sloves pravednykh (Trumpets of Righteous Words)* of 1674; see T. V. Alekseeva, ed., *Russkoe iskusstvo barokko. Materialy i issledovaniia* (Moscow, 1977), pl. 1.

92. For a short description of Ushakov's life, see A. Leonov, *Simon Ushakov. Russkii khudozhnik XVII veka, 1626–1686* (Moscow, 1945).

93. On this point, also see Filimonov, "Simon Ushakov," 35–36. The patronage of Saint Savva's monastery by the Rurikide and first two Romanov tsars is mentioned in S. Smirnov, *Istoricheskoe opisanie Savvina Storozhevskago monastyria* (Moscow, 1860), 15–26.

94. Chubinskaia, "Ikona," 302, 306.

95. Ps. 28:9. A close-up view of Aleksei Mikhailovich is produced in Kämpfer, *Herrscherbild,* 227, pl. 135. All inscriptions on the icon have been published in Filimonov, "Simon Ushakov," 33–35; for Aleksei's petition, see 34. Filimonov seems to be the only scholar to recognize the icon's message that Moscow's greatness was a function of the grace of God; see Filimonov, "Simon Ushakov," 38.

96. Filimonov, "Simon Ushakov," 33. Compare Ps. 80:14–15: "look down from heaven, and behold, and visit this vine. And the vineyard which thy right hand hath planted."

97. For examples of Byzantine and South Slavic ruler portraits, see André Grabar', *L'empereur dans l'art byzantin: Recherches sur l'art de l'empire d'Orient* (Paris, 1936); Müller, *Famous Frescoes,* 99, 121; Tanja Velmans, "Le portrait dans l'art des Paléologues," in *Art et société à Byzance sous les Paléologues.* Actes du colloque organisé par l'Association Internationale des Études byzantines à Venise en septembre 1968, Bibliothèque de l'Institut Hellénique d'Études byzantines et post-byzantines de Venise, no. 4 (Venice, 1971), pl. XLIII, fig. 18; pl. XL, fig. 11. Ivan Dujčev, ed., *The Miniatures of the Chronicle of Manasse,* trans. Marguerite Alexieva (Sofia, 1963), no. 1; Kämpfer, *Herrscherbild,* 63, no. 29.

98. Filimonov, "Simon Ushakov," 34; Chubinskaia, "Ikona," 303.

99. Muscovite rulers treated their ancestors with utmost respect and ascribed to them the ability to intercede for them from beyond the grave. In his testament Ivan IV invoked for his sons the blessings of "our entire family" from Prince Vladimir of Kiev to Vasilii III; see *DDG,* no. 104, pp. 432–33; Howes, *Testaments,* 322–24 [161].

100. Smirnova, *Moskovskaia ikona,* pl. 200. In contrast, the frontispiece of the *Spiritual Sword* depicts only Christ, the Virgin, and Saints Boris and Gleb with haloes.

101. Fr. George L. Papadeas, ed., *The Divine Liturgy of Saint John the Chrysostom* (Daytona Beach, 1988), 39, 14.

102. Filimonov, "Simon Ushakov," 34. For a close-up view of Mariia Il'inichna, see Kämpfer, *Herrscherbild,* 227, pl. 136.

103. Quoted from Chubinskaia, "Ikona," 303. Translation of quote is my own.

104. Simeon Polotskii, *Virshi,* ed. V. K. Bylinin and L. U. Zvonareva (Minsk, 1990), 300.

105. Mariia's verse represents an adaptation of verse XV.7 of the hymn ("Rejoice, you who unite virginity and child-bearing"); see Antonina Filonov Gove, *The Slavic Akathistos Hymn. Poetic Elements of the Byzantine Text and Its Old Church Slavonic Translation* (Munich, 1988), 265; Romanos Melodus, *Kontakia of Romanos, Byzantine Melodist,* trans. Marjorie Carpenter (Columbia, Mo., 1970–1973), 2:307. Filaret's scroll features verse XIII.5 of the hymn. The inscriptions on Iov's and Fotii's scrolls represent verses XXI.11 and XIII.5, respectively; Gove, *Slavic Akathistos Hymn,* 253, 269; Romanos, *Kontakia* 2:305, 308.

106. Peter Petrejus, who visited Russia in the early seventeenth century, notes that "they pray to all who according to their knowledge count among the saints, especially to the Immaculate Mother of God, the Most Holy Virgin Mary, who always shows mercy toward the human race, presents its prayers with all loving kindness, and prays for it herself that its sins might be forgiven because without her intercession, the sinners could never receive forgiveness." Peter Petrejus, "Istoriia o Velikom Kniazhestve Moskovskom, proiskhozhdenii Velikikh Russkikh Kniazei, nedavnikh smutakh, proizvedennykh tam tremia Lzhedimitriiami, i o Moskovskikh zakonakh, nravakh, pravlenii, vere i obriadakh, kotoruiu sobral, opisal i obnorodoval Petr Petrei iz Erlezunda v Leiptsige 1620 goda," trans. A. N. Shemiakin, *ChOIDR* (1867): no. 2, sect. IV, p. 424.

107. Danilova and Mneva thought the odd proportions of the image were a result of the clumsiness of the painter; Danilova and Mneva, "Zhivopis'," in

Grabar', Kemenov, and Lazarev, *Istoriia russkogo iskusstva* 4:380. The monumental features of *The Tree of the Russian Realm,* however, may well reflect Simon Ushakov's indebtedness to Byzantine traditions of icon painting; see E. S. Smirnova, "Simon Ushakov—'Historicism' and 'Byzantinism': On the Interpretation of Russian Painting from the Second Half of the Seventeenth Century," in *Religion and Culture in Early Modern Russia and the Ukraine,* ed. Samuel H. Baron and Nancy Shields Kollmann (DeKalb, Ill., 1997), 169–83.

Chapter 3: The Tsaritsa as Ruler and Dynastic Link

1. McNally, "From Public Person," 99; Zabelin, *Tsarits,* 292–93. For standard surveys of the Time of Troubles, see Platonov, *Ocherki;* R. G. Skrynnikov, *Rossiia v nachale XVII v. "Smuta"* (Moscow, 1988); R. G. Skrynnikov, *The Time of Troubles: Russia in Crisis 1604–1618,* ed. and trans. Hugh F. Graham (Gulf Breeze, Fla., 1988).

2. S. F. Platonov, *The Time of Troubles: A Historical Study of the Internal Crisis and Social Struggle in Sixteenth- and Seventeenth-Century Muscovy,* trans. John T. Alexander (Lawrence, Ks., 1976), 58; S. M. Kashtanov, "Diplomatika kak spetsial'naia istoricheskaia distsiplina," *Voprosy istorii* (1965): no. 1, p. 44. For examples of Irina's inclusion in official correspondence, see *AI,* vol. 1, no. 219, p. 415; *DAI,* vol. 1, no. 143, pp. 236–37.

3. Zimin, *V kanun,* 174; *Posol'skaia kniga,* 30, 73; Fletcher, *Rus Commonwealth,* 32.

4. *DR,* vol. 1, col. 894 (petition); *Posol'skaia kniga,* 119, 123, 127; Murav'ev, *Snosheniia Rossii* 1:159 (correspondence).

5. Rüß, "Elena Vasil'evna Glinskaja."

6. *SGGD,* vol. 1, no. 167, pp. 460–61, no. 168, pp. 463–64.

7. Hartmut Rüß, "Adel und Nachfolgefrage im Jahre 1553: Betrachtungen zur Glaubwürdigkeit einer umstrittenen Quelle," in Waugh, *Essays in Honor of A. A. Zimin,* 367–70. For a summary of the literature on the event of 1553, see ibid., 370nn.1–2.

8. For two views of the interior of the Golden Palace of the Tsaritsy, see V. Mendeleev, *Khudozhestvennye sokrovishcha Moskovskogo Kremlia* (Moscow, 1988); Markova, *Moscow Kremlin,* fig. 103. For the dispute about the date of the erection of the Golden Palace of the Tsaritsy, see N. V. Gordeev, *Bolshoi Kremlevskii Dvorets* (Moscow, 1957), 46; I. M. Snegirev, *Pamiatniki Moskovskoi drevnosti* (Moscow, 1842–1845), 251; P. Ageev, *Kratkii ukazatel' dostoprimechatel'nostei Bolshogo Kremlevskogo Dvortsa* (Moscow, 1865), 32; Zabelin, *Tsarei,* 52. For the structural changes the Golden Palace experienced through time, see Markova, *Moscow Kremlin,* 24.

9. Zabelin, *Tsarei,* 134. Short descriptions of the frescoes are found in M. P. Fabritsius, *Kreml' v Moskve. Ocherki i kartiny proshlago i nastoiashchago* (Moscow, 1883), 124; S. P. Barten'ev, *Moskovskii Kreml' v starinu i teper'* (Moscow, 1912–1916), 2:233–34; Gordeev, *Bolshoi Kremlevskii Dvorets,* 47–49; Ageev, *Kratkii ukazatel' dostoprimechatel'nostei,* 32–35. For descriptions of the room's architectural history and the history of the frescoes, see *DRG* 6:3–10; S. P. Barten'ev, *Bolshoi Kremlevskii Dvorets. Dvortsovyia tserkvi i pridvornye sobory* (Moscow, 1916), 70–75. The most detailed, though not always correct, description of the frescoes in the Golden Palace of the Tsaritsy is found in Snegirev, *Pamiatniki Moskovskoi drevnosti,* 251–54. Useful also are the accounts in Arthur Voyce, *The Moscow Kremlin* (Berkeley, 1954), 52–53; Markova, *Moscow Kremlin,* 24–25.

10. Arsenios Elassonis, *Document relatif,* 64–65. N. E. Mneva and E. S. Ovchinnikova may be too optimistic in their assumption that the decorations described by Arsenios are completely identical to the present frescoes in the room; see N. E. Mneva, "Zhivopis' kontsa XVI–nachala XVII veka," in Grabar', Kemenov, and Lazarev, *Istoriia russkogo iskusstva,* 3:636; E. S. Ovchinnikova, "Povest' o tsaritse Dinare v russkom izobrazitel'nom iskusstve," *TODRL* 22 (1966): 230.

Little is known about the fate of the Golden Palace of the Tsaritsy in the seventeenth century. Before his return to Moscow, the first Romanov tsar, Mikhail Fedorovich, in a letter from April 23, 1613, ordered his boyar Prince Fedor Ivanovich Mstislavskii to prepare the Golden Palace that once belonged to Tsaritsa Irina for his arrival; *DR,* vol. 1, Prilozheniia, no. 45, cols. 1141–42, also 1152. The Romanovs used the hall on the fourth day of a tsar's wedding; see *SGGD,* vol. 3, no. 72, p. 289; Snegirev, *Pamiatniki Moskovskoi drevnosti,* 251; RGADA, f. 135, otdel IV, rubrik 2, no. 21, fol. 66r. Tsars and tsaritsy alike received foreign dignitaries there; see *Povsiadnevnykh dvortsovykh vremeni gosudarei tsarei velikikh kniazei Mikhaila Fedorovicha, Alekseia Mikhailovicha zapisok* (Moscow, 1769), 2:206; *DR,* vol. 3, cols. 393–94; Snegirev, *Pamiatniki Moskovskoi drevnosti,* 251–52; Ageev, *Kratkii ukazatel' dostoprimechatel'nostei,* 32.

11. *DR,* vol. 1, Prilozheniia, no. 45, cols. 1141–42.

12. Ovchinnikova, "Povest' o tsaritse Dinare," 231; Markova, *Moscow Kremlin,* 24. The construction of the Church of the Crucifixion in 1681 caused further damage; possibly the installation of two tie-bars are connected with this event. An inscription on the vault in the Golden Palace mentions restorations in 1637, 1660, and in 1797 in connection with the coronation of Paul I. For the inscription and its problems, see *DRG* 6:4–5. For modern restoration efforts, see Zabelin, *Tsarei,* 134; Snegirev, *Pamiatniki Moskovskoi drevnosti,* 253; Ovchinnikova, "Povest' o tsaritse Dinare," 230, 231; Gordeev, *Bolshoi Kremlevskii dvorets,* 47; Markova, *Moscow Kremlin,* 24.

13. On this point, see Rowland, "Biblical Military Imagery," 195n.34.

14. The *life* of Constantine and Helena was included in Makarii's *Velikie chet'i minei* under the entry of May 21; see I. U. Budovnits, *Slovar' russkoi, ukrainskoi, belorusskoi pis'mennosti i literatury do XVIII veka* (Moscow, 1962), 87. The Greek Orthodox church celebrated the feast day of Saint Helena on that day; see Drijvers, *Helena Augusta,* 21.

15. A similar fresco is found on the north wall of the Cathedral of the Archangel in the Kremlin; for a reproduction, see Iu. N. Dmitriev, "Stenopis' Arkhangel'skogo sobora Moskovskogo Kremlia (Materialy k issledovaniiu)," *Drevnerusskoe iskusstvo. XVII vek,* ed. V. N. Lazarev, O. N. Podobedova, and V. V. Kostochkin (Moscow, 1964), 148. The sixteenth-century frescoes in the cathedral were repainted in the 1660s according to the layout of the older images (ibid., 141–44).

16. Eusebius Pamphilus, *The Life of the Blessed Emperor Constantine,* The Greek Ecclesiastical Historians (London, 1845), 1:26–28.

17. On the origin of the legend of the cult of the True Cross and its complex evolution in both the Christian West and in the East, see Drijvers, *Helena Augusta,* 95–117, 142–43; Hans Pohlsander, *Helena: Empress and Saint* (Chicago, 1995), 84–116. An older, but still useful account is found in A. Frolov, *La relique de la Vraie Croix: Recherches sur le développement d'un culte,* Archives de l'Orient chrétien, no. 7 (Paris, 1961).

18. Drijvers, *Helena Augusta,* 166. The Judas Cyriacus legend was the most

known and most widely distributed version of the legend of the discovery of the True Cross (Drijvers, *Helena Augusta,* 165). In Russia it was often paired with the reading for the feast day of the Elevation of the Cross on September 14; see for example RGADA, f. 181, no. 639, fols. 59–64.

19. Drijvers, *Helena Augusta,* 166–70.

20. For the iconographic manifestations of the Cyriacus legend, see Engelbert Kirschbaum and Wolfgang Braunfels, eds., *Lexikon der christlichen Ikonographie* (Rome, 1968–1976), 6:485–90; Pohlsander, *Helena,* 217–33. A Russian example is found in an icon from the late sixteenth century located in the Museum of the Trinity-Sergius Monastery (inventory no. 5719). For a detailed description and reproductions of this icon, see Nikolaeva, *Drevnerusskaia,* 136–37, fig. 235.

21. Drijvers, *Helena Augusta,* 165 (for Macarius, 177).

22. For Helena typology, see ibid., 182; Kenneth G. Holum, *Theodosian Empresses: Women and Imperial Dominion in Late Antiquity* (Berkeley, 1982), 215–16. For Ol'ga, see *PSRL,* vol. 1, col. 61; vol. 2, col. 49 (Laurentian and Hypathian versions of *Russian Primary Chronicle*); vol. 21, pt. 1, pp. 21–22 (*vita* in the *Stepennaia kniga*). For Elena, see *PSRL,* vol. 29, pp. 9–10 *(Letopisets nachala tsarstva).*

23. Murav'ev, *Snosheniia Rossii* 1:160 (Silvester quote); *Posol'skaia kniga,* 107 (Fedor Ivanovich to Jeremiah); for Irina's role in the eventual selection of Iov as Russia's first patriarch, see 119, 123, 127, 136, 142 (correspondence of Fedor Ivanovich, Iov, and Boris Godunov).

24. Ol'ga's trip to Constantinople and her conversion to Christianity in the imperial city is mentioned in the *Russian Primary Chronicle* under the year 955; see *PSRL,* vol. 1, cols. 60–64 (Laurentian version); vol. 2, cols. 49–52 (Hypathian version). The time and place of Ol'ga's conversion has been the subject of considerable scholarly controversy since Byzantine sources do not record it. Historians who accept the *Russian Primary Chronicle*'s assertion that Ol'ga was still a pagan when she arrived in Constantinople argue for a conversion date anywhere from 955 to 960. For recent treatments of the problem, see Omeljan Pritsak, "When and Where was Ol'ga Baptized?" *HUS* 9, no. 1–2 (June 1985): 5–24; J. Featherstone, "Ol'ga's Visit to Constantinople," *Adelphotes: A Tribute to Omeljan Pritsak by His Students,* ed. F. E. Sysyn, *HUS* 14, nos. 3–4 (1990): 293–312; D. Obolensky, "Ol'ga's Conversion: The Evidence Reconsidered," in *Proceedings of the International Congress Commemorating the Millenium of Christianity in Rus'-Ukraine,* ed. O. Pritsak, I. Ševčenko, and M. Labunka, *HUS* 12–13 (1988–1989): 145–58; G. G. Litavrin, "Puteshestvie russkoi kniagini Ol'gi v Konstantinopol'. Problema istochnikov," *Vizantiiskii vremennik,* n.s., 42 (1981): 35–48; and Jean Pierre Arrignon, "Mezhdunarodnye otnosheniia Kievskoi Rusi v seredine X v. i kreshchenie kniagini Ol'gi," *Vizantiiskii vremennik,* n.s., 41 (1980): 113–24. A short summary of the problem of Ol'ga's baptism is also included in Paul Hollingsworth, trans., *The Hagiography of Kievan Rus',* Harvard Library of Early Ukrainian Literature: English Translations, vol.2 (Cambridge, Mass., 1994), 169–70n.460.

25. Markova, *Moscow Kremlin,* fig. 106.

26. The image is also reproduced in Mendeleev, *Sokrovishcha Moskovskogo Kremlia.*

27. *PSRL,* vol. 21, pt. 1, p. 13.

28. I. V. Kurukin, "Sil'vestr i sostavlenie zhitiia Ol'gi Stepennoi knigi," in *Teoria i praktika istochnikovedeniia i arkheografii otechestvennoi istorii. Sbornik statei,* ed. V. T. Pashutov, A. I. Alekseev, M. V. Bibikov, V. I. Neupokoev, I. S. Chicherov, and S. O. Shmidt (Moscow, 1978), 53.

29. *PSRL,* vol. 21, pt. 1, p. 12; also see George Ostrogorsky, *History of the Byzantine State,* trans. Joan Hussey (New Brunswick, 1969), 284–85, 293. In contrast, the original account of Ol'ga's trip in the *Russian Primary Chronicle* states that the Kievan princess was received by Constantine VII Porphyrogennitus, who was not yet married; see *PSRL,* vol. 1, cols. 60–61 (Laurentian version); vol. 2, col. 49 (Hypathian version).

30. *PSRL,* vol. 21, pt. 1, pp. 12–15.

31. For both the text and the accompanying miniatures, see "Radzivilovskaia ili Kenigsbergskaia letopis'. I. Fotomekhanicheskoe vosproizvedenie rukopisi," *Pamiatniki Obshchestva liubitelei drevnei pis'mennosti i iskusstva* 118 (1902): fols. 33r, 33v. For a discussion of the chronicle, see A. V. Chernetsov, "K izucheniiu Radzivilovskoi letopisi," *TODRL* 36 (1981): 274–88.

32. The *Radzivil* miniature follows the Byzantine convention of depicting converting pagan males in the nude; see for example fol. 134v.b of the *Skylitzes Chronicle* for the baptism of the Hungarian prince Volosodes. For an example of the convention depicting females clothed, see fol. 135r.b, which shows Ol'ga fully clad and in an upright, standing position; see Sebastián Cirac Estopañán, ed., *Skylitzes Matritensis. Tomo I. Reproducciones y miniaturas* (Barcelona-Madrid, 1965), 337; for explanations of the miniatures, see 141 and 142. I am grateful to Christine Havice for alerting me to the gender-specific conventions of Byzantine baptismal scenes.

33. *PSRL,* vol. 21, pt. 1, pp. 25 (Ol'ga against paganism), 31, 19 (Ol'ga's teaching), 26 (link of chastity and intercession). The *"Slovo Pokhvalno"* ("Encomium for Saint Ol'ga") praises Ol'ga's chastity as well (ibid., 32). Both the tale of the translation of Ol'ga's relics and the *"Slovo Pokhvalno"* invoke Ol'ga as one of the intercessors for the tsar and his realm (ibid., 30). Kurukin points out that the connection of Ol'ga with the baptism of Rus' appears for the first time in the saint's *vita;* Kurukin, "Sil'vestr i sostavlenie zhitiia Ol'gi," 53.

34. *PSRL,* vol. 21, pt. 1, p. 29.

35. "O what a miracle! In heaven and on earth, as a woman first apprehends God, so through her mankind first was doomed in the Fall, and now we have found salvation through a woman" (ibid., 38). Also see ibid., 29 (comments on Eve and Mary).

36. Ibid., 37.

37. J. P. Migne, ed., *Patrologiae cursus completus, seu bibliotheca universalis, integra, uniformis, commoda, oeconomica, omnium SS. patrum, doctorum scriptorumque ecclesiasticorum sive latinorum, sive graecorum,* Series graeca (Paris, 1857–1886), vol. 109, col. 168; Ia. N. Liubarskii, trans., *Prodolzhatel' Feofana. Zhizneopisaniia vizantiiskikh tsarei* (St. Petersburg, 1992), 68. Ovchinnikova mistakenly assumes that the scene depicts the Byzantine empress Irene bringing icons of Christ and the Virgin to the sick in the first week of Lent; see Ovchinnikova, "Povest' o tsaritse Dinare," 230n.45. The texts concerning Theodora and her iconoclast husband have a complex history that is not yet fully explored. In essence they consist of a *vita* of Saint Theodora, which was written as an *encomium* for the iconodule empress, and two narrations, one about the absolution of Theophilus and another about his pious deeds. The latter two were used in Byzantine chronicles that postdate the *vita,* such as the *Chronicle of Hamartolus* and the *Chronicle of Theophanes Continuatus.* For a detailed discussion of the texts, see W. Regel, ed., *Analecta Byzantino-Russica* (New York, 1963), iii–xix (all three parts are published in their original Greek version on pp. 1–43). Excerpts of Regel's texts are published in François Halkin, ed.,

"Deux impératrices de Byzance," *Analecta Bollandiana* 106 (1988): 28–34. I would like to express my gratitude to Martha Vinson for making available to me a copy of her unpublished translation of Theodora's *vita* (BHG 1731).

On Theodora, also see Karl Krumbacher, *Geschichte der Byzantinischen Litteratur von Justinian bis zum Ende des Oströmischen Reiches (527–1453)* (Munich, 1897), 969; and Kh. M. Loparev, *Grecheskiia zhitiia sviatykh XVIII i IX vekov. Opyt klassifikatsii pamiatnikov agiografii s obzorom ikh s tochki zreniia istoricheskoi i istoriko-literaturnoi* (Petrograd, 1914), 310.

38. Regel, *Analecta,* 20–21 ("Tale"), 9–10 *(vita).* On the position of the *logothetes,* a high official at the Byzantine court who was in charge of several departments, see Kazhdan, *Oxford Dictionary of Byzantium* 2:1247.

39. *Manasses Chronicle,* fol. 155v. Dujčev, *Miniatures,* fig. 56 (fol. 155v), also provides a short description of the miniature. For general information on the *Manasses Chronicle,* its provenance and significance, see Dujčev, *Miniatures,* 17–26.

40. See Regel, *Analecta,* 33–39; Halkin, "Deux impératrices," 32–34. The *vita* of Saint Theodora does not mention the two visions.

41. The coincidence of text and image identifies the emperor depicted in the composition as Theophilus. Ovchinnikova's suggestion that the figure might represent Leo V the Armenian must be rejected (Ovchinnikova, "Povest' o tsaritse Dinare," 231).

42. See Ostrogorsky, *History of the Byzantine State,* 220.

43. Prepodobnyi Iosif Volotskii, *Prosvetitel',* translated into modern Russian by E. V. Kravets and L. P. Medvedeva (Moscow, 1993), ch. 16, pp. 362, 363.

44. See RGB, f. 113, Volokolamsk Collection, no. 522, fol. 539r; *DRV* 14:231. A version of the *life* of Theodora was included in Makarii's *Velikie chet'i minei* (February 11); see Budovnits, *Slovar' russkoi,* 96.

45. See *Blagoveshchenskii sobor,* figs. 69–70, 72–74. The frescoes date from around 1547–1551.

46. The ceremony is described in the "Tale of the Absolution of Emperor Theophilus"; Regel, *Analecta,* 38–39; see also Halkin, "Deux impératrices," 34. In Russia this event was commemorated on the first Sunday after the beginning of Lent, which came to be known as the Sunday of Orthodoxy; see V. I. Antonova, *Drevnerusskoe iskusstvo v sobranii Pavla Korina* (Moscow, 1966), 73.

47. The fresco is reproduced in Mendeleev, *Sokrovishcha Moskovskogo Kremlia.* For Byzantine images of the Triumph of Orthodoxy, see Kazhdan, *Oxford Dictionary of Byzantium* 3:2122, and André Grabar, *Iconoclasme byzantin. Dossier archéologique* (Paris, 1957), 203. The fresco in the Golden Palace closely resembles the composition in a Russian folding icon from about 1597, which depicts the fast cycle. Surrounded by a large crowd, Theodora, Michael, and Methodius worship two icons of Christ and the Virgin before an altar. The composition is entitled: "The Worship of the Holy Icons"; see Antonova, *Drevnerusskoe iskusstvo,* fig. 70.

48. See for example a polemical tract dating from 1580; A. Popov, "Drevnerusskiia polemicheskiia sochineniia protiv protestantov," *ChOIDR* (1879): no. 2, sect. IV, pp. 28–29.

49. Platonov, *Boris Godunov,* 154. Although politically the relations between Russia and its immediate neighbors to the west stabilized in the early 1590s, religious differences continued to exacerbate the interaction between the countries (ibid., 57–61).

50. Theophanes the Confessor, *The Chronicle of Theophanes,* trans. Harry

Turtledove (Philadelphia, 1982), 147 (restoration of icons); Judith Herrin, *The Formation of Christendom* (Princeton, 1987), 419 (decision of Council of Nicaea). For details of the events of 787, see Ostrogorsky, *History of the Byzantine State,* 177–79.

51. Markova, *Moscow Kremlin,* fig. 104. Irene's support of icon worship gained her the status of a saint in spite of her later involvement in the blinding of her son Constantine. The *vita* of Empress Irene, which survived in only one manuscript, is published in Halkin, "Deux impératrices," 11–66. The *vita* is based on the *Chronicle of Theophanes* and contains little new information; see Warren Treadgold, "The Unpublished Saint's Life of the Empress Irene (BHG 2205)," *Byzantinische Forschungen* 8 (1982): 237–51. Theophanes the Confessor praises Irene's support of the iconodule patriarch Tarasius, under whom iconoclasm was abolished; see Theophanes, *The Chronicle of Theophanes,* 140–41.

52. For a depiction of Irina's name saint, the martyr Irene, see Nikolaeva, *Drevnerusskaia,* 139 (fig. 238).

53. Iosif Volotskii, *Prosvetitel',* 363. Meletius cited from Regel, *Analecta,* 104. For a description of the lives of both Irenes, see Eva Catafygiota Topping, *Saints and Sisterhood: The Lives of Forty-Eight Women* (Minneapolis, 1990), 194–98, 275–81.

54. Fractions of this image can be gleaned from Markova, *Moscow Kremlin,* fig. 103.

55. Averil Cameron, "The Empress Sophia," *Byzantion* 45, no. 1 (1975): 14 (persecution), 11–13; Herrin, *Formation,* 153 (patronage).

56. Markova, *Moscow Kremlin,* figs. 103, 108. These frescoes are studied in detail by Ovchinnikova, "Povest' o tsaritse Dinare," 231–35.

57. For a summary of the tale, see Ia. S. Lur'e, ed., *Istoki russkoi belletristiki. Vozniknovenie zhanrov siuzhetnogo povestvovaniia v drevnerusskoi literature* (Leningrad, 1970), 401–2. Both Lur'e and Zimin date the tale to the mid-sixteenth century; see Lur'e, *Istoki russkoi belletristiki,* 402; Zimin, *Peresvetov,* 106. Speranskii, who believes that the tale is Armenian in origin, argues that it became known in Russia in the fifteenth century; see M. N. Speranskii, "Povest' o tsaritse Dinare v russkoi pis'mennosti," *Izvestiia Otdeleniia russkogo iazyka i slovesnosti Akademii nauk* 31 (1926), 54–61, 82.

58. L. A. Dmitriev and D. S. Likhachev, eds., *Pamiatniki literatury drevnei Rusi. Konets XV–pervaia polovina XVI veka* (Moscow, 1984), 44. Note, for example, Dinara's response to the Persian's demand that she submit to him: "You order me not to hold power, but I did not receive it from you, but it was given to me from God above" (ibid., 40).

59. Speranskii, "Povest' o tsaritse Dinare," 67. In the 1590s the story was used in redaction P of the *Kazan' Chronicle.* The tale also appears in the *Istoriia o Kazanskom tsarstve,* in later redactions of the *khronografy,* and the *Stepennaia kniga.* Another redaction, composed in the seventeenth century, emphasized the religious-didactic elements of the tale. For details of the textual history of the story, see Speranskii, "Povest' o tsaritse Dinare," 83–84; T. S. Troitskaia, "Zhanrovye transformatsii povesti o Dinare v XVI v.," in *Problemy literaturnykh zhanrov* (Tomsk, 1983), 11–12; and *Slovar' knizhnikov,* vol. 2, pt. 2, pp. 290–93.

60. For a detailed description of the first composition of the Dinara cycle, see Ovchinnikova, "Povest' o tsaritse Dinare," 231–32.

61. Dmitriev and Likhachev, *Pamiatniki . . . Konets XV,* 40–42.

62. Ibid., 42.

63. Ibid.

64. Ibid., 38.

65. The inscription follows the *"Povest' o tsaritse Dinare"*; see ibid., 42.

66. For a detailed description of the composition, see Ovchinnikova, "Povest' o tsaritse Dinare," 232. The same scene is depicted on the left half of an icon from the late sixteenth century, which is now located in the Sector of Old Russian Art of the State Historical Museum in Moscow (GIM, no. 5474, I VIII-1514). In this icon Dinara is nimbed but does not wear a crown. An inscription on the frame reads: "The pious tsaritsa Dinara came to the Sharbenskii Monastery to pray diligently [for help] against the attack of the Persian tsar on the Georgian land" (Speranskii, "Povest' o tsaritse Dinare," 88). For a detailed discussion of the icon, see Ovchinnikova, "Povest' o tsaritse Dinare," 223–27, 237–38; the icon is reproduced on p. 224.

67. Dmitriev and Likhachev, *Pamiatniki . . . Konets XV,* 42, 44.

68. The right side of the composition was covered up during the construction of the reinforcing arch in 1636.

69. Dmitriev and Likhachev, *Pamiatniki . . . Konets XV,* 44. The second redaction, composed in the 1560s, inserted an additional speech by Dinara to her boyars (ibid.). See also Troitskaia, "Zhanrovye transformatsii," 11. The same scene as in the fresco is depicted on the right side of the icon in the State Historical Museum. For a discussion of the composition, see Ovchinnikova, "Povest' o tsaritse Dinare," 225–26, 232. Ovchinnikova wrongly identified the scene on the icon with the last composition of the fresco cycle (ibid., 235).

70. Markova, *Moscow Kremlin,* fig. 107; Dmitriev and Likhachev, *Pamiatniki . . . Konets XV,* 44. The fresco was freed from its later layers in 1950. An inscription from the nineteenth century, which reads "Dmitrii Donskoi defeated Tsar Batii and cut his head off," shows that the fresco cycle and its original context were no longer understood in Imperial Russia; Ovchinnikova, "Povest' o tsaritse Dinare," 232. See also Gordeev, *Bolshoi Kremlevskii Dvorets,* 47; and Barten'ev, *Bol'shoi Kremlevskii Dvorets,* 71.

71. Dmitriev and Likhachev, *Pamiatniki . . . Konets XV,* 40.

72. Ibid., 44, 46.

73. Ibid., 46.

74. Speranskii, "Povest' o tsaritse Dinare," 89–90. The captions read: (1) "The Georgian princess Dinara came to the Sharbenskii Monastery and kneeled before the icon of the Mother of God and prayed with tears"; (2) "Tsaritsa Dinara left the church, mounted her steed and went to meet the Persians"; (3) "Tsaritsa Dinara marched against the Persian tsar and shouted with a loud voice. She beat their armies and cut off his much glorified head, put it on a spear, and brought it into the town."

75. GIM, Uvarov Collection, no. 867, fols. 258v–261v; Speranskii, "Povest' o tsaritse Dinare," 84–87.

76. The exact number of planned miniatures remains disputed; see Speranskii, "Povest' o tsaritse Dinare," 84.

77. GIM, Uvarov Collection, no. 867, fol. 259; Speranskii, "Povest' o tsaritse Dinare," 84. Speranskii argues that the extant illustrations of the Dinara cycle all go back to one prototype (91).

78. Speranskii, "Povest' o tsaritse Dinare," 85, pl. 1.

79. See ibid., 86, pl. 2.

80. See ibid., 87, pl. 3.

81. Dmitriev and Likhachev, *Pamiatniki . . . Konets XV,* 38, 40, 42; also see Speranskii, "Povest' o tsaritse Dinare," 84.

82. Dmitriev and Likhachev, *Pamiatniki . . . Konets XV,* 38.

83. Ibid., 46.

84. *PSRL,* vol. 34, p. 201 *(Piskarev Chronicle); PL* 2:265 *(Pskov Chronicle).*

85. Zimin, *V kanun,* 215.

86. *PSRL,* vol. 34, p. 201. On Irina's rejection of the rule, also see Isaac Massa, *A Short History of the Beginnings and Origins of These Present Wars in Moscow under the Reign of Various Sovereigns down to the Year 1610,* trans. G. Edward Orchard (Toronto, 1982), 38; *PSRL,* vol. 14, pt. 1, pp. 49–50 *(Novyi Letopisets).* Bussow notes that Irina bribed military leaders to support Boris's candidacy; see Konrad Bussow, *Moskovskaia khronika, 1584–1613,* ed. I. I. Smirnov (Moscow-Leningrad, 1961), 205 (German), 81 (Russian).

87. *AAE,* vol. 2, no. 1, pp. 1–6 (correspondence); vol. 2, no. 10, pp. 57–60 (oaths).

88. *PSRL,* vol. 34, p. 204 *(Piskarev Chronicle); AAE,* vol. 2. no. 1, pp. 4–5.

89. Jo Ann McNamara and Suzanne Wemple saw such a development in the West during the early Middle Ages ("Sanctity and Power"). Also see Jo Ann Hackett, "In the Days of Jael: Reclaiming the History of Women in Ancient Israel," in *Immaculate and Powerful: The Female in Sacred Image and Social Reality,* ed. Clarissa W. Atkinson, Constance H. Buchanan, and Margaret R. Miles (Wellingborough, England, 1987), 19, 25–26.

90. See for example the "Sermon of John Chrysostom about good women," in the *Izmaragd* (RGADA, f. 381, no. 199, fols. 53r–54v).

91. In recent times many scholars have exonerated Boris Godunov of the murder; see George Vernadsky, "The Death of the Tsarevich Dimitry. A Reconsideration of the Case," *OSP* 5 (1954): 1–19. For an examination of the texts that illuminate the evolution of the legend of Dmitrii's death, see A. A. Rudakov, "Razvitie legendy o smerti tsarevicha Dimitriia v Ugliche," *Istoricheskie zapiski* 12 (1941): 254–83. Unfortunately, Rudakov does not consider the evidence derived from the Commission of Inquiry headed by V. I. Shuiskii, which investigated the tsarevich's death in Uglich on May 19, 1591; see Vladimir Klein, ed., "Uglichskoe sledstvennoe delo o smerti Tsarevicha Dimitriia 15–go maia 1591 goda," *Zapiski Imperatorskago Moskovskago arkheologicheskago instituta imeni Imperatora Nikolaia II* 25 (1913).

92. William Parry, "A New and Large Discourse on the Travels of Sir Anthony Sherley, Knight, by Sea, and over Land, to the Persian Empire," in *Sir Anthony Shirley and His Persian Adventure,* ed. Sir E. Denison Ross (London, 1933), 133.

93. Massa, *Short History,* 37, 24.

94. *Posol'skaia kniga,* 141, 145; Nikolaeva, *Sobranie,* 212–13, fig. 115 (inventory no. 136), and 216–17, fig. 118 (inventory no. 415); Kapterev, "Snosheniia," 21.

95. For two icons of this type, painted by Prokopii Chirin, see *GTG. Katalog,* vol. 2, nos. 805 (GTG no. 12878), 806 (GTG no. 24821). For embroideries featuring medallions with the Godunov name saints, see Nikolaeva, *Sobranie,* 150–53, fig. 77 (inventory no. 395), and 154–55, fig. 78 (inventory no. 392).

96. Massa, *Short History,* 94.

97. *"Povest' kniazia Ivana Mikhailovicha Katyreva-Rostovskago"* ("Tale of Prince Ivan Mikhailovich Katyrev-Rostovskii"), 2d ed., in *RIB,* vol. 13, 2d ed., col. 647; also see Massa, *Short History,* 94. The authorship of Katyrev-Rostovskii's tale has been disputed. Edward Keenan makes a convincing case for its attribution to Semen

Shakhovskoi; see Keenan, *Kurbskii-Groznyi Apocrypha,* 41, 202n.60(5). I am grateful to Daniel Rowland for sharing his expertise on the literature of the Time of Troubles with me.

98. *SGGD,* vol. 2, no. 85, p. 191 (oath); no. 84, pp. 189–90 (letter). The letter dates from May 1, 1605.

99. Ibid., no. 85, pp. 191–92. Such stipulations were common in loyalty oaths demanded by Vasilii III and Ivan IV; see for example *SGGD,* vol. 1, no. 157, pp. 433–35; no. 174, pp. 474–75; no. 177, pp. 484–87; no. 182, pp. 503–6; no. 196, pp. 561–65; no. 199, p. 582; no. 201, pp. 588–91. On the political uses of witchcraft in Muscovy, see Valerie Kivelson, "Patrolling the Boundaries: Witchcraft Accusations and Household Strife in Seventeenth-Century Muscovy" in *Kamen' kraeug"l'n",* 302–23.

100. *SGGD,* vol. 2, no. 85, pp. 192–93. On the rumors concerning Semen's rivalry with the Godunovs, see Platonov, *Time of Troubles,* 63.

101. *SGGD,* vol. 2, no. 85, p. 194.

102. Ibid., p. 194.

103. Ibid., no. 83, pp. 187–88 (circular letter); also see Massa, *Short History,* 94; *AI,* vol. 2, no. 55, pp. 67–68 (*voevoda*'s letter).

104. Massa, *Short History,* 92 (rumor), 96–97 (Nagaia's isolation).

105. *RIB,* vol. 35, no. 39, pp. 52–53 (order by Mariia Grigor'evna to the Kirillo-Belozerskii Monastery concerning the monk Leonid Shirshov dating from May 7, 1605). For examples of petitions, see G. N. Anpilogov, ed., *Novye dokumenty o Rossii kontsa XVI–nachala XVII v.* (Moscow, 1967), 439–45.

106. For details of the murder of the tsaritsa and her son, see *PSRL,* vol. 14, pt. 1, p. 66 *(Novyi letopisets).* A shorter version can be found in the *Piskarev Chronicle; PSRL,* vol. 34, p. 205.

107. Platonov, *Time of Troubles,* 77.

108. *PSRL,* vol. 14, pt. 1, p. 66 *(Novyi letopisets).*

109. The church did not recognize marriages beyond the second one. After the death of his second wife, Mariia Temriukovna, Ivan IV entered into five uncanonical marital unions. His third spouse, Marfa Vasil'evna Sobakina, did not survive the wedding festivities in 1570; for the date of the wedding see M. N. Tikhomirov, *Russkoe letopisanie* (Moscow, 1979), 259. The following two wives, Anna Alekseevna Koltovskaia and Anna Vasil'chikova, incurred the tsar's displeasure and were forced by him to take the monastic habit. Little is known about Ivan's sixth wife, Vasilisa Melent'eva, who seems to have been of non-noble origin. Mariia Fedorovna Nagaia, who bore Ivan a male child, survived her husband but was tonsured in 1591 by Boris Godunov. For Ivan IV's various wives see Kaiser, "Symbol and Ritual," 249–50; R. G. Skrynnikov, *Ivan Groznyi* (Moscow, 1975), 208–13; *PSRL,* vol. 34, p. 194 *(Piskarev Chronicle).*

110. *PSRL,* vol. 34, p. 194; on the stake of the Nagie in the court politics, also see R. G. Skrynnikov, *Rossiia nakanune "smutnogo vremeni"* (Moscow, 1980), 11.

111. In many ways the cult of Anastasiia Romanovna's memory was unique. Lacking the association with the tsardom's golden days and (with the exception of Mariia Temriukovna and Mariia Nagaia) the status of motherhood, the later wives were unlikely to inspire the courtly elite. Moreover, their premature tonsure prevented them from exercising the ritual role of the tsaritsy at the court. Nevertheless, the example of Ivan IV's fourth wife, Anna Alekseevna Koltovskaia, shows that royal women continued to enjoy the title Tsaritsa and the respect that went

with it even when they were forced to take the veil. From her monastery in Tikhvin, Anna maintained her ties with the court in Moscow and even enjoyed the support of the first Romanov tsar and his family, who used their ties with a dowager Rurikide tsaritsa to bolster their legitimacy; see *PRG,* vol. 1, no. 181, p. 140; *AI,* vol. 1, no. 217, pp. 413–14.

112. The inscription and a description of the large pall (90.8 by 42.8 inches) is published in Manushina, *Khudozhestvennoe shit'e,* no. 13, pp. 68–70. The shroud is now located in the Historical Museum of the Trinity-Sergius Monastery (inventory no. 403).

113. B. Borin, "Pamiatnik zolotogo shit'ia: Pelena XVI v. tsaritsy Marii Feodorovny (1580–1584 gg.) Nagikh," *Svetil'nik,* nos. 9–12 (1915): 70–71. The tapestry is now located in the Cathedral of the Intercession of the Rogozh Cemetery in Moscow.

114. Saint Sergius, John the Baptist, and Saint Demetrius are identified by inscriptions; for a short description of the pall, see ibid., 70–71.

115. N. A. Maiasova, "Drevnerusskoe litsevoe shit'e iz sobraniia Kirillo-Belozerskogo monastyria," in *Drevnerusskoe iskusstvo. Khudozhestvennye pamiatniki russkogo Severa,* ed. G. V. Popov (Moscow, 1989), 211n.54.

116. Skrynnikov, *Rossiia nakanune "smutnogo vremeni,"* 11.

117. Vernadsky, "Tsarevich Dimitry," 2. Ivan IV, in a will he drew up during his marriage to his fourth wife, Anna Koltovskaia, already earmarked Uglich as an appanage for another son that might be born in the future; see *DDG,* no. 104, p. 443; Howes, *Testaments,* 356 [172].

118. *RIB,* vol. 13, 2d ed., cols. 1–2.

119. *PSRL,* vol. 34, p. 195 *(Piskarev Chronicle); RIB,* vol. 13, 2d ed., col. 3 *(Inoe skazanie),* col. 630 (*"Povest' kniazia Ivana Mikhailovicha Katyreva-Rostovskago,"* 2d ed.).

120. Berry and Crummey, *Rude and Barbarous Kingdom,* 321–22.

121. See for example Platonov, *Boris Godunov,* 30, 148; Vernadsky, "Tsarevich Dimitry," 3.

122. For the controversy over Dmitrii's death, see Platonov, *Boris Godunov,* 139–48; Maureen Perrie, *Pretenders and Popular Monarchism in Early Modern Russia: The False Tsars of the Time of Troubles* (Cambridge, England, 1995), 16–22.

123. Platonov, *Boris Godunov,* 135; Vernadsky, "Tsarevich Dimitry," 16. Some of Mariia's relatives who stayed with her in Uglich shared this view.

124. Vernadsky, "Tsarevich Dimitry," 16–18 (esp. 17); for the trustworthiness of the commission's findings, see 9–14, 19.

125. Ibid., 18–19. Mariia seems to have kept in touch with her connections in the capital during her stay in Uglich. The expense records of the Chudov Monastery indicate that the monastery sent a representative to the tsaritsa and her son in Uglich on February 9, 1586; see S. N. Bogatyrev, ed., *Khoziaistvennye knigi Chudova monastyria 1585–1586 g.* (Moscow, 1996), 87.

126. Klein, "Uglichskoe sledstvennoe delo," 19; Vernadsky, "Tsarevich Dimitry," 19. For the Commission's inquest, see *SGGD,* vol. 2, no. 60, pp. 103–23.

127. *RIB,* vol. 13, 2d ed., cols. 299–300.

128. Some of her relatives were tortured and imprisoned; see *PSRL,* vol. 34, p. 196 *(Piskarev Chronicle).*

129. Vladimir Arinin, "Legendy i byli devich'ei obiteli," *Pamiatniki otechestva* 30, nos. 3–4 (1993): 168. A. N. Murav'ev mentions two more chapels built by her, one to the Virgin Hodegetria and another to Saint Kirill of Beloozero; see A. N.

Murav'ev, *Russkaia fivaida na severe* (St. Petersburg, 1894), 234.

130. *RIB,* vol. 13, 2d ed., cols. 313–14.

131. *PSRL,* vol. 34, pp. 205–6 *(Piskarev Chronicle); RIB,* vol. 13, 2d ed., col. 492 *("Skazanie Avraamiia Palitsyna").* Timofeev also attributes the blame solely to the pretender; *RIB,* vol. 13, 2d ed., col. 314. The *Novyi letopisets,* clearly puzzled by Marfa's cooperation with the pretender, assumes that her actions were influenced by fear for her life; *PSRL,* vol. 14, pt. 1, p. 67.

132. Massa, *Short History,* 92.

133. On this point, also see Perrie, *Pretenders,* 82.

134. *PSRL,* vol. 34, p. 207 *(Piskarev Chronicle);* vol. 14, pt. 1, p. 67 *(Novyi letopisets).* For details of Marfa's return to Moscow, see Perrie, *Pretenders,* 82–83.

135. Massa, *Short History,* 111.

136. *PSRL,* vol. 34, p. 207; also see Massa, *Short History,* 111.

137. *PSRL,* vol. 14, pt. 1, p. 67. See also Bussow, *Moskovskaia khronika,* 236; Petrejus, "Istoriia o velikom kniazhestve," *ChOIDR* (1866): no. 2, sect. IV, p. 208; Jacques Margeret, *The Russian Empire and Grand Duchy of Muscovy: A 17th-Century French Account,* ed. and trans. Chester S. L. Dunning (Pittsburgh, 1983), 106–7; Massa, *Short History,* 111.

138. Massa, *Short History,* 111. Similar sentiments are uttered by Konrad Bussow, who does not hide his contention that Nagaia agreed to uphold Otrepiev's charade for the sole purpose of regaining her previous royal position of honor; Bussow, *Moskovskaia khronika,* 109–10, 236. Also see Petrejus, "Istoriia o Velikom Kniazhestve," *ChOIDR* (1866): no. 2, sect. IV, p. 208.

139. Massa, *Short History,* 111; Bussow, *Moskovskaia khronika,* 110, 236. Dimitrii's visits are mentioned as well in the so-called diary of Marina Mniszech; see *Dnevnik Mariny Mnishek,* trans. V. N. Kozliakov (St. Petersburg, 1995), 39, 42. For wedding negotiations, see Massa, *Short History,* 119; also *Dnevnik Mariny Mnishek,* 31. For wedding preparations, see Dmitrievskii, *Arkhiepiskop Elassonskii,* 105; compare *PSRL,* vol. 34, p. 207 *(Piskarev Chronicle).* Arsenios's memoirs end in 1619; sections of them seem to have been edited in the mid-seventeenth century.

140. *SGGD,* vol. 2, no. 91, pp. 202–3. Also see *AAE,* vol. 2, no. 35, p. 92; no. 38, p. 94.

141. On this point, also see Perrie, *Pretenders,* 82.

142. *SGGD,* vol. 2, no. 91, p. 202.

143. Ibid., no. 92, pp. 203–7 (quotation, 205).

144. Ibid., no. 146, p. 306. Marina Mniszech's diary mentions that Marfa rejected her alleged son shortly after the mob killed him; *Dnevnik Mariny Mnishek,* 238. For details of Nagaia's behavior in the riot, see Perrie, *Pretenders,* 104. The "Notes of Hetman Zolkiewski" mention that Marfa claimed to have supported the False Dmitrii because he had threatened to disinter her son in Uglich and to scatter his remains; see P. A. Mukhanov, ed., *Zapiski Getmana Zholkevskago o Moskovskoi voine* (St. Petersburg, 1871), 10–11.

145. *SGGD,* vol. 2, no. 146, p. 307.

146. For Shuiskii's legitimacy problem, see Robert O. Crummey, *The Formation of Muscovy, 1304–1613* (London, 1987), 220.

147. See for example *PSRL,* vol. 34, p. 196 *(Piskarev Chronicle); PSRL,* vol. 14, pt. 1, p. 70 *(Novyi letopisets); RIB,* vol. 13, 2d ed., col. 170 (*"Povest', kako voskhiti tsarskii prestol Boris Godonov,"* that is "Tale of How Boris Godunov Unjustly Seized the Royal Throne"), cols. 320–24 (*Vremennik* of Ivan Timofeev), cols. 1298–99

(1617 Khronograf). Scholars may have neglected the tsaritsa in the context of the translation because many sources of the event—such as the *1617 Khronograf,* the *Novyi letopisets,* the *Piskarev Chronicle,* or Timofeev's *Vremennik*—stem from the early Romanov period, when references to the meddlesome tsar mother were usually carefully avoided. Others—such as the "Tale of How Boris Godunov Unjustly Seized the Royal Throne"—focus on a subject to which Marfa's participation in the ceremonial of the translation of Dmitrii's relics was not relevant.

148. See for example *SGGD,* vol. 2, no. 147, pp. 308–15 (circular letter by Vasilii Shuiskii, June 1606) and no. 148, pp. 316–18 (circular letter by Marfa Nagaia to the town of Elets, August 1606); Massa, *Short History,* 159–61. A segment of Shuiskii's letter also appears in the *Inoe skazanie; RIB,* vol. 13, 2d ed., col. 84.

149. *SGGD,* vol. 2, no. 147, p. 311; no. 148, p. 316; *RIB,* vol. 13, 2d ed., col. 84 *(Inoe skazanie);* Massa, *Short History,* p. 159.

150. *PSRL,* vol. 14, pt. 1, p. 70 *(Novyi letopisets); RIB,* vol. 13, 2d ed., col. 322 (*Vremennik* of Ivan Timofeev).

151. Massa, *Short History,* 160.

152. On this point, see *SGGD,* vol. 2, no. 147, p. 311; no. 148, p. 316. Much work still needs to be done in establishing exact canonization procedures in Muscovite Russia; the standard interpretation is found in Golubinskii, *Istoriia kanonizatsii sviatykh,* 40–169. For more recent treatments of the subject, see Bushkovitch, *Religion,* 74–99; and Isolde Thyrêt, "Muscovite Miracle Stories as Sources for Gender-Specific Religious Experience," in Baron and Kollmann, *Religion and Culture,* 115–31.

153. *SGGD,* vol. 2, no. 147, p. 312; no. 148, pp. 316–17.

154. Ibid., no. 147, p. 312; no. 148, p. 317; *RIB,* vol. 13, 2d ed., cols. 85–86. Timofeev describes the translation of Dmitrii's relics into the Cathedral of the Archangel but omits any reference to Marfa; *RIB,* vol. 13, 2d ed., col. 322. The version of the *vita* of Tsarevich Dmitrii found in Miliutin's *minei,* which dates from the 1650s, mentions Marfa Nagaia's participation in the procession but does not refer to her confession in the Cathedral of the Archangel; *RIB,* vol. 13, 2d ed., col. 919. Since Massa was not allowed into the cathedral during the translation ceremony, we are deprived of his report; Massa, *Short History,* 160. For a summary of the event, also see Perrie, *Pretenders,* 106.

155. *SGGD,* vol. 2, no. 147, p. 312. The composer of the *Inoe skazanie* states outright that the tsar's forgiveness grew out of his own concern for his reign's success and chastises the tsaritsa for her unscrupulous complicity with the pretender, which caused her own son to remain uncommemorated for such a long time; *RIB,* vol. 13, 2d ed., col. 87.

156. *SGGD,* vol. 2, no. 147, p. 312; no. 148, p. 317; *RIB,* vol. 13, 2d ed., cols. 86–87 *(Inoe skazanie).*

157. *SGGD,* vol. 2, no. 148, pp. 317–18. In spite of Nagaia's appeal to Elets, the town continued to adhere to the camp of the False Dmitrii; see Perrie, *Pretenders,* 123.

158. *DRV* 11: 238.

159. B. A. Rybakov, ed., *Vkladnaia kniga Troitse-Sergieva monastyria* (Moscow, 1987), 30.

160. Igumeniia Ismaragda, "Uglichskii Bogoiavlenskii zhenskii monastyr'," *Iaroslavskiia eparkhial'nyia vedomosti,* no.12, March 21, 1873, neofitsial'naia chast', 100–102. The exact date of Mariia Fedorovna's death is disputed; *DRV* 11: 238 lists it as July 20.

Chapter 4: The Royal *Terem* in the Early Romanov Period

1. On Anna Vasil'evna's activities in Riazan', see L. B. Veinberg, "Lichnost' Anny Vasil'evny, velikoi kniagini Riazanskoi," *Trudy Riazanskoi uchenoi arkhivnoi kommissii* 4, no. 8 (1890): 167–69. Elena Ivanovna became the wife of Grand Prince Aleksandr of Lithuania in 1495. After her arrival in Lithuania her father, Ivan III, tried to use her to gain information about his political neighbor. See *DRV,* vol. 14, nos. I–II, pp. 1–3; Russkoe istoricheskoe obshchestvo, ed. *Sbornik Russkogo istoricheskogo obshchestva,* (Petrograd-St. Petersburg, 1867–1916), vol. 35, no. 37, pp. 196–99; no. 43, pp. 223–24; no. 49, pp. 239–42; no. 58, pp. 274–77; no. 60, pp. 278–80; no. 79, pp. 463–66. See also Pushkareva, *Zhenshchiny drevnei Rusi,* 62–65; Ia. S. Lur'e, "Elena Ivanovna, koroleva Pol'skaia i velikaia kniagina Litovskaia, kak pisatel'-publitsist," *Canadian-American Slavic Studies* 13, nos. 1–2 (1979): 111–20.

2. Zabelin, *Tsarits,* 294–95; Hughes, *Sophia,* 19–22. Technically Muscovite Russia referred to the women's quarters of a noble household as the *pokoi* (quiet rooms), but later historians prefer the term *terem.* On this point see Kollmann, "Seclusion," 172.

3. In the case of the Carolingian, Capetian, and Ottonian rulers, their female relatives played significant social and cultural roles as a direct result of the confusing of public and private spheres of influence; see Stafford, *Queens, Concubines, and Dowagers,* 93–165; Marion Facinger, "A Study of Medieval Queenship: Capetian France, 987–1237," *Studies in Medieval and Renaissance History* 5 (1968): 3–48; Leyser, *Rule and Conflict,* 49–73; Patrick Corbet, *Les saints ottoniens: Sainteté dynastique, sainteté royale et sainteté féminine autour de l'an mil* (Sigmaringen, 1986), 30–271.

4. The major proponent of the Byzantine theory is Zabelin; see Zabelin, *Tsarits,* 95–98. See also Claus, *Stellung,* 44–46. For the Mongol theory see Elaine Elnett, *Historic Origin and Social Development of Family Life in Russia* (New York, 1926), 27. For the native impact of the Muscovite autocracy and the Russian Orthodox church, see Susanne McNally, "From Public Person," 15, 143, 152; Goehrke, "Witwe," 68.

5. Kollmann, "Seclusion," 179–86 (esp. 182, 176). For a historiographical survey of the origins of the *terem,* see 171–77.

6. Philip Longworth, *Alexis, Tsar of All the Russias* (New York, 1984), 36.

7. McNally, "From Public Person," 13, 93–95, 99–100, 148, 157. This view also influenced Lindsey Hughes's interpretation of the royal *terem;* Hughes, *Sophia,* 32.

8. Kotoshikhin, *O Rossii,* 29; Zabelin, *Tsarits,* 294–97, 355.

9. Kotoshikhin, *O Rossii,* 29–30, 32; Friedrich von Adelung, ed., *Baron Meierberg i puteshestvie ego po Rossii* (St. Petersburg, 1827), 235–37; Jacob Reutenfels, "Skazaniia svetleishemu gertsogu Toskanskomu Koz'me Tret'emu o Moskovii (Padua, 1680 g.)," trans. A. I. Stankevich, *ChOIDR* (1905): no. 3, sect. II, pp. 82–85.

10. McNally, "From Public Person," 156–57; also Kotoshikhin, *O Rossii,* 32–33; Zabelin, *Tsarits,* 531. For loyalty oaths, see Zabelin, *Tsarits,* 211–12, and ibid., "Materialy," 1–4.

11. See for example the loyalty oath to the first False Dmitrii in June 1605; *SGGD,* vol. 2, no. 91, pp. 202–3. For the bureaucratization of the Russian court, see Borivoj Plavsic, "Seventeenth-Century Chanceries and Their Staffs," in W. Pintner and D. Rowney, eds., *Russian Officialdom: The Bureaucratization of Russian Society from the Seventeenth to the Twentieth Century* (Chapel Hill, N.C., 1980), 19–45.

12. Kotoshikhin, *O Rossii,* 48; Zabelin, *Tsarits,* 217–18; McNally, "From Public Person," 158.

13. A. M. Gnevushev, ed. "Smutnoe vremia Moskovskogo gosudarstva. Vyp. 2–i: Akty vremeni pravleniia tsaria Vasiliia Shuiskago (1606 g. 19 maia –17 iiulia 1610 g)," *ChOIDR* (1915): no. 2, sect. I.3, no. 124, pp. 381–82; no. 125, pp. 382–83; Novombergskii, *Slovo i delo,* no. 6, p. 7; no. 26, pp. 27–28.

14. *AI,* vol. 3, no. 45, p. 40.

15. RGADA, f. 396, Orusheinaia palata, opis'. 1, no. 3065; S. I. Kotkov, A. S. Oreshnikov, and I. S. Filippov, eds., *Moskovskaia delovaia i bytovaia pis'mennost' XVII veka* (Moscow, 1968), 62.

16. Kotoshikhin, *O Rossii,* 48, 68–69, 141; also Zabelin, *Tsarits,* 385; McNally, "From Public Person," 157. For Makrinka, see Zabelin, *Tsarits,* 558–62.

17. John Struys, *The Voiages and Travels of John Struys through Italy, Greece, Muscovy, Tartary, Media, Persia, East-India, Japan, and other Countries in Europe, Africa and Asia,* trans. John Morrison (London, 1684), 129. I am grateful to Claudia Jensen for pointing this reference out to me.

18. S. F. Platonov, ed., "Novyi istochnik dlia istorii Moskovskikh volnenii 1648 goda," *ChOIDR* (1893): no. 1, sect. III, pp. 7–8. For details of the 1648 uprising, see Longworth, *Alexis,* 38–45.

19. *DAI,* vol. 3, no. 119. XIX, p. 453; no. 119.XXVIII, p. 458; no. 119.XXX, pp. 460–61.

20. Ibid., no. 119.II, p. 443 (Pronskoi); no. 119.XXVIII, pp. 458–59 (Khilkov); N. Gibbenet, *Istoricheskoe izsledovanie dela Patriarkha Nikona* (St. Petersburg, 1882–1884), 2: 481–84. The tsaritsa requested weekly reports about the events in Moscow; see *DAI,* vol. 3, no. 119.XXX, p. 462.

21. *DAI,* vol. 3, no. 119.II, p. 443; no. 119.IV, p. 445 (blocking of roads); no. 119.XI, pp. 448–49 (checking of goods); no. 119.III, p. 444 (cancellation of supplies). For other preventive measures, such as the tsaritsa's order to quarantine the tsar's vestments and her use of middlemen in dealing with officials from potentially infected areas, see no. 119.III, p. 444; no. 119.XVII, p. 452.

22. For avoidance of capital, see ibid., no. 119.II, p. 443, no. 119.VII, p. 447; for Kremlin gates, no. 119.III, p. 444, no. 119.XXX, p. 462; for new money, no. 119.III, p. 444; for prison dead, no. 119.XXX, p. 462, no. 119.XXVIII, p. 459; for Bashmakov, no. 119.XXIX, pp. 459–60, no. 119.LXIII, pp. 491–92.

23. Ibid., no. 119.XXX, pp. 461–62; no. 119.LXI, pp. 488–90; no. 119.XIX, p. 453; no. 119.XXVIII, p. 459; Gibbenet, *Istoricheskoe izsledovanie* 2: 483.

24. The tsaritsa referred nearly all matters concerning foreigners to her husband. See *DAI,* vol. 3, no. 119.VII, p. 447; no. 119.XXX, p. 462.

25. For legal fines, see ibid., no. 119.XVII, p. 452; for head tax, see no. 119.XXX, p. 462; for food stuffs, see no. 119.XIX, p. 453; no. 119.XXVIII, pp. 458–59; no. 119.LXI, pp. 489–90; Gibbenet, *Istoricheskoe izsledovanie* 2:483; for fire, *DAI,* vol. 3, no. 119.LXI, p. 490; for instructions, see *SGGD,* vol. 3, no. 179, pp. 532–33.

26. *DAI,* vol. 3, no. 119.XLIII, pp. 475–76; also no. 119.VIII, pp. 447–48. For a direct comparison of Mariia Il'inichna's correspondence with that issued in the name of her son, also see ibid., no. 119.XIX, p. 453; no. 119.XX, p. 453.

27. For Mariia Grigor'evna Skuratova-Bel'skaia, see *RIB,* vol. 35, no. 39, pp. 52–53; Anpilogov, *Novye dokumenty,* pp. 439–45. For Mariia Fedorovna Nagaia, see *SGGD,* vol. 2, no. 146, pp. 306–7; no. 148, pp. 317–18.

28. Quoted from Kapterev, "Snosheniia," 58; also see the letter in the patriarch's own hand in RGADA, f. 52, Grecheskie dela, opis' 2, no. 196, described by B. L. Fonkich, "Ierusalimskii patriarkh Feofan i Rossiia," in *Ierusalim v russkoi kul'-ture,* ed. A. L. Batalov and A. M. Lidov (Moscow, 1994), 217. For medieval Russia's contacts with the East, see Kapterev, *Kharakter.*

29. The patriarch's letter to Mariia Il'inichna, which dates from July 1649, is cited in Kapterev, "Snosheniia," 150, 151.

30. Cited in Kapterev, "Snosheniia," 173–75. As late as 1693, an archimandrite from Mount Sinai conveyed letters from his archbishop to the tsaritsy Natal'ia Kirillovna, Praskov'ia Fedorovna, and Evdokiia Fedorovna with specific requests for liturgical objects and vestments; Kapterev, *Kharakter,* 427–30n.1.

31. For example, the tsaritsa's donation of sables to Patriarch Paisius in 1652 represented half the amount Aleksei Mikhailovich sent to Jerusalem in his own name; see Kapterev, "Snosheniia," 176. For the view that the royal women's donations were private acts, see Hughes, *Sophia,* 20.

32. For altar crosses, see N. A. Maiasova, "Dekorativno-prikladnoe iskusstvo," in *Blagoveshchenskii sobor,* 86–87. For the Royal Gate, see Nikolaeva, *Sobranie,* 100, fig. 49 (reproduction, p. 101); for the tapestry, see ibid., 164, fig. 84 (reproduction, p. 165). The tapestry is now housed in the Museum of the Trinity-Sergius Monastery (inventory no. 2441). The royal couple also sent liturgical gifts to the Kirillo-Belozerskii Monastery; see Maiasova, "Drevnerusskoe litsevoe shit'e," 223n.128.

33. *Vladimirskie gubernskie vedomosti* no. 42 (October 17, 1853): 248 (printed book); no. 38 (September 19, 1853): 217 (silver cross).

34. Kotoshikhin, *O Rossii,* 29; Adelung, *Baron Meierberg,* 236–37; Collins, *Present State,* 65; Reutenfels, "Skazaniia," *ChOIDR* (1905): no. 3, sect. II, pp. 82–83; Paul of Aleppo, *Travels* 2:39, 224; Zabelin, *Tsarits,* 295.

35. Paul of Aleppo, *Travels* 2:96, 100; Zabelin, *Tsarits,* 348 (state rituals); Paul of Aleppo, *Travels* 2:92, 100, 170 (food, holy water), 40 (gift giving), 110 (Easter eggs), 223 (chair). For royal women and gift giving see also Zabelin, *Tsarei,* 346. For the tsaritsa and religious services, see M. Kurdiumov, ed., "Zapiski o tseremoniakh, proiskhodivshikh pri dvore tsaria Alekseia Mikhailovicha po sluchaiu ob"iavleniia pokhoda protiv pol'skago korol'ia Iana-Kazimira," in *Sergeiu Fedorovichu Platonovu. Ucheniki, druzia, i pochitateli* (St. Petersburg, 1911), 317.

36. Paul of Aleppo, *Travels* 2:107–8, 80.

37. *PRG,* vol. 1, no. 8, p. 11; no. 10, p. 12; no. 76, p. 73; no. 79, pp. 74–75; no. 91, p. 82; no. 124, pp. 103–4; no. 127, p. 105, no. 140, p. 113; no. 150, p. 120 (trips to the Trinity-Sergius Monastery in August 1619, June and September 1620, September 1621, September 1622, May 1623); no. 37, p. 47 (trip to Makarii Unzhenskii Monastery in 1619); no. 63, pp. 63–64 (trip to Ugreshskii Nikolaevskii Monastery in 1620).

38. *PRG,* vol. 1, no. 196, pp. 153–54; no. 202, pp. 157–58; no. 229, p, 179; no. 236, pp. 184–85 (joint trips by Evdokiia and Marfa in June 1627, May–June 1628); no. 286, p. 225 (trip by Evdokiia Luk'ianovna with Mikhail Fedorovich in June 1629).

39. The trip took place on January 21, 1648; see *DR,* vol. 3, cols. 86–87; also see Longworth, *Alexis,* 36. On the active participation of the wives of the first two Romanov tsars in the annual pilgrimage to the Trinity-Sergius Monastery, also see Paul of Aleppo, *Travels* 2:136.

40. Longworth, *Alexis,* 63–64; Collins, *Present State,* 65; *Povsiadnevnykh,* 2:119–22; *DR,* vol. 3, col. 170.

41. Zabelin, *Tsarits,* 72; McNally, "From Public Person," 142–43; Kollmann, "Seclusion," 176, 182.

42. For the meeting in Viaz'ma, see *PRG,* vol. 5, no. 16, p. 15; *PSRL,* vol. 37, p. 177 *(Vologodskaia Chronicle).* For almsgiving, see Kotoshikhin, *O Rossii,* 102.

43. Zabelin, *Tsarits,* "Materialy," no. 3, pp. 7–14; also see Kotoshikhin, *O Rossii,* 103–4 on the tsaritsa's need to be guarded from the crowds on her way. Paul of Aleppo as well notes that during outings the tsaritsa was approached by subjects with petitions; see Paul of Aleppo, *Travels* 2:263. For a discussion of royal pilgrimages in the sixteenth century, see Kollmann, "Pilgrimage," 163–81.

44. Kotoshikhin, *O Rossii,* 28.

45. Paul of Aleppo, *Travels* 2:135.

46. Paul of Aleppo, *Travels* 1:400 (daily allowances); Collins, *Present State,* 124 (quote).

47. Paul of Aleppo, *Travels* 2:167–68.

48. For a description and a reproduction of the pall, see Roderick Grierson, ed., *Gates of Mystery: The Art of Holy Russia* (Fort Worth, Texas, 1992), 152–53, no. 40; also see L. D. Likhacheva, ed., *Drevnerusskoe shit'e XV–nachala XVIII veka v sobranii Gosudarstvennogo Russkogo muzeia. Katalog vystavki* (Leningrad, 1980), 85, no. 122.

49. Extracts from the letters are published in Zabelin, *Tsarits,* 307. On the icon of the Virgin of Kazan', see Andreas Ebbinghaus, *Die altrussischen Marienikonen-Legenden* (Veröffentlichungen der Abteilung für Slavische Sprachen und Literaturen des Osteuropa-Instituts [Slavisches Seminar] an der Freien Universität Berlin, vol. 70), Wiesbaden, 1990, 40–42.

50. The correspondence between the tsaritsa and the *protopop* is published in I. E. Zabelin, ed., "Opisanie Novgorodskoi sviatyni v 1634 godu" in *ChOIDR* (1862): no. 4, sect. V, pp. 50–56; also see Zabelin, *Tsarits,* 308.

51. Iu. I. Nikitina, A. S. Pavliuchenkova, E. K. Pagol'skaia, comps., *Novgorodskii istoriko-arkhitekturnyi muzei-zapovednik. Russkoe iskusstvo XI–nachala XX veka. Katalog* (Leningrad, 1963), 19.

52. *PRG,* vol. 1, no. 293, pp. 230–31 (prayer for Filaret); Paul of Aleppo, *Travels* 2:227.

53. Gibbenet, *Istoricheskoe izsledovanie,* 2:473–76; N. F. Kapterev, *Patriarkh Nikon i tsar Aleksei Mikhailovich* (Sergiev Posad, 1909–1912), 1:154n.1. The dissenters also expected the tsaritsa to take measures against possible heretical acts committed by foreigners in Nikon's camp.

54. Paul of Aleppo, *Travels* 2:49; also see Gibbenet, *Istoricheskoe izsledovanie,* 2:474; Kapterev, *Patriarkh Nikon i tsar Aleksei Mikhailovich,* 1:154n.1 (Pronskoi).

55. *SGGD,* vol. 3, no. 178, p. 532.

56. Patriarch Nikon left the royal family at the Trinity-Sergius Monastery and retreated to an area he considered safer from the plague; see Paul of Aleppo, *Travels* 2:49–50.

57. For October 3 letter, see *DAI,* vol. 3, no. 119.XXX, p. 461; no. 119.LXIII, p. 491; for September 7 letter, see no. 119.VI, pp. 446–47; *SGGD,* vol. 3, no. 179, pp. 532–33. The tsaritsa's authority over the holding of liturgical services is also evident in a letter by Ivan Andreevich Khilkov and Almazii Ivanov from October 1654; *DAI,* vol. 3, no. 119.LXI, p. 489.

58. *DAI,* vol. 3, no. 119.XIX, p. 453; no. 119.XVIII, pp. 458–59.

59. See for example Lindsey Hughes's statement that "it was certainly not Maria Miloslavskaia who provided a role model for the independence, determination and neglect of convention that Sophia displayed"; Hughes, *Sophia,* 28.

60. For details concerning the inquest procedure in the case of medieval Russian saints and their miracles, see Bushkovitch, *Religion,* 74–99; and Thyrêt, "Muscovite Miracle Stories."

61. Avvakum, "Zhitie Avvakuma," ed. N. S. Demkova, in *Pamiatniki literatury drevnei Rusi. XVII vek,* ed. L. A. Dmitriev and D. S. Likhachev (Moscow, 1989), 2:359; Longworth, *Alexis,* 83. The correspondence between Evdokiia Luk'ianovna and Archpriest Maksim from February 26, 1634 implies that the tsaritsa exercised a certain amount of influence over her husband when it came to changing ecclesiastical appointments. Maksim, who had lost his position in the Cathedral of the Annunciation in the Kremlin and had been transferred to Novgorod, expressed his hope to return to his previous position and urged his mistress to intercede with the tsar on his behalf; Zabelin, "Opisanie Novgorodskoi sviatyni," 51–52. The at least nominal involvement of the tsaritsa in the determination of ecclesiastical appointments can also be surmised from the fact that the tsaritsy, together with their husbands, received customary gifts by newly consecrated bishops; see Paul of Aleppo, *Travels* 2:131.

62. Avvakum, "Zhitie Avvakuma," 379; on the role of Muscovite noble women in the early Old Believer movement, see Georg Michels, "Elite Women and Old Belief," in *Kamen' kraeug"l'n",* 428–50.

63. Avvakum, "Zhitie Avvakuma," 381, 385; Longworth, *Alexis,* 185. I am grateful to Craig Bonney for his helpful comments on Avvakum's autobiography.

64. Avvakum, "Zhitie Avvakuma," 360 (Login); Longworth, *Alexis,* 89.

65. *Materialy dlia istorii raskola za pervoe vremia ego sushchestvovaniia* (Moscow, 1875–1895), vol. 1, no. VII, pp. 78–83 (quotation, 78–79). The letter is referred to also in N. S. Demkova, ed., "Zapiska o zhizni Ivana Neronova," in Dmitriev and Likhachev, *Pamiatniki literatury drevnei Rusi. XVII vek,* 2:337.

66. For information on the composition and survival of the threnodies, see V. P. Grebeniuk, "'Rifmologion' Simeona Polotskogo (istoriia sozdaniia, struktura, idei)," in *Simeon Polotskii i ego knigoizdatel'skaia deiatel'nost',* ed. A. N. Robinson (Moscow, 1982), 292–94, 259–61, 286–87; Anthony Hippisley, *The Poetic Style of Simeon Polotsky,* Birmingham Slavonic Monographs 16 (Birmingham, 1985), 48–49; Simeon Polotskii, *Virshi,* ed. V. K. Bylinin and L. U. Zvonareva (Minsk, 1990), 423–24. The text of the threnodies is published in Polotskii, *Virshi,* 297–320.

67. Polotskii, *Virshi,* 298 (tsar's lament), 305 (lament of church council), 304, 307, 314 (laments of clergy, monasteries, poor).

68. Ibid., 311. The same thought is also expressed in a eulogy composed by Polotskii and performed at the royal court on January 19, 1660, that is, during Mariia Il'inichna's lifetime. In the eulogy Polotskii praises Mariia for maintaining the Russian tsardom and its towns with "her prayers and works for God"; I. P. Eremin, "Deklamatsiia Simeona Polotskogo," *TODRL* 8 (1951): 359. Also see Hippisley, *Poetic Style,* 27.

69. Polotskii, *Virshi,* 310 (rewards), 309 (prayers). Note the wordplay in "Moisei na gore—v gornitse Mariia" ("Moses on the mountain—Mariia in the chamber"); see ibid., 309.

70. Ibid., 319.

71. Kotoshikhin, *O Rossii,* 29; McNally, "From Public Person," 68.

72. For Kseniia Godunova's prospective husbands, see W. E. D. Allen, "The Georgian Marriage Projects of Boris Godunov," *OSP* 12 (1965): 69; for Irina Mikhailovna's failed wedding to the Danish Prince Waldemar, see W. Bruce Lincoln, *The Romanovs: Autocrats of All the Russias* (New York, 1981), 37–39. Hughes points out that Irina Mikhailovna's case proves that the tsarevny in principle were allowed to marry; see Hughes, *Sophia,* 18. This is supported by Paul of Aleppo's remark that Aleksei Mikhailovich intended to marry his daughter Evdokiia to the grandson of the ruler of Georgia; see Paul of Aleppo, *Travels* 2:28.

73. Kotoshikhin, *O Rossii,* 29.

74. McNally, "From Public Person," 69, 151. On the issue of royal women as links between kin groups, see Kollmann, *Kinship and Politics,* 59, 123–34.

75. Kapterev, "Snosheniia," 144; Kapterev, *Kharakter,* 427–430n.1.

76. See, for example, *Povsiadnevnykh,* 1:15, 20, 42, 114, 120, 124, 134, 181; *DR,* vol. 2, cols. 38, 65, 121, 132, 202, 225–26, 274, 282; Paul of Aleppo, *Travels* 2:126.

77. *Povsiadnevnykh,* 1:114, 120; *DR,* vol. 2, cols. 456, 472.

78. For examples, see Zabelin, *Tsarits,* 538; Novombergskii, *Slovo i delo,* no. 262, pp. 480–83.

79. Paul of Aleppo, *Travels* 2:239, 259, 274. Also see Aleksei Mikhailovich's letters from his Smolensk campaign dated March 31, May 5, and September 1655; see *PRG,* vol. 5, no. 24, pp. 22–23; no. 30, pp. 28–29; no. 44, pp. 44–45 (RGADA, f. 27, Prikaz tainykh del, no. 91, fols. 8r, 15r, 49r). All future references to the archival fond of the Prikaz tainykh del will cite its fond number only (f.27).

80. Kotoshikhin, *O Rossii,* 19; *PSRL,* vol. 31, p. 173 *(Mazurinskii Chronicle);* see also Hughes, *Sophia,* 47.

81. *PRG,* vol. 5, no. 1, p. 1; no. 17, p. 16; no. 18, p. 17; no. 28, p. 26 (RGADA, f. 27, fols. 34r, 1r, 2r, 13r).

82. For donation, see "Uspenskii pervoklassnyi zhenskii monastyr' v gorode Aleksandrove," in *Vladimirskii sbornik,* 97. For godmother, see *Povsiadnevnykh,* 2:78; also Longworth, *Alexis,* 50.

83. *PRG,* vol. 5, nos. 1–68, pp. 1–70 (RGADA, f. 27, no. 91, fols. 1r–73r); Petr Barten'ev, ed., *Sobranie pisem tsaria Alekseia Mikhailovicha* (Moscow, 1856), 239–40; also see Longworth, *Alexis,* 25. After Aleksei Mikhailovich's marriage to Natal'ia Kirillovna Naryshkina in 1670, Irina Mikhailovna seems to have lost her prominent position in the royal correspondence; see for example *PRG,* vol. 5, no. 69, pp. 73–74.

84. Paul of Aleppo, *Travels* 2:123, 126.

85. *PRG,* vol. 5, no. 2, p. 3; also no. 8, p. 8 (letter from July 6 written near Smolensk); these letters are found in RGADA, f. 27, no. 91, fols. 18r, 24r.

86. *PRG,* vol. 5, no. 55, p. 56 (RGADA, f. 27, no. 91, fol. 60r).

87. *PRG,* vol. 5, no. 4, p. 5; no. 19, p. 18 (RGADA, f. 27, no. 91, fols. 20r, 3r).

88. *PRG,* vol. 5, no. 68, pp. 71–72 (RGADA, f. 27, no. 91, fols. 73r–73v).

89. See for example *PRG,* vol. 5, no. 1, p. 1; no. 4, p. 5; no. 6, p. 6; no. 7, pp. 6–7; no. 17, pp. 16–17; no. 20, pp. 18–19; no. 22, pp. 20–21; no. 36, pp. 34–36; no. 41, pp. 41–43; no. 48, pp. 48–49; no. 51, pp. 51–52; no. 54, pp. 55–56; no. 62, pp. 63–64 (RGADA, f. 27, no. 91, fols. 34r, 20r, 22r, 23r, 1r, 4r, 6r, 38r, 46r–46v, 53r, 56r, 59r, 67r).

90. For road conditions: *PRG,* vol. 5, no. 1, p. 1; no. 17, pp. 16–17; no. 23,

pp. 21–22; no. 54, pp. 55–56 (RGADA, f. 27, no. 91, fols. 34r, 1r, 7r, 59r). See also Barten'ev, *Sobranie pisem,* 239. For reconnaissance: *PRG,* vol. 5, no. 2, pp. 2–3; no. 29, pp. 27–28; no. 36, pp. 34–36; no. 54, pp. 55–56 (RGADA, f. 27, no. 91, fols. 18r–18v, 14r, 38r, 59r). For coordination of troops: *PRG,* vol. 5, no. 9, pp. 8–9; no. 30, pp. 28–29; no. 36, pp. 34–36; no. 37, pp. 36–38; no. 40, pp. 40–41; no. 41, pp. 41–43; no. 68, pp. 71–72 (RGADA, f. 27, no. 91, fols. 25r, 15r, 38r, 42r–42v, 45r–45v, 46r–46v, 73r–73v). For fortifications: *PRG,* vol. 5, no. 12, pp. 11–12; no. 36, pp. 34–36; no. 60, pp. 61–62; no. 61, pp. 62–63 (RGADA, f. 27, no. 91, fols. 28r, 38r, 65r–65v, 66r). For maintenance of supplies: *PRG,* vol. 5, no. 1, p. 1; no. 36, pp. 34–36; no. 41, pp. 41–43 (RGADA, f. 27, no. 91, fols. 34r, 38r, 46r–46v). For siege tactics: *PRG,* vol. 5, no. 12, pp. 11–12; no. 60, pp. 61–62; no. 61, pp. 62–63 (RGADA, f. 27, no. 91, fols. 28r, 65r–65v, 66r).

91. *PRG,* vol. 5, no. 1, p. 1; no. 2, pp. 2–3; no. 29, pp. 27–28 (RGADA, f. 27, no. 91, fols. 34r, 18r–18v, 14r).

92. For reports of battles and the capitulation of enemy positions: *PRG,* vol. 5, no. 6, p. 6; no. 7, pp. 6–7; no. 8, p. 8; no. 9, pp. 8–9; no. 10, pp. 9–10; no. 12, pp. 11–12; no. 14, p. 13; no. 23, pp. 21–22; no. 61, pp. 62–63 (RGADA, f. 27, no. 91, fols. 22r, 23r, 24r, 25r, 26r, 28r, 30r, 7r, 66r). For reports of losses: *PRG,* vol. 5, no. 12, pp. 11–12; no. 60, pp. 61–62; no. 61, pp. 62–63 (RGADA, f. 27, no. 91, fols. 28r, 65r–65v, 66r).

93. *PRG,* vol. 5, no. 6, p. 6; no. 7, pp. 6–7; no. 29, pp. 27–28; no. 36, pp. 34–36; no. 37, pp. 36–38; no. 50, pp. 50–51 (RGADA, f. 27, no. 91, fols. 22r, 23r, 14r, 38r, 42r–42v, 55r–55v).

94. Kotoshikhin, *O Rossii,* 29; Zabelin, *Tsarits,* 376, 459.

95. On the relationship of the provincial elite to the Russian ruler in the seventeenth century, see Valerie Kivelson, *Autocracy in the Provinces: The Russian Gentry and Political Culture in the Seventeenth Century* (Stanford, 1996).

96. For traitor, see *PRG,* vol. 5, no. 2, p. 3 (RGADA, f. 27, no. 91, fols. 18r–18v); for Sheremetev, no. 7, pp. 6–7 (RGADA, f. 27, no. 91, fol. 15r); for Sheremetev's maneuvers, also see no. 36, pp. 34–36; no. 37, pp. 36–38 (RGADA, f. 27, no. 91, fols. 38r, 42r–42v); for references to Sheremetev and other individuals, also see no. 3, p. 4; no. 30, pp. 28–29; no. 36, pp. 34–36; no. 37, pp. 36–37; no. 40, pp. 40–41; no. 50, pp. 50–51 (RGADA, f. 27, no. 91, fols. 19r, 15r, 39r, 42r–42v, 45r–45v, 55r–55v). On Sheremetev in general, see Robert O. Crummey, *Aristocrats and Servitors: The Boyar Elite in Russia, 1613–1689* (Princeton, N.J., 1983), 185.

97. For Shein, see *PRG,* vol. 5, no. 34, p. 32 (RGADA, f. 27, no. 91, fo. 36r); for Odoevskii, no. 59, p. 60 (RGADA, f. 27, no. 91, fol. 64r); for Pronskoi, *DAI,* vol. 3, no. 119.LXIII, pp. 491–92.

98. Kotoshikhin, *O Rossii,* 29. See also Meyerberg, *Relation d'un voyage,* 1:136. On the evaluation of Kotoshikhin's work in general, see George G. Weickhardt, "Kotoshikhin: An Evaluation and Interpretation," *RH* 17, no. 2 (Summer 1990): 127–54.

99. Paul of Aleppo, *Travels* 2:39; see 2:249 for another example. On the concept of *umilenie,* see G. P. Fedotov, *The Russian Religious Mind* (Cambridge, Mass., 1946–1966), 1:393, 2:249.

100. For letter of May 1654, see *PRG,* vol. 5, no. 1, p. 1 (RGADA, f. 27, no. 91, fol. 1); for regular praying, no. 3, p. 4; no. 8, p. 8; no. 9, p. 8; no. 10, p. 9; no. 11, p. 10; no. 12, p. 11; no. 14, p. 13; no. 15, p. 14; no. 16, p. 15; no. 37, pp. 37–38 (RGADA, f. 27, no. 91, fols. 19r, 24r, 25r, 26r, 27r, 28r, 30r, 31r, 32r[?], 42r–42v).

101. *PRG,* vol. 5, nos. 18–31, pp. 17–30; nos. 33–60, pp. 31–62; nos. 63–65, pp. 64–66 (RGADA, f. 27, no. 91, fols. 2r–16r, 35r–38r, 42r–46v, 48r–65v, 68r–70r).

102. For the cross of Constantine, see *PRG,* vol. 5, no. 33, p. 31 (RGADA, f. 27, no. 91, fol. 35r); for communion, no. 7, p. 7; no. 35, p. 33; no. 61, p. 62 (RGADA, f. 27, no. 91, fols. 23r, 37r, 66r); for vision, no. 61, pp. 62–63 (RGADA, f. 27, no. 91, fol. 66r). Aleksei Mikhailovich obeyed the saint's command and even named the captured town after Saint Dmitrii.

103. See, for example, the letters from the Savvino-Storozhevskii Monastery and the Trinity-Sergius Monastery in *PRG,* vol. 5, nos. 66, 69, pp. 67–68, 73–74 (RGADA, f. 27, no. 91, fols. 71r, 74r).

104. Avvakum, "Zhitie Avvakuma," 400.

Chapter 5: Sofiia Alekseevna, the Tsarevna as Ruler

1. For an excellent survey of attitudes toward Sofiia Alekseevna from the late seventeenth century to the present, see Hughes, *Sophia,* 263–76.

2. Lindsey Hughes, "'Ambitious and Daring above her Sex': Tsarevna Sophia Alekseevna (1657–1704) in Foreigners' Accounts," *OSP* 21 (1988): 65–89; Lindsey Hughes, "Sofiya Alekseyevna and the Moscow Rebellion of 1682," *SEER* 63, no. 4 (1985): 518–39; Lindsey Hughes, "Sophia, 'Autocrat of All the Russias': Titles, Ritual and Eulogy in the Regency of Sophia Alekseevna (1682–89)," *Canadian Slavonic Papers* 28, no. 3 (1986): 265–86; A. P. Bogdanov, "Politicheskaia graviura v Rossii perioda regentstva Sof'i Alekseevny," in *Istochnikovedenie otechestvennoi istorii. Sbornik statei. 1981,* ed. V. I. Buganov (Moscow, 1982), 225–46; A. P. Bogdanov, "Sil'vestra Medvedeva panegirik tsarevne Sof'e 1682g.," in *Pamiatniki kul'tury. Novye otkrytiia, 1982* (Leningrad, 1984), 45–52; Elizabeth Kristofovich Zelensky, "'Sophia the Wisdom of God': The Function of Religious Imagery during the Regency of Sofiia Alekseevna of Muscovy," in *Women and Sovereignty,* 192–211.

3. Hughes, *Sophia,* xvii; Hughes, "Sophia, 'Autocrat,'" 266–67.

4. On this point, see Nancy Shields Kollmann, review of *Sophia, Regent of Russia 1657–1704,* by Lindsey Hughes, in *RR* 52, no. 2 (April 1993): 270–71.

5. Hughes, *Sophia,* 275; Elizabeth Kristofovich Zelensky, "'Sophia the Wisdom of God' as a Rhetorical Device during the Regency of Sof'ia Alekseevna, 1682–1689" (Ph.D. diss., Georgetown University, Washington, D.C., 1992), 1:15, 7–8; Zelensky, "Sophia . . . Religious Imagery," 193.

6. On the dual coding of Russian culture in the second half of the seventeenth century, see B. A. Uspenskii, *Semiotik der Geschichte* (Vienna, 1991), 153–55. For the impact of Ukrainian cultural trends embodying Western features on Russian court culture, see Bushkovitch, *Religion,* 134–45, 150–75.

7. In view of Sofiia Alekseevna's medieval background, Hughes's search for Sofiia as a modern individual—her possible role models, tastes, and cosmopolitan interests—is fraught with problems; see Hughes, *Sophia,* 27–30.

8. See for example Hughes, "Sophia, 'Autocrat,'" 216; Hughes, *Sophia,* 16–17, 20; Hughes, "Moscow Rebellion," 522; Zelensky, "Sophia . . . Religious Imagery," 193; Zelensky, "Sophia . . . Rhetorical Device," 2:201; N. Moleva, "Tsar-Devitsa," *Znanie–sila* (1971): no. 1, p. 34.

9. Hughes, *Sophia,* 19 (quote). D. Mordovtsev, *Russkie istoricheskie zhenshchiny. Populiarnye rasskazy iz russkoi istorii* (St. Petersburg, 1874), 306; Lindsey Hughes, "Portraits of Tsarevna Sof'ia Alekseevna," *Study Group on 18th-century Rus-*

sia. Newsletter 14 (1988): 3. On Natal'ia Kirillovna, see Hughes, "Ambitious and Daring," 66–67; Reutenfels, "Skazaniia," *ChOIDR* (1905): no. 3, sect. II, pp. 82–83.

10. Hughes, *Sophia,* 104; Kollmann, *Kinship and Politics,* 124–25.

11. On the notion of throne-worthiness in the medieval West, see Fritz Kern, *Kingship and Law in the Middle Ages* (Oxford, 1956), 12–17; William A. Chaney, *The Cult of Kingship in Anglo-Saxon England* (Berkeley, 1970), 12–42; Ian Wood, *The Merovingian Kingdoms, 450–751* (New York, 1994), 55–60; J. M. Wallace-Hadrill, *Early Germanic Kingship in England and on the Continent* (Oxford, 1971), 17–20.

12. For the loyalty oath, see *SGGD,* vol. 2, no. 85, p. 191. On Kseniia Godunova's fate, see N. A. Maiasova, "Literaturnyi obraz Ksenii Godunovoi i pripisyvaemye ei proizvedeniia shit'ia (k voprosu o vzaimo-otnoshenii literatury, iskusstva i deistvitel'nosti)," *TODRL* 22 (1966): 297–302.

13. See for example a document from February 3, 1676, announcing to the Don Cossacks Fedor Alekseevich's accession to the throne; *SGGD,* vol. 4, no. 103, pp. 333–35; Hughes, *Sophia,* 44. Hughes intuitively assumes that the Romanov women enjoyed a "sanctity of royal blood"; see *Sophia,* 67.

14. V. I. Buganov, ed., *Vosstanie v Moskve 1682 g. Sbornik dokumentov* (Moscow, 1976), no. 204, pp. 257–59. For other examples of oaths sworn to royal women in 1682, see *SGGD,* vol. 4, no. 146, p. 441; *PSZ,* vol. 2, no. 932, p. 441.

15. A. A. Prozorovskii, ed., "Sil'vestra Medvedeva Sozertsanie let kratkoe 7190, 91, i 92, v nikh zhe chto sodeiasia vo grazhdanstve," *ChOIDR* (1894): no. 4, sect. II, p. 66; Hughes, *Sophia,* 83.

16. For court poetry, see for example Sil'vestr Medvedev's congratulatory ode on the occasion of Sofiia's name day, composed between 1681 and 1685 in A. M. Panchenko, ed., *Russkaia sillabicheskaia poeziia XVII–XVIII v.v.,* Biblioteka poeta (Leningrad, 1970), no. 186, pp. 190–91. For tapestry, see L. D. Likhacheva, comp., *Drevnerusskoe shit'e XV–nachala XVIII v. v sobranii Gosudarstvennogo Russkogo muzeia. Katalog vystavki* (Leningrad, 1980), 99.

17. Hughes, *Sophia,* pp. 251–52. Sofiia Alekseevna was tonsured on October 21, 1698, and given the monastic name Susanna. Marfa lived out her life in the Monastery of the Dormition in Pereslavl' as the nun Margarita. Twenty-one extant letters by her to her natal sisters, members of the Naryshkin family, and other Naryshkin supporters document her continued struggle with the court in Moscow, which denied her food and medical care. In spite of these adversities, the tsarevna worked hard for the erection of a church and the ordination of a local priest in her monastery; see Arkhimandrit Leonid, "Blagovernaia tsarevna, velikaia kniazhna Marfa Alekseevna," *Russkii arkhiv* 20 (1882): 27.

18. Peter I, *Pis'ma i bumagi Imperatora Petra Velikogo* (St. Petersburg, 1887–1919), vol. 1, no. 254, pp. 268–69; Hughes, *Sophia,* 255, also 246.

19. Paul of Aleppo, *Travels* 2:123; *PRG,* vol. 5, no. 66, p. 67; no. 67, p. 69; no. 68, p. 71; no. 69, pp. 73–74 (RGADA, f. 27, no. 91, fols. 71–74). The letters including Sofiia date from 1659, 1660, 1670, and 1674–1675, respectively.

20. For Medvedev, see Bogdanov, "Sil'vestra Medvedeva panegirik," 51; Hughes, "Sophia, 'Autocrat,'" 280–81. For Rimskii-Korsakov, A. P. Bogdanov and V. I. Buganov, eds., *Pamiatniki obshchestvenno-politicheskoi mysli v Rossii kontsa XVII veka. Literaturnye panegiriki* (Moscow, 1983), vol. 2, no. 32, pp. 235, 309.

21. S. Brailovskii, "K voprosu o literaturnoi deiatel'nosti russkikh pisatelei XVII stoletiia, nosivshikh imia 'Karion'," *Izvestiia Otdeleniia russkago iazyka i slovesnosti Imperatorskoi Akademii nauk* 14 (1910): 26. On Pulcheria's achievements, see

Kenneth G. Holum, *Theodosian Empresses: Women and Imperial Dominion in Late Antiquity* (Berkeley, 1982), 91–111. The Latin inscription on Sofiia Alekseevna's portrait by Abraham Bloteling from ca. 1688 also makes reference to the similarity of the regent's mental acumen to that of Pulcheria; see M. A. Alekseeva, "Portret tsarevny Sof'i gravera Tarasevicha," in *Pamiatniki kul'tury. Novye otkrytiia, 1975* (Moscow, 1976), 240–49 (reproduction, 242).

22. *DRV* 14:105 (Medvedev); Brailovskii, "K voprosu," 52 (Istomin in September 1687); Bogdanov and Buganov, *Pamiatniki,* vol. 2, no. 32, p. 239 (Rimskii-Korsakov); Brailovskii, "K voprosu," 26 (Istomin in 1682–1683); Bogdanov and Buganov, *Pamiatniki,* vol. 1, no. 14, p. 138 (Istomin in March 1687).

23. Zabelin, *Tsarits,* 152–92; Hughes, *Sophia,* 176.

24. For examples, see *DR,* vol. 4, cols. 373–478; also *SGGD,* vol. 4, no. 174, pp. 505–9; nos. 176–191, pp. 514–85; nos. 193–94, pp. 587–94; no. 196, p. 596; no. 198, p. 599; E. Lermontova, "Samoderzhavie Tsarevny Sof'i Alekseevny po neizdannym dokumentam (iz perepiski, vozbuzhdennoi grafom Paninym)," *Russkaia starina* 149 (1912), bk. 2, p.435; bk. 3, pp. 539, 541, 542, 544; Hughes, "Sophia, 'Autocrat,'" 271–74. For a discussion of Sofiia's appropriation of the title Autocrat, see Hughes, "Sophia, 'Autocrat,'" 271–72.

25. Hughes, "Moscow Rebellion," 535.

26. John Keep, ed. and trans., "Mutiny in Moscow, 1682: A Contemporary Account," *Canadian Slavonic Papers* 23, no. 4 (December 1981): 439–40, 422, 430–32; Hughes, *Sophia,* 66; Hughes, "Ambitious and Daring," 73; Hughes, "Moscow Rebellion," 535.

27. For a summary of the events of May 15–18, see Hughes, "Moscow Rebellion," 533–35.

28. Hughes, *Sophia,* 11, 176 (quote). For patronage of religious art and architecture, see ibid., 146–57; Zelensky, "Sophia . . . Religious Imagery," 198–203. For Istomin, see Brailovskii, "K literaturnoi deiatel'nosti," 53. For pilgrimages and processions, see *DR,* vol. 4, cols. 402, 431, 434, 436, 439, 453, 455, 457, 461–62, 466, 471–72, 474, 477; also Hughes, "Sophia, 'Autocrat,'" 274.

29. This throne was located to the left of the Royal Gate; see Lukian Iakovlev, ed. *Russkiia starinnyia znamena* in *Drevnosti rossiiskago gosudarstva. Dopolnenie k III otdeleniiu* (Moscow, 1865), II, sect. I, no. 3572, p. 5; also see *DRV* 11:163–65; F. Tumanskii, *Sobranie raznykh zapisok i sochinenii sluzhashchikh k dostavleniiu polnogo svedeniia o zhizni i deianiakh gosudaria imperatora Petra Velikogo* (St. Petersburg, 1787), 2:311–20.

30. See, for example, the banners sent to Ivan Samoilovich, hetman of the Zaporozhian regiment, on June 27, 1682; to V. V. Golitsyn on November 3, 1687; to V. V. Golitsyn and A. V. Golitsyn on January 4, 1687; to V. I. Shveikovskii on January 5, 1687; to *stol'nik* Tsykler and the Ivanov regiment on January 19, 1687; to M. A. Golitsyn on February 23, 1687; and to I. F. Volynskii on September 11, 1688; Iakovlev, *Russkiia starinnyia znamena,* I, pp. 97–98; "Prilozheniia," no. 7, pp. 14–20; "Prilozheniia," no. 36, pp. 75–76; I, p. 79; "Prilozheniia," no. 34, pp. 70–72; "Prilozheniia," no. 30, p. 59; II, sect. II, no. 12, p. 74.

31. Iakovlev, *Russkiia starinnyia znamena,* II, sect. I, no. 3612, p. 44; a copy of the banner is found in Lukian Iakovlev, ed., *Risunki k izdaniiu russkiia starinnyia znamena* (Moscow, 1865), no. VIII.

32. Hughes, *Sophia,* 226–29.

33. N. G. Ustrialov, *Istoriia tsarstvovaniia Petra Velikogo* (St. Petersburg,

1858–1863), vol. 1, "Prilozheniia," no. X, pp. 382–84; *DR,* vol. 4, cols. 433–40. A summary of the content of the letters is found in Hughes, *Sophia,* 227–28.

34. On this point, also see Hughes, "Sophia, 'Autocrat,'" 275.

35. Iakovlev, *Russkiia starinnyia znamena,* II, sect. I, no. 3572, p. 5.

36. See for example A. A. Matveev, "Zapiski Andreia Artamonovicha grafa Matveeva," in N. Sakharov, ed., *Zapiski russkikh liudei. Sobytiia vremen Petra Velikogo* (St. Petersburg, 1841), 52.

37. *Pis'ma i bumagi Imperatora Petra Velikogo,* vol. 1, no. 10, pp. 13–14.

38. Hughes, "Sophia, 'Autocrat,'" 286.

39. Prozorovskii, "Sil'vestra Medvedeva Sozertsanie," 76–80, 84. On the disputed identity of the tsarevny attending the meeting in the Palace of Facets, see Hughes, *Sophia,* 76.

40. Prozorovskii, "Sil'vestra Medvedeva Sozertsanie," 81.

41. Ibid., 83 (quote), 86–91 (Sofiia and dissenters). For Istomin, see Brailovskii, "K voprosu," 19, 29, 30.

42. For contemporary accounts, see V. S. Rumiantseva, *Narodnoe antitserkovnoe dvizhenie v Rossii v XVII veke* (Moscow, 1986), 24, 188, 197, 240; Georg Schleusing's account in L. P. Lapteva, trans., "Rasskaz ochevidtsa o zhizni Moskovii kontsa XVII veka," *Voprosy istorii* (1970): no. 1, pp. 117–18. For holiday, see *DR,* vol. 4, col. 358 (commemoration of 1685); also see cols. 391, 456 (commemorations of 1688 and 1689); Hughes, "Sophia, 'Autocrat,'" 274–75. See also Hughes, *Sophia,* 122–23 for details of the persecution of Old Believers during Sofiia's regency.

43. For characterization of Tatars, see *PSZ,* vol. 2, no. 1224, pp. 835–42; Hughes, *Sophia,* 197. For Sofiia's commitment, see *PSZ,* vol. 2, no. 1186, p. 777. For processions, see *DRV* 11:163–72; *DR,* vol. 4, cols. 461–66; Tumanskii, *Sobranie raznykh zapisok,* 2:311–20. Also see Hughes, "Sophia, 'Autocrat,'" 276–77.

44. *DR,* vol. 4, cols. 466–67 (service). On the second Crimean campaign, see Hughes, *Sophia,* 211–17. For Sofiia's religious policies, see *PSZ,* vol. 2, no. 1144, pp. 702–7 (charter of rights of the metropolitan of Kiev, December 15, 1685); no. 1191, pp. 795–97 (letter from the Muscovite rulers to the patriarch of Constantinople, Dionysius IV Mouselimes, May 1686); no. 1196, pp. 805–7 (letter by Greek hierarchs, June 1686); no. 1186, p. 777 (treaty of 1686 with Poland).

45. Bogdanov, "Politicheskaia graviura," 241. For other examples, see Bogdanov and Buganov, *Pamiatniki,* vol. 2, no. 32, p. 234; Alekseeva, "Portret tsarevny Sof'i," 242; Panchenko, *Russkaia sillabicheskaia poeziia,* 381, 201–2.

46. Huneycutt, "High-Medieval Queen," 129–34.

47. For Medvedev, see A. A. Prozorovskii, "Sil'vestr Medvedev (Ego zhizn' i deiatel'nost')," *ChOIDR* (1896): no. 2, sect. IV, p. 76. See also V. K. Bylinin and V. A. Grikhin, "Simeon Polotskii i Simon Ushakov. K probleme estetiki russkogo barokko," in *Barokko v slavianskikh kul'turakh,* ed. A. V. Lipatov (Moscow, 1982), 196, for Polotskii's interest in apocryphal literature. For first play, see Hughes, *Sophia,* 37.

48. Prozorovskii, "Sil'vestra Medvedeva Sozertsanie," 58 (Medvedev); Brailovskii, "K voprosu," 19 (Karion Istomin); Bogdanov and Buganov, *Pamiatniki,* vol. 1, no. 9, p. 107 (Titov); no. 15, pp. 150–51 (Rimskii-Korsakov), and vol. 2, no. 17, p. 183 (Likhudes); Kapterev, *Kharakter,* 370–71 (Dionysius).

49. Zelensky, "Sophia . . . Rhetorical Device," 2:238, 257–58.

50. For the apocryphal Book of Judith, see Edgar J. Goodspeed, trans., *The*

Apocrypha. An American Translation (New York, 1959), 133–64.

51. Prozorovskii, "Sil'vestra Medvedeva Sozertsanie," 58 (Medvedev); Brailovskii, "K voprosu," 19–20 (Istomin).

52. Bogdanov and Buganov, *Pamiatniki,* vol. 2, no. 9, p. 265. Bogdanov assumes that Titov and the illustrator worked closely together; ibid., pp. 265–66.

53. Rowland, "Moscow" (Jerusalem theme); Bogdanov and Buganov, *Pamiatniki,* vol. 1, no. 9, pp. 105–7 (quote, 107). Bogdanov points out that this phrase is highlighted in the text. Titov includes Sofiia Alekseevna in his initial address of the Russian rulers on fol. 3v; see Bogdanov and Buganov, *Pamiatniki,* vol. 1, no. 9, pp. 107n.d., 105.

54. On Deborah's position in the Old Testament, see Bogdanov and Buganov, *Pamiatniki,* vol. 2, no. 9, p. 266; for Titov's praise, see vol. 1, no. 9, p. 109.

55. Brailovskii, "K voprosu," 47 (Istomin). Patriarch cited from Kapterev, *Kharakter,* 270–71. For oration of Likhudes brothers, see Bogdanov and Buganov, *Pamiatniki,* vol. 2, no. 17, p. 183; also Zelensky, "Sophia . . . Rhetorical Device," 169–70.

56. Zelensky, "Sophia . . . Rhetorical Device," 1:iv; Hughes, *Sophia,* 140; A. P. Bogdanov, "Literaturnye panegiriki kak istochnik izucheniia sootnosheniia sil v pravitel'stve Rossii perioda regentstva Sof'i (1682–1689 gg.)," *Materialy XVII vsesoiuznoi nauchnoi studencheskoi konferentsii "Student i nauchno-tekhnicheskii progress,"* ed. Ministerstvo vysshego i srednego spetsial'nogo obrazovaniia RSFSR Novosibirskii gosudarstvennyi universitet im. Leninskogo Komsomola (Novosibirsk, 1979), 71–72 (also 73–79).

57. For examples of Sofiia's association with the martyr saint, see A. A. Pavlenko, "Karp Zolotarev i Moskovskie zhivopistsy poslednei treti XVII v.," *Pamiatniki kul'tury. Novye otkrytiia, 1982* (Leningrad, 1984), 314–15; Iakovlev, *Russkiia starinnyia znamena,* II, sect. I, no. 3612, p. 44; Bogdanov and Buganov, *Pamiatniki,* vol. 1, no. 14, p. 134; also see Hughes, *Sophia,* 24–25.

58. Polotskii, *Virshi,* 285; the book dates from 1670.

59. Polotskii, *Virshi,* 285. For Istomin, see Bogdanov and Buganov, *Pamiatniki,* vol. 1, no. 2, p. 77; S. Smirnov, *Istoriia Moskovskoi Slaviano-Greko-Latinskoi Akademii* (Moscow, 1855), Prilozheniia, no. 1, pp. 396–97. For Medvedev, see Prozorovskii, "Sil'vestr Medvedev," *ChOIDR* (1896): no. 4, sect. III, Prilozheniia, no. 2, p. 385; Panchenko, *Russkaia sillabicheskaia poeziia,* no. 187, pp. 193–94 (on the historical background of the struggle over the academy, 379–80n.187). The term *male courage* is specifically used by Karion Istomin; see Bogdanov, *Pamiatniki,* vol. 1, no. 2, p. 77; Smirnov, *Istoriia Moskovskoi Slaviano-Greko-Latinskoi Akademii,* 397.

60. For the application of the concept of liminality to Sofiia Alekseevna, see Zelensky, "Sophia . . . Religious Imagery," 192–97.

61. Smirnov, *Istoriia Moskovskoi Slaviano-Greko-Latinskoi Akademii,* 398–400.

62. Prozorovskii, "Sil'vestr Medvedev," *ChOIDR* (1896): no. 4, sect. III, Prilozheniia, no. 2, p. 386; also see Panchenko, *Russkaia sillabicheskaia poeziia,* no. 187, p. 194.

63. On the theological concept of Sophia in medieval Russia, see Donald M. Fiene, "What is the Appearance of the Divine Sophia?" *SR* 48, no. 3 (fall 1989): 449–76; Priscilla Hunt, "Ivan IV's Mythology of Kingship," *SR* 52, no. 4 (winter 1993): 778–88.

64. Polotskii, *Virshi,* 285 (quote); Hughes, "Sophia, 'Autocrat,'" 280. Medvedev's eulogy is reproduced in Bogdanov, "Sil'vestra Medvedeva panegirik," 48–51.

65. Bogdanov, "Sil'vestra Medvedeva panegirik," 48. See Prov. 9:1—"Wisdom hath builded her house, she hath hewn out her seven pillars." The "house of the sun" was used as a religious metaphor already in Lazar Baranovich's *Spiritual Sword;* see Chubinskaia, "Ikona," 305.

66. Bogdanov, "Sil'vestra Medvedeva panegirik," 49; "The Book of Judith," 11:1–13:10 in *The Apocrypha,* 153–57; also see Zelensky, "Sophia . . . Rhetorical Device," 2:277. In his dedication of the *Dialogi premudrosti voploshcheniia Syna Bozhiia (Dialogues about the Wisdom of the Incarnation of the Son of God),* a play in verse for twelve young men, Luk'ian Golosov declared that the eternal wisdom of God resided in Sofiia's royal soul "as in her chosen house." See I. A. Shliapkin, "Tsarevna Natal'ia Alekseevna i teatr eia vremeni," *Pamiatniki drevnei pis'mennosti* 128 (1898): 42. The dedication occurred on December 23, 1682. On the performance of Golosov's piece, see A. M. Panchenko, *Russkaia stikhotvornaia kul'tura XVII veka* (Leningrad, 1973), 211.

67. Bogdanov, "Sil'vestra Medvedeva panegirik," 50, 51.

68. Zelensky, "Sophia . . . Rhetorical Device," 2:281, 284; Prozorovskii, "Sil'vestr Medvedev," *ChOIDR* (1896): no. 4, sect. III, Prilozheniia, no. 2, pp. 384–85; Panchenko, *Russkaia sillabicheskaia poeziia,* no. 187, pp. 191–93; also see Zelensky, "Sophia . . . Rhetorical Device," 2:285–86.

69. Bodganov, "Sil'vestra Medvedeva panegirik," 49–50.

70. See for example Zelensky, "Sophia . . . Rhetorical Device," 2:280.

71. Ibid., 1:44–49.

72. Polotskii, *Virshi,* 33. For further examples, see the *Dialog Kratkii (Short Dialog),* a congratulatory ode to the newborn Tsarevna Mariia Alekseevna, and verses to Mariia Il'inichna composed by Polotskii in 1660; Panchenko, *Russkaia sillabicheskaia poeziia,* no. 14, p. 104; Polotskii, *Virshi,* 67–68, 41; N. I. Prashkovich, "Iz rannykh deklamatsii Simeona Polotskogo ('Metry' i 'Dialog kratkii')," *TODRL* 21 (1965): 38.

73. Bogdanov, "Sil'vestra Medvedeva panegirik," 50. See Ps. 45:9: "King's daughters were among thy honorable women: upon thy right hand did stand the queen in gold of Ophir." On Medvedev's elaboration of Polotskii's tsar-sun analogy, see A. P. Bogdanov, "Sil'vestr Medvedev," *Voprosy istorii* (1988): no. 2, p. 88. Also see Medvedev's Easter greeting to the regent from April 7, 1685; Panchenko, *Russkaia sillabicheskaia poeziia,* no. 189, p. 201. A. M. Panchenko, "Pridvornye virshi 80–kh godov XVII stoletiia," *TODRL* 21 (1965): 72–73. For the dating of the text and its attribution to Medvedev, see ibid., 65–67.

74. Bogdanov and Buganov, *Pamiatniki,* vol. 1, no. 14, p. 133.

75. See Matt. 25: 1–13. Cited from A. S. Eleonskaia, *Russkaia oratorskaia proza v literaturnom protsesse XVII veka* (Moscow, 1990), 138 (Eleonskaia's punctuation of the passage is incorrect). The manuscript (GIM, Synodal Collection no. 658) was written in stages between 1668 and 1676; ibid., 131–36.

76. Polotskii, *Virshi,* 272.

77. See, for example, Smirnova, *Moskovskaia ikona,* fig. 78; *GTG. Katalog,* vol. 2, no. 605, fig. 70 (inventory no. 12802).

78. Brailovskii, "K voprosu," 20, 35, 36 (Istomin); M. Semevskii, "Sovremennye portrety Sofii Alekseevny i V. V. Golitsyna," *Russkoe slovo* (1859): no. 12, 422 (Dionysius).

79. Brailovskii, "K voprosu," 47 (quotation), 50. For another example of Istomin's fertility theme, see the draft of a eulogy he composed for the regent in

March 1687; Bogdanov and Buganov, *Pamiatniki,* vol. 1, no. 14, p. 134; Zelensky, "Sophia . . . Rhetorical Device," 2:235.

80. The engraving is reproduced in M. A. Alekseeva, "Zhanr konkliuzii v russkom iskusstve kontsa XVII–nachala XVIII v.," in *Russkoe iskusstvo barokko. Materialy i issledovaniia,* ed. T. V. Alekseeva (Moscow, 1977), fig. 2. For a short description, see D. A. Rovinskii, ed., *Podrobnyi slovar' russkikh gravirovannykh portretov* (St. Petersburg, 1889), vol. 2, cols. 1520–21, no. 2; cols. 1657–58, no. 3. Baranovich's book represents a eulogy to the two young tsars Ivan and Peter. Discussions of the symbolism of the image and its relation to Baranovich's text are found in Bogdanov, "Politicheskaia graviura," 231–34; Hughes, "Sophia, 'Autocrat,'" 279–81; Zelensky, "Sophia . . . Rhetorical Device," 2:307–12.

81. About a hundred copies of the engraving were printed; many copies circulated separately from the book; Bogdanov, "Politicheskaia graviura," 234.

82. On the regalia worn by the first Romanov tsars, see M. V. Martynova, "K voprosu ob atributsii regalii tsaria Mikhaila Fedorovicha," *Pamiatniki kul'tury. Novye otkrytiia, 1981* (Leningrad, 1983), 392–403.

83. Bogdanov, who interprets the city as Kiev, sees in the engraving an attempt by the Ukrainian pro-Muscovite faction to counter Polish intentions to exploit the dynastic instability in Moscow and to push for unification with Russia while maintaining religious autonomy; Bogdanov, "Politicheskaia graviura," 234. Also see Zelensky, "Sophia . . . Rhetorical Device," 2:309–10; Hughes, *Sophia,* 140.

84. Although the engraving features Western stylistic influences, evident in the angels' classical armor and the perspective drawing in the lower register, its iconography reflects Russian Orthodox norms common in the seventeenth century. Compositional models can be found in Simon Ushakov's *The Tree of the Russian Realm* (see Smirnova, *Moskovskaia ikona,* fig. 199), the frontispiece of Baranovich's *Spiritual Sword* of 1666 (see Chubinskaia, "Ikona," 305), the frontispiece of *The Trumpets of Righteous Words* of 1674 (see Alekseeva, "Zhanr konkliuzii," fig. 1), and seventeenth-century Ukrainian depictions of Sophia in the shape of the woman of the Apocalypse (see Rovinskii, *Podrobnyi . . . portretov,* vol. 2, col. 1520, no. 2; cols. 1657–58, no. 3; Bogdanov, "Politicheskaia graviura," 232). The woman of the Apocalypse is referred to in Rev. 12:14.

85. Bogdanov, "Politicheskaia graviura," 233–34. The inscriptions on the composition are deciphered in Rovinskii, *Podrobnyi . . . portretov,* vol. 2, cols. 1520–21, no. 2. All but two of them are biblical.

86. On the idea of Moscow representing the Third Rome or a successor of Byzantium in the seventeenth century, see Daniel Clarke Waugh, "'Odolenie na Turskoe tsarstvo'—pamiatnik antituretskoi publitsistiki XVII v.," *TODRL* 33 (1979): 88–107, and Rowland, "Moscow," 594–95.

87. Eschatological imagery is also contained in bands of inscriptions in the lower parts of the image: "The kings of the earth set themselves, and the rulers take counsel together against the Lord, and against his anointed" (Ps. 2:2); "And the battle increased that day: howbeit the King of Israel stayed himself up in the chariot against the Syrians until the even" (2 Ch. 18:34); "So let all thine enemies perish, O Lord: but let them that love him be as the sun when he goeth forth in his might" (Judg. 5:31); "And Moses stretched forth his hand over the sea [and the Egyptians fled against it; and the Lord overthrew the Egyptians in the midst of the sea]" (Exod. 14:27); "A thousand shall fall at thy side, and ten thousand at thy right hand; but it shall not come nigh thee" (Ps. 91:7); "I have pursued mine ene-

mies, and destroyed them; and turned not again until I had consumed them" (2 Sa. 22:38); "Thou shalt tread upon the lion and adder: the young lion and the dragon shalt thou trample under feet" (Ps. 91:13).

88. Zelensky, "Sophia . . . Rhetorical Device," 2:310–11. Both Bogdanov and Hughes treat the wisdom figure as an iconographic rendition of Sofiia Alekseevna's adopted name saint; Hughes, *Sophia,* 140; Bogdanov, "Politicheskaia graviura," 232.

89. Bogdanov, "Politicheskaia graviura," 237.

90. Rovinskii noted the tsar figures in the medallions; see Rovinskii, *Podrobnyi . . . portretov,* vol. 2, col. 1520, no. 2; col. 1658, no. 3. Zelensky mistakes them for angels; "Sophia . . . Rhetorical Device," 2:309.

91. This contradicts Zelensky's view that the two monarchs stand between heaven and earth; see Zelensky, "Sophia . . . Rhetorical Device," 2:308.

92. Bogdanov, "Politicheskaia graviura," 233.

93. On the inclusion of Sofiia's name in royal rescripts, see Hughes, *Sophia,* 68–70.

94. Lermontova, "Samoderzhavie tsarevny Sof'i," bk. 2, pp. 441–44 (also see bk. 3, pp. 540–41 for Sofiia's reception of Polish ambassadors in 1686); Hughes, *Sophia,* 189–90, 193.

95. Hughes, "Sophia, 'Autocrat,'" 277. For Sofiia's prominent role in the Muscovite diplomatic protocol, see Hughes, *Sophia,* 189–196; Hughes, "Ambitious and Daring," 80–81.

96. Bogdanov, "Sil'vestr Medvedev," 89–90; Bogdanov, "Politicheskaia graviura," 237–38; Hughes, *Sophia,* 69–70; Hughes, "Sophia, 'Autocrat,'" 271–73.

97. For examples of inscriptions on banners, see Iakovlev, *Russkiia starinnyia znamena,* "Prilozheniia," no. 44, p. 95; II, sect. I, no. 3708, pp. 57–58. For the association of the title Autocrat with Sofiia on coins, see I. G. Spasskii and E. S. Shchukina, eds., *Medali i monety Petrovskogo vremeni* (Leningrad, 1974), no. 1 (fig. 1). See also V. I. Petrov, *Catalogue des monnaies russes de tous les princes, tsars et empereurs depuis 980 jusqu'à 1899* (Graz, 1964), no. 278, p. 8; for other examples, see no. 137, p. 8; no. 283, p. 9; no. 279, p. 8 (illustrations all on pl. 12). For a short description of the gold coins, which were meant to be worn from a chain around the neck, see Ovchinnikova, *Portret,* 102–3.

98. In the mid-seventeenth century, the tsarevny wore different crowns than the one found in Sofiia's coin portraits. Sofiia's crown resembles that of her mother, Mariia Il'inichna; see Meyerberg, *Al'bom Meierberga. Vidy i bytovyia kartiny Rossii XVII veka,* 40, fig. 78; 42, fig. 81. For male ruler portraits found in the so-called *Titularniki (Books of State),* see Ovchinnikova, *Portret,* 65–85.

99. On Sofiia's ambitions, see Hughes, "Ambitious and Daring," 70–88; Hughes, "Sophia, 'Autocrat,'" 267. On Western influences in the monarchical discourse in Russia, see Zelensky, "Sophia . . . Rhetorical Device," 1:186; 2:205–10, 284, 343.

100. On Sofiia's plans for coronation and her eagle portraits, see Bogdanov, "Politicheskaia graviura," 239–46; Hughes, "Sophia, 'Autocrat,'" 278–84; Hughes, *Sophia,* 142–44, 224; Zelensky, "Sophia . . . Rhetorical Device," 2:313–22; Ovchinnikova, *Portret,* 103–5; Rovinskii, *Podrobnyi . . . graverov,* vol. 2, cols. 986–87, no. 5; Rovinskii, *Podrobnyi . . . portretov,* vol. 2, cols. 1658–65, nos. 5–23; Alekseeva, "Portret tsarevny Sof'i," 240–49. On the personifications of the imperial virtues in the Sofiia portraits, see Bogdanov, "Politicheskaia graviura," 242; Alekseeva, "Portret tsarevny Sof'i," 242–48. For the association of the classical imperial values

with early medieval Western rulers, see Ernst Kantorowicz, *The King's Two Bodies: A Study in Mediaeval Political Theory* (Princeton, N.J., 1981), 113–14.

101. Arkheograficheskaia kommissiia, ed., *Rozysknye dela o Fedore Shaklovitom i ego soobshchikakh* (St. Petersburg, 1884–1893), vol. 1 (1884), cols. 165–67.

102. Kapterev, *Kharakter,* 375–77n.1.

103. *Rozysknye dela,* vol. 1, no. 52, cols. 655–56, 659–62.

104. Ibid., no. 50, cols. 595–96. Also see Bogdanov, "Politicheskaia graviura," 339–40; Zelensky, "Sophia . . . Rhetorical Device," 2:314–16; Alekseeva, "Zhanr konkliuzii," 14; Alekseeva, "Portret tsarevny Sof'i," 240–42.

105. *Rozysknye dela,* vol. 1, no. 25, cols. 546–47.

106. *Pis'ma preosviashchennago Lazaria Baranovicha* (Chernigov, 1865), no. 145, p. 227.

107. Bogdanov and Buganov, *Pamiatniki,* vol. 2, no. 32, pp. 234–38 (brief discussion, 309–10); Bogdanov, "Politicheskaia graviura," 233; Zelensky, "Sophia . . . Rhetorical Device," 2:293–96.

108. Panchenko, *Russkaia sillabicheskaia poeziia,* no. 190, pp. 202, 380. See also Zelensky, "Sophia . . . Rhetorical Device," 2:320.

109. For the inscriptions on the Bloteling and Afanas'ev portraits of the regent, see Alekseeva, "Portret tsarevny Sof'i," 242–43; also see Panchenko, *Russkaia sillabicheskaia poeziia,* 201–2.

110. Peter I, *Pis'ma i bumagi,* vol. 1, no. 10, pp. 13–14; also see Hughes, "Sophia, 'Autocrat,'" 284–85.

Conclusion

1. See, for example, Richard Pipes, *Russia under the Old Regime* (New York, 1974).

2. Kollmann, *By Honor Bound* and *Kinship;* Kivelson, *Autocracy;* Donald Ostrowski, *Muscovy and the Mongols: Cross-Cultural Influences on the Steppe Frontier, 1304–1589* (Cambridge, England,1998).

Selected Bibliography

Archival Material

Library of the Academy of Sciences, St. Petersburg (BAN)
Sobranie Petra Pervogo.
A 6: composition by Sil'vestr Medvedev.
A 37: *vita* and miracles of Nikita of Pereslavl'. *Poluustav.* Seventeenth-century watermarks. Cropped folio.

Russian National Library, St. Petersburg (RNB)
Pogodin Collection.
no. 647: *vita* of Kornilii Komel'skii.
Sophia Cathedral Collection.
no. 1491: miscellany, containing miracles of Metropolitan Iona. *Poluustav,* multiple hands. Watermarks from second part of sixteenth century. Quarto.
F. XVII. 16: miscellany, containing *vita* of Solomoniia Saburova. *Skoropis',* multiple hands. Watermarks from late seventeenth, early eighteenth century. Folio.
O. IV. 17: miscellany, containing Patriarch Iov's letter to Irina Godunova. *Skoropis',* multiple hands. Watermarks from seventeenth century? Octavo.
Q. I. 365: miscellany, containing *Skazanie o Kamennom monastyre. Poluustav,* multiple hands. Quarto.
Q. XVII. 142: *vita* of Khristofor Koriazhemskii.

Russian State Archive of Ancient Acts, Moscow (RGADA)
f. 27, no. 91: letters by Tsar Aleksei Mikhailovich to his family.
f. 135, otdel IV, rubrik 2, no. 5: materials concerning wedding of Ivan IV and

Anastasiia Romanovna; and otdel IV, rubrik 2, no. 21: wedding roster of planned wedding of Aleksei Mikhailovich and Evfimiia Vsevolozhskaia.
f. 181, no. 582: *Zlatoust. Poluustav,* sixteenth century? Folio; and no. 639: miscellany, containing Russian *vitae,* story of Elevation of the Cross. *Poluustav,* multiple hands. Folio.
f. 197, opis' 51, no. 62: *vita* and miracles of Solomoniia Saburova.
f. 381, no. 199: miscellany, containing *Izmaragd. Poluustav,* multiple hands. Watermarks from first half of seventeenth century. Folio.
f. 396, opis' 1, no. 3065: petition to Evdokiia Luk'ianovna.

Russian State Library, Moscow (RGB)
f. 37, Bolshakov Collection, no. 26: P. N. Krekshin—deeds of Peter the Great; and no. 422: *vita* of Antonii Siiskii.
f. 113, Volokolamsk Collection, no. 522: sermon of Metropolitan Makarii on Ivan IV's wedding to Anastasiia Romanovna.
f. 256, Sobranie Rumiantseva, no. 164: *vita* and miracles of Solomoniia Saburova; and no. 264: letters by Maksim Grek.
f. 304, I. Collection of the Trinity-Sergius Monastery, no. 200: letters by Maksim Grek; no. 562: *chet'i minei* of Tulup; no. 673: miscellany, containing *chet'i minei* of Tulup, including *vita* of Gennadii Vologodskii. Written in 1630 according to note on fol. 449v.
f. 310, Undol'skii Collection, no. 1153: *vita* of Genadii Kostromskii i Liubimogradskii.

State Historical Museum, Manuscript Division, Moscow (GIM)
Synodal Collection.
no. 658: Sermon on the Day of Gregory of Neokaisareia
Uvarov Collection.
no. 867: *Povest' o tsaritse Dinare*

Published Primary Sources

Adelung, Friedrich von, ed. *Baron Meierberg i puteshestvie ego po Rossii.* St. Petersburg, 1827.
Akty istoricheskie, sobrannye i izdannye Arkheograficheskoi kommissiei. 5 vols. St. Petersburg, 1841–1842.
Akty sobrannye v bibliotekakh i arkhivakh Rossiiskoi imperii Arkheograficheskoiiu ekspeditsieiu Akademii nauk. 4 vols. St. Petersburg, 1836.
Amfilokhii, archimandrit, ed. "Vypiska iz podrobnoi opisi imushchestvu Voskresenskago Novoierusalimskago monastyria, 1680 goda." *Izvestiia Imperatorskago arkheologicheskago obshchestva* 4 (1863): cols. 25–60.
Anpilogov, G. N., ed. *Novye dokumenty o Rossii kontsa XVI–nachala XVII v.* Moscow, 1967.
The Apocrypha: An American Translation. Trans. Edgar J. Goodspeed. New York, 1959.
Arkheograficheskaia kommissiia, ed. *Pis'ma russkikh gosudarei i drugikh osob tsarskago semeistva.* Vol. 1. Moscow, 1848.
_____. *Pis'ma russkikh gosudarei i drugikh osob tsarskago semeistva.* Vol. 5. Moscow, 1896.
_____. *Rozysknye dela o Fedore Shaklovitom i ego soobshchikakh.* 4 vols. St. Petersburg, 1884–1893.

Arsenios Elassonis. *Document relatif au patriarchat moscovite 1589.* Trans. Prince Augustin Galitzin. Paris, 1857.

Avvakum. "Zhitie Avvakuma." Ed. N. S. Demkova. In *Pamiatniki literatury drevnei Rusi. XVII vek.* Ed. L. A. Dmitriev and D. S. Likhachev. Vol. 2. Moscow, 1989. 351–97.

Azar'in, Simon. "Kniga o chudesakh pr. Sergiia." Ed. S. O. Platonov. In *Pamiatniki drevnei pis'mennosti i iskusstva.* Vol. 70. St. Petersburg, 1888.

Barten'ev, Petr, ed. *Sobranie pisem tsaria Alekseia Mikhailovicha.* Moscow, 1856.

Berry, Lloyd E., and R. O. Crummey, comps. *Rude and Barbarous Kingdom: Russia in the Accounts of Sixteenth-Century English Voyagers.* Madison, 1968.

Bogatyrev, S. N., ed. *Khoziaistvennye knigi Chudova monastyria 1585/86 g.* Moscow, 1996.

Bogdanov, A. P., and V. I. Buganov, eds. *Pamiatniki obshchestvenno-politicheskoi mysli v Rossii kontsa XVII veka. Literaturnye panegiriki.* 2 vols. Moscow, 1983.

Brailovskii, S. "K voprosu o literaturnoi deiatel'nosti russkikh pisatelei XVII stoletiia, nosivshikh imia 'Karion.'" *Izvestiia Otdeleniia russkago iazyka i slovesnosti Imperatorskoi Akademii nauk* 14 (1910): 12–58.

Buganov, V. I., ed. *Vosstanie v Moskve 1682 g. Sbornik dokumentov.* Moscow, 1976.

Buganov, V. I., and M. P. Lukichev, eds. *Posol'skaia kniga po sviaziam Rossii s Gretsiei (pravoslavnymi ierarkhami i monastyriami) 1588–1594 gg.* Moscow, 1988.

Bulanin, D. M., ed. *Perevody i poslaniia Maksima Greka.* Leningrad, 1984.

Bussow, Konrad. *Moskovskaia khronika, 1584–1613.* Ed. I. I. Smirnov. Moscow-Leningrad, 1961.

Cherepnin, L. V. *Dukhovnye i dogovornye gramoty velikikh i udel'nykh kniazei XIV–XVI vv.* Moscow, 1950.

Chteniia v Imperatorskom obshchestve istorii i drevnostei rossiiskikh pri Moskovskom universitete. 264 vols. Moscow, 1846–1918.

Collins, Samuel. *The Present State of Russia, in a Letter to a Friend at London.* London, 1671.

Dimitrijević, M., ed. "Dokumenti koji se tiču odnosa između srpske crkve i Rusije u XVI veku." *Spomenik.* Ed. Srpska Kraljevska Akademija. Vol. 39, drugi razred, br. 35 (1903): 16–42.

Dmitriev, L. A., and D. S. Likhachev, eds. *Pamiatniki literatury drevnei Rusi. Konets XV–pervaia polovina XVI veka.* Moscow, 1984.

_____. *Pamiatniki literatury drevnei Rusi. Vtoraia polovina XVI veka.* Moscow, 1986.

_____. *Pamiatniki literatury drevnei Rusi. XVII vek.* 3 vols. Moscow, 1988–1994.

Dnevnik Mariny Mnishek. Trans. V. N. Kozliakov. St. Petersburg, 1995.

Dopolneniia k Aktam istoricheskim, sobrannym i izdannym Arkheograficheskoi kommissiei. 12 vols. St. Petersburg, 1846–1872.

Dujčev, Ivan, ed. *The Miniatures of the Chronicle of Manasse.* Trans. Marguerite Alexieva. Sofia, 1963.

Dvortsovye razriady po vysochaishemu poveleniiu izdannye II otdeleniem sobstvennoi ego Imperatorskago velichestva kantseliarii. 4 vols. St. Petersburg, 1850–1855.

Eremin, I. P. "Deklamatsiia Simeona Polotskogo." *TODRL* 8 (1951): 352–61.

Estopañán, Sebastián Cirac, ed. *Skylitzes Matritensis. Tomo I. Reproducciones y miniaturas.* Barcelona-Madrid, 1965.

Eusebius Pamphilus. *The Life of the Blessed Emperor Constantine.* The Greek Ecclesiastical Historians, vol. 1. London, 1845.

Fedorov, Ananiia. "Istoricheskoe sobranie o grade Suzhdale." *Vremennik Imperatorskago Moskovskago obshchestva istorii i drevnostei rossiiskikh* 22 (1855): Materialy, 1–208.

Fletcher, Giles. *Of the Rus Commonwealth.* Ed. Albert J. Schmidt. Ithaca, N.Y., 1966.

Gibbenet, N. *Istoricheskoe izsledovanie dela Patriarkha Nikona.* 2 vols. St. Petersburg, 1882–1884.

Gnevushev, A. M., ed. "Smutnoe vremia Moskovskogo gosudarstva. Vyp. 2-i: Akty vremeni pravleniia tsaria Vasiliia Shuiskago (1606 g. 19 maia–17 iiulia 1610 g)." *ChOIDR* (1915): no. 2, sect. I.3, pp. I–XIX; 1–422.

Grekov, B. D., ed. *Akty sotsial'no-ekonomicheskoi istorii severo-vostochnoi Rusi kontsa XIV–nachala XVI v.* 3 vols. Moscow, 1952.

Halkin, François, ed. "Deux impératrices de Byzance." *Analecta Bollandiana* 106 (1988): 5–34.

Herberstein, Sigismund von. *Notes Upon Russia: Being a Translation of the Earliest Account of that Country, entitled Rerum Moscoviticarum Commentarii.* Ed. and trans. R. H. Major. 2 vols. 1851–1852. Reprint, New York, 1963.

Hollingsworth, Paul, trans. *The Hagiography of Kievan Rus'.* Harvard Library of Early Ukrainian Literature: English Translations, vol. 2. Cambridge, Mass., 1992.

Howes, Robert Craig, ed. and trans. *The Testaments of the Grand Princes of Moscow.* Ithaca, N. Y. 1967.

Iosif Volotskii, prepodobnyi. *Prosvetitel'.* Trans. into modern Russian by E. V. Kravets and L. P. Medvedeva. Moscow, 1993.

Keep, John, ed. and trans. "Mutiny in Moscow, 1682: A Contemporary Account." *Canadian Slavonic Papers* 23, no. 4 (December 1981): 410–42.

Klein, Vladimir, ed. "Uglichskoe sledstvennoe delo o smerti Tsarevicha Dimitriia 15–go maia 1591 goda." *Zapiski Imperatorskago Moskovskago arkheologicheskago instituta imeni Imperatora Nikolaia II* 25 (1913).

Klitina, E. N., T. N. Manushina, and T. V. Nikolaeva, eds. *Vkladnaia kniga Troitse-Sergieva monastyria.* Moscow, 1987.

Korb, Johann Georg. *Diary of an Austrian Secretary of Legation at the Court of Czar Peter the Great.* Ed. and trans. Count Mac Donnell. 2 vols. London, 1863.

Kotkov S. I., A. S. Oreshnikov, and I. S. Filippov. *Moskovskaia delovaia i bytovaia pis'mennost' XVII veka.* Moscow, 1968.

Kotoshikhin, Grigorii. *O Rossii v carstvovanie Alekseija Mixailoviča.* Ed. A. E. Pennington. Oxford, 1980.

Krekshin, Petr. "Kratkoe opisanie blazhennykh del Velikago Gosudaria, imperatora Petra velikago, samoderzhtsa vserossiiskago." In *Zapiski russkikh liudei. Sobytiia vremen Petra Velikogo.* Ed. N. Sakharov. St. Petersburg, 1841. 1–124.

Kurbskii, Andrei. "Istoriia o velikom kniaze Moskovskom." In *Pamiatniki literatury drevnei Rusi. Vtoraia polovina XVI veka.* Ed. L. A. Dmitriev and D. S. Likhachev. Moscow, 1986. 218–399, 605–17.

Kurdiumov, M., ed. "Zapiski o tseremoniakh, proiskhodivshikh pri dvore tsaria Alekseia Mikhailovicha po sluchaiu ob"iavleniia pokhoda protiv pol'skago korol'ia Iana-Kazimira." In *Sergeiu Fedorovichu Platonovu. Ucheniki, druzia, i pochitateli.* St. Petersburg, 1911.

Liubarskii, Ia. N., trans. *Prodolzhatel' Feofana. Zhizneopisaniia vizantiiskikh tsarei.* St. Petersburg, 1992.

Margeret, Jaques. *The Russian Empire and Grand Duchy of Muscovy: A 17th-Century French Account.* Ed. and trans. Chester S. L. Dunning. Pittsburgh, 1983.

Massa, Isaac. *A Short History of the Beginnings and Origins of These Present Wars in Moscow under the Reign of Various Sovereigns down to the Year 1610.* Trans. G. Edward Orchard. Toronto, 1982.

Materialy dlia istorii raskola za pervoe vremia ego sushchestvovaniia. 9 vols. Moscow, 1875–1895.

Matveev, A. A. "Zapiski Andreia Artamonovicha grafa Matveeva." In *Zapiski russkikh liudei. Sobytiia vremen Petra Velikogo.* Ed. N. Sakharov. St. Petersburg, 1841. 1–94.

Meyerberg, Augustin Baron de. *Al'bom Meierberga. Vidy i bytovyia kartiny Rossii XVII veka.* Ed. A. M. Loviagin. St. Petersburg, 1903.

____. *Al'bom Meierberga. Vidy i bytovyia kartiny Rossii XVII veka. Ob"iasnitel'nyia primechaniia k risunkam.* Ed. A. M. Loviagin. St. Petersburg, 1903.

____. *Relation d'un voyage en Moscovie.* Trans. Prince Augustin Galitzin. 2 vols. Bibliothèque russe et polonaise. Paris, 1858.

Michell, Robert, and Nevill Forbes, eds. and trans. *The Chronicle of Novgorod, 1016–1471.* Camden Third Series, vol. 25. London, 1914.

Migne, J. P., ed. *Patrologiae cursus completus, seu bibliotheca universalis, integra, uniformis, commoda, oeconomica, omnium SS. patrum, doctorum scriptorumque ecclesiasticorum sive latinorum, sive graecorum.* Series graeca. Paris, 1857–1886.

Mukhanov, P. A., ed. *Zapiski Getmana Zholkevskago o Moskovskoi voine.* 2d ed. St. Petersburg, 1871.

Nasonov, A. N., ed. *Pskovskie letopisi.* 2 vols. Moscow, 1941–1955.

Novikov, N. I., ed. *Drevniaia rossiiskaia vivliofika.* 2d ed. 20 vols. Slavistic Printings and Reprintings 250. 1788–1791. The Hague, 1970.

Novombergskii, N., ed. *Slovo i delo gosudarevy. Protsessy do izdaniia Ulozheniia Alekseia Mikhailovicha 1649 goda.* Vol. 1. Moscow, 1911.

Olearius. *The Travels of Olearius in Seventeenth-Century Russia.* Ed. and trans. Samuel H. Baron. Stanford, 1967.

Panchenko, A. M., ed. *Russkaia sillabicheskaia poeziia XVII–XVIII v.v. Biblioteka poeta,* 2d ed. Leningrad, 1970.

Papadeas, Fr. George L., ed. *The Divine Liturgy of Saint John the Chrysostom.* Daytona Beach, 1988.

Parry, William. "A New and Large Discourse on the Travels of Sir Anthony Sherley, Knight, by Sea, and over Land, to the Persian Empire." In *Sir Anthony Shirley and His Persian Adventure.* Ed. Sir E. Denison Ross. London, 1933. 98–136.

Paul of Aleppo. *The Travels of Macarius, Patriarch of Antioch, written by his Attendant Archdeacon, Paul of Aleppo, in Arabic.* Trans. F. C. Belfour. 2 vols. London, 1836.

Pavlov, A. S., ed. *Pamiatniki drevne-russkago kanonicheskago prava, vol. 1: Pamiatniki XI–XV v.* In *RIB.* Vol. 6. St. Petersburg-Leningrad, 1880.

Peter I. *Pis'ma i bumagi Imperatora Petra Velikogo.* 12 vols. St. Petersburg, 1887–1919.

Petrejus, Peter. "Istoriia o Velikom Kniazhestve Moskovskom, proiskhozhdenii Velikikh Russkikh Kniazei, nedavnikh smutakh, proizvedennykh tam tremia Lzhedimitriiami, i o Moskovskikh zakonakh, nravakh, pravlenii, vere i obriadakh, kotoruiu sobral, opisal i obnorodoval Petr Petrei de Erlezunda v Leiptsige 1620 goda." Trans. A. N. Shemiakin. *ChOIDR* (1865): no. 4, sect. IV, pp. 1–88; (1866): no. 1, sect. IV, pp. 89–184; (1866): no. 2, sect. IV, pp. 185–280; (1866): no. 3, sect. IV, pp. 281–342; (1867): no. 2, sect. IV, pp. 343–578.

Pis'ma preosviashchennago Lazaria Baranovicha. 2d ed. Chernigov, 1865.

"Pis'mo tsaritsy Evdokii Luk'ianovny k ee sestre Fedos'e Luk'ianovne Streshnevoi." *Vremennik Moskovskogo obshchestva istorii i drevnostei rossiiskikh* 1 (1849): sect. III, p. 15.

Platonov, S. F., ed. "Novyi istochnik dlia istorii Moskovskikh volnenii 1648 goda." *ChOIDR* (1893): no. 1, sect. III, pp. 3–19.

Platonov, S. F., and V. V. Maikov, eds. "Fedora Griboedova Istoriia o tsariakh i velikikh kniaziakh zemli russkoi." In *Pamiatniki drevnei pismennosti i iskusstva* 121 (1896): I–XVI, 1–69.

Polnoe sobranie russkikh letopisei. 41 vols. to date. St. Petersburg-Moscow, 1846–1995.

Polnoe sobranie zakonov Rossiiskoi imperii. Sobranie pervoe. 45 vols. St. Petersburg, 1830.

Polotskii, Simeon. *Izbrannye sochineniia.* Ed. I. P. Eremin. Moscow, 1953.

____. *Virshi.* Ed. V. K. Bylinin and L. U. Zvonareva. Minsk, 1990.

Ponyrko, N. V., ed. *Voinskie povesti drevnei Rusi.* Leningrad, 1985.

Povsiadnevnykh dvortsovykh vremeni gosudarei tsarei velikikh kniazei Mikhaila Feodorovicha, Alekseia Mikhailovicha zapisok. 2 vols. Moscow, 1769.

Prozorovskii, A. A., ed. "Sil'vestra Medvedeva Sozertsanie let kratkoe 7190, 91, i 92, v nikh zhe chto sodeiasia vo grazhdanstve." *ChOIDR* 1894. No. 4. Section II. Pp. I–LII, 1–197.

Putilov, B. N., and B. M. Dobrovol'skii, comps. *Istoricheskie pesni XIII–XVI vekov.* Moscow-Leningrad, 1960.

"Radzivilovskaia ili Kenigsbergskaia letopis'. I. Fotomekhanicheskoe vosproizvedenie rukopisi." *Pamiatniki Obshchestva liubitelei drevnei pis'mennosti i iskusstva* 118 (1902).

Regel, W., ed. *Analecta Byzantino-Russica.* 1891–1898. Reprint, New York, 1963.

Reutenfels, Jacob. "Skazaniia svetleishemu gertsogu Toskanskomu Koz'me Tret'emu o Moskovii (Padua, 1680 g.)." Trans. A. I. Stankevich. *ChOIDR* (1905): no. 3, sect. II, pp. 1–128; (1906): no. 3, sect. III, pp. 129–228.

Romanos Melodus. *Kontakia of Romanos, Byzantine Melodist.* Trans. Marjorie Carpenter. 2 vols. Columbia, Mo., 1970–1973.

Romanov, S. "Istoriia o vere i chelobitnaia o strel'tsakh Savvy Romanova." *Letopisi russkoi literatury i drevnosti* 5 (1863): sect. II, 111–48.

Russkaia istoricheskaia biblioteka. 39 vols. St. Petersburg-Leningrad, 1872–1927.

Rybakov, B. A., ed. *Vkladnaia kniga Troitse-Sergieva monastyria.* Moscow, 1987.

Sakharov, N., ed. *Zapiski russkikh liudei. Sobytiia vremen Petra Velikogo.* St. Petersburg, 1841.

Schleussing, Georg. "Rasskaz ochevidtsa o zhizni Moskovii kontsa XVII veka." Trans. L. P. Lapteva. *Voprosy istorii* (1970) no. 1, pp. 103–26.

Sluzhba i akafist prepodobnomu ottsu nashemu Gennadiiu, Kostromskomu i Liubimogradskomu chudotvortsu: S prisovokupleniem skazaniia o zhitii ego i chudesakh. Moscow, 1888.

Sluzhba i zhitiia Sergiia i Nikona. Moscow: Moskovskii pechatnyi dvor, 27.XI.1646.

Sobranie gosudarstvennykh gramot i dogovorov khraniashchikhsia v Gosudarstvennoi kollegii inostrannykh del. 5 vols. Moscow, 1813–1894.

Struys, John. *The Voiages and Travels of John Struys through Italy, Greece, Muscovy, Tartary, Media, Persia, East-India, Japan, and other Countries in Europe, Africa and Asia.* Trans. John Morrison. London, 1684.

Subbotin, N., ed. *Tsarskiia voprosy i sobornyia otvety v mnogo-razlichnykh tserkovnykh chinekh (Stoglav).* Moscow, 1890.

Sumarokov, A. P. *Polnoe sobranie vsekh sochinenii v stikhakh i proze.* Ed. N. Novikov. 10 vols. Moscow, 1787.

Theophanes the Confessor. *The Chronicle of Theophanes.* Trans. Harry Turtledove. Philadelphia, 1982.

Zabelin, I. E., ed. "Opisanie Novgorodskoi sviatyni v 1634 godu." *ChOIDR* 1862, no. 4, sect. V, pp. 50–56.

SECONDARY SOURCES

Ageev, P. *Kratkii ukazatel' dostoprimechatel'nostei Bolshogo Kremlevskogo Dvortsa.* Moscow, 1865.

Alef, Gustave. "Aristocratic Politics and Royal Policy in Muscovy in the Late Fifteenth and Early Sixteenth Centuries." *Forschungen zur osteuropäischen Geschichte* 27 (1980).

Alekseeva, M. A. "Portret tsarevny Sof'i gravera Tarasevicha." In *Pamiatniki kul'tury. Novye otkrytiia, 1975.* Moscow, 1976. 240–49.

____. "Zhanr konkliuzii v russkom iskusstve kontsa XVII–nachala XVIII v." In *Russkoe iskusstvo barokko. Materialy i issledovaniia.* Ed. T. V. Alekseeva. Moscow, 1977. 7–29.

Alekseeva, T. V., ed. *Ot Srednevekov'ia k Novomu vremeni. Materialy i issledovaniia po russkomu iskusstvu XVIII–pervoi poloviny XIX veka.* Moscow, 1984.

____. *Russkoe iskusstvo barokko. Materialy i issledovaniia.* Moscow, 1977.

Allen, W. E. D. "The Georgian Marriage Projects of Boris Godunov." *OSP* 12 (1965): 69–79.

Anan'eva, T. A. *Simon Ushakov. Masters of World Painting.* Leningrad, 1971.

Antonova, V. I. *Drevnerusskoe iskusstvo v sobranii Pavla Korina.* Moscow, 1966.

Antonova, V. I., and N. E. Mneva. *Gosudarstvennaia Tret'iakovskaia Gallereia. Katalog drevnerusskoi zhivopisi XI–nachala XVIII vv.* 2 vols. Moscow, 1963.

Arinin, Vladimir. "Legendy i byli devich'ei obiteli." *Pamiatniki otechestva* 30, nos. 3–4 (1993): 166–71.

Arrignon, Jean Pierre. "Mezhdunarodnye otnosheniia Kievskoi Rusi v seredine X v. i kreshchenie kniagini Ol'gi." *Vizantiiskii vremennik,* n.s., 41 (1980): 113–24.

Art et société à Byzance sous les Paléologues. Actes du colloque organisé par l' Association Internationale des Études byzantines à Venise en septembre 1968. Bibliothèque de l'Institut Hellénique d'Etudes byzantines et post-byzantines de Venise, no. 4. Venice, 1971.

Atkinson, Dorothy. "Society and the Sexes in the Russian Past." In *Women in Russia.* Ed. Dorothy Atkinson, Alexander Dallin, and Gail Lapidus. Stanford, 1977. 3–38.

Bakhrushin, S. V. "Politicheskie tolki v tsarstvovanie Mikhaila Fedorovicha." In *Trudy po istochnikovedeniiu, istoriografii i istorii Rossii epokhi feodalizma (nauchnoe nasledie).* Ed. B. V. Levshin. Moscow, 1987. 87–118.

Baron, Samuel H., and Nancy Shields Kollmann, eds. *Religion and Culture in Early Modern Russia and Ukraine.* DeKalb, Ill., 1997.

Barsukov, N. P. *Istochniki russkoi agiografii. Izdaniia.* Ed. Obshchestvo liubitelei drevnei pis'mennosti, 81. St. Petersburg, 1882.

Barten'ev, S. P. *Bolshoi Kremlevskii Dvorets. Dvortsovyia tserkvi i pridvornye sobory.* Moscow, 1916.

____. *Moskovskii Kreml' v starinu i teper'.* 3rd ed. 2 vols. Moscow, 1912–1916.

Bassein, Beth Ann. *Women and Death: Linkages in Western Thought and Literature.* Westport, 1984.

Batalov, A. L. "Molenie o chadorodii i obetnoe stroitel'stvo tsaria Fedora Ivanovicha." In *Zakazchik v istorii russkoi arkhitektury.* Ed. G. I. Revzin and V. V. Sedov. *Arkhiv arkhitektury,* vol. 5, no. 1. Moscow, 1994. 117–40.

Batalov, A. L., and A. M. Lidov, eds. *Ierusalim v russkoi kul'ture.* Moscow, 1994.

Begunov, Iu. K. "Povest' o vtorom brake Vasiliia III." *TODRL* 25 (1970): 105–18.

Bekeneva, N. G. *Simon Ushakov, 1626–1686.* Leningrad, 1984.

Bloch, Marc. *The Royal Touch. Monarchy and Miracles in France and England.* Trans. J. E. Anderson. New York, 1961.

Bogdanov, A. P. "Literaturnye panegiriki kak istochnik izucheniia sootnosheniia sil v pravitel'stve Rossii perioda regentstva Sof'i (1682–1689 gg.)." *Materialy XVII vsesoiuznoi nauchnoi studencheskoi konferentsii "Student i nauchno-tekhnicheskii progress."* Ed. Ministerstvo vysshego i srednego spetsial'nogo obrazovaniia RSFSR Novosibirskii gosudarstvennyi universitet im. Leninskogo Komsomola, Novosibirsk, 1979. 71–79.

____. "Politicheskaia graviura v Rossii perioda regentstva Sof'i Alekseevny." In *Istochnikovedenie otechestvennoi istorii. Sbornik statei. 1981.* Ed. V. I. Buganov. Moscow, 1982. 225–46.

____. "Sil'vestr Medvedev." *Voprosy istorii* (1988): no. 2, pp. 84–98.

____. "Sil'vestra Medvedeva panegirik tsarevne Sof'e 1682 g." In *Pamiatniki kul'tury. Novye otkrytiia, 1982.* Leningrad, 1984. 45–52.

Boiare Romanovy i votsarenie Mikhaila Fedorovicha. Izdanie Komiteta dlia ustroistva prazdnovaniia trekhsotletiia tsarstvovaniia Doma Romanovykh. St. Petersburg, 1913.

Borin, B. "Pamiatnik zolotogo shit'ia: Pelena XVI v. tsaritsy Marii Feodorovny (1580–1588 gg.) Nagikh." *Svetil'nik,* nos. 9–12 (1915): 70–73.

Boškovska, Nada. *Die russische Frau im 17. Jahrhundert.* Cologne, 1998.

Briusova, V. G. *Russkaia zhivopis' 17 veka.* Moscow, 1984.

Brown, Peter. *The Body and Society: Men, Women and Sexual Renunciation in Early Christianity.* New York, 1988.

Budovnits, I. U. *Slovar' russkoi, ukrainskoi, belorusskoi pis'mennosti i literatury do XVIII veka.* Moscow, 1962.

Buseva-Davydova, I. L. "Ob ideinom mysle 'Novogo Ierusalima' patriarkha Nikona." In *Ierusalim v russkoi kul'ture.* Ed. A. L. Batalov and A. M. Lidov. Moscow, 1994. 174–81.

Bushkovitch, Paul A. "The Epiphany Ceremony of the Russian Court in the Sixteenth and Seventeenth Centuries." *RR* 49, no. 1 (January 1990): 1–17.

____. *Religion and Society in Russia. The Sixteenth and Seventeenth Centuries.* New York, 1992.

Bylinin, V. K., and V. A. Grikhin. "Simeon Polotskii i Simon Ushakov. K probleme estetiki russkogo barokko." In *Barokko v slavianskikh kul'turakh.* Ed. A. V. Lipatov. Moscow, 1982. 191–219.

Bynum, Caroline. *Fragmentation and Redemption: Essays on Gender and the Human Body in Medieval Religion.* New York, 1991.

____. *Holy Feast and Holy Fast: The Religious Significance of Food for Medieval Women.* Berkeley, 1987.

Cameron, Averil. "The Empress Sophia." *Byzantion* 45, no. 1 (1975): 5–21.

Chaney, William A. *The Cult of Kingship in Anglo-Saxon England.* Berkeley, 1970.

Cherepnin, L. V. *Russkie feodal'nye arkhivy XIV–XV vekov.* 2 vols. Moscow, 1948–1951.

Chernetsov, A. V. "K izucheniiu Radzivilovskoi letopisi." *TODRL* 36 (1981): 274–88.

Cherniavsky, Michael. *Tsar and People: Studies in Russian Myths.* 2d ed. New York, 1969.

Chubinskaia, V. G. "Ikona Simona Ushakova 'Bogomater' Vladimirskaia,' 'Drevo Moskovskogo gosudarstva,' 'Pokhvala Bogomateri Vladimirskoi' (opyt istoriko-kul'turnoi interpretatsii)." *TODRL* 38 (1985): 290–308.

Claus, Claire. *Die Stellung der russischen Frau von der Einführung des Christentums bei den Russen bis zu den Reformen Peter des Großen.* Munich, 1959.

Clements, Barbara Evans, Barbara Alpern Engel, and Christine D. Worobec, eds. *Russia's Women: Accommodation, Resistance, Transformation.* Berkeley, 1991.

Corbet, Patrick. *Les saints ottoniens: Sainteté dynastique, sainteté royale et sainteté féminine autour de l'an mil.* Sigmaringen, 1986.

Cracraft, James. *The Petrine Revolution in Russian Imagery.* Chicago, 1997.

Crummey, Robert O. *Aristocrats and Servitors: The Boyar Elite in Russia, 1613–1689.* Princeton, 1983.

____. "Court Spectacles in Seventeenth-Century Russia: Illusion and Reality." In *Essays in Honor of A. A. Zimin.* Ed. Daniel Clarke Waugh. Columbus, Ohio, 1985. 130–58.

____. *The Formation of Muscovy, 1304–1613.* London, 1987.

Danilova, I. E., and N. E. Mneva. "Zhivopis' XVII veka." In I. E. Grabar', V. S. Kemenov, and V. N. Lazarev, eds. *Istoriia russkogo iskusstva.* 13 vols. Moscow, 1953–1969. 4:345–466.

Diehl, Ch. "La légende de l'empereur Theophile." *Seminarium Kondakovianum* 4 (1931): 33–37.

Dmitriev, Iu. N. "Stenopis' Arkhangel'skogo sobora Moskovskogo Kremlia (Materialy k issledovaniiu)." *Drevnerusskoe iskusstvo. XVII vek.* Ed. V. N. Lazarev, O. N. Podobedova, and V. V. Kostochkin. Moscow, 1964. 138–59.

Dmitrieva, R. P., and O. A. Belobrova. "Petr i Fevroniia muromskie v literature i iskusstve drevnei Rusi." *TODRL* 38 (1985): 138–78.

Dmitrievskii, A. *Arkhiepiskop Elassonskii Arsenii i memuary ego iz russkoi istorii po rukopisi trapezuntskago sumeliiskago monastyria.* Kiev, 1899.

Dobriakov, A. V. *Russkaia zhenshchina v do-mongol'skii period.* St. Petersburg, 1864.

Doty, William G. *Mythography: The Study of Myths and Rituals.* University, Ala., 1986.

Drijvers, Jan Willem. *Helena Augusta: The Mother of Constantine the Great and the Legend of the Finding of the True Cross.* Leiden, 1992.

Ebbinghaus, Andreas. *Die altrussischen Marienikonen-Legenden.* Veröffentlichungen der Abteilung für Slavische Sprachen und Literaturen des Osteuropa-Instituts [Slavisches Seminar] an der Freien Universität Berlin, vol. 70. Wiesbaden, 1990.

Eck, Alexandre. "La situation juridique de la femme russe au moyen âge." *Recueils de la Société Jean Bodin pour l'histoire comparative des institutions* 12 (1962): 405–20.

Eleonskaia, A. S. *Russkaia oratorskaia proza v literaturnom protsesse XVII veka.* Moscow, 1990.

Elnett, Elaine. *Historic Origin and Social Development of Family Life in Russia.* New York, 1926.

Erler, Mary, and Marianne Kowalevski, eds. *Women and Power in the Middle Ages.* Athens, Ga., 1988.

Evangulova, O. S. *Izobrazitel'noe iskusstvo v Rossii pervoi chetverti XVIII v.* Moscow, 1987.

Fabritsius, M. P. *Kreml' v Moskve. Ocherki i kartiny proshlago i nastoiashchago.* Moscow, 1883.

Facinger, Marion. "A Study of Medieval Queenship: Capetian France, 987–1237." *Studies in Medieval and Renaissance History* 5 (1968): 3–48.

Featherstone, J. "Ol'ga's Visit to Constantinople." *Adelphotes: A Tribute to Omeljan Pritsak by His Students.* Ed. F. E. Sysyn. In *HUS* 14, nos. 3–4 (1990): 293–312.

Fedotov, G. P. *The Russian Religious Mind.* 2 vols. Cambridge, Mass., 1946–1966.

Felicetti-Liebenfels, Walter. *Geschichte der russischen Ikonenmalerei.* Graz, 1972.

Fennell, J. L. I. *The Emergence of Moscow, 1304–1359.* Berkeley, 1968.

_____. *A History of the Russian Church to 1448.* London, 1995.

Fiene, Donald M. "What is the Appearance of the Divine Sophia?" *SR* 48, no. 3 (Fall 1989): 449–76.

Filaret, arkhiepiskop. *Russkie sviatye, chtimye vseiu tserkoviu ili mestno. Opyt opisaniia zhizni ikh.* 3rd ed. St. Petersburg, 1882.

Filatov, V. V. "Ikona s izobrazheniem siuzhetov iz istorii Russkogo gosudarstva." *TODRL* 22 (1966): 277–93.

Filimonov, G. "Simon Ushakov i sovremennaia emu epokha Russkoi ikonopisi." In *Sbornik na 1873 god.* Ed. Obshchestvo drevne-russkago iskusstva pri Moskovskom publichnom Muzee. Moscow, 1873. Sect. I. "Izsledovaniia." 3–104.

Fine, John V. A., Jr. "The Muscovite Dynastic Crisis of 1497–1502." *Canadian Slavonic Papers* 8 (1966): 198–215.

Flier, Michael S. "Breaking the Code: The Image of the Tsar in the Muscovite Palm Sunday Ritual." In *Medieval Russian Culture.* Vol. 2. Ed. Michael S. Flier and Daniel Rowland. California Slavic Studies 19. Berkeley, 1994. 213–42.

_____. "The Iconography of Royal Procession: Ivan the Terrible and the Muscovite Palm Sunday Ritual." In *European Monarchy: Its Evolution and Practice from Roman Antiquity to Modern Times.* Ed. Heinz Duchhardt, Richard A. Jackson and David Sturdy. Stuttgart, 1992. 109–25.

_____. "The Iconology of Royal Ritual in Sixteenth-Century Muscovy." In *Byzantine Studies: Essays on the Slavic World and the Eleventh Century.* Ed. Speros Vryonis, Jr. New Rochelle, 1992. 53–76.

Fonkich, B. L. "Ierusalimskii patriarkh Feofan i Rossiia." In *Ierusalim v russkoi kul'ture.* Ed. A. L. Batalov and A. M. Lidov. Moscow, 1994. 212–18.

Fradenburg, Louise Olga, ed. *Women and Sovereignty.* Cosmos: The Yearbook of the Traditional Cosmology Society, vol. 7. Edinburgh, 1992.

Frolov, A. *La relique de la Vraie Croix: Recherches sur le développement d'un culte.* Archives de l'Orient chrétien, no 7. Paris, 1961.

Gaidarova, E. M., ed. *Znamenitye Rossianki.* Moscow, 1991.

Gal'kovskii, N. *Bor'ba khristianstva s ostatkami iazychestva v drevnei Rusi.* 2 vols. Kharkov, 1913–1916.

Gallas, Klaus, Klaus Wessel, and Manolis Borboudakis. *Byzantinisches Kreta.* Munich, 1983.

Geertz, Clifford. "Centers, Kings, and Charisma: Reflections on the Symbolics of Power." In *The Rites of Power.* Ed. Sean Willenz. Philadelphia, 1985. 13–38.

Georgievskii, V. *Pamiatniki starinnogo russkogo iskusstva Suzdal'skogo Muzeia.* Moscow, 1927.

Goehrke, Carsten. "Die Witwe im alten Rußland." *Forschungen zur osteuropäischen Geschichte* 38 (1986): 64–96.

Golubinskii, E. *Istoriia kanonizatsii sviatykh v russkoi tserkvi.* 2d ed. Moscow, 1903.

Gordeev, N. V. *Bolshoi Kremlevskii Dvorets.* Moscow, 1957.

Gosudarstvennyi istoriko-kul'turnyi muzei-zapovednik "Moskovskii Kreml'," ed. *Moskovskii Kreml'. Patriarshie palaty.* N.P., 1994.

Gove, Antonina Filonov. *The Slavic Akathistos Hymn. Poetic Elements of the Byzantine Text and Its Old Church Slavonic Translation.* Munich, 1988.

Grabar, André. *L'empereur dans l'art byzantin. Recherches sur l'art de l'empire d'Orient.* Paris, 1936.

____. *Iconoclasme byzantin. Dossier archéologique.* Paris, 1957.

Grabar', I. E. *Istoriia russkago iskusstva.* 6 vols. Moscow, 1909–1913.

Grabar', I. E., V. S. Kemenov, and V. N. Lazarev, eds. *Istoriia russkogo iskusstva.* 13 vols. Moscow, 1953–1969.

Grebel'skii, P. Kh., and A. B. Mirvis. *Dom Romanovykh. Biograficheskie svedeniia o chlenakh tsarstvovavshego doma, ikh predkakh i rodstvennikakh.* 2d ed. St. Petersburg, 1992.

Grebeniuk, V. P. "'Rifmologion' Simeona Polotskogo (istoriia sozdaniia, struktura, idei." In *Simeon Polotskii i ego knigoizdatel'skaia deiatel'nost'.* Ed. A. N. Robinson. Moscow, 1982. 259–308.

Grierson, Roderick, ed. *Gates of Mystery: The Art of Holy Russia.* Forth Worth, 1992.

Grossman, Joan Delaney. "Feminine Images in Old Russian Literature and Art." *California Slavic Studies* 11 (1980): 33–70.

Habermas, Jürgen. *The Structural Transformation of the Public Sphere: An Inquiry into a Category of Bourgeois Society.* Trans. Thomas Burger. Cambridge, Mass., 1989.

Hackett, Jo Ann. "In the Days of Jael: Reclaiming the History of Women in Ancient Israel." In *Immaculate and Powerful: The Female in Sacred Image and Social Reality.* Ed. Clarissa W. Atkinson, Constance H. Buchanan, and Margaret R. Miles. Wellingborough, G.B., 1987. 15–38.

Havice, Christine. "The Hamilton Psalter in Berlin, Kupferstichkabinett 78.A.9." Ph.D. diss., Pennsylvania State University, 1978.

Herrin, Judith. *The Formation of Christendom.* Princeton, 1987.

Hippisley, Anthony. *The Poetic Style of Simeon Polotsky.* Birmingham Slavonic Monographs, no. 16. Birmingham, 1985.

Holum, Kenneth G. *Theodosian Empresses: Women and Imperial Dominion in Late Antiquity.* Berkeley, 1982.

Hughes, Lindsey. "The 17th-Century 'Renaissance' in Russia: Western Influences in Art and Architecture." *History Today* (February 1980): 41–45.

____. "'Ambitious and Daring above her Sex': Tsarevna Sophia Alekseevna (1657–1704) in Foreigners' Accounts." *OSP* 21 (1988): 64–88.

____. "Portraits of Tsarevna Sof'ia Alekseevna, 1657–1704." *Study Group on 18th-century Russia. Newsletter* 14 (1988): 3–4.

____. "Sofiya Alekseyevna and the Moscow Rebellion of 1682." *SEER* 63, no. 4 (1985): 518–39.

____. "Sophia, 'Autocrat of All the Russias': Titles, Ritual and Eulogy in the Regency of Sophia Alekseevna (1682–89)." *Canadian Slavonic Papers* 28, no. 3 (1986): 266–86.

____. *Sophia, Regent of Russia 1657–1704.* New Haven, 1990.

Huneycutt, Lois L. "Intercession and the High-Medieval Queen: The Esther Topos." In *Power of the Weak: Studies on Medieval Women.* Ed. Jennifer Carpenter and Sally-Beth MacLean. Urbana, Ill., 1995. 126–46.

Hunt, Priscilla. "Ivan IV's Mythology of Kingship." *SR* 52, no. 4 (Winter 1993): 774–809.

Iakovlev, Lukian, ed. *Risunki k izdaniiu russkiia starinnyia znamena.* Moscow, 1865.

____, ed. *Russkiia starinnyia znamena.* In *Drevnosti rossiiskago gosudarstva. Dopolnenie k III otdeleniiu.* Moscow, 1865.

Iaroslavskiia eparkhial'nyia vedomosti. Neofitsial'naia chast', 1873.

Ikonnikova, A. "Tsaritsy i tsarevny iz doma Romanovykh." *Russkii arkhiv* (1913): 156–73, 345–71, 489–503.

Il'in, M. A. *Podmoskov'e.* Moscow, 1974.

____. *Zagorsk. Trinity-Sergius Monastery.* Trans. Natasha Johnstone. Moscow, 1967.

Ingham, Norman W. "The Groza of Ivan Groznyi in Russian Folklore." *RH* 14, nos. 1–4 (1987): 225–45.

Iosif, arkhimandrit. *Podrobnoe oglavlenie Velikikh Chetiikh Minei vserossiiskogo mitropolita Makariia khraniashchikhsia v Moskovskoi Patriarshei (nyne Sinodal'noi) biblioteke.* 2 vols. Moscow, 1892.

Ismaragda, igumeniia. "Uglichskii Bogoiavlenskii zhenskii monastyr'." *Iaroslavskiia eparkhial'nyia vedomosti.* No. 10, March 7, 1873, neofitsial'naia chast', 79–94; no. 12, March 21, 1873, neofitsial'naia chast', 95–102; no. 13, March 28, 1873, neofitsial'naia chast', 103–7.

Izvestiia Imperatorskago arkheologicheskago obshchestva. 10 vols. St. Petersburg, 1857–1884.

Johnstone, Pauline. *The Byzantine Tradition in Church Embroidery.* Chicago, 1967.

Kachalova, I. Ia., N. A. Maiasova, and L. A. Shchennikova, eds. *Blagoveshchenskii sobor Moskovskogo Kremlia. K 500–letiiu unikal'nogo pamiatnika russkoi kul'tury.* Moscow, 1990.

Kaidash, Svetlana. *Sila slabykh. Zhenshchiny v istorii Rossii (XI-XIX vv).* Moscow, 1989.

Kaiser, Daniel. "Symbol and Ritual in the Marriages of Ivan IV." *RH* 14, nos. 1–4 (1987): 247–62.

Kamentseva, E. I. *Khronologiia.* Moscow, 1967.

Kamen' kraeug"l'n": Rhetoric of the Medieval Slavic World. Essays presented to Edward L. Keenan on his Sixtieth Birthday by his Colleagues and Students. Ed. Nancy Shields Kollmann, Donald Ostrowski, Andrei Pliguzov, and Daniel Rowland. *HUS* 19. Cambridge, Mass., 1995.

Kämpfer, Frank. "Ivan Groznyj und Hilandar." *Jahrbücher für Geschichte Osteuropas* 19, no. 4 (December 1974): 499–519.

____. *Das russische Herrscherbild von den Anfängen bis zu Peter dem Großen.* Recklinghausen, 1978.

Kantorowicz, Ernst. *The King's Two Bodies. A Study in Mediaeval Political Theology.* Princeton, N. J., 1981.

Kapterev, N. F. *Kharakter otnoshenii Rossii k pravoslavnomu vostoku v XVI i XVII stoletiiakh.* 2d ed. Slavistic Printings and Reprintings 107. 1914. Reprint, The Hague, 1968.

____. *Patriarkh Nikon i tsar Aleksei Mikhailovich.* 2 vols. Sergiev Posad, 1909–1912.

____. "Snosheniia ierusalimskikh patriarkhov s russkim pravitel'stvom s poloviny XVI do kontsa XVIII stoletiia." *Pravoslavnyi palestinskii sbornik* 15, no. 1 (1895): 1–508.

Karamzin, N. M. *Istoriia gosudarstva Rossiiskago.* 12 vols. Slavistic Printings and Reprintings 189/1–12. 1892. Reprint, The Hague, 1969.

Kashtanov, S. M. "Diplomatika kak spetsial'naia istoricheskaia distsiplina." *Voprosy istorii* (1965): no. 1. 39–44.

Kazakova, N. A. *Ocherki po istorii russkoi obshchestvennoi mysli. Pervaia tret' XVI veka.* Leningrad, 1970.

Kazhdan A. P., ed. *The Oxford Dictionary of Byzantium.* 3 vols. New York, 1991.

Keenan, Edward L. "Ivan the Terrible and His Women. Pt. 2: Dowagers, Nannies, and Brides." Typescript. Cambridge, Mass., 1981.

____. *The Kurbskii-Groznyi Apocrypha: The Seventeenth-Century Genesis of the "Correspondence" Attributed to Prince A. M. Kurbskii and Tsar Ivan IV.* Appendix by Daniel C. Waugh. Cambridge, Mass., 1971.

____. "Putting Kurbskii in His Place, or: Observations and Suggestions concerning the Place of the *History of the Grand Prince of Muscovy* in the History of Muscovite Literary Culture." *Forschungen zur osteuropäischen Geschichte* 24 (1978): 131–61.

Kern, Fritz. *Kingship and Law in the Middle Ages.* Oxford, 1956.

Kivelson, Valerie. *Autocracy in the Provinces: The Russian Gentry and Political Culture in the Seventeenth Century.* Stanford, 1996.

____. "Patrolling the Boundaries: Witchcraft Accusations and Household Strife in Seventeenth-Century Muscovy." In *Kamen' kraeug"l'n": Rhetoric of the Medieval Slavic World. Essays presented to Edward L. Keenan on his Sixtieth Birthday by his Colleagues and Students.* Ed. Nancy Shields Kollmann, Donald Ostrowski, Andrei Pliguzov, and Daniel Rowland. *HUS* 19. Cambridge, Mass., 1995. 428–50.

____. "Private Property à la Russe: Maps and the Outlines of Ownership in the Seventeenth Century." Paper delivered at Privacies Seminar, University of Michigan, Ann Arbor, October 3, 1998.

Kleimola, Ann M. "'In Accordance with the Canons of the Holy Apostles': Muscovite Dowries and Women's Property Rights." *RR* 51 (April 1992): 204–29.

Kliuchevskii, V. O. *A Course in Russian History: The Seventeenth Century.* Trans. Natalie Duddington. Armonk, N.Y., 1994.

____. *Drevnerusskiia zhitiia sviatykh kak istoricheskii istochnik.* 1871. Reprint, The Hague, 1968.

Kloss, B. M. *Nikonovskii svod i russkie letopisi XVI–XVII vekov.* Moscow, 1980.

Kollmann, Nancy Shields. *By Honor Bound: State and Society in Early Modern Russia.* Ithaca, N.Y., 1999.

____. "Consensus Politics: The Dynastic Crisis of the 1490s Reconsidered." *RR* 45, no. 3 (July 1986): 235–67.

____. *Kinship and Politics: The Making of the Muscovite Political System, 1345–1547.* Stanford, 1987.

____. "The Meaning of the Private in Seventeenth-Century Russia." Paper delivered at Privacies Seminar, University of Michigan, Ann Arbor, October 3, 1998.

____. "Pilgrimage, Procession, and Symbolic Space in Sixteenth-Century Russian Politics." In *Medieval Russian Culture.* Vol. 2. Ed. Michael S. Flier and Daniel

Rowland. California Slavic Studies 19. Berkeley, 1994. 163–81.

____. "The Seclusion of Elite Muscovite Women." *RH* 10, pt. 2 (1983): 170–87.

Kol'tsova, T. M. "'Krestovyi obraz' Kiiskogo Krestnogo monastyria." In *Nauchno-issledovatel'skaia rabota v khudozhestvennom muzee: sbornik statei.* Ed. E. I. Ruzhnikova. Arkhangelsk, 1998. 14–32.

Komitet dlia izdaniia Drevnostei Rossiiskago gosudarstva. *Drevnosti Rossiiskago gosudarstva.* 6 vols. Moscow, 1849–1853.

Kondakov, N. P. *Pamiatniki khristianskago iskusstva na Afone.* St. Petersburg, 1902.

Krumbacher, Karl. *Geschichte der Byzantinischen Litteratur von Justinian bis zum Ende des Oströmischen Reiches (527–1453).* 2d ed. Munich, 1897.

Kurukin, I. V. "Sil'vestr i sostavlenie zhitiia Ol'gi Stepennoi knigi." In *Teoria i praktika istochnikovedeniia i arkheografii otechestvennoi istorii. Sbornik statei.* Ed. V. T. Pashuto, A. I. Alekseev, M. V. Bibikov, V. I. Neupokoev, I. S. Chicherev, and S. O. Shmidt. Moscow, 1978. 51–60.

Kusheva, E. *Iz publitsistiki Smutnogo vremeni.* Saratov, 1926.

Laporte, Jean. *The Role of Women in Early Christianity.* New York, 1982.

Lenhoff, Gail. "Canonization and Princely Power in Northeast Rus': The Cult of Leontij Rostovskij." *Die Welt der Slaven* 37, nos.1–2 (1992): 359–80.

Leonid, arkhimandrit. "Blagovernaia tsarevna, velikaia kniazhna Marfa Alekseevna." *Russkii arkhiv* 20 (1882): 27–41.

Leonov, A. *Simon Ushakov. Russkii khudozhnik XVII veka, 1626–1686.* Moscow, 1945.

Lermontova, E. "Samoderzhavie Tsarevny Sof'i Alekseevny po neizdannym dokumentam (iz perepiski, vozbuzhdennoi grafom Paninym)." *Russkaia starina* 149 (1912): bk. 2, pp. 425–45; bk. 3, pp. 539–47.

Levin, Eve Rebecca. *Sex and Society in the World of the Orthodox Slavs, 900–1700.* Ithaca, N.Y., 1989.

Lewitter, L. R. "Women, Sainthood and Marriage in Muscovy." *Journal of Russian Studies* no. 37 (1979): 3–11.

Lexikon der christlichen Ikonographie. 8 vols. Ed. Engelbert Kirschbaum and Wolfgang Braunfels. Rome, 1968–1976.

Leyser, Karl. *Rule and Conflict in an Early Medieval Society: Ottonian Saxony.* Oxford, 1989.

Likhachev, D. S., ed. *Slovar' knizhnikov i knizhnosti drevnei Rusi.* 3 vols. in 5 parts to date. Leningrad, 1987–1993.

Likhacheva, L. D. *Drevnerusskoe shit'e XV–nachala XVIII veka v sobranii Gosudarstvennogo Russkogo muzeia. Katalog vystavki.* Leningrad, 1980.

____. "Pokrov Pafnutiia Borovskogo iz Gosudarstvennogo Russkogo Muzeia." In *Pamiatniki kul'tury. Novye otkrytiia. Ezhegodnik 1977.* Moscow, 1977. 269–73.

Lincoln, W. Bruce. *The Romanovs. Autocrats of All the Russias.* New York, 1981.

Litavrin, G. G. "Puteshestvie russkoi kniagini Ol'gi v Konstantinopol'. Problema istochnikov." *Vizantiiskii vremennik,* n.s., 42 (1981): 35–48.

Longworth, Philip. *Alexis, Tsar of All the Russias.* New York, 1984.

Loparev, Kh. M. *Grecheskiia zhitiia sviatykh VIII i IX vekov. Opyt klassifikatsii pamiatnikov agiografii s obzorom ikh s tochki zreniia istoricheskoi i istoriko-literaturnoi.* Petrograd, 1914.

Lur'e, Ia. S. *Dve istorii Rusi 15 veka.* St. Petersburg, 1994.

____. "Elena Ivanovna, koroleva Pol'skaia i velikaia kniagina Litovskaia, kak pisatel'-publitsist." *Canadian-American Slavic Studies* 13, nos. 1–2 (1979): 11–20.

____, ed. *Istoki russkoi belletristiki. Vozniknovenie zhanrov siuzhetnogo povestvovaniia v drevnerusskoi literature*. Leningrad, 1970.

Lur'e, Ia. S., and Iu. D. Rykov. *Perepiska Ivana Groznogo s Andreem Kurbskim*. Leningrad, 1979.

Maiasova, N. A. "Drevnerusskoe litsevoe shit'e iz sobraniia Kirillo-Belozerskogo monastyria." In *Drevnerusskoe iskusstvo. Khudozhestvennye pamiatniki russkogo Severa*. Ed. G. V. Popov. Moscow, 1989. 203–24.

____. *Drevnerusskoe shit'e*. Moscow, 1971.

____. "Literaturnyi obraz Ksenii Godunovoi i pripisyvaemye ei proizvedeniia shit'ia (k voprosu o vzaimo-otnoshenii literatury, iskusstva i deistvitel'nosti)," *TODRL* 22 (1966): 294–310.

____, ed. *Srednevekovoe litsevoe shit'e. Vizantiia, Balkany, Rus'. Katalog vystavki. XVIII mezhdunarodnyi kongress vizantinistov. Moskva, 8–15 avgusta, 1991 g*. Moscow, 1991.

Makhan'ko, Mariia. "Sobiranie v Moskve drevnikh ikon i relikvii v XVI veke, ego istoriko-kul'turnoe znachenie." *Iskusstvoznanie* 1 (1998): 112–42.

Mansikka, V. J. *Die Religion der Ostslaven*. Helsinki, 1922.

Manushina, T. N., ed. *Khudozhestvennoe shit'e drevnei Rusi v sobranii Zagorskogo muzeia*. Moscow, 1983.

Markova, G., comp. *The Great Palace of the Moscow Kremlin*. Trans. M. Wilkinson. Leningrad, 1981.

Martynova, M. V. "K voprosu ob atributsii regalii tsaria Mikhaila Fedorovicha." *Pamiatniki kul'tury. Novye otkrytiia, 1981*. Leningrad, 1983. 392–403.

Maslenitsyn, S. I. *Iaroslavskaia ikonopis'*. Moscow, 1973.

____. *Pereslavl-Zalessky*. Trans. N. Johnston. Leningrad, 1975.

____. *Souzdal. Monuments d'architecture*. Trans. Vladimir Maksimov. Leningrad, 1985.

McCartney, Elizabeth. "Ceremonies and Privileges of Office: Queenship in Late Medieval France." In *Power of the Weak. Studies on Medieval Women*. Ed. Jennifer Carpenter and Sally-Beth MacLean. Urbana, Ill., 1995. 178–219.

McKitterick, Rosamond. *The Frankish Kingdoms under the Carolingians, 751–987*. London, 1983.

McNally, Susanne. "From Public Person to Private Prisoner: The Changing Place of Women in Medieval Russia." Ph.D. diss., State University of New York at Binghamton, 1976.

McNamara, Jo Ann, and Suzanne F. Wemple. "Sanctity and Power: The Dual Pursuit of Medieval Women." In *Becoming Visible: Women in European History*. Ed. Renate Bridenthal and Claudia Koonz. Boston, 1977. 90–118.

Mendeleev, V. *Khudozhestvennye sokrovishcha Moskovskogo Kremlia*. 2d ed. Moscow, 1988.

Meyendorff, John. *Byzantium and the Rise of Russia*. Crestwood, N.Y., 1989.

Michels, Georg. *At War with the Church: Religious Dissent in Seventeenth-Century Russia*. Stanford, 1999.

____. "Elite Women and Old Belief." In *Kamen' kraeug"l'n": Rhetoric of the Medieval Slavic World. Essays presented to Edward L. Keenan on his Sixtieth Birthday by his Colleagues and Students*. Ed. Nancy Shields Kollmann, Donald Ostrowski, Andrei Pliguzov, and Daniel Rowland. *HUS* 19. Cambridge, Mass., 1995. 428–50.

Miller, David. "The Cult of Saint Sergius of Radonezh and Its Political Uses." *SR* 52, no. 4 (winter 1993): 680–99.

____. "The Velikie Chetii and the Stepennaia Kniga of Metropolitan Makarii and the Origins of Russian National Consciousness." *Forschungen zur osteuropäischen Geschichte* 26 (1979): 263–382.

Mneva, N. E. "Shit'e XVI–nachala XVII veka." In I. E. Grabar', V. S. Kemenov, and V. N. Lazarev, eds. *Istoriia russkogo iskusstva.* 13 vols. Moscow, 1953–1969. 3:676–88.

____. "Zhivopis' kontsa XVI–nachala XVII veka." In I. E. Grabar', V. S. Kemenov, and V. N. Lazarev, eds. *Istoriia russkogo iskusstva.* 13 vols. Moscow, 1953–1969. 3:635–43.

Moleva, N. "Tsar-Devitsa." *Znanie–sila* (1971): no. 1. 32–36.

Mordovtsev, D. *Russkiia istoricheskiia zhenshchiny. Populiarnye rasskazy iz russkoi istorii.* St. Petersburg, 1874.

Mordvinova, S. B. "Istoriko-khudozhestvennye predposylki vozniknoveniia i razvitiia portreta v XVII v." In *Ot Srednevekov'ia k Novomu vremeni. Materialy i issledovaniia po russkomu iskusstvu XVIII–pervoi poloviny XIX veka.* Ed. T. V. Alekseeva. Moscow, 1984. 9–35.

Müller, Paul Johannes. *Famous Frescoes.* Trans. Una Tomašević. Belgrade, 1986.

Murav'ev, A. N. *Russkaia fivaida na severe.* St. Petersburg, 1894.

____. *Snosheniia Rossii s Vostokom po delam tserkovnym.* 2 vols. St. Petersburg, 1858–1860.

Nasonov, A. N. *Istoriia russkogo letopisaniia XI–nachala XVIII v. Ocherki i issledovaniia.* Moscow, 1969.

____. "Materialy i issledovaniia po istorii russkogo letopisaniia." *Problemy istochnikovedeniia* 6 (1958): 235–74.

Nekrasov, A. I. *Drevnerusskoe izobrazitel'noe iskusstvo.* 1937. Reprint, The Hague, 1969.

Nikitina, Iu. I., A. S. Pavliuchenkova, and E. K. Pagol'skaia, comps. *Novgorodskii istoriko-arkhitekturnyi muzei-zapovednik. Russkoe iskusstvo XI–nachala XX veka. Katalog.* Leningrad, 1963.

Nikolaeva, T. V. *Drevnerusskaia zhivopis' Zagorskogo muzeia.* Moscow, 1977.

____. *Prikladnoe iskusstvo Moskovskoi Rusi.* Moscow, 1976.

____. "Proizvedeniia russkogo prikladnogo iskusstva s nadpisiami XV–pervoi chetverti XVI v." *Arkheologiia SSSR. Svod arkheologicheskikh istochnikov* E 1–49 (1971).

____. *Sobranie drevnerusskogo iskusstva v Zagorskom Muzee.* Leningrad, 1968.

____. "Troitskii zhivopisets XVI v. Evstafii Golovkin." In *Kul'tura drevnei Rusi.* Ed. A. L. Mongait. Moscow, 1966. 177–83.

Obolensky, Dimitrii. *The Byzantine Commonwealth: Eastern Europe, 500–1453.* Crestwood, 1974.

____. "Ol'ga's Conversion: The Evidence Reconsidered." In *Proceedings of the International Congress Commemorating the Millenium of Christianity in Rus'-Ukraine.* Ed. O. Pritsak, I. Ševčenko, and M. Labunka. In *HUS* 12–13 (1988–1989): 145–58.

____. "Some Notes concerning a Byzantine Portrait of John VIII Palaeologus." *Eastern Churches Review* 4, no. 2 (1972): 141–46.

Oikonomides, Nicolas. "John VII Palaeologus and the Ivory Pyxis at Dumbarton Oaks." *Dumbarton Oaks Papers* no. 31 (1977): 329–37.

Ostrogorsky, George. *History of the Byzantine State.* Trans. Joan Hussey. Rev. ed., New Brunswick, 1969.

Ostrowski, Donald. *Muscovy and the Mongols: Cross-cultural Influence on the Steppe-Frontier, 1304–1589*. Cambridge, England, 1998.
Ovchinnikova, E. S. *Portret v russkom iskusstve XVII veka. Materialy i issledovaniia*. Moscow, 1955.
____. "Povest' o tsaritse Dinare v russkom izobrazitel'nom iskusstve." *TODRL* 22 (1966): 222–38.
____. *Tserkov' Troitsy v Nikitnikakh. Pamiatnik zhivopisi i zodchestva XVII veka*. Moscow, 1970.
Pagels, Elaine. *Adam, Eve and the Serpent*. New York, 1988.
Panchenko, A. M. "Pridvornye virshi 80–kh godov XVII stoletiia." *TODRL* 21 (1965): 65–73.
____. *Russkaia stikhotvornaia kul'tura XVII veka*. Leningrad, 1973.
Papas, Tano. *Studien zur Geschichte der Messgewänder im byzantinischen Ritus*. Munich, 1965.
Parsons, John Carmi. "The Queen's Intercession in Thirteenth-Century England." In *Power of the Weak: Studies on Medieval Women*. Ed. Jennifer Carpenter and Sally-Beth MacLean. Urbana, Ill., 1995. 147–77.
____. "Ritual and Symbol in the English Medieval Queenship to 1500." In *Women and Sovereignty*. Ed. Louise Olga Fradenburg. Cosmos: The Yearbook of the Traditional Cosmology Society, vol. 7. Edinburgh, 1992. 60–77.
____, ed. *Medieval Queenship*. New York, 1993.
Pavlenko, A. A. "Karp Zolotarev i Moskovskie zhivopistsy poslednei treti XVII v." *Pamiatniki kul'tury. Novye otkrytiia, 1982*. Leningrad, 1984. 301–16.
Pelenski, Iaroslav. "The Origins of the Official Muscovite Claims to the 'Kievan Inheritance'." *HUS* 1 (March 1977): 29–52.
Perrie, Maureen. *Pretenders and Popular Monarchism in Early Modern Russia: The False Tsars of the Time of Troubles*. Cambridge, England, 1995.
Petrov, V. I. *Catalogue des monnaies russes de tous les princes, tsars et empereurs depuis 980 jusqu'à 1899*. Graz, 1964.
Philipp, Werner. "Heiligkeit und Herrschaft in der Vita Aleksandr Nevskijs." *Forschungen zur osteuropäischen Geschichte* 18 (1973): 55–72.
Piltz, Elisabeth. *Trois sakkoi byzantins. Analyse iconographique*. Stockholm, 1976.
Pipes, Richard. *Russia under the Old Regime*. New York, 1974.
Platonov, S. F. *Boris Godunov: Tsar of Russia*. Trans. L. Rex Pyles. The Russian Series, vol. 10. Gulf Breeze, 1973.
____. *Ocherki po istorii smuty v Moskovskom gosudarstve XVI–XVII vv. (Opyt izucheniia obshchestvennogo stroia i soslovnykh otnoshenii v smutnoe vremia)*. Moscow, 1937.
____. *The Time of Troubles: A Historical Study of the Internal Crisis and Social Struggle in Sixteenth- and Seventeenth-Century Muscovy*. Trans. John T. Alexander. Lawrence, Ks., 1970.
Plavsic, Borivoj. "Seventeenth-Century Chanceries and Their Staffs." In *Russian Officialdom: The Bureaucratization of Russian Society from the Seventeenth to the Twentieth Century*. Ed. W. Pintner and D. Rowney. Chapel Hill, N. C. 1980. 19–45.
Pohlsander, Hans. *Helena: Empress and Saint*. Chicago, 1995.
Popov, A. "Drevnerusskiia polemicheskiia sochineniia protiv protestantov." *ChOIDR* (1879): no. 2, sect. IV, pp. 1–80.
Popov, G. V. *Zhivopis' i miniatiura Moskvy serediny XV–nachala XVI veka*. Moscow, 1975.
Prashkovich, N. I. "Iz rannykh deklamatsii Simeona Polotskogo ('Metry' i 'Dialog

kratkii')," *TODRL* 21 (1965): 29–38.

Presniakov, A. E. *The Formation of the Great Russian State: A Study of Russian History in the Thirteenth to Fifteenth Centuries*. Trans. A. E. Moorhouse. Chicago, 1970.

Pritsak, Omeljan. "When and Where was Ol'ga Baptized?" *HUS* 9, no. 1–2 (June 1985): 5–24.

Prozorovskii, A. A. "Sil'vestr Medvedev (Ego zhizn' i deiatel'nost')." *ChOIDR* (1896): no. 2, sect. IV, pp. 1–148; no. 3, sect. IV, pp. 149–378; no. 4, sect. III, pp. 379–606.

Pushkareva, N. L. *Zhenshchiny drevnei Rusi*. Moscow, 1989.

Réau, Louis. *Iconographie de l'art chrétien*. 3 vols. Paris, 1955–1959.

Rollason, David. *Saints and Relics in Anglo-Saxon England*. Oxford, 1989.

Roman, Stanislaw. "Le statut de la femme dans l'Europe Orientale (Pologne et Russie) au moyen âge et aux temps modernes." *Recueils de la Société Jean Bodin pour l'histoire comparative des institutions* 12 (1962): 389–403.

Roozemond–Van Ginhoven, Hetty J. *Ikon: Inspired Art: Icons from "De Wijenburgh."* Echteld, Netherlands, 1980.

Rovinskii, D. A. *Podrobnyi slovar' russkikh graverov XVI–XIX vv.* 2 vols. St. Petersburg, 1895.

____. *Podrobnyi slovar' russkikh gravirovannykh portretov*. 2 vols. St. Petersburg, 1889.

Rowland, Daniel. "Biblical Military Imagery in the Political Culture of Early Modern Russia: The Blessed Host of the Heavenly Tsar." In *Medieval Russian Culture*. Vol. 2. Ed. Michael S. Flier and Daniel Rowland. California Slavic Studies 19. Berkeley, 1994. 182–212.

____. "Did Muscovite Literary Ideology Place Limits on the Power of the Tsar (1540s–1660s)?" *RR* 49, no. 2 (April 1990): 125–55.

____. "Ivan the Terrible as a Carolingian Renaissance Prince." In *Kamen' kraeug"l'n": Rhetoric of the Medieval Slavic World. Essays presented to Edward L. Keenan on his Sixtieth Birthday by his Colleagues and Students*. Ed. Nancy Shields Kollmann, Donald Ostrowski, Andrei Pliguzov, and Daniel Rowland. *HUS* 19. Cambridge, Mass., 1995. 594–606.

____. "Moscow—the Third Rome or the New Israel?" *RR* 55, no. 4 (October 1996): 591–614.

____. "Toward an Understanding of the Political Ideas in Ivan Timofeyev's *Vremennik*." *SEER* 62, no. 3 (July 1984): 371–99.

Rudakov, A. A. "Razvitie legendy o smerti tsarevicha Dimitriia v Ugliche." *Istoricheskie zapiski* 12 (1941): 254–83.

Rumiantseva, V. S. *Narodnoe antitserkovnoe dvizhenie v Rossii v XVII veke*. Moscow, 1986.

Rüß, Hartmut. "Adel und Nachfolgefrage im Jahre 1553: Betrachtungen zur Glaubwürdigkeit einer umstrittenen Quelle." In *Essays in Honor of A. A. Zimin*. Ed. Daniel Clarke Waugh. Columbus, Ohio, 1985. 345–78.

____. "Elena Vasil'evna Glinskaja." *Jahrbücher für Geschichte Osteuropas* 19, no. 4 (December 1971): 481–98.

Russkoe istoricheskoe obshchestvo, ed. *Sbornik Russkogo istoricheskogo obshchestva*. 148 vols. Petrograd [St. Petersburg], 1867–1916.

Rydén, L. *Bemerkungen zum Leben des heiligen Symeon von Leontius von Neapolis*. Uppsala, 1970.

Rzhiga, V. F. "Neizdannye sochineniia Maksima Greka." *Byzantinoslavica* 6 (1936): 85–109.

Savva, V. I. *Moskovskie tsari i vizantiiskie vasilevsy. K voprosu o vliianii Vizantii na obrazovanie idei tsarskoi vlasti moskovskikh gosudarei.* Kharkov, 1901.

Schulenburg, Jane Tibbetts. "Female Sanctity: Public and Private Roles, ca. 500–1100." In *Women and Power in the Middle Ages.* Ed. Mary Erler and Maryanne Kowaleski. Athens, Ga., 1988. 102–25.

Semevskii, M. "Sovremennye portrety Sofii Alekseevny i V. V. Golitsyna." *Russkoe slovo* (1859): no. 12. 411–58.

Shahar, Shulamith. *Childhood in the Middle Ages.* Trans. Chaya Galai. London, 1992.

Shchepkina, M. V. *Izobrazhenie russkikh istoricheskikh lits v shit'e XV veka.* Moscow, 1954.

Shliapkin, I. A. "Tsarevna Natal'ia Alekseevna i teatr eia vremeni." *Pamiatniki drevnei pis'mennosti* 128 (1898): I–LVIII; 1–85.

Shmidt, S. O. "O vremeni sostavlenii 'Vypisi' o vtorom brake Vasiliia III." In *Novoe o proshlom nashei strany. Pamiati akademika M. N. Tikhomirova.* Ed. V. A. Aleksandrov. Moscow, 1967. 110–22.

Skrynnikov, R. G. *Ivan Groznyi.* Moscow, 1975.

____. *Perepiska Groznogo i Kurbskogo. Paradoksi Edvarda Kinana.* Leningrad, 1973.

____. *Rossiia nakanune "smutnogo vremeni".* Moscow, 1980.

____. *Rossiia v nachale XVII v. "Smuta".* Moscow, 1988.

____. *The Time of Troubles: Russia in Crisis 1604–1618.* Ed and trans. Hugh F. Graham. Gulf Breeze, Fla., 1988.

Smirnov, S. *Istoricheskoe opisanie Savvina Storozhevskago monastyria.* Moscow, 1860.

____. *Istoriia Moskovskoi Slaviano-Greko-Latinskoi Akademii.* Moscow, 1855.

____. "O predislovii k zhitiiu prepodobnago Sergiia pisannom kelarem Simonom Azar'inym." *Vremennik Imperatorskago Moskovskago obshchestva istorii i drevnostei rossiiskikh* (1851): section III, 1, pp. 1–13.

Smirnova, E. S. *Moskovskaia ikona XIV–XVII vekov.* Leningrad, 1988.

____. "Simon Ushakov—'Historicism' and 'Byzantinism': On the Interpretation of Russian Painting from the Second Half of the Seventeenth Century." In *Religion and Culture in Early Modern Russia and Ukraine.* Ed. Samuel H. Baron and Nancy Shields Kollmann. DeKalb, Ill., 1997. 169–83.

Snegirev, I. M. *Pamiatniki Moskovskoi drevnosti.* Moscow, 1842–1845.

Spasskii, I. G., and E. S. Shchukina, eds. *Medali i monety Petrovskogo vremeni.* Leningrad, 1974.

Speranskii, M. N. "Povest' o tsaritse Dinare v russkoi pis'mennosti." *Izvestiia Otdeleniia russkogo iazyka i slovesnosti Akademii nauk* 31 (1926): 43–92.

Stafford, Pauline. *Queens, Concubines, and Dowagers: The King's Wife in the Early Middle Ages.* Athens, Ga., 1983.

Stasov, V. V. "Zametki o drevnei russkoi katapetasme." *Izvestiia Imperatorskago arkheologicheskago obshchestva* 4 (1863): cols. 534–51.

Steindorff, Ludwig. *Memoria in Altrußland: Untersuchungen zu den Formen christlicher Totensorge.* Quellen und Studien zur Geschichte des östlichen Europa, vol. 38. Stuttgart, 1994.

Stökl, Günther. "Staat und Kirche im Moskauer Rußland. Die vier Moskauer Wundertäter." *Jahrbücher für Geschichte Osteuropas*, n.s., 29, no. 4 (1981): 481–93.

Svirin, A. N. *Drevnerusskoe shit'e.* Moscow, 1963.

____. *Iuvelirnoe iskusstvo Drevnei Rusi XI–XVII vekov.* Moscow, 1972.

Thompson, Ewa M. *Understanding Russia: The Holy Fool in Russian Culture.* Lanham, 1987.

Thyrêt, Isolde. "'Blessed Is the Tsaritsa's Womb': The Myth of Miraculous Birth and Royal Motherhood in Muscovite Russia." *RR* 53, no. 4 (October 1994): 479–96.

____. "The Construction of the Tsar's Image at the Court of Ivan IV: The Case of the *Katapetasma* of 1555." Paper presented at the Twenty-Seventh National Convention of the American Association for the Advancement of Slavic Studies. Washington, DC, October 26–29, 1995.

____. "The Grand Princesses of Moscow and the Ideology of Dynastic Continuity." Paper presented at the Early Russian History Workshop. Illinois Summer Research Laboratory on Russia and Eastern Europe. University of Illinois, Urbana, June 15–19, 1998.

____. "The Grand Princesses of Moscow and the Rise of the Medieval Russian State." Paper presented at the Thirty-Seventh Annual Meeting of the Midwest Medieval History Conference. University of Notre Dame, October 26–27, 1998.

____. "Muscovite Miracle Stories as Sources for Gender-Specific Religious Experience." In *Religion and Culture in Early Modern Russia and Ukraine.* Ed. Samuel H. Baron and Nancy Shields Kollmann. DeKalb, Ill., 1997. 115–31.

Tikhomirov, M. N. *Russkoe letopisanie.* Moscow, 1979.

Tikhonravov, K., ed. *Vladimirskii sbornik. Materialy dlia statistiki, etnografii, istorii i arkheologii Vladimirskoi gubernii.* Moscow, 1857.

Tokmakov, I. *Istoricheskoe i arkheologicheskoe opisanie Pokrovskago devich'iago monastyria v gorode Suzdale.* Vladimir, 1913.

Tolstoi, Count M. V., ed. "Kniga glagolemaia opisanie o Rossiiskikh sviatykh." *ChOIDR* (1887): no. 4, sect. II, pp. 1–288.

Topping, Eva Catafygiota. *Saints and Sisterhood: The Lives of Forty-Eight Women.* Minneapolis, 1990.

Treadgold, Warren. "The Unpublished Saint's Life of the Empress Irene (BHG 2205)." *Byzantinische Forschungen* 8 (1982): 237–51.

Treitinger, Otto. *Die oströmische Kaiser- und Reichsidee nach ihrer Gestaltung im höfischen Zeremoniell.* Bad Homburg, 1969.

Troitskaia, T. S. "Zhanrovye transformatsii povesti o Dinare v XVI v." In *Problemy literaturnykh zhanrov.* Tomsk, 1983. 11–12.

Trutneva, N. F., and M. M. Shvedova. *Russkie mastera zhivopisi i graviury XVI–XVIII vv. Katalog vystavki. Gosudarstvennyi ordena Lenina Istoricheskii Muzei.* N.P., 1989.

Trutovskii, V. "'Romanovskaia' tserkovno-arkheologicheskaia vystavka v Moskve." *Starye gody* 2 (1913): 36–43.

Tumanskii, F. *Sobranie raznykh zapisok i sochinenii sluzhashchikh k dostavleniiu polnogo svedeniia o zhizni i deianiakh gosudaria imperatora Petra Velikogo.* 10 vols. St. Petersburg, 1787.

Turner, Kay F. "Contemporary Feminist Rituals." In *The Politics of Women's Spirituality.* Ed. Charlene Spretnak. New York, 1982. 219–33.

Uspenskii, B. A. *Semiotik der Geschichte.* Vienna, 1991.

____. *The Semiotics of the Russian Icon.* Ed. Stephen Rudy. Lisse, Belgium, 1976.

Uspenskii, L., and V. Losskii. *Der Sinn der Ikonen.* Bern and Olten, 1952.

Ustrialov, N. G. *Istoriia tsarstvovaniia Petra Velikogo*. 6 vols. St. Petersburg, 1858–1863.

Vasenko, P. G. *Boiare Romanovy i votsarenie Mikhaila Feodorovicha*. St. Peterburg, 1913.

Vasiliev, A. A. *History of the Byzantine Empire, 324–1453*. 2 vols. 2d ed. Madison, 1964.

Veinberg, L. B. "Lichnost' Anny Vasil'evny, velikoi kniagini Riazanskoi." *Trudy Riazanskoi uchenoi arkhivnoi komissii* 4, no. 8 (1890): 167–69.

Velmans, Tanja. "Le portrait dans l'art des Paléologues." In *Art et société à Byzance sous les Paléologues*. Actes du colloque organisé par l'Association Internationale des Études byzantines à Venise en septembre 1968. Bibliothèque de l'Institut Hellénique d'Études byzantines et post-byzantines de Venise, no. 4. Venice, 1971. 91–148.

Vernadsky, George. "The Death of the Tsarevich Dimitry. A Reconsideration of the Case." *OSP* 5 (1954): 1–19.

Vernadskii, M. G. "Note sur les vêtements sacerdotaux du patriarche Nikon." *L'art byzantin chez les Slaves. Les Balkans*, vol. 1, pt. 2. Ed. Gabriel Millet. Orient et Byzance IV. Paris, 1930. 412–15.

Veselovskii, S. B. "Dukhovnoe zaveshchanie Ivana Groznogo kak istoricheskii istochnik." *Izvestiia Akademii nauk SSSR. Seriia istorii i filosofii* 4, no. 6 (1947): 505–20.

Vladimirskie gubernskie vedomosti. 1844, 1852, 1853, 1854.

Vlasov, A. N. "O pamiatnikakh Ustiuzhskoi literaturnoi traditsii XVI–XVII vv." In *Knizhnye tsentry drevnei Rusi XI–XVI vv*. Ed. D. S. Likhachev. St. Petersburg, 1991. 313–43.

Voronin, N. N., and V. V. Kostochkin, eds. *Troitse-Sergieva Lavra. Khudozhestvennye pamiatniki*. Moscow, 1968.

Voyce, Arthur. *The Art and Architecture of Medieval Russia*. Norman, Ok., 1967.

____. *The Moscow Kremlin*. Berkeley, 1954.

Wallace-Hadrill, J. M. *Early Germanic Kingship in England and on the Continent*. Oxford, 1971.

Waugh, Daniel Clarke, ed. *Essays in Honor of A. A. Zimin*. Columbus, Ohio, 1985.

____. "'Odolenie na Turskoe tsarstvo'—pamiatnik antituretskoi publitsistiki XVII v." *TODRL* 33 (1979): 88–107.

Weickhardt, George G. "Kotoshikhin: An Evaluation and Interpretation." *RH* 17, no. 2 (Summer 1990): 127–54.

Wemple, Suzanne. *Women in Frankish Society: Marriage and the Cloister, 500 to 900*. Philadelphia, 1981.

Wessel, Klaus. "Konstantin und Helena". *Reallexikon zur byzantinischen Kunst*. Vol. 4. Stuttgart, 1990. 358–66.

Wieczynski, Joseph, ed. *Modern Encyclopedia of Russian and Soviet History*. 59 vols. Gulf Breeze, Fla., 1976–1996.

Wood, Ian N. *The Merovingian Kingdoms, 450–751*. New York, 1994.

Wortman, Richard. *Scenarios of Power. Myth and Ceremony in Russian Monarchy*. Vol. 1. Princeton, New Jersey, 1995.

Zabelin, I. E. *Domashnii byt russkikh tsarei v XVI i XVII st*. 2d ed. Moscow, 1872.

____. *Domashnii byt russkikh tsarits v XVI i XVII st*. 2d ed. Moscow, 1872.

____. *Troitskie pokhody russkikh tsarei*. Moscow, 1847.

Zagorsk State Museum–Preserve of History and Art: An Illustrated Guidebook. Moscow, 1988.

Zapasko, Iakim, and Iaroslav Isaevich, eds. *Pamiatki knizhkovogo mistetstva.* 2 vols. L'viv, 1984.

Zelensky, Elizabeth Kristofovich. "'Sophia the Wisdom of God' as a Rhetorical Device during the Regency of Sof'ia Alekseevna, 1682–1689." 2 vols. Ph.D. diss., Georgetown University, Washington, DC, 1992.

____. "'Sophia the Wisdom of God': The Function of Religious Imagery during the Regency of Sofiia Alekseevna of Muscovy." In *Women and Sovereigny.* Ed. Louise Olga Fradenburg. Cosmos: The Yearbook of the Traditional Cosmology Society, vol. 7. Edinburgh, 1992. 192–211.

Zimin, A. A. *Formirovanie boiarskoi aristokratii v Rossii vo vtoroi polovine XV–pervoi treti XVI v.* Ed. V. I. Buganov. Moscow, 1988.

____. *Gosudarstvennyi arkhiv Rossii XVI stoletiia. Opyt rekonstruktsii.* Vol. 1. Moscow, 1978.

____. *I. S. Peresvetov i ego sovremenniki.* Moscow, 1958.

____. "O metodike izuchenii povestvovatel'nykh istochnikov XVI v." *Istochnikovedenie otechestvennoi istorii* 1 (1973): 187–211.

____. "O politicheskoi doktrine Iosifa Volotskogo." *TODRL* 9 (1953): 160–74.

____. *Oprichnina Ivana Groznogo.* Moscow, 1964.

____. *Rossiia na poroge novogo vremeni (Ocherki politicheskoi istorii Rossii pervoi treti XVI v.).* Moscow, 1972.

____. *Russkie letopisi i khronografy kontsa XV–XVI vv.* 1960. Reprint, The Hague, 1969.

____. *V kanun groznykh potriasenii, predposylki pervoi krest'ianskoi voiny v Rossii.* Moscow, 1986.

____. *Vitiaz' na rasput'e. Feodal'naia voina v Rossii XV v.* Moscow, 1991.

____. "Vypis' o vtorom brake Vasiliia III." *TODRL* 30 (1976): 132–48.

Index